BLACK EXCEL

AFRICAN AMERICAN STUDENT'S COLLEGE GUIDE

**BLACK
EXCEL**

AFRICAN AMERICAN STUDENT'S COLLEGE GUIDE

Your One-Stop Resource for Choosing the Right
College, Getting In, and Paying the Bill

ISAAC BLACK

JOHN WILEY & SONS, INC.

New York ■ Chichester ■ Weinheim ■ Brisbane ■ Singapore ■ Toronto

This book is printed on acid-free paper. ∞

Published by John Wiley & Sons, Inc.
Published simultaneously in Canada

Design and production by Navta Associates, Inc.

This publication is designed to provide accurate and authoritative information in regard to the subject matter covered. It is sold with the understanding that the publisher is not engaged in rendering professional services. If professional advice or other expert assistance is required, the services of a competent professional person should be sought.

Library of Congress Cataloging-in-Publication Data

Black, Isaac, 1943–
    African American student's college guide : your one-stop resource for choosing the right college, getting in, and paying the bill / Isaac Black.
        p. cm.
    ISBN 0-471-29552-3 (pbk.)
    1. Afro-Americans—Education (Higher)   2. Universities and colleges—United States—Admission.   3. Student aid—United States.   4. Student loan funds—United States. 5. Universities and colleges—United States—Directories.   I. Title.

    LC2781 .B4635   2000
    378.1'61—dc21   99-088892

Printed in the United States of America

10 9 8 7 6 5 4 3

In memory of my parents,
who attended historically black colleges
and gave us gifts, insight,
and the path.
"When you finish college—," they began.

CONTENTS

ACKNOWLEDGMENTS

"So what if they're taller? We'll play big!"

> —George Ireland, ex-basketball coach,
> Loyola U. of Chicago

I love that quote, and have used it when talking to students. This book was a tall order, but the nucleus of the family—Barbie J, Eric, and Kris—was encouraging and supportive. They believed. Special thanks, too, must go to the thousands of students and parents I have met, lectured, and sometimes personally counseled at seminars and college fairs. Often I would think "give it your all," my voice actually hoarse at day's end. I could play "big" because I was truly energized. In this guide, I hope you feel the carryover.

With heartfelt gratitude I must thank Shana Bridgeman, a student at the University of Florida. Our cyber conversations were yearlong and inspirational. She told a national magazine that her experience with Black Excel was like interacting "with family." And wow, she hadn't even read our mission statement!

Special thanks to B. Keith Fulton, the former web site and technology coordinator for the Urban League. He sent us his very useful master's honors thesis, "Black Students/White Campus," and was really encouraging. Also, my gratitude goes to Thomas Landerfeld, Ph.D., an associate dean at California State University (Dominguez Hills), for his continuous moral support. Helpful was Dr. Aprille Ericsson-Jackson, an engineer at NASA, who amazingly had time to provide scholarship information via e-mails.

I am greatly indebted to Cherreka Montgomery, who does research for The United Negro College Fund, for sending me updated data and material. She made me focus and try to get it right. Thanks for the contribution of Victor K. Wilson, an assistant to the president at the University of Georgia, whose work I hope to use at our web site. His offering helped me along.

I am indebted to Thomas Hubschman, a fine novelist and dear friend, for his writer's perspective. Due respect and appreciation goes to Chris Jackson, my editor at Wiley. He did a yeoman's job, made me smile, and kept me from writing an encyclopedia. A sincere thanks to Marie Brown, who I had met many years ago and who I knew would be my agent. Kudos to the many students, graduates, and educators who filled my mailbox with ideas and insights. Many of you are quoted between these pages.

Lastly, let me give a second shoutout to Kris. She has been the perfect partner, helping shape Black Excel, A thru Z. Imagine that, while making stopovers at Cornell, Mount Sinai School of Medicine, and Harvard as an Arthur Ashe Fellow.

Thanks to all for the inspiration, thoughtful help, and support.

African American
Student's
College Guide

INTRODUCTION

"Help at Last!"

That was the headline of one early magazine story on Black Excel: The College Help Network. Later, when *Emerge* magazine was gathering information for an article on us, a writer spoke to one high school student with whom we'd worked. Shana Bridgeman, now a junior at the University of Florida, didn't hesitate. She said, "Black Excel has the resources of a large company and the feel of a closely knit family."

Shana is part of a growing roll call of students who have used Black Excel to help them navigate the college admissions maze. Sherice is heading to Penn, Kimberly is at Hampton, Tracy is a senior at John C. Smith, and Alex has just graduated from Johns Hopkins. Shana had it right! "Treat every aspiring student like it's *your own son or daughter*" has been our motto from the beginning. As founder of Black Excel, I believe I've lectured to, shook hands with, or interacted with well over 10,000 students and parents since 1988. Speaking at college fairs and for groups such as the Urban League, I've seen at firsthand the deep hunger among our students and their parents for good information on the college process.

From observation and experience, we knew our young people were often overlooked, misguided, and left discouraged when it came time to think about college and how to apply. *How do you pick a school? Can I get in? And if I get in, where will the money come from?* Just three of hundreds of questions. But who would supply the answers? Unfortunately, in many cases it wasn't high school grade advisers, who sometimes have more than 500 students in their caseloads at one time. For whatever reason, it has been that age-old story: *neglect!* The *African American Student's College Guide* is intended to supply all the answers you need. Our method has garnered positive, undeniable results. Looking back, we can say we have helped all kinds of students at all levels—from super students shooting for the Ivy League, to high school underachievers who need a "second chance." Students we've worked with write us from a variety of colleges, including Yale, Spelman, Temple, and even little Miles College in Alabama. We agree with the old cliché, "A journey of a thousand miles must begin with a single step." But in what direction do you head, and are there specially designed shoes that should be worn?

The startling fact is that even when a black student is a National Merit finalist, he or she usually has pivotal questions. Often students have no clue as to what to do next. That's a fact. But the college decision shouldn't be made in a haphazard way, with students feeling like they're throwing darts at a board. Your decisions, after all, will decide the next four to six years of your life and will certainly impact your future. Well, this guide aims to be your tutorial as you make those decisions.

First off, we're going to help you navigate the admissions process. That's the first step. We try to "keep it real," as our young people say. In this book we'll tell you how to rock the admissions process and get in! If there's a way to maximize your chances, this guide will lay out a plan. If your position looks futile, the A, B, C's of recovery are here to use. No matter what your position, today, with more students than ever entering college, this guide will give you an edge. It will be an education about admission strategy and how to make the college review teams STOP and discuss your specific application. You don't want to be onstage for 60 seconds—not with your future *on the line.*

And if money is an issue—and when hasn't it been?—part two of this guide is going to be a lifesaver. Our 350-plus scholarship list, often cited in magazines, will point you to the best money sources and how to get the cash in this section.

Not only will you get a basic overview of the admissions and financial aid process, but also the scoop on specific schools. In part three, the top historically black colleges (from Howard to Xavier) and mainstream, predominantly white schools (from Amherst to the Ivy League) are put under scrutiny. With these profiles we paint a picture that will give you crucial information to help decide about these colleges.

At any given time about 1.4 million African American students are in college. That's about 10% of all the students who are enrolled. We can do better. *We must do better.* Sure, our goal is an ambitious one. If we could, here, we would shout out the names of two dozen colleges the way we sometimes do at lectures. *Howard. Wesleyan. North Carolina A&T. Cornell.* "You've gotta believe," we often say. We try to inspire high school students. But we would not be telling you the truth if we didn't confess: we intend to try to reach all our young folks, even those in junior high school and elementary grades.

During a recent college fair here in New York, I must have personally stopped and talked to 100 students, often with a parent or two voicing their concerns. I think I covered just about every topic: SATs, school rankings, picking schools, the application process, aid, and scholarship money. It was another marathon question-and-answer session. I was left hoarse. Heading home, I wondered if folks would recall what I'd said, the good advice, the warnings, the tips. Now, with the *African American Student's College Guide,* I can start by placing a finger on the book.

Good luck, best wishes, and get that edge,

Isaac Black
Black Excel
ijblack@blackexcel.org
web site: www.blackexcel.org

PART ONE

GETTING IN

Navigating the Admissions Process

CHAPTER I

GETTING STARTED

Answers to Frequently Asked Questions

At Black Excel, our aim has always been to cram as much helpful information and guidance about the college selection, admissions, and payment processes as we can in a session; we try to demystify the process and provide students and parents with answers to all their key questions. Too often, black high school students—especially when they're the first in their families with the opportunity to go to college—begin the process with almost zero information about what to expect; we're still at the starting line while everybody else is off and running!

When I was in high school, a grade adviser told my parents I wasn't college material. Luckily my parents had attended small, historically black colleges in the South, and "can't" wasn't in their vocabulary. Or mine. But with the wind knocked out of us by my adviser, we proceeded on our own in a haphazard way, as if lost in a desert. Nevertheless, two months after high school graduation, I was in a college classroom. That was a start! I would go on to attend seven colleges and attain three degrees. Thinking about my own hit-or-miss beginning, and after a decade of interacting with thousands of students and their families, one thing has become crystal clear: Information is power, and all too often, we don't have it. Good grades and test scores are important, but strong guidance, insiders' tips, and knowing "the rules" matter.

But never fear: we'll put a compass in your hands, boots on your feet, and tools in your pack to help you reach the elusive mountaintop of a college education. This Q&A session offers examples of some of the most frequently asked questions we've encountered in our meetings with parents, students, and others, along with our insights, suggestions, and opinions based on more than a decade's work. It will provide a snapshot overview of some of the material you'll find in the book. If you want more information on any of these topics immediately, you can simply follow the chapter references at the end of the answers.

Question 1: *"My daughter is a good student. She wants to apply to Spelman, but she has heard that half the students who apply are rejected. Is this true? What can she do to improve her chances?"*

It's true that Spelman accepts only about 50% of the students who apply, making it one of the most selective historically black colleges and universities (HBCUs). The average combined SAT (Scholastic Aptitude Test) scores at that school are about 1,075. Spelman is undoubtedly looking for the "cream of the crop." Students who fall short in SAT scores and GPA (grade-point average) should try to present impressive records in other areas such as leadership, special talents and extracurricular achievements to get noticed. Outstanding recommendations by teachers also are a must, along with a superior application essay. In a nutshell, your daughter's strategy should be to demonstrate that she is a standout, even if her overall academic record is a bit below Spelman's norm. And we almost always encourage students who like Spelman to also apply to Hampton. Both schools attract a similar kind of student and provide a similar learning environment.

For more information on the getting into selective schools, see chapter 9.

Question 2: *"I am finally a senior in high school. But I messed up big time, failing and repeating many courses. I also suspect that I'm going to do poorly on the SATs. Still, I feel like I'm now ready to get serious and work. Is college beyond my reach?"*

No, college is not beyond your reach. You should apply along with everyone else. There are more than 3,000 four-year colleges in the United States, and many schools have "open admissions"—that is, they accept any student who graduates from high school and forwards an application. Also, there are noncompetitive schools, both historically black and mainstream, that will offer you that second chance if you give indications of being ready to accept it. A community college is yet another option. All you need is a positive attitude and the desire. We have helped many students who have done poorly in high school. Many now have their degrees. Think of yourself as a runner starting an entirely new race. Then step up to the starting line. It's a race you can win.

For more information on college strategies for "second-chance students," see chapter 10.

Question 3: *"If an African American student has an SAT score that's clearly below the average scores at a specific college, should that student still apply? Does he or she have a chance of getting an accept?"*

Never count yourself out. Instead ask yourself, "Am I in the ballpark?" Indeed, when you see an average SAT score, that means that in all likelihood half the admitted students have scored lower than the published score. Note, too, that there have been articles about how colleges sometimes pad the scores they report to college guides. Even if your score is lower than the average, you might be a desirable candidate. If your total package is strong, there's no telling what might happen. Your GPA, special talents, extracurricular activities, recommendations, and other attributes could flag your folder. And, of course, there may be other variables. Are you involved in high school government? Do you play an instrument? Were you the editor of the yearbook? Showing marked improvement in the 11th grade could also signal that you've become a maturing student.

Of course, you've got to be prudent too. If a college or a university reports SAT scores in the 1300 range, and you're nowhere near 1000, you might be facing a wall that can't be climbed. You want to try for "a reach," but not recklessly toss away application fees, which can run from $25 to $60 a pop. Finally, are you ready (if accepted) to sit next to scholars who might study around the clock and sleep with Albert Einstein (or Benjamin Banneker) T-shirts on? Think about it. We've seen students do the impossible when given the chance. Whatever you decide to do, showcase all your positives, no matter where you apply and what your standardized test scores are. You never know.

For more information on standardized tests, see chapter 5.

Question 4: *"What strategies or suggestions do you recommend in regard to taking SAT or ACT tests?"*

Of course, the stronger your high school preparation (e.g., taking honors or advanced placement courses), the better prepared you'll be to tackle the tests. Still, no matter what level you're at, you should always go in knowing the rules of engagement. You should know what the tests entail, the varying sections, and what to expect. Walking in blind is foolhardy. The very least you should do is study and review the guidebooks. Less than a month's preparation will not be enough. Time yourself while taking practice tests. Take no shortcuts.

Hopefully, your high school will be giving you guidance. If not, study and practice on your own. Do not go in without a clue. One key is pacing. You should have a feel for how fast or slow you should be moving from question to question. Remember that the results of these tests, for better or worse, will be as important as your GPA and your four years of coursework to many admissions officers.

A must—particularly if you are a super student looking at those prestigious schools—is to take the best prep course you can find, even if it means some sacrifice of time and money. Top students of other cultures routinely do this. You shouldn't concede any advantage to anyone.

If you can get into the prestigious ballpark with your score (perhaps 1200 or over) and you have been taking a strong college preparatory track courseload, there is no need to keep taking the test over. If you have a solid GPA, concentrate on other facets of your application, particularly polishing your essay and obtaining superlative recommendations, rather than retaking the test in search of a few more points.

If you're "not ready" and know it, study as hard as you can, and even if you don't get a top score, take the test only once. Let that score stand. Over and over, we see students retaking the test in the hope that a miracle will occur. It rarely does. Amazingly, a good deal of the time the do-it-again student has done absolutely nothing to improve his or her score. It's better to have one low score—perhaps you had a bad day!—than three or four test scores that confirm that you were ill-prepared. You only retake the test if you have been seriously prepping for a rematch.

In regard to the PSAT, which is usually given as a prep test in the 11th grade, treat it seriously. In fact, we recommend that be your first strike in your college campaign. Take your prep courses before you take that test. Do well, and you're eligible for National Merit Scholarship and other awards. Do well and the highly ranked and strong colleges will start sending you "Congratulations" and "recruit" mail.

Here are some excerpt samples from colleges after you do well on those SAT and PSAT tests:

> Williams: *"Congratulations on your impressive academic achievements!"*
>
> Brandeis: *"You're in the top ranks of the nation's rising high school seniors. . . ."*
>
> Stevens Institute of Technology: *"Congratulations. Your excellent PSAT scores and interest in humanities are a winning combination."*
>
> Simon's Rock of Bard College: *" . . .consider applying for a W. E. B. Du Bois Scholarship . . ."*
>
> Wellesley College: *"I hope that Wellesley College is one of the schools on your list."*

Get the point?
For more information on standardized tests, see chapter 5.

Question 5: *"How are the SAT, PSAT, and ACT tests different?"*

The SAT is a three-hour test, with seven sections. There are three math and three verbal parts. Also, there is an experimental section.

The PSAT (usually given in October in your junior year) is often called a "practice" test. Don't practice here. We recommend that if you are not ready, skip it. Get books and practice at home.

These "practice" scores show up in your college folders. The three sections here will focus on math, verbal, and writing skills.

The ACT is usually given and used in the midwestern states. Most schools, however, will accept it. Here you're find four pivotal sections: math, English, writing, and science.

Your high school should provide info in regard to taking all these tests. If not, call (609) 921-9000 for SAT instructions/timetables or (319) 337-1000 for ACT guidance.

For more information on standardized tests, see chapter 5.

Question 6: *"I have taken advanced placement courses and did well on the exams. Folks are saying that I can jump over a semester to a year's college work if I apply for the credits. They say, too, that I can cut my college costs, because I would be reducing the time and credits I would need to get my degree. What's your opinion?"*

We have worked with many students who have taken advanced placement courses and done well on the tests. We have also worked with students in international baccalaureate programs (i.e., students who are pursuing college credits in high school). The positive in pursuing advanced credit in college is that you can save money and time. The negative is that you might be jeopardizing your eventual GPA. If you are a "super student" who is thinking of medical or law school, we would advise you to forget about the tempting positives.

In regard to medical school, for example, getting an acceptance is almost tantamount to climbing Mount Everest. Sound strategy is to do everything and anything to keep your GPA as high as possible, start to finish. If you have advanced credits skills, you want to put that knowledge into play in beginning 101 classes. We say "Hedge your bets and try for A's." If you are given advanced placement credits in biology, calculus, physics, or chemistry (to name a few heavy-hitting courses), you don't want to willy-nilly "jump" to the next level.

With each upgrade, the rigor, content, and pace of a course can sometimes be maddening. Why not advance along with other students who are also freshman? In regard to medical school admission, that C+ in a course or two could signal the end. Note that some medical schools will actually have GPA cutoffs—a 3.2, let's say. And if you don't reach that, they don't even look at your folder. In a nutshell, don't risk forfeiting everything for a semester or a year. Your advanced placement strategy should depend on what you'll be shooting for down the road.

Of course, if you're an aspiring journalist or artist or are pursuing a goal that isn't dependent on some final do-or-die analysis of the numbers, then it might pay to take advantage of the opportunity for quicker advancement.

For more information on standardized tests, see chapter 5.

Question 7: *"How many colleges should I apply to? Is there a formula, or a best strategy?"*

We've always recommended that more is better than less. Often we've said six to eight is a good number range, depending on your finances and resources. In regard to some public college systems, a single application can sometimes leave you eligible for a half a dozen schools. Count that application as one. When the process is over you want to have several admits, as well as a number of financial aid offers to consider. One or two of these might be that super school that's a "tough admit." That's your dream school. Two others should be "probable admits" based on your record and test scores. The final two should be "certain" accepts. In a nutshell, you want to cover all bases and be left with a college you can attend.

Tip: If you are a super student you might want to increase your overall number of applications. Apply to a cluster of highly regarded schools in addition to a few "probable" and "certain" admits. Take no chances.

For more information on application strategies, see chapters 2 and 3.

Question 8: *"My son is an honors student with great grades and test scores. Would it be to his advantage to apply to a college 'early decision' if they have such a program?"*

Generally, students we have worked with have not chosen the early-decision route. If you opt for an early-decision try, you must attend your targeted school if accepted. You can't change your mind. Also, whatever financial aid package they award you, that's generally it, since you have no leverage for negotiation. Of course, if you are a super student and have the money, and one very special school is your dream choice, you might want to go that way. Schools such as Wellesley, Oberlin, Bowdoin, the University of Chicago, and Notre Dame always seem to be partial to any strong student of color. In fact, any highly ranked school with a relatively low percentage of black students will probably throw out the welcome mat if you're an impressive candidate. Still, it is our opinion that students of color who are "highly desirable" are in a win-win situation. Why have one stellar pick when you can have five bargaining for your attention? Why not pick and choose and then negotiate for the best deal? Maybe one of your selections will want to foot a large portion of the bill.

For more information on application strategies, see chapters 2 and 3.

Question 9: *"I am a high school senior and want to go to a black college. My father thinks I should go to a predominantly white college, but my mother thinks a historically black college would be better. What do you say?"*

There is no easy answer or objectively superior choice. For more than a decade we have helped students get into both historically black and mainstream colleges. Students we have counseled have applied to Cornell, Morehouse, Bennett, Johns Hopkins, Florida A&M, UPenn, Howard, Emory, and Clark-Atlanta, as well as more than a hundred other schools across the spectrum. Our thinking is simple: the selection of a college should depend on the individual student's personality, attitude, ability, social skills, and needs. We encourage parents to ask this question: "What does my son or daughter require to be happy and successful?" The next question should be: "What does each individual college offer to meet those needs?" For example, if a student needs a "nurturing environment" (some personal attention, perhaps tutoring), it would be foolish to ignore the historically black colleges. Our experience has generally been that personal attention, hands-on help, and aggressive mentoring are more likely at a historically black college, where extra encouragement and counseling are freely offered, particularly if you run into academic difficulty. At too many mainstream schools, students of color are left to sink or swim. Although statistics show that there are more students of color at mainstream schools, the HBCU graduation rate suggests that they often offer more support. Of course, at mainstream schools you are more likely to find fully equipped, state-of-the-art laboratories, computers, libraries, famous-name faculty, and big endowments. But while one black student might fare very well at Ohio State, another does better at Florida A&M. Each student must factor into his or her college picks considerations such as a school's reputation, racism, social life, majors, levels of course difficulty, on-site support systems, cost, campus employment, and work-study opportunities, as well options for graduate study.

For more information on the white college/black college decision, see chapter 8.

Question 10: *"If I pick a predominantly white college, will I feel isolated?"*

The answer to this question has a lot with to do with "who" you are. On some campuses there is a friendly cultural mix. Students of all colors seem to adjust. Elsewhere, you might feel alone. Your personality and attitude are key factors. Remember, too, that many schools actually have a "college within a college" feel. Cultural groups find their "own thing." Often black students have their own preferred hangouts and organizations, including the Black Student Union and related groups. The reality is that we are often segregated once we leave the classroom. Still, we feel that you can find whatever you are looking for. The wise thing is to try to pick a school where you'll feel most comfortable. Choices span the entire social and cultural gambit, A to Z.

For more information on the white college/black college decision, see chapter 8.

Question 11: *"If I pick a historically black college, will I be at a disadvantage in regard to career and graduate and professional school options?"*

Really, we have watched graduates from historically black colleges and mainstream schools both excel. Frankly, there is a wide range of varying schools with stellar reputations and track records. There are, to be sure, different tiers of historically black schools. In regard to the schools at the top, rest assured that you can reach your destination, whatever it is. For example, the students we have worked with who went to Spelman or Morehouse or Hampton (to name a few of our top HBCU picks) are arriving at the same peaks reached by our Ivy Leaguers when it comes to careers and graduate school options.

Also, at many of the lesser-known schools, we see students excelling and reaching targeted goals. We are sure about one thing: a lot of what happens depends on the drive and resourcefulness of a particular student, whatever type of school he or she picks.

The above said, there are a relatively small number of historically black or predominantly white schools—fewer than 100—that can open doors for graduates on their reputations alone. Spelman graduates, for example, are well respected and received at the top graduate schools and in industry. And, of course, having a Harvard degree has never hurt anyone's prospects.

For more information on the white college/black college decision, see chapter 8.

Question 12: *"My child is heading to college in a few months. We need a scholarship. How do we get one ASAP?"*

Many students and families have misconceptions about the idea of scholarships. They mistakenly think that finding that money is going to offer "salvation" and a quick fix. They want somebody who can point them to the gold in a wink. Unfortunately, it doesn't happen that way.

First, the student must have an impressive résumé (grades, test scores, extracurricular activities, or special talents). You've got to impress a money-giver. Contrary to what a few books imply about an average Joe or Jane walking away with the cash, it's not happening. These awards, grants, and giveaways are competitive. Every student is trying to get a piece of the pie.

Going head to head with others, you've got to sell yourself. Frankly, we see strong and/or talented students winning scholarships all the time. But it's not a one-week or a 30-day process. Generally, you've got to send for applications, follow instructions, and forward your personal package back to the scholarship source. Often that includes an essay, recommendations, and other extras. To get a "yes" or a "no" can take months. Still, the effort of completing this taxing process often reaps big rewards. No half hearted approach is likely to work. You've got to be on a mission and start early.

For more information on getting scholarship money, see chapter 14.

Question 13: *"Okay, I've won a scholarship or two. What happens next?"*

We've received notes like this: "Yeeeaaaahhh, I've won a scholarship! After my student loan and the college grant, the college still wanted $2,000, and the scholarship was for $2,000. Now we don't have to pay anything. It's free!" Wrong!

After you complete your FAFSA (Financial Aid Form for Student Aid), an analysis of what you and your family can pay for tuition is calculated. Student/parent federal income tax returns, W-2s, and bank savings are part of the equation. If the calculations say you are capable of paying $2,000 a year, that's generally the ballpark figure you will be expected to pay.

That said, the college will create "a package" for you. The package will include federal Pell aid, a college grant, state money, a loan, and (maybe) work-study. If total tuition and board are $10,000, the college will subtract the $2,000 (you can theoretically pay) and create "a package" for you that includes the above. In this case the package will be worth about $8,000. The balance would be your responsibility.

Okay, you then win a scholarship worth $2,000. Generally, colleges will then subtract that total from your package side. Perhaps they'll reduce your grant or the loan. You will still be responsible for the $2,000 due. Got it?

The plus side in the above scenario is that the scholarship money will likely reduce your future debt.

For more information on financial aid and scholarships, see chapters 12 and 14.

Question 14: *"Can you be more specific about the financial aid package that will be put together? What's 'typical,' or to be expected?"*

Generally, the federal government foots the major portion of your bill by giving you a loan. The first-year limit is usually about $2,600. In the second year you can get about $3,500. After that, the loan can go as high as $5,500 per year. If you need more than four years, the debt ceiling can reach $23,000.

The Pell grant is also a key yearly giveaway for students who fall under specific income totals. That can amount to as much as $3,000 (it varies every year). You don't have to pay this back.

A federal Perkins loan is also available to students who fall under certain income lines. That's about $4,000 a year.

Individual states usually have grants ("incentive awards") and other money extras that are available to its resident students.

Generally colleges offer most students who are admitted additional grants or scholarships to cut some of the cost. In *Money* magazine's college edition, for example, you can find out what the average giveaway totals are at individual schools. Remember that the stated price tag for a college is often nowhere near the actual cost. After the "discount," the tuition at most schools can be 30% or more less than the published tuition. The average discount at prestigious Duke is 50%. At historically black Tuskegee University, it's about 28%. Work-study can help with some of the financial burden, as well as other campus jobs students often find independently.

Parents can apply for PLUS (Parent Loans for Undergraduate Students) and other loans to pay the bill if necessary. Some parents with the means and homes do refinance their mortgages to help pay tuition. Finally, there are payment plans that can help you pay in monthly installments.

A key thing to remember is that just about every student/family who is aspiring to get a college degree will go through this "money" crisis. It's a sacrifice, however, that will reap benefits.

For more information on putting together a financial package, see chapter 13.

Question 15: *"We've picked about a dozen colleges we like, but some have huge price tags. We only have a modest income. Would applying just be an exercise in futility?"*

Oftentimes that highly endowed, more expensive college, will give you a better financial deal than the school with the much cheaper price tag. Note our answer about price tags in the previous response. You never know. If you are a strong student, you would be wise to apply to whatever colleges you like, and see what happens. If it's a prestigious school, that institution will often attempt to meet your need or even sweeten the pie. And again, always back up your college picks with at least a couple of obvious bargain buys. Many of the public, state universities are excellent selections.

For more information on financial aid strategies, see chapters 12 and 13.

Question 16: *"My child has gotten that 'accept' and is college-bound. We are rejoicing. Are there any helpful suggestions or advice you can give us?"*

First, congratulations! It's a great moment, to be sure. We think the following comments (a bit abbreviated) by Jay Ento, director of the Oakland and National Chapters of JSHC and coordinator of the FOCUS 2000 and Heir Apparent Programs for junior and senior high school students, will be helpful:

THROW YOUR COLLEGE-BOUND YOUNGSTER a "scholarship shower" and invite family and friends to celebrate your child's achievement. The invitations can be made up on the computer or purchased at any Hallmark shop. Enclose a list of gift suggestions the young person will need, especially if they are going to be staying in a dorm. A laundry basket filled with detergent, bleach, softener, and $20 worth of quarters is a great gift.

Your youngster will need blankets, mattress pads, pillows, sheets (dorm size), clothes hangers, personal and hygienic products, towels, a wastebasket, desk lamp, pens, a dictionary, and a thesaurus.

Also: nonperishable food items (including crackers, juice, and bottled water), posters, picture frames, stationery, luggage, umbrella, backpack, room deodorizer, Roach Motels (just in case), iron, clock, radio, and a laptop or PC computer with diskettes and a printer.

Note that most students also have the following in their rooms (I couldn't believe it when I saw it myself!): minirefrigerators, microwave ovens, CD players with BIIIIGGG speakers, televisions, and VCRs—all the comforts of home. For girls: hair care is important, so when you visit the college of your choice, check out the nearest black-owned beauty spot near campus, or wear braids, locks, or an Afro unless you can do it yourself. If you plan to perm and style, you better make sure you bring all the hair-care products you will need for the entire semester.

Tip: do not sign up for credit cards that will be offered to you (especially during your first two weeks of your freshman year) unless you have a good-paying part-time job. After all, students tend to charge stupid things on their new Visa and MC cards: CDs, clothes, food, shoes, stuff for their dorm rooms, and more clothes.

Have your youngsters stick to a budget. If they do that (they won't), they'll be all right. Only pay for your child's $200 + phone bill once!! Emphasize they are to call you once a week for the first few weeks; then once a month is sufficient. They are not to call their homies, girl, or boyfriends at another college 300 + miles away or their favorite cousin who is attending college 3,000 miles away. Kids tend to think they are just talking across the room, not across time zones and area codes!

Last, if your child has a medical condition, make sure he or she has all the necessary medication for the semester, including prescriptions for refills.

Let me add that getting your child an "emergency" debit card is a good idea. Also, providing an answering machine is highly recommended, as your child will not spend most of his or her time in the room.

CHAPTER 2

PICKING A COLLEGE

What You Know Can Help You

Often the first question a student will ask us when they come in for a consultation is this: "Can I get into college?" Fortunately, the answer to that question, almost without exception, is easy: "Yes, you can get into college." The second question they ask is invariably: "Where?" Now, that's a tougher one to answer.

Picking a college isn't easy. There are more than 3,000 four-year colleges in the United States and nearly 4,000 two-year schools, and we can honestly say from experience that most parents and students aren't even aware of a fraction of them. We often hear students mention Spelman or Harvard or their state university or the college their brother, uncle, or mother went to—but when we ask them for specific reasons why they're interested in those colleges, we often get blank stares. But picking the right college is more than just choosing among the few colleges that you already know about, or limiting your sights to the colleges in your local area. The right college for you is the college that gives you the academic and social experience you want and that prepares you for the career you're seeking (or opens you up to career choices you hadn't even thought about). And let's not forget: the right college is also the college that will accept you and whose tuition fits your ability to pay! But to pick the right school, you have to start early.

PUT ON YOUR RACING SHOES: YOU'RE AT THE STARTING LINE

You should begin thinking seriously about choosing a college as early as elementary or junior high school. Of course, if you're already in 9th, 10th, 11th, or even 12th grade, you better get on it. It's better to be early than late, and it's never too early to start getting a feel for the terrain. It's important to realize that the students you'll be competing with for those coveted seats at the college you want to attend are already preparing themselves.

Here is a true story: A white woman who knows that I run a college help service recently approached me. Two months before, she had given birth to a baby boy. Her questions: What are the best colleges? How important is the SAT? Should she begin a college savings plan now? Believe it. Whether you're a student or a parent, it's never too soon to be proactive about college selection.

On the other hand, as late as the beginning of senior year, we find lots of our students in a tizzy. The sad truth is that making a college choice at that point is like throwing dice. There are a number of important factors that students and their parents should be very familiar with by this point. See if you can answer the following questions:

- What's your GPA?
- What's the name and location of the state university (or universities) in your state?
- What's your class rank?
- What's the Ivy League?
- How does financial aid work?
- What's the FAFSA?
- Can you name ten historically black colleges?
- How important is your ability to write a good essay? To have extracurricular activities?
- What is advanced placement?
- What is early admissions?

Consider this a preparedness test. If you don't know the answers to these questions yet, you should start looking for them. (Don't worry: you'll find them all in this book.)

USE YOUR HIGH SCHOOL COUNSELORS—BUT NOT TOO MUCH!

It makes sense to use your high school counselors as much as possible to help you make the right decision. That's what they're there for. But be careful. While there are great counselors out there—and we've interacted with some truly remarkable ones—note the following from a recent *Time/Princeton Review* college edition: "Most counselors are great, but all counselors, and especially those in large public schools, are swamped with work." Pat Ordovensy, author of *College Planning for Dummies,* takes it a step farther: "Poor high school counselors know as much about the admissions process as you. Maybe less."

The point is, when it comes to choosing a school, you need to be proactive and not just react to the guidance of your high school counselors. In our counseling sessions with students and their parents, we repeatedly see very strong African American candidates referred by their counselors to "acceptable" or "good" state colleges when, in fact, they are capable of being accepted at the top-ranking schools in the country. Often when faced with good to stellar records, some counselors seem to have lower aim and poorer expectations than the students themselves. Also, many high school counselors are not properly aware of the best HBCUs—many with remarkable track records—and direct their top black students away from these fine schools.

An absence of good advice can be hazardous. Bad advice can be worse. Picking the wrong school can be traumatic and affect you for the rest of your life. The bottom line? Take advantage of whatever counseling you get, but in the end, you have to make an educated choice about which school is right for you. But how?

GET THOSE CATALOGS!

As early as possible, you should start sending for college catalogs, viewbooks, and applications. A simple request letter to the university will usually do the trick (see the model letter below). If possible, ask for a copy of the school's newspaper as well. Why the newspaper? Looking at a school's newspaper gives you a firsthand idea of what's going on on campus. It's a great way to find out about special programs, student morale, and even issues such as campus safety and crime. And folks, we're not talking about sending requests to two or three colleges; we're suggesting that you create a master request letter and forward it to fifteen to twenty different schools of different sorts, including both predominantly white institutions (PWIs) and historically black colleges. You can find school names and addresses by referring to the profiles presented in part three of this guide.

Here's a sample of a letter requesting a catalog and other information:

[Insert date]

Dr. Elizabeth Mitchell
Office of Admissions
Rutgers University
P.O. Box 2101
New Brunswick, NJ 08903-2101

Dear Dr. Mitchell:

I am an African American student considering applying to your university. Please send me your catalog, an application, your minority viewbook, and a copy of your school newspaper, if possible. Please forward the material to:

Derek Smith
123 Main Street
New City, CA 98765

Thank you.

Sincerely,
Derek Smith

Catalogs

College catalogs come in all shapes and sizes. We have seen hundreds and, trust us, they are an amazing phenomenon. Some are very creative, and many of them are glossy and full of lovely pictures of buildings with ivy-colored walls and green lawns—and, of course, those very attractive students running around the campus.

But the key thing is that the catalogs contain vital information about the college, including general information about the university's mission, campus (often including maps and directories), academic requirements, available majors, and a cost overview. Don't be overwhelmed or unduly influenced by the photos and the copy—many of these catalogs, especially from well-endowed schools, function as advertisements designed to sell you on the spot. Even as they are making their emotional pitch through words and pictures, keep your bearings and glean the important information you need.

The Viewbook

Usually the viewbook is a quicker, much more snappy promotional piece designed to tell you about the college. We call some of these shorter booklets "the lazy man's catalog." They offer a quick read with illustrations, including, occasionally, poster-size foldouts. Sometimes colleges offer viewbooks aimed at African American or minority students. These viewbooks often touch on issues such as how you would fit in, the college environment, cultural resources, course offerings, exchange programs, aid, and other opportunities for your group. Of course, it's a biased point of view. Nevertheless, these publications can be useful in telling you what a college thinks about itself and what its priorities are.

> If you take the PSAT or the SAT and receive a good score (more about these tests in later chapters), you might be sent something extra from colleges. One of the students we worked with did well on his college boards and received a slew of information from colleges, including student journals, home videos, and a prospectus.

THE X FACTOR: FINDING SCHOOLS AT THE RIGHT LEVEL FOR YOU

Now you've got a couple of dozen catalogs, but how do you start narrowing your search? Well, to pick a college, there are a few basic facts and realities you must digest. Colleges are different in many ways, some as opposite as night and day. For example, at some schools a student might actually raise his or her hand and question a theory by a Pulitzer or Nobel Prize winner teaching the course. At another college, introductory classes might be taught at an almost remedial level (perhaps equivalent to the work you aced in high school). So be aware; it's been our experience that many African American students think of "college" as if it's a standardized situation, when in fact the differences among colleges are profound.

A college's "admit" level is the X factor. It's a key consideration when picking schools. In the college admissions game, knowing where a school is ranked is as important as a scientist knowing about Einstein's theory of relativity. It's 30% of the ball game. Black Excel, after a decade of analyzing the X factor, has broken the college levels into five categories. We have given each category a tag name with explanations for better understanding:

1. Climbing Everest: Very Competitive
2. Designer Clothes: Competitive
3. As the World Turns: Average
4. Wheel of Fortune: Noncompetitive
5. You've Come a Long Way: Open Admissions

Following are detailed descriptions of each level of school. This overview will help you in your assessment of how and where you should attack when you're ready. The trick is to target the best schools for you while simultaneously factoring in your chances for getting accepted.

CLIMBING EVEREST: VERY COMPETITIVE SCHOOLS

If you are applying to the *very competitive* schools, you are definitely taking on a task akin to climbing Everest. At the very peak, there are about fifty schools, including the cluster of Ivy League schools (Harvard, Princeton, Penn, Brown, Yale, Cornell, Dartmouth, and Columbia) and such brand-name institutions as Chicago, Stanford, Northwestern, Emory, and MIT. Schools at this challenging level are obviously looking for overachievers. Students accepted to these prestigious universities have usually taken and excelled at the most rigorous courses available at their high schools, including honors and advanced courses and even college-level courses taken at local colleges. They have also made a point of engaging in a variety of extracurricular activities and acing the necessary college boards.

The Ethnic Factor

Despite the sterling reputations of some very competitive colleges, students should always consider the "ethnic factor." Will you be welcome? Can you adjust to whatever the environment might be? For example, consider the California Institute of Technology. It consistently ranks as one of the top academic schools in the nation; however, its black enrollment has historically been less than 1%. Does that matter to you? On the other hand, a top college such as the University of North Carolina at Chapel Hill has a wonderful reputation, quality academics, and their enrollment is approximately 10% African American annually. The numbers could be telling.

Be aware that your minority status might help you in getting admitted to some top universities, many of which are actively trying to diversify their student population. So, if you are a student who has excelled, but don't think your standardized test scores measure up, don't be deterred. If you are in the test score ballpark, and you believe you can compete against anyone in a classroom environment, prepare your application. A recent study from the *Journal of Blacks in Higher Education* found that at schools such as Harvard, Princeton, Vassar, Amherst, and Haverford, African Americans are graduating at a pace that indicates we are competing successfully, no matter what the standardized test scores say.

So don't let anyone "dumb down" your application choices. One essential factor that is often forgotten by counselors is the fact that in many cases, black students have already overcome odds, including the need to play "catch-up" in some areas due to poor training at the primary and secondary levels. When you put an African American catch-up student into the battle, they often adapt, adjust, and excel. We've found that to be the case with students we've helped get into institutions such as Duke, Harvard, Penn, and Smith. We can compete.

Super Black Colleges

While schools such as Spelman, Morehouse, and Hampton have been given high praise in standard college references, HBCU rankings in general don't really reflect their true quality. Black schools are, to put it mildly, at a considerable disadvantage when the mainstream methodology is put into play. For example, at *US News,* the creator of one of the most influential college rankings, 25% of a school's score is based on "academic reputation," which even they admit is highly subjective. To qualify a school's academic reputation, their research team polls the president, provost, and deans of admissions at other colleges and universities. Are these educators even remotely aware of what's going on at the top HBCU campuses, let alone at the average schools? Another key consideration added into the *US News* rating is "financial resources," which weights the ratings toward schools with large endowments. This excludes most HBCUs and, at any rate, is of debatable importance to the individual student. The bottom line? If you feel that you're ready for a very competitive school, don't forget to consider the top HBCUs (see part three for descriptions of the top HBCUs).

Looking in the Mirror: Competitive Students

All right, now it's time to look in the mirror to see if you measure up to the admissions profile of the very competitive colleges and universities. Your shouldn't see any warts here, or excess baby fat. You should have the look and the gait of a winner. You—and the admissions officers at the very competitive schools—should see as many of the following as possible.

- B+ or higher grade average
- honors/advanced placement courses
- top 10% class rank
- 1300 or higher SAT score (or in the ballpark)
- strong to super application essay
- strong to super recommendations
- strong to super extracurricular activities
- special talents
- proven leadership qualities
- proven success potential
- community service
- summer work or volunteer experience
- intangible qualities that suggest you'll be adding positive karma to the campus environment

Here's what you *shouldn't* see in the mirror:

- academic lapses
- indicators of a lack of goals or motivation
- intellectual malingering (i.e., taking easy or "general" courses)
- a problematic disciplinary background (e.g., suspensions, arrests)
- no signs of being a potential contributor to campus life

If you don't see yourself as ready for the very competitive schools, don't worry: most people aren't. But there are still a wide range of schools that can offer you a strong academic environment and a great launching pad for your career and your life.

DESIGNER CLOTHES: COMPETITIVE SCHOOLS

Many of you have heard that oldie "There's a Thin Line between Love and Hate." Well, very often there's a thin line between what it takes to get into a very competitive school and a merely competitive school. There's usually a dip in the median SAT scores at the competitive schools, and they are more willing to accept students with strong, promising records. But remember, if you've been a good student, you'll find yourself in a buyer's market. A transcript that indicates your ability to take on courses such as chemistry, physics, or calculus is like a beacon to admissions officers. Toss in a solid grade average, strong college boards, and good intangibles and there's an excellent chance doors will open. And even if you're not a top student in terms of grades and test scores, you can reach if you have other strengths and talents.

The competitive schools take 50% to 80% of their applicants. In this grouping are schools that are fairly picky, looking for only prepared, motivated, and capable students. This group includes good state universities such as second-tier University of California and State University of New York schools, the University of Maryland at College Park, and Pennsylvania State University. It includes private institutions like Fordham University (NY), American University (DC), and Seattle University (WA). This category also includes such HBCUs as Xavier University of Louisiana, Tuskegee University (AL), and Florida A&M.

Looking in the Mirror: Competitive Schools

Okay, now it's your turn to look in the mirror to see if you've got what it takes to make the cut at a competitive school. Here's what you should see:

- at least a B average, with some A's thrown in
- some honors/advanced placement/college-level courses
- rank in the top 30% to 40% of your class
- SAT score over 1000
- solid application essay
- solid recommendations
- good extracurricular activities
- indications of strong potential
- intangible qualities that suggest you'll be adding positive karma to the campus environment

Here's what you shouldn't see:

- same negatives as for very competitive students
- any indications that you can't do the work or have dropout potential

AS THE WORLD TURNS: AVERAGE SCHOOLS

These schools make up the bulk of the nation's colleges—more than 2,500—and include schools that may have some local or regional obligations to some students. These are degree-granting universities that accept the vast majority—60% to 90%—of candidates. Some have name recognition and good reputations. A passable record and show of promise may be all it takes to get accepted. Schools in this category include third-tier state schools such as the University of Nevada at Las Vegas, small private colleges and universities such as the Philadelphia College of Textiles and Science, and second-tier HBCUs such as Grambling State University (LA), North Carolina Central, and Clark-Atlanta University.

Even if you consider yourself only an "average" student, you should definitely keep your college hopes alive and think seriously about "reaching." Follow these steps:

1. Go to your grade adviser. Ask which colleges are likely to accept you and which colleges he or she recommends based on your overall record. Make a list.
2. Find out which local colleges your high school "feeds" students with records similar to yours. Make a list.
3. Find out which "side door" programs are available. Ask your adviser about the SEEK (Search for Education, Elevation, and Knowledge) program, College Discovery, and HEOP (Higher Education Opportunity Program). If you come from an economically disadvantaged background, there may be wonderful options open to you. Make a list.
4. Go to the section of this book on historically black colleges. More than 140 schools are listed, including "mainstream" schools where the student body is more than 75% black. The majority of these schools welcome "average" students.
5. Reassess yourself. We've worked with many students who at first considered themselves only average, but after some coaching were able to beat out students with better academic credentials for spots at good schools. Could your nonacademic credentials or exceptional social activities and contributions make you more attractive?

From this process you should be able to develop a list of desirable colleges.

WHEEL OF FORTUNE: NONCOMPETITIVE SCHOOLS

Noncompetitive schools offer excellent opportunities for a second chance—you *can* recover your fumbles! Noncompetitive schools are, for many, a godsend. They offer an excellent opportunity to I-am-ready-to-turn-it-around students. Sometimes students look at their transcripts and wish they could erase entire sections. We've looked at numerous transcripts that mix areas of hope with passages of despair; we call them "report card enigmas." A line of English courses might end with an accumulated average of 82, let's say. Good! A math column might point to a 66 average, with two failures and two summer school retakes. Bad!

Other areas on your transcript might show a yo-yo effect. For example, a student might get an 80 in algebra during the first semester and a 65 in the second. SAT scores might be marginal: 810 combined on a first test; maybe the same or even less on the second. Then, during the senior year, the student admits to not taking anything seriously. Is all lost? No way. Noncompetitive schools offer a chance to work out the "enigma" and develop academic consistency. Generally schools in this category accept 85 to 90%—or more—of students who apply. These schools include HBCUs such as Virginia State University, Norfolk State University, and Albany State College, as well as many state and city colleges.

YOU'VE COME A LONG WAY: OPEN ADMISSIONS

Open admissions schools are schools that accept 100% of students who apply. The open admission schools are great second or even third chances at going to college. A student who has had serious academic problems but is still determined to get into college should consider this option. Such schools can become an essential turning point in your life, that pivotal key to future opportunities.

Open admissions schools include HBCUs and state- and city-funded colleges, including Wilmington College (DE), Northern Kentucky University, Southern University at New Orleans, Indiana University Southeast, Lincoln University (MO), Thomas Edison State College (NJ), Rush College (MS), New College of California at Miles City, and Medgar Evers College of the City University of New York.

You Can Be a Pauper Today but a Prince (or a Princess) Tomorrow

I used to incessantly study catalogs from historically black colleges. I would place them in stacks and then read them, one after the other. I would often read the listings of faculty. What a lesson I learned! Take, for instance, the Tuskegee faculty: one department head got his B.S. from Rush College (a small HBCU in Mississippi). He then went on to get his master's and Ph.D. from Purdue University. Another professor got his B.S. from very small Paul Quinn College in Texas, another HBCU. He ended up getting his Ph.D. from the University of Michigan.

Here again the saying "The longest journey begins with one step" rings true. No matter what your record says today, no matter how far you've fallen, you get up, shake yourself off, and climb to the mountaintop. That college that nobody has ever heard of could be your oasis, the catalyst that sends you soaring to fame and fortune. The key is to get in somewhere and go from there.

I have a number of "come from behind" stories to tell, including my own, but for now let me just tell you of two gentlemen I've worked with who desperately lost their ways as teenagers: both were high school dropouts, petty criminals, and addicted to drugs. But they never said "never." Fighting back, one eventually was awarded an M.S.W. from Columbia University; the other a master's degree from Harvard. The lesson? Nobody can count you out if you're willing to fight.

Whether it's a noncompetitive or an open admissions opportunity, if options are limited it's time to get to steppin'. The key is to make the move that allows you to recover and put that bad start or wrong turn behind you. Smile, because every student who has experienced social or academic problems can still get into the get-that-degree sweepstakes. All you need is desire.

KNOW YOURSELF: THE NINE KEYS FOR COLLEGE SELECTION

Now that you're aware of the different levels of colleges out there, the next step to finding the right college is to *know yourself*. By the time you begin your senior year in high school, you should already have begun your self-assessment. What kind of student have you been? On the Dean's List? All honors? Top quarter of your class? That average Joe or Jane (or Malik or Kyesha)? Someone who, for whatever reason, needs a second chance? Indeed, what does your transcript look like? Does it say "success" or "potential" or "oops"? Don't kid yourself; be real, be honest. Have you made a contribution to your school? To your community? Were you the class president, a hospital volunteer, cheerleader, or just a face in the crowd? Were you the editor who helped put that fabulous yearbook together, a chorus soloist? Did awards or recognition come to you? Or were you like most students in high school—virtually invisible? An honest self-assessment is essential. We'll be returning to that theme at each stage of the admissions process.

Here are nine key things you must consider about yourself and your needs in order to pick the right college for you:

1. your academic profile: test scores, GPA, and class rank
2. your special talents and qualities
3. your motivation and readiness
4. your nirvana—finding a match for your major and career goals
5. the "black factor"
6. dating and dancing: your social life
7. the intangibles: location, size, food, climate, and racism
8. playing it smart: your visit and admissions drop-ins
9. the winner's circle: your lotto picks, or "you can't win it unless you're in it!"

The First Key: Your Academic Profile

There are three main components to your academic profile: your scores on the college boards, your grade-point average, and your class rank.

First, consider your ACT or SAT scores. Just comparing your scores on these tests to the reported average scores at various schools will give you a general idea of which schools you should target. When you're checking a school's "average" scores, just remember that at the more prestigious mainstream schools, our "get in" scores are generally less than the average or median scores reported in catalogs and college guidebooks. At some places, including such highly ranked schools as Johns Hopkins, MIT, and Princeton, an African American student can score 150 or more points less than the reported average score and still be accepted. Why? Because these schools—despite the recent affirmative action backlash—put more emphasis on a black student's potential, as demonstrated by other factors, than in their cold test results. We'll talk more about this later in the book.

The second thing to consider is your GPA and courseload, as indicated on your transcript. This is perhaps the single most important key to how a college admission team views your application. We call the transcript your student DNA.

Aside from the raw grade averages, admissions officers also factor in the rigor of your courseload. The powerhouse schools expect to see a demanding courseload, with correspondingly good grades. Your courses signal where you want to go; your grades signal how likely you are to get there.

The third factor in your academic self-portrait is your class rank. In a nutshell, the admissions people want to see how you stack up against your classmates. Are you simply another Joe or Jane, or do you stand out?

Usually, your transcript will have a section indicating your class rank or percentile. For example, the transcript might indicate that there are 233 graduating seniors in your class and that based on a comparison of GPAs, you are ranked 13th. In other words, you had a better GPA than 220 of your classmates. That rank would also place you in the top 7% of the graduating seniors at your school. If you went to a high school with a strong reputation, that's a mighty plus; but even if you went to a less highly regarded school, a high rank works in your favor.

Since different universities have different standards for class rank, knowing your class rank is another good way to narrow your college search. For instance, if you rank in the lower 20% of your class, you probably shouldn't set your heart on Yale, where 95% of the students accepted graduated in the top 10% of their class. Here's a quick sampling of the average number of students graduating in the top 10% of their class at some other schools:

Amherst College: 84%

City College of the City University of New York: 7%

North Carolina Central University: 8%

Rochester Institute of Technology: 27%

South Carolina State University: 14%

Stanford University: 95%

Syracuse University: 33%

University of Maryland, College Park: 26%

University of Southern California: 43%

Wesleyan University: 63%

Now imagine you're a fly on the wall as admissions officers are examining your test scores, GPA, and class rank. They're asking themselves, "At our college, can this student do the work? Can he or she, based on what we're looking at, be reasonably expected to graduate? If not, has this student shown the potential to rise to the occasion?" It's better to ask yourself those questions first, and answer them honestly, *before* applying.

The Second Key: Your Special Talents and Qualities

A total overview of who you are, and what you've done, is a pivotal part of your self-assessment. While your academic profile is important, sometimes you've got to think beyond academics; make sure you play your complete hand. Sometimes it's those intangibles that will allow you to reach for a higher level and get accepted to better schools than your academic profile might suggest.

Here's a true story: A student sat with me to discuss her college picks. She wanted to apply to a couple of Ivy League schools, Wesleyan, Spelman, Hampton, Smith, and a few other academic "shrines." (Notice that her application attack takes the crossover approach—i.e., she shot for elite schools from both the predominantly white and historically black categories.)

I checked her file and found that while her SAT scores weren't bad, they were clearly below the Ivy League threshold. Her academic average wasn't even close to the 92+ range of most students accepted to Ivy League schools, including those of her fellow black students also trying to land spots in the top schools. On the plus side, she had taken honors and advance placement courses; she was also in the gifted program in her high school and had generally strong grades. Our assessment was that she had a better-than-average shot at getting into all the schools she wanted to, with the exception of the Ivy League schools. There she'd be facing heavy, heavy odds.

However, that was before we looked at her special talents and leadership qualities. There we found a gold mine of activities in nonacademic areas, including a variety of achievements, talents, and contributions in school and beyond. Her essay captured her spirit and made her case persuasively, telling her story in grand fashion. I told the student that it would be her extras, not the standardized test scores or academic average, that would be deciding factors. Her talents and leadership qualities in a sense added 50 points to her SAT score and 10 points to her academic average.

The sister got a clean sweep of accepts and could barely believe it. Neither could her embarrassed high school adviser, who had warned her that the Ivies were too high a reach for her. The lesson? Carefully consider your intangibles. Never fold simply because you feel your test scores or academic average may not be able to take you all the way.

"Okay," you say, "but I've been a marginal student," or perhaps even worse. It doesn't matter! At whatever level you're at, you must consider the bigger picture; intangible extras do make a difference. They can get you into a better school or might mean a better grant, a better financial package, a specific dorm, or some other added bonus. Make them know that you're worthy of special attention if you're a musician, an editor, an artist, someone who is involved in the community or the school, someone who will be an asset to campus life.

The Third Key: Your Motivation and Readiness

Where's your head? What's your state of mind? Are you motivated? Are you ready? And at what level?

When you pick schools to apply to, these questions need to be answered. For example, if I shot back in time and was told that I could go to MIT or Cornell, I would still pass. Not because I don't think I'm smart enough. But these schools—two powerful, get-the-job-done institutions of the highest rank—wouldn't fit my personality and preferred study pace. These are schools with very challenging academic environments that inevitably put students under a certain amount of academic stress along the way. On the other hand, there are plenty of students who are motivated and ready for that sort of challenge. The old adage is true: When the going gets tough, the tough get going!

I have a treasured picture in my photo album of me standing next to a sister who had just graduated from Harvard. Her high school was not one with a national reputation, and she was the first from her school to make it to Harvard. Before she applied, someone warned her that she might be going head-to-head in her classes with top young scholars from the best prep schools in the nation and around the world. She didn't blink. Yes, she ended up having to overcome numerous obstacles, but she endured it all with grace, because she was ready for the challenge.

We sometimes hear comments like this from students we work with:

"It's easier than junior high school. I am not learning anything!"

> —a student who enrolled at a small, academically "safe" southern school without considering that he might be ready for a higher level of challenge.

"The homework in one class alone amounts to about 50 pages of reading a night! I have no clue as to what's going on and the professor seems to be saying 'tough.'"

> —a student who "reached up" to get an accept at a very tough school, but who now feels as though she is in over her head.

"It's tough, but I'm hanging in there. I just got a B+ on a test and the professor praised my thinking on my last paper."

> —a student who got into a better school than her high school record indicated she could handle, but who is adapting and persevering.

The point is that knowing your state of motivation and readiness before you start targeting schools is pivotal. Be careful not to choose a school that will frustrate you academically. Don't settle for a "safe" school if it means you'll be academically stymied. And you should only reach up to tougher schools if you're ready to step it up when you get there. With 3,000 colleges to choose from, it's in your best interest to make a choice that you're comfortable with and can live with for four years. A college divorce, after all, can get messy (transfers and start-overs are emotionally upsetting and sometimes financially disastrous).

The Fourth Key: What's Your Nirvana?: Finding a Match for Your Major and Career Goals

You may already have a major and career choice in mind, whether it's business, education, prelaw, premedicine, computer science, journalism, or engineering. On the other hand, if you're like the average student, you're probably still a little unsure about your major and, ultimately, your career.

So how does a major factor into your self-assessment and your college pick? Well, consider that 50% to 60% of freshmen are undecided as to their majors. And if they have made a decision, the majority will change their minds two or even three times. Chances are you'll begin your college career taking courses tied to the school's core curriculum—courses such as English Composition, History of Civilization, or Communication Skills—even if you've been asked to target a major. At most colleges you won't need to officially declare your major until your sophomore year or later.

It's also important to remember that at some colleges, you might be accepted into a school tied to specific professional training—for instance, a school of engineering, education, business, or art. At some colleges the different schools or departments will review applications directed toward related majors and apply a different set of standards to those applications. For example, you shouldn't check "Engineering" or "Accounting" as your desired major if you have marginal math grades; an art student who submits a slide portfolio with his or her application might be forgiven a C in a math course, but a math C turned in by an aspiring engineering student will raise eyebrows. Likewise, you shouldn't check "premed" if you haven't ably handled or even aced your biology and chemistry courses. In short, don't get daring if your record can't stand the heat. Students who identify themselves as undecided, or liberal arts, majors sometimes have an easier road to an accept.

So, for instance, if you're a very strong student interested in becoming a doctor, we would advise you to consider listing premed on your application. If you're a student with more marginal grades with the same goal, it might be better to indicate "undecided."

Colleges, in their catalogs and viewbooks, often lay down the ground rules. For instance, this is what the University of Southern California has to say about majors in their catalog:

> *"While some students are dedicated to a certain discipline upon enrollment, many others are not. Academic advisors are available to students with defined interests . . . in the College of Arts and Sciences, in the professional schools, and in pre-professional programs such as medicine or law. Students who are undecided about their courses of study are encouraged to apply 'undecided' and take advantage of the counseling services."*

This from Smith College:

> *"Whether you come to Smith with a specific career goal in mind or are unsure of your educational direction, you'll be encouraged to explore many fields of knowledge before making a choice."*

Finally, here's what South Carolina State, an HBCU, has to say on the matter:

> *"South Carolina State offers more than sixty major fields of study. We can help you learn enough about yourself to know which major (by sophomore year) will not only lead to a rewarding career, but hold your interest."*

Of course, if you're already sure of what your intended major is, it is important that you find a school that offers a competitive program in that area. If you have a long-term career goal already in mind that requires an advanced degree (e.g., physician), it's important that you find a school that offers the kind of training that will position you for acceptance into the right professional or graduate school.

The Fifth Key: The Black Factor

One of the most frequently asked questions we hear is: Is it better to go to a historically black college or a predominantly white college? In chapter 8 we give you some information to help you tackle that tough question, along with comments from students, alumni, and experts on the subject. But the quick answer to the question is that it all depends on what you're looking for and what you're willing to adapt to. Don't fool yourself into thinking you can go to an HBCU if what you're really looking for is an ethnically diverse campus experience. And don't fool yourself into thinking you'd prefer a predominantly white institution if you what you're really looking for is the HBCU experience.

The Sixth Key: Dating and Dancing—Your Social Life

A few years ago, I remember attending the annual Urban League–sponsored college football classic. The game pitted Grambling against Hampton University, and I could feel the electricity in the air. I had a great time; though I don't remember who won the game, I do remember the fun of sitting only seats behind the Grambling band and student body. The band members, when not on the field, played spontaneously, shouted, hooted, high-fived, and generally seemed to be having the time of their lives. I realized that the young people there were not just getting an education, but also having a good time and developing a sense of camaraderie that would last them a lifetime. On the other hand, at some colleges we've heard students of color complain that there is no social life.

The point is, there are other things besides the academic environment that matter when we think of schools. While some people complain about the "party obsession" of students, engaging in social activities—particularly in freshman year—is like a rite of passage. These activities will be an integral part of your orientation, whether it's Welcoming Day, all-university picnics, receptions, bazaars, Homecoming, Black History Month, Kwanzaa celebrations, intramural sports programs, happy hours, and maybe even a spades tournament! You'll find most of these sorts of activities at schools where black students form a fairly large contingent.

Wherever you go, there will be some sort of social life, more often than not energized and driven by the presence of Greek-letter organizations: the AKA's, the Deltas, the Ques. These groups are not for everyone, but they do offer the possibility of forming important relationships that will last your entire life.

You should factor in your social expectations when selecting a college, or you might face a culture shock when you get there. Are you a social butterfly? Well, there are colleges with continuous social outlets: perhaps a lively black student union with opportunities for chatting or just profiling. There may be, too, numerous clubs and organizations to get involved with, frequent step shows and talent contests. One thing is clear from the feedback we get from students: having a social outlet is very important to a student's sense of whether he or she is having a happy, well-rounded college experience.

On the other hand, some students are not as concerned with having constant social activities. If you're focused intently primarily with your intellectual needs, you may be able to adjust to a campus where there are more limited social opportunities. Even then, it's important to consider how barren the cultural and social terrain might be; for example, at some schools it's hard to even find contemporary black music on the radio, and campus concerts may infrequently include black music. If you're a young woman looking to focus on personal and academic development away from the pressures of a coed environment, perhaps a woman's college is the ticket. It's vital to take all of that into consideration or risk being stuck in a bad situation. Remember, what you experience after your four or five hours in class is going to shape you and your attitude, for better or for worse. And the odds are high that your environment will be a factor in how you do in school, for better or for worse.

The Seventh Key: The Intangibles—Location, Size, Food, Climate, and Racism

When picking a college, look beyond the glossy catalog and viewbook. The catalogs generally present you with a storybook image of collegiate bliss: beautiful buildings, fountains, tree-lined walks, footbridges, and plenty of winsome, attractive students everywhere. Often these images are confirmed after an actual visit to the campus; indeed, we're big fans of Hampton's seaside vistas (thus "the College by the Sea"), the gorges at Cornell, and the lush greenery of the University of North Carolina at Chapel Hill. But sometimes even pictures can lie (or at least shade the truth a little).

At Wesleyan University, for instance, the lovely campus feels minuscule compared to the look and feel of its viewbook. At Howard University (in the District of Columbia) you can actually look out the windows of some school buildings and see scenes of urban blight. At Lincoln University in Pennsylvania, whose graduates include Supreme Court justice Thurgood Marshall, students acknowledge that they feel isolated, far from any city, and in need of a car. That's why it's vital that once you start getting serious about your college search, you personally visit the campus.

Another question to ask yourself is this: Do I want to be a big fish in a little pond, or a little fish in a big pond? Does it matter? If you took a walk through the campus of Penn State, the University of Maryland at College Park, or Cornell University, you would probably think, "This place is huge!" It might be a little intimidating, to say the least. Furthermore, in some college towns, the school really extends beyond its actual campus; it is the central focus of everything that happens in the surrounding community. Frankly, you might feel like a speck of dust when you arrive.

But the truth is, there are social and academic benefits and negatives to going to a big school. Positives at a big school include:

- most, if not all, conceivable majors offered
- a correspondingly large choice of courses
- top-ranked programs
- large libraries, including a satellite system of smaller, targeted branches on campus
- good computer networking systems
- honors programs
- almost unlimited choice of clubs and organizations
- large Greek-letter networks
- competitive varsity sports programs (and corresponding team frenzy)
- intramural sports
- on-campus athletic facilities, including tracks, pools, and workout equipment
- top-quality labs and equipment
- game rooms
- lots of dorms or off-campus housing options

Negatives at a big school include:

- the potential for getting "lost in the crowd"
- little nurturing or hands-on counseling support
- poor faculty accessibility
- large introductory classes (sometimes with more than 100 students)
- impersonal feel
- maddening bureaucracy

On the other hand, imagine being at a college where you recognize almost every face. Or better still, where you might know most of your fellow classmates by name. Imagine, too, that the campus feels like home and that everybody—students, faculty, administration—feels like part of an extended family. Got a problem? You feel comfortable enough to drop in on your resident adviser, or slip a note under a professor's door. Need help? Tutoring services are widely accessible to meet your needs.

You get the point. There are actually colleges out there, both predominantly white institutions and historically black institutions, where you never feel like a number. Fisk University, for instance, an HBCU that counts W. E. B. Du Bois among its alumni. One student at Fisk told us after her first semester that she'd already found a mentor and lauded the school for the close-knit community feel that exists on its relatively small 32-acre campus. That close-knit feel and personal attention may be one reason why Fisk does such a good job—proportionately speaking—of sending graduates on to their doctorates.

Again, there are positives and negatives to going to a small school. The positives include:

- smaller, more intimate classes that allow for more discussion
- easy-to-access academic tutoring and remedial help
- more hands-on support
- more networking opportunities
- generally better student-to-faculty ratios
- a stronger sense of camaraderie

The negatives include:

- occasionally inadequate facilities (e.g., labs and related equipment)
- small or sparse libraries
- small endowments that have a negative impact on the amount of financial aid available
- everybody's in your business!

There are other intangibles you'll need to think about when choosing a school. How's the food, for instance? Can you adapt to a regional menu very different from the one you're accustomed to? What's the climate like? Can you handle a New England winter or a Texas summer? Some campuses have a decidedly conservative feel to them, which sometimes spills over into veiled racism among the student body—particularly on campuses that are not very ethnically diverse. Are there indicators of racism on campus? Check the student newspapers to get a sense of how your politics will jibe with that of your classmates. Check for a preponderance or even any presence of Confederate flags. Is the on-campus socializing strictly, if informally, segregated? Can you handle that? Is the surrounding community hostile to African Americans? These are all things to seriously consider.

CROSSOVER: DESIGNING AN ADMISSIONS ATTACK STRATEGY

You should not feel limited to where you apply. When you are deciding where to apply, remember to keep in mind the potential for "crossover"—that is, your ability to cross over from one category of school to another. The set of schools you finally apply to should include a diverse mix of schools from the following categories:

Reaching: If you feel you are a student who has proven your ability to get into a school in the "competitive" range, you still might want to apply to one or two schools in the "very competitive" category. Go for it if you think you're capable and ready to compete at a higher level. Once your application is in, you can never be sure what will happen. We'll talk more about tricks and tips for "reaching" in the following chapters.

Niche: These are the best schools where you are most likely to get accepts and feel comfortable. These are schools where your academic profile falls squarely into the range of the student body. A sound strategy is always to target most of your applications to this category.

Stepping down: Always select one or two "sure admits." These are schools where your admissions factors (test scores, GPA, extracurriculars, class rank, etc.) are better than for their average accepted student. This might include your neighborhood community college, which might even have an open admissions policy. Remember: always cover your back!

An average student's application attack might look like this:

reaching: two applications

niche: four applications

stepping down: two applications

Remember: this may be one of the most important decisions you make in your life. Start early so you can take your time, do the research, analyze your own feelings and attitudes, and then go for it!

CHAPTER 3

PACKAGING YOUR APPLICATION

Now that you've decided which schools you're going to apply to, it's time to knock the admissions people out with a brilliant application. To effectively stop the show and throw that perfect admissions punch, you've got to package your application the right way. Your application should reflect a great deal of skill and precision.

The key thing to keep in mind is that your application *is* you as far as admissions officers are concerned, and it has to tell your story to your best advantage. It's like when it's time to take a photograph, you make sure you smile a certain way, tilt your head to the most flattering angle, and turn to your best side to make sure you get the best results on film. Well, you should think of your application the same way. Remember, a strong application can make a difference, even if your test scores and GPA are not all you'd like them to be. Here are the steps to putting together a tight application that will get you into the best school for you.

GET THE APPLICATIONS

As we mentioned in the previous chapter, the first thing you need to do is get your hands on the applications. During your junior year, at the latest, you should begin writing for catalogs, viewbooks, and applications. The worst thing you can do is wait. If they don't know you're there, colleges won't send applications to you! Be proactive.

Once you start getting the catalogs and applications, create a filing system so you can keep track of it all. It will get a little hectic with all those catalogs and financial aid forms and applications floating around! After you have the applications, review them to see what the colleges are looking for in terms of information, essays, and application format.

Every college has its own application or set of applications for you to fill out. If you're applying to a targeted school within a university (e.g., the university's school of music or arts), you may need to fill out a separate application. Sometimes schools have a two-part application process. The first application requires you to fill out a basic statistical application; after you've completed and returned that application, the university will send you the second—and more involved—part of the application. Many colleges offer you the option of filling out a common application, which allows you to send the same application to a number of schools, although many colleges require a supplementary piece designed just for their school. There are also lots of electronic options that allow you to send the same application to more than one school at a time. It's important that you understand these options and choose wisely.

GET READY FOR THE KEY QUESTIONS

Regardless of the specific application format you choose, your application will require you to sell yourself. When your applications are reviewed, it's like you are under a microscope. People will be looking closely, digesting the material, making judgments, and comparing you with other students. Your edge is that you will address all of their questions by coming full force and never playing yourself short.

This subjective review of who you are will, in the admissions committee's mind at least, give them the complete story of:

- your character
- your leadership potential
- your concern for others
- your personal initiative
- your self-confidence and maturity
- your talents and special skills
- your potential
- how you will fit in at their campus

Here are four crucial questions you should be prepared to answer in the application:

1. What activities, clubs, and/or special events did you participate in or contribute to while in high school?
2. Have you participated in activities outside of school during the past few years? (e.g., community, religious, or volunteer organizations).
3. What scholastic distinctions, honors, or recognitions of special talent have you received?
4. Have you held any jobs—including full-time, part-time, and summer work—during the past few years?

Be prepared for these questions! You should start compiling a list right now with the answers to those questions, and you've got to invest some time in compiling the right answers. Let's get to it!

School Activities

Let's start by compiling all of your school activities on a sheet of paper. Remember, even if you were not the person spearheading the project or the activity, you may be able to mention it if you played a role in assisting. Here are some possibilities:

Are you (or have you ever been):

- an editor or a writer for the school newspaper?
- a member of the yearbook staff?
- part of a cultural or academic group?
- on an intramural or varsity team?
- a member of the school band or orchestra?
- an artist?
- in any honor societies?
- part of the drama club?
- a member of the choir or glee club?
- a tutor assigned to work with other students?

- involved in class government?
- involved in fund-raising?
- a cheerleader or a booster?
- on the debate team?
- a performer in talent shows?
- an audio visual assistant?
- an introductory speaker for any invited guest?
- a school monitor?
- an assistant to a teacher on a pet project?
- an assistant for the PTA?
- an assistant or a helper during Open School Day or Night?
- an assistant for a team, club, or organization—did you travel with them, man a table, handle tickets, etc.?

Outside Activities

Now let's look at the activities you engaged in outside of school. Again, compile a list on a sheet of paper. Here are some possibilities:

Are you (or have you ever been):

- a youth member of the NAACP, the Urban League, the United Negro College Fund, or other civil rights organizations?
- a volunteer at a hospital? (note that hospitals, nursing homes, and nonprofit organizations always need volunteers)
- a volunteer at your church?
- a volunteer in a political campaign?
- involved in a community clean-up campaign?
- a mentor to a younger student?
- involved in starting and running your own business?
- an intern at any company or organization?
- A Sunday school teacher or assistant?
- someone who has worked with little children in any capacity?
- the designer of a flyer or newsletter for any group?
- a summer camp counselor?
- involved in a travel experience that has in some way shaped you?
- involved in any other activity that has contributed to the community?

Special Honors and Awards

Now let's look at any special honors or awards you may have received. You may have more than you think.

Are you (or have you ever been):

- an entrant in the Westinghouse Science Fair? (believe it or not, just entering makes a statement)
- national achievement finalist?
- in the honor society?
- in the student council?
- published by the school literary magazine?

- the winner of any school competitions?
- the class president?
- a varsity athlete?
- an artist?

Work Experience

Sometimes you may feel that your work experience is irrelevant to your college application, particularly if you "only" worked in an informal setting or a service position (e.g. behind the counter at McDonald's). But it's all in how you present it—you can add flavor, even a bit of humor, when discussing your work experience. Each job sends a message to the school. Here are some examples from students we've worked with:

Job: "Bunny Tail," a costumed mascot, at Charley's Cookie Place. The student added the line, "The children loved me!"

Message to college: I am a fun person with personality!

Job: Freelance car mechanic over summer vacation. The student wrote that he was his neighborhood's "Mr. Fix-It." He then embellished the entry with an essay that indicated he was, at 17, an expert car mechanic who was often called on to look at or fix neighbor's cars for modest fees, if not for free.

Message to college: I am a resourceful, intelligent, and hardworking person, and have had an impact in my neighborhood.

Job: Actor. This student went to an announced audition in New York for a role in a movie produced by Quincy Jones's production company and got a callback.

Message to college: I am a young man with acting ability and, in all likelihood, charisma.

Thinking about Your Lists

Now you should have drafted four lists: School Activities, Outside Activities, Awards/Honors, and Work. This should not be a simple list of one- or two-word descriptions. We implore you to think smart and enhance your list. It's not unethical to present your story in the most favorable way possible. Your extra activities should stamp you as a winner, someone special, someone who will be getting involved on campus in a positive way. If you're a strong student targeting the most selective schools, your presentation should definitely have sparkle! But whatever level you're at, maximum impact is your goal.

This also means that the list should not just be a laundry list of random activities. While there's nothing wrong with flipping hamburgers or being a teacher's monitor, too many of those kinds of entries back-to-back may look like filler. Quantity for quantity's sake can be a turnoff. You don't want someone thinking, "This student is everywhere, but doesn't really appear to have achieved or accomplished anything noteworthy." Remember, one slam dunk says more than a dozen weak dribbles.

PREPARING THE ACTUAL APPLICATION

Your first draft will not do. When you are ready to type it up—this is after you've completed the exercises above and thought long and hard about the answers to the key questions—stick a new, black ribbon in your typewriter. Don't handwrite anything unless specifically asked to do so. It might be best to make a photocopy of the application, or to have an extra one on hand, in case you make any mistakes.

On the final copy, a minimal amount of Wite-Out should be used (if any!). Your application should have a very clean look. If the instructions on the application ask you to use the space provided, use it. For the essay and any other extra narratives that may be required, you'll need 20-pound bond paper. Erasable bond is a no-no. And the color of the paper should be white, not pink, yellow, or any other "pretty" color. You should use a standard typeface, nothing fancy— and certainly no cursive or dot-matrix print. Neatness and legibility are essential; misspellings are inexcusable.

Getting the Specifics Right

Entering your legal name on the application is important. That name must correspond to the name on your high school transcript and, hopefully, your birth certificate. Some applications will also ask for "other legal names" or your a. k. a.—"also known as." Needless to say, don't reveal any nicknames that sound too "street" or controversial—you know, Foxxy, Sugar G, or any of that initial stuff: T. J., W. B., Big L. Keep it to yourself. Once on campus, you can reveal your charming a. k. a.

You will have to list your Social Security number. If you don't have one, you're in limbo. At most colleges today, that number will serve as your college ID number in all matters: financial aid, work-study, loans, and so on. At larger campuses it will also help to separate you from other students with the same name. One student we worked with reported arriving at school for the first time, only to discover that another student had already registered in his name and went to his dorm room! The Social Security number was the key to straightening the mess out. So make sure you have your Social Security number before filling out your applications.

Race and Ethnic Background: Don't Leave It Blank

Usually you will find a box that asks for your racial/ethnic identification. Colleges usually indicate that checking the box is optional. However, if you're black, you should always check it— it will only work to your benefit. Note that both parents don't have to belong to a racial or ethnic group for a student to identify himself or herself in that group.

Danger Signals

Just about all applications ask these two questions or variations of them:

- "Have you ever been placed on academic or social probation, suspended, or dismissed?"
- "Have you ever been convicted of a crime?"

If you must answer "Yes" to either of these questions, don't be flippant or quick with your answer. Your reply is going to be as important as your required essay. Attach a sheet of paper and respond as if your life depended on it.

Dress to Impress

The key to packaging your application is to put a power spin on every piece of information included. You have to be determined not to get lost in the shuffle. Fine-tune the language and presentation so you stand out and beat the odds.

In the next four chapters we're going to go through four of the key components of your application package: Your high school record, your test scores, your all-important essay, and recommendations.

CHAPTER 4

HAVE YOU BEEN NAUGHTY OR NICE?

Your High School Record

It's time to look at the most important part of your application package: your high school record. If you've been nice, you can smile: you're on your way. If you've been naughty—perhaps malingering a bit, not performing up to your capacity, and generally underachieving—you might feel as though you've dug a hole for yourself. And you have. Can you get out? Of course. Remember, it's never too late. The key is to find out what your high school record says about you before you start applying to schools.

DRESSING YOU UP OR DRESSING YOU DOWN?

We've said it before and we'll say it again: your record is your academic DNA. The transcript will give admissions people all the components—the rigor of your courseload, your grade-point average, and, in some cases, your unofficial standardized test scores—that add up to the sum total of your academic performance. Many admissions experts agree that the high school record—more than any SAT or ACT score—is the best predictor of college performance. So when admissions officers see that high school record, be forewarned that it will be reviewed, studied, analyzed, and dissected like a cadaver in an autopsy room. So it's important that you review it so you can better understand how you look on paper before those admissions officers get a crack at it.

We can't tell you the number of times we've reviewed a student's record—the total transcript, list of extracurricular activities, exemplary talents, etc., and said, "Why are you shooting for John Doe U.? Your record is strong enough to make a Yale, Stanford, Emory, Brown, or one of the public Ivies!" Your record will tell you what your options are. Here are some tips for analyzing your record and previewing the reactions it will get from admissions officers.

THE GOLD STANDARD: THE SUPER STUDENT RECORD

Super students are those with almost unlimited selection possibilities for college, who would be wise to consider the highest-ranked colleges, including the Ivy League schools, top-rated private and public universities, and the cream of the HBCU crop. So, if you're a super student, what does your transcript look like?

First of all, you've taken the most challenging courses you can. Your transcript will show consistently high grades in challenging courses. Here's what your courseload over your high school career might include:

9th grade

   English (honors)

   Biology

   French (first year)

   Algebra

   Social Studies

10th grade

   English (honors)

   French (second level)

   Chemistry

   Geometry

   World History

11th grade

   English (honors)

   French (third level)

   Tough elective

   Physics

   American History

   Trigonometry

12th grade

   English (advance placement)

   College-level social studies course (e.g., Economics, Comparative Religions)

   Tough elective

   Calculus

   French Literature

Notice that the super student's transcript lists tougher courses, including Physics, Calculus, and advanced language courses. Note, too, that the super student takes college-level, advance placement, and honors courses. Here are some advance placement and college-level courses that indicate to top schools that a student can meet the demands of college work:

- Political Science
- French Literature
- History of Art
- Computer Science
- Calculus
- Music Theory
- Studio Art

You can often get credit for these courses once you get into college, usually by taking an exam. We've worked with a number of students who have been in "baccalaureate programs" in high school, where they are trained to do college-level work for which they often receive credit once in college. If your school offers such a program, and you're interested in getting into a highly competitive university, you should definitely take advantage of the opportunity to get your feet wet with college-level work.

If you are taking a courseload similar to the one above and getting B's or higher, you are in a good position, so don't sell yourself short. You are probably going to be considered by admissions officers as a super student if your grade-point average is higher than a B (80 to 89), and you've navigated the "fast track" as outlined above. In fact, as an African American student, you'll be a sought-after commodity with those kinds of academic credentials (assuming the rest of your application package is also on point).

Remember, too, that your transcript will include your class rank, to give admissions officers a look at how you compared to your peers. To make the cut as a super student, you should be in the top 10% of your class. Also note that your grade adviser might list your standardized test scores on your actual transcript. THIS IS UNOFFICIAL. The testing service still needs to send your official scores to the colleges.

What kind of courses go into the strong college prep load? Well, admissions officers will look at your record favorable if you've done adequately or better in these key courses:

- English Literature, Composition, and Creative Writing courses
- a math sequence that includes Algebra, Geometry, and Trigonometry
- a strong plus is an elective math course, such as a Pre-calculus or Calculus or Statistics course
- a history sequence that includes American History and World History
- a science sequence of Biology, Chemistry, and Physics
- a three-year language sequence studying French, Spanish, or other language (extra points for difficult languages such as Mandarin Chinese, Japanese, or Russian)
- a well-rounded elective selection that includes courses in Art and Music
- honors and advanced placement electives
- a Computer Science course or a research project for credit (adds spice to your transcript)

SEARCHING FOR THE MAGIC FORMULA: THE GOOD STUDENT RECORD

The good student's transcript is also impressive to admissions officers, if not as challenging as the super student's. If you're a good student, you've been taking a college preparatory course-load, perhaps with an honors course here and there. You've shown signs of being capable, bright, and able to rise to the occasion, but you may also have the occasional "dip" in your grades and have not taken the initiative to go after the *really* tough courses. Your GPA, as a good student, might be in the 80 to 85 range, taking a standard college preparatory courseload. Avoid, if at all possible, frivolous courses and electives (e.g., History of Comic Books). If you've done well, if not "super," with a college prep courseload, you are in a favorable position; if you add to that extracurriculars, special talents, impressive test scores, and strong recommendations—all of which are covered in other chapters—and add your personal determination to the mix, you can make a reach for an elite school, even if your transcript is not perfect.

LOST SOULS OR SALVATION? THE AVERAGE STUDENT RECORD

It's rare to see a guide that addresses the needs of the average (or just below average) student with an average transcript. This is surprising, because great numbers of our students nationwide—for a litany of reasons—fall into this category: they have not particularly distinguished themselves, but do intend to go to college. But we've seen enough of these "average" students to know that today's so-so student is tomorrow's mover and shaker!

If you are an average student, your transcript will feature some of the college prep courses already mentioned, including the basic math, English, and Social Studies sequences: in other words, the basics. What you won't find on your transcript are the higher-level science and math courses, honors courses, or challenging Social Studies, English, and Art electives. Your academic average may be in the 75 to 80 range, and the impression admissions officers may get is that you haven't really challenged yourself, have demonstrated questionable academic preparedness, and have basically drifted to a degree. And if you've gone to a large public school, chances are you've run across indifference from your overworked counselors.

But here's a guarantee: you can still get in to a quality school and make a turnaround. See chapter 2, on making a college choice, to see your options for college. It's important that you couple your mediocre transcript with solid test scores (if possible), recommendations, and a good essay, all of which will be covered in the next few chapters.

WHEN? WHERE? HOW?
THE "NEED A SECOND CHANCE" STUDENT RECORD

Many students whom grade advisers typically count out, we count in! As a student, it's never, ever too late to initiate a change and begin a new journey. We've found "need a second chance" students everywhere, from inner-city public high schools to the top prep schools in the country. How do you know if you're in this category?

Well, if you're a second-chance student, you probably know it already. Your transcript is probably lacking in some major way: it may show a pattern of yo-yoing grades, going up only to come crashing down. Your academic average may be in the mid-60s to low 70s range. You may even have failed courses—sometimes we see so many summer classes on a student's transcript, we get the feeling the student thought going to school in June and July was the thing to do! We've given these transcripts distinct categories: The Frankenstein Transcript; The Summer School Makeover; The Believe It or Not! We might have smiled, but we were concerned.

But the truth is that every need-a-second-chance student we've ever worked with has had a story behind the dismal transcript that made us realize there were extenuating circumstances. And while it's hard to get a foot in the door when you have a bad record, the key is not to look at it as the end of the world, and remember to market what you have. Some college somewhere will give you a chance; you can bet on it.

Take the story of one student we worked with who brought with her one of the worst transcripts we had ever seen. Her academic average was 67, but her SAT score was better than would have been expected given her record, close to 1000 points combined. Her high school record looked very bad, but there were flashes of greatness—a few of the grades amid the wreckage of her transcript were quite impressive. She had also missed 80 days of school, according to her transcript. Even though she insisted to her high school adviser that she was going to college, the adviser did not have a lot of faith in her ability to make it. When she met with us her for a consultation, she told us of her volunteer service with homeless women at a shelter. She also spoke of often visiting museums and studying in libraries around the city. We wondered how she had time for all of this, given her frequent absences from school. She was an enigma, to be sure.

Eventually we found out her whole story. She was living with her grandmother, a mother who couldn't even read, a brother and a sister, and a little niece who was classified "learning disabled" and was also sickly. Since her mother and grandmother spent many days and nights at the hospital, she was often left in charge of her younger siblings. She was also called on to help with the adult problems of the household—including helping to keep track of bills and dealing with bill collectors. Formal education in this family unit was clearly secondary.

Since there was always noise in the cramped apartment, and no real study space, she actually studied on the outside stoop a good deal of the time—in dim light and under varying weather conditions. The libraries were her paradise, and volunteer work was something she cared about deeply whenever she had free time. So while her transcript said "this is a loser," that wasn't really the case. She was someone who had developed sterling personal qualities:

tolerance, determination, self-motivation, and more. But none of that appeared on her feeble little transcript. Our message to her was to tell her story, using the essay. She's now attending a small college away from home and is planning on going to graduate school. The point is, if you know the challenges raised by your transcript, be proactive about answering those challenges through the other application tools at your disposal.

Now let's take on the tests!

CHAPTER 5

YOUR TEST SCORES

Beat the Bell Curve!

If you're already a junior or a senior in high school, many of your grades and class selections are already etched in the stone of your transcript. While those scores and your developing GPA are crucial, your SAT and other standardized tests can still make or break you.

WHY THE TESTS MATTER

We don't want to alarm you, but we do want you to understand the standardized test battle to come. Your mission is to put yourself in the most advantageous position possible for these tests—whether you're planning on taking the PSAT, SAT, ACT, or achievement tests—by studying and strategizing to maximize your scores. And just showing up for the test doesn't count as a strategy. If you've been following the affirmative action battles declared in states such as California and Texas, you realize that standardized test scores are one of the chinks in the armor of African American applicants, making them more vulnerable in the admissions battle.

At Black Excel we've seen how irrelevant standardized test scores (sometimes!) can be in predicting student performance. We know that when it comes to the quality of a student, many other factors are just as important, if not more important, including the GPA, the rigor of the courseload, and the intangibles of character. We also recall that Martin Luther King Jr. turned in a very mediocre score on the GRE test to get into graduate school, yet went on to make history. So remember, you are more than your SAT score, and your potential is not limited by a poor showing on one test.

That said, the SAT score does have value when wisely factored into a student's total assessment. We acknowledge there's a cultural bias embedded in some questions and test formats. Still, we see test scores as useful tools for (1) indicating your academic readiness; (2) your willingness and ability to *prepare* for academic challenges; and (3) suggesting options, strategies, and possible colleges for you to attend (see chapter 2 on selecting a college).

WHAT DOES IT TAKE TO ACE THE TESTS?

To turn that question around a little, let's first consider this question: Why do African Americans seems to score lower on these tests than the general population? Here are a few theories:

1. We do not prepare.
2. The tests do not become a central priority until it's time to take them.
3. We don't understand how important test scores are to college admissions.

The key to success is preparation, and we cannot overemphasize its importance. If you want to hit a home run on these tests, your preparation has to include private self-testing, a preparation course (particularly if such a course is available from your school or a community organization at little or no cost), and a rigorous high school courseload, particularly in English and math subjects. Without that sort of preparation you will be at a distinct disadvantage when the test rolls around; you should assume that the students you're competing with have been taking prep courses, have been taking the tough classes at school, and have been thinking about these tests since they were small children! That should pump up your motivation to prepare.

WHAT THE SCORES MEAN

Here's the way we generally assess scores. If you've already taken the tests and received your score, you can find out here what that score means and what you may do to improve it. If you haven't already taken the test, you can look below and see what it takes to get your score to each level.

High Scorers: 1100+ on the SAT

Among students who have scored 1100 or above on the SATs, the common denominator is strong preparation. We're not saying they're smarter than other students. What we are saying is that their superior preparation makes them better equipped academically to navigate college-level courses with stronger basic skills in math and language. The high SAT score alone makes them in demand among top colleges. If you haven't taken the test yet, the profile of a high scorer is:

1. The student is taking a college prep courseload (see chapter 4 for a description of the college prep courseload) and is usually taking a few college-level courses in science, English, or a foreign language.

2. The student is usually taking the strongest academic program available in his or her school, no matter how strong the school's overall academic reputation is.

3. In many cases the student has taken a test prep course, whether one of the commercially available courses or one offered at his or her school.

4. The rest of the student's application package (including the application itself, the essay, and the recommendations) is also well put together and indicates preparation and attention to detail.

Good Scorers: 900 to 1100 on the SATs

Winners abound in this category as well. Students in this group usually prove themselves to be as capable and motivated as the group above. If you haven't taken the test yet and want to hit this mark, see the profile below for what it takes. If you've taken the test already and scored in this range, the key for you is to put together a strong package of supplemental material—including a transcript featuring a rigorous courseload and strong GPA—to be considered for the competitive universities.

The profile of a good scorer is:

1. Usually carrying some college prep courses, although overall courseload might be a step weaker than for a high-scoring student.

2. The student has his or her sights set on getting into college and has taken steps to ensure that goal's fulfillment, including possibly taking test prep courses.

3. Some students in this range might be classic underachievers who can make the difference by putting together strong application packets indicating their potential to become super students.

Stand-by-Me Scorers: 800 to 900 on the SATs

This is an intriguing group. Sometimes we run into students who bring home reasonably good grades with a fairly tough courseload, including some college prep courses, but then go out and score a meager 820 on the test of their lives. Why does this happen? The problem is often a lack of personal focus and, again, preparation. A lot of times, even if a student is pulling in good grades, he or she may be riding on natural ability, instead of on strong study habits, and may lack the academic fundamentals necessary. Particularly if you go to a school where the classes feel easy or even dumbed down, you have to take it on yourself to push harder to prepare yourself for the standardized tests—or risk scoring in this mediocre range.

Try-it-Again Scorers: 700 to 800 on the SATs

If you score in this range, you have to ask yourself: Am I applying myself? If you are a student giving your all, there's no need to panic, pout, or shout. But a test score in this range means that your academic preparation has been poor, even if you've been getting good grades. It may mean that you're not taking a tough enough courseload featuring the standard college preparatory classes. A low SAT score may be sending you a signal. But it's not too late to catch up. If you feel like you may be about to fall into this category, now's the time to get to those test prep books and courses to try to bring your score to a high level. If you've already taken the tests, there's still hope for college (see chapter 2 on choosing a college to find out what to do if your academic performance falls to this level).

Missing-the-Boat Scorers: 600 to 700 on the SATs

Perhaps the heart is willing. We get plenty of applications from people in this category—many have strong college aspirations, and a lot are first-generation potential students. Sometimes these students have transcripts with lines of 75's and 80's and a general courseload. They also have teacher recommendations that say things like, "Shirline is a personable young lady" or "Raheem is respectful and attentive" but don't really address the issue of academic readiness.

Why does a student turn in a score like this? Here is a story of one such student: She was an 11th-grader who came to Black Excel with an SAT score in the mid-600 range. She was disheartened, because her grade adviser informed her that such a score limited her options. She was aware that there was a small group of students in her school on a college prep track, who were considered "smarter" than the rest of the students, and who filled the honors classes. Still, she felt that she was making progress, doing okay, and figured she'd get a "passable" score on the SAT.

However, she, like a lot of first-in-their-family college aspirants, hadn't familiarized herself with the test. She didn't know it was three hours long, that it had seven sections, that the verbal section required you to read and analyze many long passages, and that the math section required knowledge of arithmetic, algebra, and geometry. When she opened the test book with the clock ticking, it was like culture shock.

If you haven't taken the test yet, how do you avoid falling into this pit? Again, the key is to prepare well. That preparation starts at the beginning of your high school career by choosing a program and meaningful courses. Then get busy with specific test preparation tools; at least make sure you're familiar with the nature of the test (how long it takes, which subjects to expect, etc.).

If you have taken the test already and scored in this low range, you need to get busy with the other aspects of your application. If you score this low on the SAT, chances are you will need help in writing a crisp, articulate essay. Get whatever counseling and tutoring you need to make sure you're able to put together a winning essay. Also, take the test again; you really have nothing to lose. But this time, prepare better—your score may not rise to 1000 or higher, but if you show improvement, it will make you a more attractive college candidate. That student we talked about above? We worked with her on putting together a strong essay and coached her to a higher SAT score. Now she's in her junior year of college and considering graduate school. Remember, it's never too late!

TEST CHECKLIST

Here are some questions you should be ready to answer *well before* you take the test:

- When is the test offered?
- How long is the SAT? (or ACT?)
- How do I pace myself?
- What subjects are covered?
- Where are my weaknesses, and how can I improve them?
- Is there a "best test" strategy?
- Should I take a prep course?

Remember, the key is preparation, and the preparation starts as early as possible. Make sure you take the right courseload, take the necessary prep courses, and familiarize yourself with the test itself. And then all you have to do is ace the test—easy!

CHAPTER 6

THE ESSAY

Your Life Preserver

Your essay is a major weapon in the admissions war. Your essay is your lance, your sword, your ace in the hole, your life preserver. That's how importantly you should view it. As a student of color, you will be particularly scrutinized when it comes to the essay. Your transcript will not answer all of the questions of the admissions committee—this is your chance to shape and color (no pun intended) their opinion and clarify any doubts they may have about your value to their campus.

Sure, the quality of your academic work is an all-important factor, as well as the crucial test scores. But admissions personnel are human, curious—nosy, even—so you should use this opportunity to let them into your house, let them see the furniture, your baby pictures if need be; let them know how wonderful you'd be as a leader, a dorm personality, someone's roommate. Make them look at and discuss you. They don't want to just evaluate the competency of your writing, they want to guess, speculate, and theorize about the content of your character. Your essay—what you have to say and how you say it—is your sermon and testimony on the subject.

You should check the appendix for some sample essays that have worked, but first go over the following tips on making your essay the best it can be.

WHAT DIFFERENCE DOES AN ESSAY MAKE?

If the rest of your academic profile (GPA, test scores, etc.) is peaches and cream, you can catapult yourself to the top of the line with those one or two pages of added revelation. Some "testperts" say that the SAT and the ACT don't measure creativity, motivation, or special talents, so you better take this chance to tell your story. If you're already a super student, and you finesse this right, the Harvards of the world might just send a limo for you!

On the other hand, if there are substantial chinks in your armor, you can actually create a shift in the admissions team's perception with a strong essay. Perhaps you can explain a mediocre grade (or grades), a course retake, the reason for this or that course selection—maybe you had asthma, a death in the family, or a crisis that, without your essay, no one would have a clue about. Your patchwork of words can impress, maybe even bring tears to someone's eyes. While a masterpiece here might not completely override a mediocre or a questionable record, it can sometimes help you jump that thin line that distinguishes accepts from rejects.

WRITING THE ESSAY: BLACK EXCEL'S TOP 10 TIPS

Here are 10 tips to help you ace the essay, based on our work with thousands of students:

1. **Never write the essay in one day or one week.** The best essays we've seen take weeks to conceive, write, and polish.

2. **Revise and revise some more**. Never think that you can get away with a first draft. And don't settle for a second draft either. Take as long as it takes to revise your essay.

3. **Read your essay aloud.** Choose a friend or a family member you feel comfortable with and read the essay to that person. Then have him or her read the essay to you. How does it sound? How are the rhythm, the language, the grammar?

4. **Get input.** Another successful method we've found is to have a family-and-friends round-table discussion of your essay. You read the essay one sentence or one paragraph at a time. Ask your roundtable for their feedback. The more discussion, the more tips you'll get for creating an essay with maximum impact.

5. **Avoid topics that might offend or slight.** Topics such as sex, religion, abortion, mercy killing, your first fight, your last fight, the day you stole something, etc.

6. **Put a new spin on time worn topics such as "My summer vacation" or themes such as, "Why I want to go to college."** A routine handling of one of these topics might put a reader to sleep. Remember, no matter what the college gives you as a theme, *you* must be clever enough to put yourself into the essay. For instance, Dartmouth asks, "What prominent person (past or present) do you particularly admire? Why?" Don't just write about that person as if you were a biographer. Be original. Incorporate your thoughts, ideas, and plans into your answer. Wellesley asks, "We are creating a time capsule to launch into space and would like you to contribute five items; what would you contribute and why?" Maybe you can include your diary. You have to touch the reader, make him or her sympathetic to you, make sure that person realizes that you're special and personable and a resource. Always sell yourself!

7. **Put some jazz into your essay.** Remember, admission officers have to read dozens of essays a day and sometimes are bored to death; make their jobs interesting, and they will reward you. Make sure your use of language and word choices show thought and creativity.

8. **Avoid opening-sentence posturing.** We find that most students open their essays trying to sound "intellectual" by emptying their thesaurus of big words. Don't do it. The key is to be engaging and clear with your writing.

9. **If you can, open with a "hook," an opening sentence that grabs the reader's attention.** And once you've got that attention, hold on to it. Remember, you have a story to tell. What is a good hook? Here are some examples from essays we've reviewed:

   My first day at Jackson High, someone called me "Doogie Howser."

   I could recite the names even after I woke up: Galileo, Albert Einstein, Charles Drew, and me.

   When I graduated from junior high school, no one could see that my shoes had no soles.

10. **Demonstrate that you can write on a college level.** Show that you understand sentence structure, can write grammatically correct English, can handle a theme, and know the differences among words such as "their," there," and "they're."

ESSAY CHECKLIST

What should your essay accomplish? Well, you should have convinced the admissions folks to answer "yes" to each of these questions:

- Do we have a feel for you as an individual?
- Does the college need you?
- Can you do the work?
- Is your essay more revealing, creative, and impressive than those of the competition?
- Do you deserve a second chance if your high school performance was weak?
- Can you reasonably be expected to overcome any negatives that might be visible in your record?
- Will you add to the diversity and richness of the campus?
- Will you make a positive contribution to the school?

The answer should be "no" to each of these questions:

- Will you likely fail out?
- Will you "just be there," not contributing to campus life?
- Was the essay just average or ordinary?
- Were there grammatical mistakes or misspellings?
- Can the college afford *not* to have you?

The Importance of the Rewrite

No matter how good your first draft was, you've got to take another look. Think good, better, best. Perhaps where there's a whisper, you really wanted a shout. Sometimes the shift of a single phrase can make the difference between the sixty-second read most students will get and a five-minute read. If you're really going for it, take the time it takes to polish and finish the essay. Other students will see the essay as an opportunity to show and tell—make sure you don't fall asleep on your opportunity to tell your story.

As you're rewriting, focus on making your essay as simple and as clear as possible. Every point you make should emphasize *your* special qualities. The first paragraph in particular should be simple and ring out with your particular qualities, pulling the reader into your story. Make sure you've used clear, basic language, and eliminate any attempts to be fancy or impressive with overstuffed words or concepts. You should write from the heart.

Beyond the first paragraph, make sure you've included specific details in the essay. One essayist we worked with didn't just say that she played in a band in junior high school; she wrote that her favorite tune was Mozart's Seventh and explained why. That's the sort of detail that will catch the attention of the reader. Be aware of portions of the essay where the power dips or the clarity fades. Keep working at it until the essay has wings to carry your application to a higher level. Also, remember to check the appendix of sample essays for examples of essays that worked.

CHAPTER 7

RECOMMENDATIONS

You'd Better Beware!

Recommendations are a key part of your application package. Nearly every school requests at least one or two recommendations; for instance, Spelman asks for two, Colgate wants three, Fisk wants two, Emory wants one, and Harvard wants two.

The recommendation might be requested as a narrative, a completed form, or a combination of the two. Many colleges also ask for a personal profile/academic recommendation from the school's guidance counselor that factors in the collected opinions of three or four teachers. And some schools ask for peer recommendations.

WHAT DO RECOMMENDATIONS TELL SCHOOLS?

Their are eight areas that colleges typically want addressed in a recommendation. They want to know about your:

1. motivation
2. industry
3. initiative
4. influence and leadership
5. concern for others
6. responsibility
7. integrity
8. emotional stability

Other questions that might be addressed in a recommendation include: Do you have significant physical, social, or mental limitations? Is your future performance most likely to be "superior," "average," "difficult," or "unsuccessful"?

If the recommendation is in checklist form, your teachers and grade advisors will be faced with a jigsaw of options that can either sink you or send you flying:

highly motivated

actively creative

assumes responsibility

vacillating

excitable

consistently self-reliant

indifferent

> conscientious
>
> not dependable
>
> unreliable
>
> cooperative but retiring
>
> trustworthy
>
> apathetic
>
> needs occasional prodding

The form closes with the ultimate multiple choice: "recommended," "not recommended for this university," and the damning "prefer not to make a recommendation."

WHO LOVES YA, BABY? GETTING THE RIGHT RECOMMENDATION

Too often, getting the right recommendation is not easy. In our experience, about 75% of the time students either (1) get shortchanged in some way, (2) don't understand the significance of pushing for a strong recommendation, or (3) don't do or say the right thing when approaching a teacher or an adviser for a recommendation. When we say that students are shortchanged, we mean that a recommender just didn't deliver. Yes, advisers and teachers are very busy, but something is wrong when you get a recommendation that is merely "standard," or worse, shallow and completely lacking in substance. What went wrong?

Sometimes it's clear that the recommender didn't really know the student. When that happens, it reflects that the *student* made a mistake. Don't just approach *anyone* to make a recommendation. If you are a John or a Jane Doe in a class—the kind of student who inspires a "were you in my math class?" response when you ask for the recommendation—what kind of message do you think will arrive on the admission officer's desk? Most likely, an ineffective one that says something like, "Andrea received a B in my geometry class and seemed like a nice young lady," which an admissions officer will read as, "I haven't a clue as to who this student really is."

And even when the recommender does know the student, he or she may fail to properly dress the student up—presenting recommendation letters that are tear-jerkers and profiles of future leaders. The sad fact is that many recommendations reflect writers who are merely going through the motions; they can be too shallow, too short, and not good enough to convey authentic support.

Another problem is when a recommendation is requested at the last minute. Writing a recommendation is hard work and takes time. If you're forced to ask for a recommendation at the last minute, chances are you'll get a rush job, a generic letter with little impact.

What Kind of Recommendation Do You Want?

In our experience, recommendations come in three categories: the good, the bad, and the ugly.

The Good

The hallmarks of a good recommendation are when the recommendation:

- is from someone who knows you, and cares enough to be your advocate
- confirms that your are worthy, intelligent, personable, an asset
- positively explains a flaw, if any, in your record
- says or implies "take this student!"

The Bad

You know you got a bad recommendation when:

- it's a general, lame, generic letter that could have gone out to about any student
- it indicates that the teacher obviously didn't know you very well
- the writer or the adviser completely lacks enthusiasm about you

The Ugly

Then there's the ugly recommendation that:

- undermines you and your ability
- essentially says to the college "you better beware, this student has serious flaws"
- tells the college not to accept you

WHAT YOU MUST DO TO LAND A WINNING RECOMMENDATION:

Here are our insider's tips on getting a great recommendation:

1. Don't take anything for granted. It's nice to think that your favorite teacher will write a wonderful endorsement for you with no prodding, but don't assume! Be proactive.

2. Cultivate relationships with teachers and advisers throughout your high school career. Don't be a seat warmer in class. Be seen, be heard.

3. Start early. It's better to be the first to ask for a recommendation than the 25th, 50th, or 100th. Get busy!

4. Select teachers and advisers who will be amenable to your cause. This is the best way to avoid the generic recommendation.

5. If you're really going for the gusto—admission to an elite college—it's often wise to ask your parents to meet with the teachers and advisers who have agreed to write your recommendations. Don't leave your fate to chance. A little concern from a caring family often gets sterling results. It's prudent to touch all bases.

6. Remember, as an African American student, colleges will take a close look at your recommendations. Make sure your recommenders emphasize that you're intelligent and personable.

7. Understand that every recommendation will matter in your application's review. Do everything you can to get the best picture on display.

THE PRESENTATION PACKAGE

Now that you understand what's at stake and who you will need to get involved in your quest for a good recommendation, the question is: How do I approach my teachers and advisers? The answer is: with a strong presentation package.

The presentation package should tell your story in the most favorable light. Anyone looking at the package should be left enlightened as to who you are and what you have accomplished in your life thus far. It should serve as a quick snapshot of your exploits in high school, in the community, and beyond. You goal is to create an "I can copy that" pullout of material that recommenders can use when writing on your behalf. Our experience is that recommenders will use the material you have provided, sometimes word for word, or echo your perspective as they write about you.

How do you create a presentation package? If you've followed our advice in this book so far, you should have all you need at your fingertips.

- a résumé that's good enough to land you a job
- a short essay that reveals important facts about your life and academic career
- copies of any other recommendations you have
- a sheet with your standardized test scores (if they're impressive)
- an unofficial transcript

Put the package in a clear, plastic folder so it's easy to handle and attractive to look at. This package should be presented to every teacher and grade adviser whom you've asked to write a recommendation. You should also explain what's inside and include any necessary envelopes, forms, and stamps. If the recommendation comes in a form, always waive your rights to review the recommendation by checking the appropriate box on forms and applications.

Recommendations are the final key element to your application package. Don't fall asleep. Start early, follow through, and stay proactive to make sure you get the strongest recommendation possible.

CHAPTER 8

BLACK COLLEGE VS. WHITE COLLEGE

Which Is Better for You?

I am a high school senior and want to go to a black college. One of my parents thinks I should go to a white college, the other thinks I should go to a black school. Which would be better?

This question—in one variation or another—is one of the major issues students inevitably grapple with at our counseling sessions. We refer to it as the *black college/white college debate,* and for as long as we can remember, counselors and other commentators have stepped forward to try to clarify the issue, if not put closure on the discussion. But there is no easy answer.

The good news is that students, depending on their needs and sensibilities, have a choice. At Black Excel we are committed to helping our students get into both historically black colleges and universities (HBCUs) and predominantly white institutions (PWIs). Students we have counseled have been accepted to Cornell and Morehouse, Bennett and USC, North Carolina Central and Syracuse University.

We encourage every student (and every parent) to ask this question: "What do I [or my son or my daughter] require to be happy and successful at college?" The next question should be: "What does what each individual college offer in the way of meeting these needs?" For example, if a student needs a nurturing environment with personal attention, it would be foolish to ignore or only lightly consider the HBCUs, which have established a wonderful reputation for nurturing black students through their college years. On the other hand, if a student wants a premier engineering school with state-of-the-art resources or an art school with a famous instructor, perhaps, the options do widen. In the end, our thinking is pretty simple: the selection of a college should depend on a particular student's personality, attitude, ability, life skills, and needs.

MAKING THE CHOICE

If you decided to go search for answers at the library, you might be in for a surprise. In fact, you'd probably come away as puzzled as ever. You'd actually find newspaper and magazine articles such as James A. Lawson's, "Black Colleges on the Rise" and then discover something like James F. Alsbrook's piece, "Are Black Colleges Halfway Houses?" both of which were published in local African American newspapers. Then there's the series of articles "Black Colleges: Will They Survive?" written by Ernest Suggs and published in by the *Herald Sun.* You could get a headache trying to juggle opinions and facts and reach a conclusion. Confusing matters, too, are the myriad of statements that have been made by many of our academic leaders.

Norman C. Francis, the president of historically black Xavier University for more than 30 years, points out that black colleges have delivered "30% of all bachelor's and 15% of all master's degrees awarded to African Americans," while representing only 3% of all the nation's colleges. He says, proudly, that black colleges are "ideal environments for learning, for growing, for sharing, and for achieving."

Black Enterprise publisher Earl G. Graves mentioned in a 1990 Howard University commencement address that when his magazine did a feature on the top 15 black doctors in America, he discovered that five were graduates of Howard University. Few realize that as a college student, Jesse Jackson first enrolled at the University of Illinois but faced racism—the school couldn't accept a black quarterback—and headed into the welcoming arms of an HBCU, North Carolina A&T University. The rest is history.

Thomas Sowell, conservative columnist and author of the now out-of-print *Choosing a College* (Harper & Row, 1989), on the other hand, often makes the point that HBCUs don't measure up academically to elite mainstream schools. Sowell, interestingly, began his undergraduate work at Howard University, one of our premier black schools, and then transferred to Harvard. After making the academic transition from a flagship black school to the world-renowned Harvard, he realized that what he thought were good study habits were not. His point is that historically black colleges must make stronger academic demands on our students and that they should demand higher standards for themselves.

In his memoir *Days of Grace,* Arthur Ashe makes some thought-provoking comments about historically black colleges. He writes that they "must be preserved." He mentions that he grew up across the street from Virginia Union and not far from Hampton University. It's telling that our late hero also goes on to say this: "Such colleges are curators of our culture just as, whether we like to admit it or not, Harvard is a curator of Anglo-Saxon culture in the United States." He says we have "Howard, Tuskegee, and Spelman, and should help them."

Ashe courageously turned down Yale to teach at a historically black college. But before long, he found himself deeply troubled. At this "fourth tier" school (so ranked by *US News & World Report* in 1998), the students handed in papers that he felt lacked organization, "logic, and argumentation." Some students, he wrote, actually showed up late for class, didn't seem to care, and the experience left him disenchanted. Too many students, to Ashe, didn't take their education seriously; he also observed academic deficiencies and an absence of basic academic skills.

Marian Wright Edelman, president of the Children's Defense Fund, also gave a wonderful speech at a past Howard University commencement. She called it "Beating the Odds." At one point in her speech she said, "A black boy today has a 1 in 4,000 chance of getting a Ph.D. in math, Engineering, or Physics, a 1 in 684 chance of becoming a physician, a 1 in 372 chance of becoming a teacher." She then gave the odds of that same black boy becoming a drug abuser (e.g., 1 in 45), a prisoner, or a dropout. Anyone listening could realize what these odds would be if the nurturing environment of black colleges were suddenly erased from the face of the earth.

"There's still a role for black colleges," says former governor L. Douglas Wilder. A graduate of historically black Virginia Union University, his alma mater, he makes some poignant points. One, that about 40% of all the students of color at Virginia's public four-year

> "The mission of black colleges is not only to educate students but also to improve quality of life for black families. [When] a student comes out of here and goes to law school, that family may never have to see difficult days again . . ."
> —CALVIN W. BURNET, PRESIDENT, COPPIN STATE

colleges attend either Norfolk or Virginia State, two historically black colleges. He says, finally, that those two schools produce more black graduates than the 13 other public colleges in Virginia combined. So it's a given that the black colleges have a rich historical legacy and are both vital and necessary today.

THE PROS AND THE CONS

At mainstream colleges of all levels and ranks, you are likely to find more amenities. When our students arrive at HBCU Clark-Atlanta, then look at the University of Georgia, they discover that the other side has what some might consider awesome advantages—modern buildings, fully equipped, state-of-the-art computers, laboratories, and libraries. Looking deeper, you find big-time faculty names and larger endowments. The less astute might immediately want to go to the Hilton, and wonder why they're staying in a motel off the highway. Again, the debate rages on. Some argue that they

> "There are pros and cons of both black and white colleges. I have taken classes at Haverford, Swarthmore, Bryn Mawr, Penn, Spelman, Morehouse, Yale, and Cambridge University in England. Due to historical and financial advantages, white colleges often had better facilities and may be able to recruit the 'big name' profs, but black colleges provide a nurturing, comfortable atmosphere in which to learn. Weigh your options wisely. I did study away at Spelman for a semester and had the time of my life! There is nothing more refreshing than a nurturing, comfortable community of learning."—JOY ZAREMBKA, GRADUATE, YALE UNIVERSITY

might as well get used to the "real world" and its challenges. Translation: go to a white school. Others factor in all the parts and say "The HBCUs do more with less!"

The choice, of course, is yours. Here are some specific pros and cons to help you make your decision.

Predominantly White Institutions: The Positives

Here are some of the advantages of pursuing your education at a predominantly white college. Remember, these are all generalizations; it's important to check on each school individually:

- Many have endowments of more than $64 million, according to a report published in *The Chronicle of Higher Education Almanac,* based on 1996 figures provided by the National Association of College and University Business Officers. Some schools, such as Harvard, the University of Notre Dame, and Emory, have "market values" of more than $1 billion. No HBCUs even approach such figures. Why does the endowment matter? Quite simply, colleges with higher endowments tend to have more stability, better facilities, and star-studded faculties. Because of rich endowments many prestigious PWIs generally do not have to depend on tuition to survive. In fact, even the endowments of second-tier PWIs look impressive compared to those of most black schools. Because of an obvious financial advantage, many mainstream schools can recruit "the best and the brightest" of our African American scholars. Former Spelman president Dr. Johnnetta Cole, has often spoken about the realities of recruiting head-on against the Ivy League and Seven Sisters schools. At times such schools have been able to offer great financial aid and scholarship packages that Spelman, try as it may, couldn't match. Of course, colleges with lesser endowments can often offer a top-notch experience, and a college's rich endowment is no guarantee that it's the best school for you. But it's a factor that should be considered.

- A good number of highly ranked or elite PWIs can deliver a "gold card" to the best professional and graduate schools, top jobs, and high salaries upon graduation. An MIT degree, for instance, opens doors.

- Many PWIs offer better equipment and facilities than our schools. Some offer very beautiful campuses (University of North Carolina at Chapel Hill, Princeton), relatively plush dorms, and even cafeterias offering *good* meals with a

> **Comparing the Endowments of top PWIs and HBCUs**
>
> - Harvard: $8,811,785,000
> - University of Texas system: $5,697,150,000
> - Yale University: $4,853,010,000
>
> - Howard: $176,186,000
> - Spelman: $142,884,000
> - Hampton: $113,046,000

choice on the menu (Cornell). You might find, too, superior libraries, professional-looking sports stadiums, gyms, swimming pools, on-campus movie theaters, and more. Being "better equipped" also applies to research and laboratory facilities that are often important to science and engineering programs, to cite two areas. State-of-the art equipment is always a plus in getting those lucrative multimillion-dollar contracts and support awards.

- More PWIs are "wired"—that is, students have access to computers around campus, in their dorms, and sometimes can surf and do research in their rooms. At many schools you get your own e-mail account, as well as the option of creating your own web site on the university's server, and the computer-to-student ratio is 1 to 18 or better.

- PWI schools can seek, pay, and hire elite professors, including some of the top African American scholars around. Maya Angelou is at Wake Forest, Henry Louis Gates and Cornel West are at Harvard, Charles V. Hamilton and Manning Marable are at Columbia. These are just a few, but the list of top black professors at predominantly white institutions is long indeed.

- Generally, PWIs have more programs available for artistic studies: theater, art, film, and dance. Among PWIs you'll find such institutions as Juilliard (dance and music), Parsons School of Design (art), University of California at Los Angeles (film), and Yale (theater), each the top school in its area. When pursuing these sorts of studies at other schools, you might find the offerings hard to find or limited.

- Finally, mainstream colleges contend that they are working toward achieving desirable integrated environments. Some argue that the mainstream setting is closer to "the real world," which students will eventually have to integrate into.

> **"** I was surprised and honored to be chosen as valedictorian of my graduating class as well as the speaker for the universitywide commencement. I never imagined that I would have such opportunities in a school so large, but I found multiple outlets for my interest and incredible encouragement and support from many administrators and faculty—black and white alike . . ." —RACHEL LYN JOHNSON, GRADUATE, NEW YORK UNIVERSITY, CURRENTLY A GRADUATE STUDENT AT JOHNS HOPKINS UNIVERSITY

Predominantly White Institutions: The Downside

Okay, now that you've see the upside of going to a mainstream college, here are some of the problems you may run into:

- Racism. Even though colleges have done a lot to create a positive environment for all students, there are still innumerable examples of overt and subtle on-campus racism. They can range from the rare cases of overt physical attacks on black students by white students, or the more frequent belittling of black student achievement by members of the faculty, campus newspapers, and small-minded students. We're not going to name schools or document the problems here, but suffice to say that problems have occurred and do occur—in some schools more than in others.

> "**A**s an educator, I think it's beyond crisis when in our citadels of rational thought and wisdom—our colleges and universities—we find that since 1986, there have been 300 incidents of harassment and violence involving race, religion, ethnicity or sexual orientation." —DR. JOHNNETTA B. COLE, FORMER PRESIDENT OF SPELMAN UNIVERSITY

- Feelings of isolation. Chances are that you could be the only black person in your dormitory wing or one of a very small number of black students on campus, which can be a major adjustment, particularly if you're coming from a predominantly black community or school. A further problem is that when the percentage of blacks on campus is low, social and cultural events are usually not targeted to our interests or needs. Looking for a gospel choir? You may be out of luck. On some campuses the odds are high that you will need to seek solace/fun away. Sometimes the students of Alabama's Auburn University head to Tuskegee for parties or social events. Our folks at Davidson College often find themselves at North Carolina A&T.

The Legacy of Leaders from Predominantly White Colleges

- Neurosurgeon Benjamin Carson (University of Michigan)
- Professor Manning Marable (Michigan State University)
- The discoverer of blood plasma Charles Drew (Amherst College)
- Former head of the NAACP Benjamin Hooks (DePaul University)
- Basketball legend Kareem Abdul-Jabbar (UCLA)
- Tennis legend Arthur Ashe (UCLA)
- Daughter of Martin Luther King Jr. Yolanda King (Smith College)
- Actor James Earl Jones (University of Michigan)
- Chief CEO and president, Black Entertainment Network, Robert Johnson (University of Illinois)
- Former president of the Urban League Vernon Jordan (Depauw University)
- Singer Natalie Cole (University of Massachusetts)

- At the very top schools, when black students experience academic difficulty, our experience has been that students are reluctant to say anything to the college's counselors and advisers. Students have told us that the unspoken vibe they often pick up when they are experiencing adjustment problems is "Well, you shouldn't be here!" or a variation of that theme. The attitude they face is "You're here, now perform or get out."

Historically Black Colleges: The Positives

> "The best antidote to racism is excellence."
> —JOURNALIST CLARENCE PAGE, FROM HIS BOOK *SHOWING MY COLOR*

We've already talked a bit about the shortcomings of HBCUs, but don't be misled: the best HBCUs still provide a top-line educational experience. If you're talking about producing scholars in the natural sciences, including engineering, you can't help but mention Fisk, Howard, Tuskegee, and Spelman, for example. Unquestioned are the undergraduate achievements of Xavier University in preparing its students for medical school and Florida A&M and Howard in garnering record numbers of achievement scholars. Fisk offers a UNCF Premedical Summer Institute that leads our students to M.D. degrees. Spelman is an academic beacon in the national rankings and has been picked as a "best money buy" in the well-regarded *U.S. News* rankings. You can clearly see the value of such schools even when you take a narrower state-by-state focus. "Southern and Grambling are only two of the state's institutions, but we provide about half of the black bachelorette graduates in the state every year," says Southern's president Delores Spikes. That's telling.

Here are some more specific positives to think about when considering an HBCU:

- A larger percentage of students who enroll at historically black colleges will go on to graduate. While fewer than 20% of all black college students choose an HBCU, approximately 34% of our graduates get their degrees from HBCUs.

> "We try very hard to incubate in our students a belief that they can overcome odds and win!"—FORMER MOREHOUSE PRESIDENT HUGH M. GLOSTER

- Large percentages of students graduating from black schools go on to get advanced degrees, often at elite graduate schools. Time and time again, we have seen the journey: From Spelman to Duke (medical), from North Carolina Central to Boston College (law), from Howard to Florida A&M (business).
- There is often ample opportunity for self-realization and growth in all areas—academic, cultural, social—without the stress of trying to fit into the often less-welcome environment of PWIs.
- There are also better opportunities to hold positions of leadership (class president, Homecoming queen, editor of the school newspaper).
- The college cost to you (unless you are selecting a public school) is generally less expensive. (The gap, however, is closing. Look for continued increases of tuition and fees at HBCUs.)
- Admissions requirements are less stringent. Application officers take into consideration a student's potential, and the possibility of late blooming is often factored into the application process. If necessary, you'll also find better remedial backup. At HBCUs, in other words, you're more likely to get a second chance.
- There's little racial intolerance, at least for black students, as racial problems are minimized. Course presentations are also less likely to be unremittingly Eurocentric. Furthermore,

generally speaking, economically disadvantaged students are not treated as if they have a stigma.

- You'll find more black role models and mentors. You'll also have a rich legacy of black achievers.

- When it's all over (your degree in hand), the odds will be that you will have a better alumni networking base. It's probable, too, that you will have made more lifelong friends. You will return for Homecoming. Black college graduates seem to have a stronger bond.

Historically Black Colleges: The Downside

Here's the bad news about HBCUs. Remember, these are all generalizations and don't necessarily apply to every HBCU. It's important to check on each school individually.

- You will find a lack of racial diversity and few opportunities to interact with people of other races.

- Black colleges have low endowments and are frequently dependent on state and outside support. In regard to day-to-day-operations, academic and other resources are often lacking.

- There are occasionally administrative problems. Major complaints? Long lines to register and financial aid support/problems.

- Often, black schools cannot afford to hire and keep professors with the best reputations and credentials. This is not to say that HBCUs don't have fine professoriat, only that you are less likely to find the academic superstars there.

> "In many instances, black institutions are not eligible for research grants simply because they do not have the laboratory resources or academic horsepower necessary to conduct projects."
> —*JOURNAL OF BLACKS IN HIGHER EDUCATION*

- Buildings and libraries are sometimes described by students as "old" or "inadequate." Too often, students complain about "second-class" dorms. Of course, the quality of the facilities varies from school to school.

- Many schools are not properly wired in regard to computers. At top schools such as Fisk and Howard you can get e-mail and create home pages, but computers are not located in the dorms.

- Believe it or not, few predominantly black colleges offer African American Studies majors.

SOME OTHER THINGS TO THINK ABOUT

Even at PWIs, you will very often find "schools within schools." The odds are high that you will find a Black Student Union or Center, Offices of Minority Affairs, hangouts, and "hot spots" particular to your needs.

At some mainstream schools you will find "theme" houses where sizable numbers of black students reside, in order to feel at home. At Amherst there is a "Charles Drew House"; at Cornell, "Ujamaa." Such dorms also exist at Brown and Wesleyan. Of course, some colleges don't permit such obvious segregation, but still students manage to stay close. At MIT, one floor where our students used to hang out was called "Chocolate City."

In 1995, after reviewing a study by the National Research Council (NRC), the *Journal of Blacks in Higher Education* made this assessment: "It appears that many academically gifted students who choose the nurturing environment of a Black college or university for

---

The Legacy of Leaders from Historically Black Colleges

- Civil rights activist the Reverend Jesse Jackson (North Carolina A&T)
- The late NASA astronaut Ronald E. McNair (North Carolina A&T)
- *Black Enterprise* publisher Earl G. Graves (Morgan State)
- Filmmaker Spike Lee (Morehouse)
- Nobel Prize laureate the Reverend Dr. Martin Luther King Jr. (Morehouse)
- Opera singer Leontyne Price (Central State)
- Former UN ambassador and Atlanta mayor Andrew Young (Howard University)
- Supreme Court justice Thurgood Marshall (Lincoln University)
- *60 Minutes* commentator Ed Bradley (Cheyney University)
- Former U.S. Secretary of Health and Human Services Dr. Louis Sullivan (Morehouse)
- Editor of *Ebony* and historian Lerone Bennet (Morehouse)
- Talk show host Oprah Winfrey (Tennessee State)
- Actress and dancer Debbie Allen (Howard University)
- Pulitzer Prize–winning author Toni Morrison (Howard University)
- President of the Children's Defense Fund Marian Wright Edelman (Spelman). She was the valedictorian of her class!
- First woman U.S. Air Force brigadier general Marcelite J. Harris (Spelman)

---

undergraduate studies are opting for graduate programs in which academic strength and reputation are prime considerations." Sadly, the resources HBCUs have generally had available at the graduate level have been limited. There are Howard, Clark-Atlanta, Tennessee State, and a very short list of other competing schools. About five HBCU graduate programs award more than 20 Ph.D.'s a year.

A WORD TO THE WISE

Each student of color is unique. That's a fact. Talking to, lecturing to, and interacting with thousands of aspiring freshmen-to-be's, we can honestly say that we have pointed—without prejudice—to the best option for the individual student. There's no route that is etched in granite or paved with gold. There are households today where you can find a brother going to the University of Michigan, and a sister from the same household studying at Howard.

On a counseling form that Black Excel often uses to assist students to arrive at sensible choices, at least 40% of our clientele when asked to list four schools they are considering give us crossover lists. A student might express interest in Hampton, Spelman, Wesleyan, and Boston College. Test the waters, consider your options. Of course, there are groups of students who feel strongly that they want to go one way or another. Whatever your need, there are roads you can travel leading to wherever you want to go at a speed that is amenable to your emotional, cultural, or mental speedometer. That's the important thing.

To be sure, historically black colleges fill a need. Not a year goes by that at least a couple of students have not told us that they have had dinner at a professor's house. Sometimes our students get an opportunity to shake hands with a college president, or deans, and there is constant talk of finding mentors. It's not that unusual. Certainly, we hear stories that echo similar themes/stories from the mainstream institutions, but honestly, not nearly as often. The fact is, at too many mainstream schools, students of color are left to sink or swim.

But even at the most PW of the PWIs, if you take a close look you will often find, somehow, a "black thing." Our students seem to create safe havens at predominantly white colleges. Black student centers, clubs, associations, hangouts, and Greek-

> "North Carolina A&T is one of the few schools with a spirit that transcends students and alumni. From the first day on campus, you are considered a member of the Aggie Family and you instantly have a bridge of contacts worldwide. A&T offers small classes with caring professors. Where else would a professor call you to offer special tutoring because he noticed you were struggling? Where else would the dean of your school call you after you graduate to find out how the university prepared you for life outside of school? . . ." —MATTHEW BARNHILL, GRADUATE, NORTH CAROLINA A&T

letter systems have (over decades) taken on lives of their own. And if you ask, you'll find that our students are constantly inviting guests who have particular interest to them, some even controversial: Louis Farrakhan, Spike Lee, and Dr. Jawanza Kunjufu are examples who come to mind.

Aside from these buffers, many of our students coexist, strive, and are happy at PWIs such as Haverford, where students of all cultures appear to get along. Many who hope to navigate the college admissions process do not realize that there are more African Americans students—by a large margin—studying at mainstream schools than at historically black colleges. Check and you will find that there are no HBCUs in states such as Minnesota, Connecticut, or Illinois. The list is long. There are more than 3,000 PWIs compared to just over 100 HBCUs. In fact, in most college guides the HBCUs are barely mentioned. They are "invisible," to quote Ralph Ellison's word.

Black Excel has been around long enough to know that you can't put closure on the black college/white college debate without bringing each individual student front and center first. Let us emphasize again: one student might fare very well at Ohio State, another does better at Florida A&M. Each student must factor into his or her decision such factors as racism, campus social life, a school's reputation, majors offered, levels of course difficulty, on-site support systems, cost, campus employment, and options for graduate and professional school study.

Ultimately, the debate—and your school selections—are about who you are and what you are striving for. So choose carefully.

CHAPTER 9

THE TOP SCHOOLS

Can You Do a Four-Minute Mile?

I f, after reviewing the previous chapters on choosing a college and preparing your application, you discover that you fall into the category of "super student," you may decide to go for an elite college or university—perhaps Yale or Princeton of the Ivy League, a super private school such as Emory in Atlanta or Stanford in Palo Alto, a well-regarded public school such as SUNY Binghamton in New York or UCLA, or one of the HBCU giants such as Spelman. You should know by now that it's not going to be easy. Those prestigious, all-knowing admissions selectors at the top universities—and don't tell them otherwise—want the "best and the brightest," and will try to pick their latest freshman class with that goal in mind.

THE BEST NATIONAL UNIVERSITIES AND LIBERAL ARTS COLLEGES

The first question might be: What are the top national universities and liberal arts colleges? Different sources will give you slightly different lists, but here we will provide you with the *U.S. News & World Report* list, which is perhaps the most widely used and quoted—sometimes by dissenters. We think the list is generally sound and will give you a good idea of which schools are considered the cream of the crop (although we do not endorse the list). Aside from the 50 schools listed here, there are another 100 or so that would qualify as highly competitive, including other competitive public universities and HBCUs.

In the past, HBCUs such as Spelman, Hampton, and Morehouse have gotten favorable press and mention in rankings, but generally it's been our opinion that HBCUs have been overlooked here. The deciding criteria for placement, in our opinion, often overlook the ingredients that make some black schools particularly strong and far more competitive than some experts report.

Very often, we have been impressed by what we have seen. In the Spring 1996 edition of our newsletter *Black Excel News* (vol. 3, no. 1–2), we picked our top 10 historically black colleges. We did not place our picks in any particular ranking order, but our ten picks are essentially the same as the top 10 grouping picked by *Black Enterprise* in its January 1999 issue. The exception is that *BE* didn't include Fisk among its premier selections, but we did.

Here's our top 10 (in alphabetical order) based on more than a decade of looking at and assessing schools:

- Clark-Atlanta University (GA)
- Fisk University (TN)
- Florida A&M University (FL)
- Hampton University (VA)
- Howard University (DC)

- Morehouse College (GA)
- North Carolina A&T University (NC)
- Spelman College (GA)
- Tuskegee University (AL)
- Xavier University (LA)

National Universities

National universities are defined by Carnegie Foundation for Advancement of Teaching as universities that offer a full range of undergraduate majors, as well as master's and doctoral degrees. Here are the top national universities, in alphabetical order, according to the 1999 *U.S. News & World Report* rankings:

- Brown University (RI)
- California Institute of Technology (CA)
- Carnegie Mellon University (PA)
- Columbia University (NY)
- Cornell University (NY)
- Dartmouth College (NH)
- Duke University (NC)
- Emory University (GA)
- Georgetown University (DC)
- Harvard University (MA)
- Johns Hopkins University (MD)
- Massachusetts Institute of Technology (MA)
- Northwestern University (IL)
- Princeton University (NJ)
- Rice University (TX)
- Stanford University (CA)
- Tufts University (MA)
- University of California at Berkeley (CA)
- University of California at Los Angeles (CA)
- University of Chicago (IL)
- University of Michigan at Ann Arbor (MI)
- University of North Carolina at Chapel Hill (NC)
- University of Notre Dame (IN)
- University of Pennsylvania (PA)
- University of Virginia (VA)
- Vanderbilt University (TN)
- Washington University at St. Louis (MO)
- Yale University (CT)

National Liberal Arts Colleges

These are defined as schools that emphasize undergraduate education and award at least 40% of their degrees in the liberal arts:

- Amherst College (MA)
- Barnard College (NY)
- Bates College (ME)

- Bowdoin College (ME)
- Bryn Mawr College (PA)
- Carleton College (MN)
- Claremont McKenna College (CA)
- Colby College (ME)
- Colgate University (NY)
- Colorado College (CO)
- Davidson College (NC)
- Grinnell College (IA)
- Hamilton College (NY)
- Haverford College (PA)
- Macalester College (MN)
- Middlebury College (VT)
- Mount Holyoke College (MA)
- Oberlin College (OH)
- Pomona College (CA)
- Smith College (MA)
- Swarthmore College (PA)
- Trinity College (CT)
- University of the South (TN)
- Vassar College (NY)
- Washington and Lee University (VA)
- Wellesley College (MA)
- Wesleyan University (CT)
- Williams College (MA)

Again, it's worth knowing that at the California Institute of Technology—known as Cal Tech—black enrollment is a measly 1%; at MIT—the Massachusetts Institute of Technology—black enrollment is a more acceptable 6%.

YOUR ODYSSEY: BEATING THE ODDS AND GETTING IN

The key thing to remember here is that you don't want to be just another number. You've got to begin your quest knowing that perhaps only 150 colleges in the country can legitimately be called "very competitive" in regard to admissions and that the odds are that nearly every smart kid in the country with a strong academic profile is thinking the way you are: "I want to get accepted." Although we might smile at an article such as "Give Me Harvard or Give Me Death" (*New York Times Magazine,* 1997), many students (and their parents) have been waiting about 16 or 17 years to cash in on a dream. Some have had a road map. Others, by hook or by crook, facing daunting and sometimes unmentionable disadvantages—inferior schools, teacher apathy and neglect, perhaps a single parent who is exhausted but carrying on—have studied and worked long and hard to get a piece of the pie. And why not? But these are the people against whom you'll be competing.

What Are the Odds?

Even if you have always been a high achiever, you're going to have to run a four-minute mile during the selection and application process if you want to win the race. Some freshman accept-ance rates to the very competitive schools will make you swallow hard. The top schools have acceptance rates that range from 13% (Harvard) to 34% (University of Virginia). For every 100 applications Georgetown University will accept approximately 23 students. At Spelman, fewer than half of those 100 will make the cut. At the University of Pennsylvania, about 29. At Stanford, about 13.

At Yale, in an average year, the school will hear from more than 12,000 applicants and accept only 2,144. At MIT, a first-year application pool of about 8,000 will generate about 2,000 accepts. Even when some of the rates seem favorable, it's part illusion. Some schools attract a very smart and competitive application pool: the University of Chicago (61%), Georgia Institute of Technology (61%), and University of Michigan at Ann Arbor (69%), for example. And certainly, the acceptance rates to the best HBCUs will continue to decline as the number of applicants increases. Hampton University, for example, with an application pool near the 6,000 range, can accommodate only about 52% who apply. At the premier black schools, many of us are no longer guaranteed a sure admit.

What Are Your Odds as a Black Student?

Despite the intimidating figures above, you must remember that there is a hierarchy of qualified students. For serious, honor track students with good grades, there are options galore. And if you are one of about 1,500 black students—perhaps 1% of the total—who score over 1,200 on the SAT, you're a commodity, all other things being satisfactory. You will get recruitment letters from dozens of schools.

But even if you're not presently one of the very rare academic "stars"—based on objective stats—there is still wonderful news. You may not be a Charles Drew yet, and your standardized test scores may not be stratospheric, but the evidence says that you could be a strong admissions candidate at many of the highest-ranked schools. Point of fact: our 1200-point test takers can't fill the seven Ivy League slots we usually garner annually. The University of Pennsylvania, for example, accepts about 400 blacks each year. Cornell accepts more than 325, with Columbia totaling about 275. Harvard accepts about 180 blacks.

Check out these additional accept figures for highly ranked schools:

The University of Virginia: about 750 accepts a year. The University of Michigan: about 900 accepts a year. Emory University: about 500 accepts a year. Massachusetts Institute of Technology: about 132 accepts a year. Stanford University: about 250 accepts a year. Carnegie Mellon University: about 300 accepts a year.

In this little overview, we have named 10 highly ranked mainstream schools. They accept about 3,000 black students annually. Factor in 100-plus other very selective or prestigious schools and it's clear to see that if you're a strong student, a good college will likely put out the welcome mat.

Now factor in the top HBCUs—Spelman, Howard, Xavier, Florida A&M—and you can see how your odds greatly increase. Florida A&M University: about 2,900 accepts yearly. Howard University: about 3,200 accepts yearly. Spelman College: about 1,400 accepts yearly. Morehouse College: about 1,350 accepts a year. So if you're a strong student who has demonstrated that you can handle the work, it's a buyer's market. But that doesn't mean it's going to be easy.

Who's Your Competition? Your Brothers and Sisters

At the highest-ranked schools, if you check "black" or "African American" on your application submission, the odds are very high that you will be competing against other students of color, our best and brightest. No, this is not something that is usually said in catalogs, phone conversations, or discussed in other guides. But it's a fact.

In Michele A. Hernandez's good book, *A Is for Admission: The Insider's Guide to Getting into the Ivy League and Other Top Schools* (Warner Books, 1997), she mentions that black Dartmouth applicants are given "red tags" to distinguish their folders. In *Questions and Admissions: Reflections on 100,000 Admissions Decisions at Stanford* (Stanford University Press, 1995), by Jean Fetter, a former dean of undergraduate admissions at Stanford, we learn that black applicants to Stanford get a special look from an "appropriate minority director." At other schools, too, minority applications are sorted and reviewed differently, whether black, Asian, or Native American. This will likely continue; even as the affirmative action debate continues and legislation passes making "race-based admissions" unacceptable, the odds are still high that most admissions officers will make an effort to maintain diversity on their campuses.

DON'T GET WEEDED OUT

All schools, of course, have their "weed out" methods. We feel that if you're simply a stat or a number, you could be at a considerable disadvantage. Many of the large public colleges use computer-generated formulas that simply factor in GPAs and standardized test scores. The question of "who you are" is set aside. Special talent, and students with unlimited potential, can be (and are) easily overlooked. Some of the University of California colleges—with huge applicant pools—have used statistical cutoffs, even before the anti-affirmative action rules said scores of one kind or another should be primary. A school such as the University of Illinois at Urbana-Champaign is another example of an admit system that sometimes feels impersonal. Admission is dependent on class rank and College Board scores. So even to get considered at these schools, you must have outstanding grades and test scores.

Even when they don't use strict formulas, most of the top colleges have screening systems—like radar—where applications are immediately routed to Definite Accept, Possible Accept, Borderline, Reject, and other piles of folders by first-step reviewers. You get the idea. At a school such as Harvard, perhaps 150 to 350 of an enormous pool of applicants (18,000) present stats and extras that are so awesome that it's no contest: admit, admit, admit. Here you will probably find a Westinghouse winner or finalist, to name one area that undoubtedly gets instant attention. If you fall into that category, congratulations—somebody probably has contacted you. But if not, what kind of application will get you in the right pile?

Well, just to get into the right pile, your record and personal attributes have to be impressive. For example, a school might use a 1 to 5 rating system to size up your academic capability/performance on one side, and your personal/extracurricular level on the other. In the academic arena, a 5 might mean that you're clearly "superior"—a very strong student academically. A 4 might say you're a "strong student." A 3? You're "acceptable." A 2, that you "have limitations." A 1, that you are a clear "reject." On the personal/extracurricular side, the numbers might have similar tags. A 5 might mean that you are a star (perhaps there's been national recognition for creating a community project). A 4? That you are clearly "a contributor." A 3 might mean that your overview is "simply average." A 2? That you "fall below average," and a 1 that you present "nothing special" or noteworthy. Translation: reject.

In the presented scenario, any applicant strong enough to get a 5/5, or perfect score, would be in outstanding shape. It's likely that an admissions committee reviewing such a case would say: "Accept, without reservation!"

But inevitably, most applicants will be 3/3's, or thereabouts. And hitting the jackpot might mean that you generally need a 7, or higher using a 5/5 system (where a combined 10 might be the ultimate). To get a 7 you need to have something special; you need to touch a nerve, write a brilliant and amusing essay, demonstrate a steady climb in grades from the 10th year on, presenting outstanding recommendations. A no or wait list call, even after you're tagged a 7, might mean that one admissions officer felt uncomfortable because of a lukewarm recommendation from your Literature teacher. Or simply that he or she was more excited about another candidate: the person whose application was tighter, whose demeanor was more determined.

I Am Somebody: Distinguishing Yourself from the Pack

The point is, once you've gotten into the right pile, you need to do something to make your application stand out. A *U.S. News & World Report* story headline (April 14, 1997) read, "How to Get into a Great College." Writer Alvin P. Sanoff spent five days studying admissions deliberations at the University of Pennsylvania. Not the least of his revelations is that "the process at this Ivy League school is thorough, even painstaking. It is also a process that is driven by subjectivity, numbers, and chance. . . ."

So pump your gas pedal! If you hope to gain a prestigious admit, make that maximum, go-for-the-gold-effort. One director of admissions noted that "of 11 candidates I see, eight are interchangeable." Without question there is often a thin line between the winners and the losers in the admissions game. You don't want to second-guess yourself—make every dot, comma, sentence, and paragraph count.

How Important Is Your Record?

Certainly, a great record of grades in rigorous courses is always a major factor at this level. Accomplishments in honors, advance placement, and college preparatory courses in general do impress. Also, your commendable test scores will carry substantial weight in any admissions assessment. Your grade-point average, curriculum, and test scores have to signal "I can do the work." If your grades don't cut the mustard, being Mr. or Ms. Congeniality isn't going to matter. Still, remember that the very top schools in the nation routinely reject the majority of valedictorians and salutatorians who apply, in all likelihood because they are one-dimensional. A main offense is presenting a package that doesn't inspire anyone. Be spiritual, maybe even shout a little. If your application effort is indistinguishable from others, why should Rice or Morehouse or Northwestern accept you?

Stanford University, for instance, claims to favors applicants who have performed well in a strong, broad high school curriculum but who have also "shown energy and persistence in extracurricular activities." For the black applicant, we think the comments and insights of the former dean of undergraduate admissions at Stanford are particularly meaningful. As author of *Questions and Admissions: Reflections on 100,000 Admissions Decisions at Stanford,* Jean Fetter says, "SAT's do not predict such human qualities as leadership, creativity, motivation, energy, persistence, compassion, and sensitivity." She states, too, that picking a freshman class involves "considerable subjectivity." So while grades are very important, it's still crucial that you sell yourself as a complete person, one whose potential is only suggested by mere grades.

THE SUPER STUDENT PORTFOLIO: HOW IT SHOULD LOOK

When the admissions officers see your offering, you want them to nod, smile, and discuss your attributes. You don't want a 30-second accept/deny. If you can, you want to stop the show. Remember, too, that often there is a subjective element in the decisions made. There's an oldies record called "Will You Still Love Me Tomorrow?" Well, will they remember your name at the day's end? The next day?

Here's what they should find in you, the super student:

- an academic average in the B+/A range
- a full slate of college preparatory courses, including lab sciences: chemistry, biology, and physics, and two or more years of foreign-language study
- good course selection (the depth and scope of your curriculum)
- senior year courses at the local college are always a plus, if possible
- extracurricular achievements in school
- community service
- in the ballpark SAT scores. There's a wide range here, depending on your portfolio's overall impact. We've seen scores from 1100 to well over 1200 do the job.
- two or three Achievement Test (SAT II) scores—perhaps in English (writing), math, or social studies
- a high class rank, preferably, in the top 5 to 10% of your class
- high character, morals, personality, and seriousness of purpose, as demonstrated in extracurricular activities and expressed in your essay
- strong letters of recommendation
- an above-average essay, one that tells your story in a way that resonates while also demonstrating strong grammar, vocabulary, and writing skills

Things that will put you in an even better position include:

- a strong interview (if a school recommends interviews, and you have the gift of gab and personality, ask for one; if it's a strain—perhaps you're shy, or not the talkative type—pass)
- evidence of special talent in the arts, music, drama, athletics, writing, or some other area
- consistently strong grades or consistent grade improvement: B, B+, A
- a high school that is a "feeder" school—with successful students—already at your selected college
- strong peer references; you know what they say, Birds of a feather . . .

Other Intangibles in Your Favor

Aside from already discussed factors, including grades, extracurriculars, recommendations, and your essay, there are other intangibles that might swing things in your favor:

- Your geographical location. If it's a regional or in-state school, you might be that rare and desirable traveler. Applying to your public state college or university is always wise. Hedge your bets. Usually the state school has a primary obligation to accept more students from its state.

- Picking a major at your selected school that has a short supply of applicants.

- A school's need for diversity. Good schools want students with varied talents, interests, and backgrounds.

- Being a federally recognized minority (black, Native American) helps. Again, despite affirmative action rollbacks, schools still want racial diversity (but stay tuned as affirmative action debate and legislation evolve).

Increase Your Admission Odds to the Powerhouse Schools

If you're committed to getting into a powerhouse school, there are some things you can do to increase your odds.

1. *Your Self-Assessment*
   The first step is to make an honest self-assessment. If the elements of the super student portfolio listed above are completely alien to you, perhaps you should aim for a school that better suits your needs. On the other hand, if your credentials are at least in the ballpark of the super student portfolio outlined above, give it a shot. We've worked with applicants whose advisers have discouraged them from applying to top schools when it's a borderline call. We say GO FOR IT.

   You have nothing to lose but the application fee and nothing to gain but an exceptional educational experience that might give you an edge for the rest of your life. You don't want to second-guess yourself later.

2. *Take an SAT/ACT Prep Course*
   Top students nearly always take SAT/ACT prep courses. They spare no expense, nor should you if you have the money. Don't concede any advantage to anyone. The stories about training raising scores 50 to 200 points higher have some validity. We have seen it happen to students we have worked with.

3. *Take Achievement Test (SAT II) Prep Courses*
   Top students also take Achievement Test (SAT II) prepping if required. Again, if you can afford it, spare no expense. Some of the very best schools require two or three of these tests. At last count, there were 23 academic subject areas you could test in, including biology, American history, math, physics, chemistry, and writing.

4. *Get to Know Your Best Friend, the Grade Adviser*
   Early on, get to know your college grade adviser. You don't want him or her to know you simply as student "365." That adviser (who sometimes has to write a collaborative evaluation, using the comments of two or three of your teachers) usually has as much clout as anyone writing you a recommendation. If your school adviser is not tooting your horn, what does that say? If an admissions officer has any questions about you, needing clarification about your personality, grades, or purposefulness, the pivotal call will be to your grade adviser.

5. *Use the School's Application Form*
   As we mentioned in the previous chapter, when it's application time, do it hands-on, the old-fashioned way. With your top college selections, use the school's actual application, not the alternate, generic common application or online electronic applications that students sometimes use to save time and apply to many colleges.

   If a top college is receiving 1000 applications, and 950 applicants are responding to/on the school's actual application, do we want to be in the smaller grouping, perhaps answering an essay question that is not as relevant? Can we chance any possible bias?

6. *Think about Early Admissions*
   Many of the elite colleges are filling large portions of their freshman class with "early admissions" applications. As we mentioned in the previous chapter, as a super and very capable student, you can apply early (November 1–15) and get a yes/no reply by mid-December. But remember, once you accept, it's binding. Since the powerhouse schools are now filling a large percentage of their freshman classes with such students (more than 30% at schools such as Cornell, Columbia, Princeton, Stanford, Penn, Williams, and Amherst, to name several), you might want to take advantage of a favorable early reception, since the demand for academically strong black students is high.

The danger? With one school in the basket, your financial aid options are limited. Can you afford to not play the field? It's telling that the *Journal of Blacks in Higher Education (JBHE)* found that black students were opting not to apply early. After all, "well-prepared black applicants have discovered that they may win a better financial aid package if they wait for the regular admissions sweepstakes and take advantage of the competitive process." In short, get as many offers as you can.

Here are some early-admissions figures from the *JBHE* (for the 1997 entering class) that you might want to keep in mind, as you consider your options:

High-Ranked Universities

Massachusetts Institute of Technology (40 applied, 15 admitted)—37.5%

Brown University (103 applied, 47 admitted)—45.6%

University of Chicago (20 applied, 11 admitted)—55.0%

University of Pennsylvania (34 applied, 15 admitted)—44.1%

Cornell University (71 applied, 15 admitted)—21.1%

University of Notre Dame (25 applied, 18 admitted)—72.0%

Washington University (31 applied, 12 admitted)—38.7%

Emory University (25 applied, 10 admitted)—40.0%

High-Ranked Liberal Arts Colleges

Swarthmore College (8 applied, 3 admitted)—37.5%

Wellesley College (8 applied, 7 admitted)—87.5%

Haverford College (1 applied, 0 admitted)—0.0%

Bowdoin College (5 applied, 3 admitted)—60%

Carleton College (4 applied, 4 admitted)—100.0%

Davidson College (7 applied, 6 admitted)—85.7%

Oberlin College (7 applied, 7 admitted)—100.0%

7. It's a Team Game

You can't do it alone! Your parent or parents, mentor, or advocate should visit and talk to your college adviser at least once, if not more. You should also be present. You're a serious student with college aspirations and goals, and you want the idea that you need support tantamount in everyone's mind. Similarly, your parent or parents or others should make their presence and concern felt during all open school nights. Like the grade adviser, teachers you are looking to for recommendations should be courted—and be very conscious of your needs.

8. Stay Black

Check "black," "African American," or "minority" whenever there's an inquiry. If somebody is going to route your folder, you want it to land in the proper file.

9. Apply, Apply, Apply

Don't be afraid to apply to a large number of schools if you can. In the end you want options, choices. Nothing feels better than having two or three accepts from top schools. Imagine:

"Well, I've been accepted to Spelman, Boston College, and the University of Virginia. No, I didn't decide yet. But I'm leaning towards . . ." Wouldn't this be wonderful?

Imagine that you were planning to buy your first home, and the agent took you to look at two houses. In the end, the agent is going to show you dollar figures and talk about required fees and down payments. The odds are strong that each money package will be different. College accepts are the same way. You want to be able to have several options before the final call. One school might want $6,000 per year, while another might be offering a free ride.

Several years ago, the president of Florida A&M University offered a student a full-tuition scholarship, the cost of books, and a $1,000 per semester stipend to attend the HBCU in Tallahassee. The student, who had scored a perfect 800 on the math section on the SAT, picked FAMU over Cornell and Dartmouth because of its offer of support. Powerhouse mainstream schools also often decide to sweeten the pot. You've got to factor in everything— what you want, what you're looking for—then ponder, compare, and crunch the numbers.

GETTING IT DONE

If you're that super student with a great SAT and a 4.0 GPA, you may have a pretty easy time of it. On the other hand, students we have counseled have beaten competitors with higher grades and/or test scores. It can and does happen. When we actually talk to a student with a strong record, an eye on a super school, who is willing to eyeball the odds and do the work, we put it bluntly. We might say, "Jenn, you want to go to Amherst. Okay, imagine there is one slot and you're competing against one other student. That student has an SAT score that's 100 points higher than yours. Her 93.4 academic average beats you by 3 points. She's in the top 10% of her class, coming from a very reputable high school. You can bet that her family is behind her, and she'll go all out to present herself to best advantage." That's the kind of background info we need to be aware of—that we are not just going to waltz in and take that seat at the top college; we have to be ready to compete.

We might go on: "Okay, do you want to pass? To pick another school, to maybe sidetrack this opportunity? Or do you believe you are competitive, that perhaps you have more to offer than this rival? Despite the numbers?" At this level I can tell you that many of our students believe in themselves. It's evident. They understand that possibly it might be a miss. But they're at that crossroads. It's life. If you are going to be a doctor, lawyer, engineer, artist, accountant, teacher, social worker, a success, whatever, you've got to rise to the occasion. It could be Harvard or Stanford or MIT, but if it's not, it's your second choice or your third. You're not going to be side-tracked. Others won't be. You go in blasting—giving it everything you have—and hope for the best.

CHAPTER 10

IF YOU'VE MESSED UP JUST A LITTLE

"Need a Second Chance" Students

Y ou're the "Invisible Man" or woman, as the novel says. Look at your typical college guide. If you didn't know better, you're think that the world was filled with students who were scholars, had 3.4 to 4.0 grade point averages, and were all considering admission to highly ranked, prestigious schools with names such as Harvard, Rensselaer Polytechnic Institute, or the University of California at Berkeley.

If you are a "need a second chance" student, our guess is that your college grade adviser has given you little or no attention. At best, you've probably been given an instructional sheet or two with dates and warnings. That'll be information on the PSAT, SAT, FAFSA form (financial aid), and final application deadlines. Where do you turn? You're thinking, "I've been counted out." And perhaps you and even your family suspect/feel as much. It's a closed case: your career, your future. You need help, if not a miracle.

IF YOU WANT A COLLEGE DEGREE . . .

First, count your blessings. If this were a baseball game, you'd be scoreless in the third inning, but with six innings left to score. If you've read this guide from page one, you know that we've known students who came from nowhere, were classified "losers" and worse, and went on to get graduate degrees from Columbia and Harvard. You can make a 360-degree turnaround. In due time you can overcome whatever is on your transcript—low grades, standardized test scores, a slate that looks "abominable," if that's what you've created.

Yes, maybe you've had a legitimate excuse or two. Or perhaps you know you've been cheating yourself. We're heard it all: I'm disadvantaged. It's a racist society. My teachers don't like me and/or don't teach. At home, there's no place to study. Or: I've had to baby-sit for my mom, who's a single parent. My little brother is ill. I'm ill. Or honestly: I didn't care, I was lazy, or I didn't know what I wanted to do. We can list a million reasons.

Despite all of that, you can still make it. Perhaps your college journey will begin on a road less traveled. That road might have steeper inclines, sharper turns, and may never be considered a shortcut. But if you hold steady, you'll surely see road signs ahead: Admission, Freshman Year, Graduation.

You can take your first step if you are motivated, if you care enough, if you are tired of making excuses. And yes, first and foremost, if you are now ready!

Where Do You Fit In?

The first step is to make a quick self-assessment. See if you identify yourself in any of these categories:

Average student (college prep level): any student who has taken a college preparatory courseload but who, for whatever reason or reasons, has "messed" up. That is, your academic average is between 65 (at the lowest) to about 75 (at the highest). Your record indicates one or more of the following: poor performance, lack of motivation, wavering focus, attendance problems, and obvious failure to live up to your potential.

Average student (general courseload): any student with between a 70 and 80 academic average and who is taking a curriculum that is often described as "basic" or "regular." That is, you are taking courses such as General Math, English, and American Government. Your load is "no frills," with few or no courses falling in the college prep range. Honors or advance placement courses such as Biology or Physics are not factors.

Mediocre student: any student who is barely getting by. You are languishing between a 65 and a 70 academic average, while taking—leisurely—only general and no-frills courses. Effort is marginal.

"Need a second chance" student: any student who falls in the mediocre range with very low grades but who has repeatedly failed courses, occasionally going to summer school to make up work.

The dropout: any student who, for whatever reason or reasons—academic, social, or otherwise—has *temporarily* stopped going to school.

Of course, there really are no lines or cutoffs etched in stone in this list of categories. The students who are performing poorly—too often below their capabilities—know who they are.

YOUR ROAD MAP TO RECOVERY AND COLLEGE ADMISSIONS

Here are your next steps to preparing yourself for colleges admissions:

- Send for catalogs like everybody else. Get a general overview.
- Meet with your grade adviser. Your question: Are there any "sleeper" schools that would be receptive to a "need a second chance" student? There always are. For example, in New York City there's Medgar Evers College of CUNY (my father's alma mater) and Borough of Manhattan Community College, which has been an excellent option—and pathway—for many students of color.
- Whatever time you have left, study as hard as you can. A couple of B's, for example, couldn't hurt. Somebody might notice.
- If there's time, do something worthwhile. If the extracurricular, work, and community service spots on your application are blank, what does that say to any reviewing committee?
- Create a tentative list of schools that will likely accept you. Every student should be able to write sizable columns of target school names. Lists will include both "might" and "definite" admit possibilities.

It's important to realize that there are vastly different admissions standards at different schools. Consider these stats: Columbia University (NY)—an Ivy League school—generally accepts about 23% of the students who apply; Bennett College (NC)—a historically Black women's college—accepts about 70%; Cleveland State University (OH) usually accepts about 97% (this school would fall in the noncompetitive category); Miles College (AL)—a historically black college—accepts 100% of all applicants (this is an open admissions school). There are more than 300 quality schools in this country that are minimally difficult to get into. Here's just a sampling of schools—and admit possibilities—that we think should be considered by any student who needs a second chance. Remember, too, to always consider your state school system. Often at the public schools, students are guaranteed a spot (grades and test scores aside) in at least one two-year community college if they graduate. Use what you have. See the colleges listed in chapter 2 that are designed for "need a second chance" students.

Students, too, should write to the United Negro College Fund, because (as their slogan says), "A mind is a terrible thing to waste." The 41 UNCF schools have a rich and colorful history of serving students of all levels of academic standing. These schools offer a world of majors, including Law, Business, Engineering, Veterinary Medicine, Pharmacy, and more. And not only do the schools have very nurturing environments, but also many will readily accommodate a student who has potential, needs some initial close attention, is motivated, and needs a second chance.

Write for your UNCF student handbook for a listing of school profiles and majors offered at: United Negro College Fund, Inc., Educational Services Department, 500 East 62nd Street, New York, NY 10021.

Your Application

Aside from the tips offered in the previous chapters about preparing your application, here are some additional ideas that are specific to your situation:

Do

- Give the admissions team some attribute or asset (e.g., you have potential, you're personable), to work with.
- Let your essay "dress you up." Sell yourself. Perhaps you've made missteps and work has been marginal, but you're ready to turn it around.
- Get any positives (special talents, accomplishments, if any) into your presentation.
- Talk about where you're going—and why—as opposed to where you've been. You're at that crossroads, changing the course of your life.

Don't

- Confirm a lack of skills in your package. An ineffective essay can sink you. Don't use improper grammar or make spelling mistakes. If your offering looks/reads disorganized or seems like an elementary school student could have written it, you're done.
- Give them an easy excuse to reject you. In your essay, avoid topics such as romance, sex, abortion, politics, religion, or anything controversial. You might love Khalid Muhammad, Dennis Rodman, or Lil' Kim, but this isn't the time to say so.
- Undersell yourself or present mediocrity as an accomplishment. You don't want to write: "I got a 65 in English in my sophomore year, and then a 70. I wasn't focused." Better: "Last week, Ms. Brown looked startled when I received a 95 on her literature test. A few minutes later she probably noted that look in my eye when I raised my hand and said a few words about Macbeth. She nodded, and perhaps wondered if she was looking at a twin." A student could actually signal a sincere transformation in his or her essay. It could matter!

The Black College Tour

If you can, go on a black college tour. Usually several of the colleges on the itinerary will be receptive to a student who needs a second chance. If you can discreetly discuss your particular case with an administrator or guide, do it. If you have personality and aplomb, asking for an interview won't hurt. If you're reading this and saying "I don't think so," pass.

Parental Involvement

Especially in regard to the historically black colleges, I have generally found that school administrators listen and respond to parents who inquire, get involved, and advocate for their child/potential student if there's a problem. Sometimes a visit to a school—with the student in tow— will do wonders. Often a parent will help you get an ear—and suggestions—if not some desirable consideration and help.

Alumni Involvement

If there's a special problem or concern, it never hurts to contact the alumni association representative residing in your state, if not your community (alumni chapters can be found at college web sites, or in this guide at profile locations). Schools such as Johnson C. Smith and South Carolina State, for example, have many chapters around the country. Our experience has been that old graduates love to get involved. Many have helped their schools with recruiting at college fairs and beyond. If a representative from an alumni chapter calls his or her college about a perspective student and/or incoming application, it's all the better. After all, when you're more than just a folder and print on a page or two, you are at an advantage.

Your Daily Paper

Read the papers. Many colleges are bending over backward to find students. School begins in the fall, but this ad ran in the *New York Daily News* on July 19. This is an ad for a community college that's been a lifesaver for many students needing an opportunity. Here's the text:

Come to BMCC for ON THE SPOT ADMISSIONS

Bring your GED or high school diploma/college transcript (if applicable); and a money order for $40 ($50 for transfers) to BCMM, and be admitted on the spot.

The Tests: SAT/ACT

Don't keep taking these tests, hoping to improve your score. You can't hope. If you've gotten a 710 or 820 or 910 combined SAT score, for example, and you don't feel you were prepared— or that you've done your absolute best—let your score ride. Researchers have found that students generally don't improve their scores by more than insignificant numbers on second or third tries. In fact, there's a reasonable chance that you'll get a lower score.

A 710, standing alone, might look like you've simply had a bad day. A 710 sitting beside a 690, 670, and 720 on your ETS (Educational Testing Service) transcript, however, might leave (unfairly) the impression that you're a "borderline" student, perhaps inadequately prepared.

The College Board says that the SAT "measures developed verbal and mathematical abilities" and not intelligence. The key word here is "developed." We believe that a student who is focused and determined can play catch-up, learn how to read for comprehension, improve his or her vocabulary, solve mathematical equations, write better, and generally improve analytical and reasoning skills. So don't keep taking tests in the hope that a miracle will happen, not if you don't have a plan. Concentrate on what you know you can improve: your essay, community service, perhaps that résumé.

But if you know you can do better on the SAT or the ACT—and perhaps intend to take a prep course or attack a review book or two—go for it. Joel Rubin of the *Princeton Review* says it best: "Understand the test: know as much as possible about the structure, format, and material to be tested before going in. There shouldn't be any surprises." Using tutors and/or studying with focus, we've seen students raise their scores 100 points and more. And yes, the better your score, the better your options.

There are, by the way, more than 280 colleges that don't require SAT or ACT scores. Relatively, it's a very small number of schools, having very little impact on what black students should or shouldn't do. We don't recommend passing over these tests as part of any strategic plan. Many colleges use the scores for academic assessment/placement purposes, and they are required.

The following sampling of no SAT/ACT required historically black colleges, should be considered for your "get in" lists, because (tests aside) these schools are more often amendable to our special needs:

> Bethune College (FL)
> Norfolk State University (VA)
> Texas Southern University (TX)
> Benedict College (SC)
> Tougaloo College (MS)
> Wilberforce University (OH)
> Voorhees College (SC)
> Grambling State University (LA)
> University of Arkansas at Pine Bluff (AR)
> Wiley College (TX)
> Miles College (AL)
> University of D.C. (DC)
> Lincoln University (MO)
> Stillman College (AL)

Don't Disintegrate

Don't think, "What's the use?" Whatever your story is, they've seen worse and then some. Humans will be looking at your application. Once you get in—and you will—it's even-steven. That is, the instant you take your seat in class, your high school record will depreciate like a newly purchased car. You can, literally, rewrite history. After one semester of good grades, your college work will be what's pivotal—even if you transfer early on (perhaps after 15 credits) and your high school record is still required for review. Transfer news? After 30 credits you'll often find that decisions are made based on your college work. After taking 10 or more college-level courses your high school record will generally be considered "old news." After all, your high school transcript was predictive. Your college performance is/will be the true measure—you've been tested under fire!—of your capability.

Give It That "I Am Somebody" Try

That's a must. The admissions committee will have to shape their freshman class. If there's agreement that you can do the work, and can be reasonably expected to graduate, many intangibles might come into play when your application is reviewed and/or discussed. Maybe your supplemental material will say that you'll be a "personality" and add to a school's spirit. Perhaps that marching band needs a trumpet or tuba player. Maybe you're from an underrepresented geographical area. Or maybe there's a need for another art or drama major. Were you an "organizer" in high school? A yearbook contributor, perhaps? A dancer in the chorus line? A ticket taker, even? Be aware: a bench warmer at Hillcrest High might be a potential basketball starter at Paine or a Division II or III school. That singer in the community church choir might meet a crying need somewhere. Colleges want scholars, personalities, artists, jocks, students with vision and potential (from all economic backgrounds) who will enrich/enhance the quality of life on campus. Many prospective students won't be paper perfect. Often something will say that "growth" is around the corner. A strong grade or two? A paragraph in a single recommendation? Perhaps the obvious odds you've been facing? You never know. Consider, too, that some colleges might find you appealing if you've been a mentor—because Big Brother/Big Sister programs are important on or around campus.

The point is that some colleges want a vibrant, exciting atmosphere for their students. You might be a "discovery," another intricate part of the campus puzzle. Who says a need-a-chance student doesn't have something to offer? If you have a horn, lift it and give a toot. No telling who will hear.

THE COMMUNITY COLLEGES: SHOULD YOU GO THERE?

On Chambers Street in New York City, not far from the World Trade Center, sits the Borough of Manhattan Community College. If you take a seat on the elevated steps before the school's entrance, you can watch thousands of students come and go. It's a steady flow of young, aspiring faces. On weekdays in the morning hours and later, after 5:00 P.M., it's clear that large numbers of students are fighting the odds, studying and often simultaneously working. It's a sight to behold.

Often I have watched the procession and nodded proudly. What an opportunity for perhaps 14,000-plus students (the majority of color). BMCC, the largest two-year school in the City University of New York system, is undoubtedly meeting a need. If the statistics are correct, 66% of the students who graduate will go on to four-year colleges. Many others, getting their degrees in areas such as Respiratory Therapy or Office Operations, will successfully begin employment. Who can knock this? Indeed, if more than 1,100 two-year community colleges didn't exist, where would these students have gone?

The two-year experience often marks an auspicious beginning, rife with all kinds of possibilities. Sometimes it is a second chance. Some of these schools have wonderful support systems—tutorial programs, study skills workshops, computer labs, and many of the extras we sometimes only associate with the four-year schools. At BMCC there are social and ethnic clubs, varsity sports, even an Olympic-size swimming pool. And you've also got majors galore—from Accounting to Computer Technologies to Tourism and Travel.

At BMCC graduates often head to some of the fine schools in the City University system (Hunter, Queens, and Brooklyn Colleges, to name a few). Others go on to private schools such as Long Island and New York Universities. The point is that the two-year experience can begin a journey that can deliver you wherever you desire to go.

The Community College Option: The Positives

The journey can eventually deliver you wherever you desire to go. Aerospace Sciences? Hospitality Services? Robotics? A Ph.D., anyone? Law? To be a certified public accountant? It's your call. At whatever academic level, there's usually a welcoming mat. Very often you're look-ing at open admissions or, at the least, a sympathetic admissions review.

- You can pick a school such as Miami-Dade Community College (FL), which is gigantic (online applications, corporate partnerships, the Internet, clubs, 40,000-plus students), or get close and personal with no more than 600 classmates.
- Depending on your personal circumstances, you can study toward your degree full-time or part-time, whether employed or not.
- Often your specialized training and majors are top-notch and lead to certificates, diplo-mas, and certification in many areas. Usually you are gaining employable skills. You can become a registered nurse, learn those electrical and electronics technologies, get into banking, communications, the arts, and more.
- You can stay close to home.
- The cost is considerably less than the cost of two years at a four-year school. Savings can be a real factor.
- Remedial assistance and support are generally available.
- Getting that associate degree—quickly—is often a great motivator. You have achieved.
- That job or a bachelor's degree can be in your sights every step of the way.
- You can hone your skills, your writing, and your analytical thinking before the next step.
- You're progressing, even if your destiny is unclear. When and if you decide to shift sails, you can.
- Sometimes the possibly of internships or "practicums" off campus are real. Other options: cooperative education (study/work), individualized majors, maybe even study abroad.
- At many two-year schools you will find feelings of camaraderie—with drama/theater groups, intercollegiate sports, and an "I belong" atmosphere.

The Two-Year Downside

- If your career goal calls for a bachelor's degree or higher, the hurdle ahead (transferring, credit questions) could be a hassle. It might not be fun, to say the least.
- If you intend/try to transfer to a four-year school, the financial aid hurdles (Will you get more? Will you get less?) are still another headache.
- Sometimes that two-year degree isn't enough to boost and/or secure your career goals.
- Sometimes when you get that transfer accept, you lose credits and time.
- Often, the step up to a four-year college means more study, stronger competition in class, and greater academic rigor and demands.
- In most cases, housing is not available. Note, however, that at some of the public two-year colleges, room and board is an option.

AND IF YOU'RE A DROPOUT?

Don't let it be your last hurrah. If you've been irresponsible in the past, we can't condone it. If you've made little or no effort: shame, shame. If there's a reason for not doing your school-work—and walking away from it—we hope it involved life-and-death issues. That's our atti-tude. That saying, "A mind is a terrible thing to waste" can't be said enough. That said, we suggest that you shake away the academic cobwebs, take a sigh or two, and digest what's going to be said next. You can drop in. Not to a trade school, or a GED program, but to a fully accred-ited, two- or four-year college! Yes, you may have messed up, and done it in grand style, *kaput.*

And if you were actually sitting with us this minute, we would eyeball you. You'd hear a word or two about what could conceivably lie ahead. It's called a "dead-end job." The fact of the matter is that dropouts don't get a lot of respect in the job market. Employers will ask you questions like "Can you handle MS Word, Excel, PowerPoint? Can you handle multiple tasks, prioritize, be a team player?" They are looking for workers who can produce—and have a track record of sticking to it—whether you're targeted for the mailroom or to be a worker at NASA, in the nuclear lab.

Be aware: at best, a dropout will make $200,000 less than a high school graduate over his or her lifetime. The dropout, too, will make at least $800,000 less than the student who goes on to get that four-year degree.

If this section applies to you, we hope you're thinking "This is it, I've got to do something." No magician on earth can change what happened yesterday, so worrying about what you "could've, should've done" isn't going to help. The reality of past performance, low academic achievement, absenteeism, failure, or just plain laziness, must be all filed away—like a bad dream. Are you ready, motivated, and committed to change? That's the pivotal question. When the answer has been a resounding "Yes!" we've seen students like you go from feeling like an academic pauper to a scholarly prince. No, it didn't happen overnight. Sure there were obstacles: mindset adjustments, often some remedial focusing. Whatever the case the first battle will take place in your head. "Can I do it?" Of course you can.

If you're reading this guide, there are already a set of keys in your pocket. The door is just a few steps ahead. There are many other schools across the United States that offer "special" or "alternative" admissions options that include remedial programs that will help you get on track for college-level work. In many cases these "best-kept secrets" are not widely advertised. If you pick up *Lovejoy's College Guide* (Macmillan), and just take the time to flip through some of the data-driven profiles of 4,200-plus colleges, you'll note that after the "Freshman Admissions" caption you won't always see "Graduation from secondary school required." Sometimes you'll see "Graduation from secondary school recommended." Do some research; in the New York City area alone there are numerous colleges, including Long Island University, Touro and Monroe Colleges, FIT, and the College of New Rochelle, where you can begin your college journey without that certificate or GED. There are doubtlessly equally fine choices in your area.

In New York State, if a student can successfully complete 24 college credits, he or she can apply to the Board of Regents for an automatic GED—General Equivalency Diploma—without the need for a test. It's possible to proceed while in college (heading for your degree) while eventually removing what some might perceive as a blemish on your record. There are similar programs around the country.

If you are accepted into a no high school diploma/college or remedial program, always immediately find out which department administers the placement tests. Then go and get a sample test and study materials. Familiarize yourself with everything in those pamphlets/guides, such as basic math, division, subtraction, elementary algebra, and grammar. Find out about scoring, test times, whatever you can.

You will be asked to take several tests, probably covering verbal and math areas. Also, the college will ask you to write an essay on a given topic. Your scores (competency) on these tests will decide whether you must take remedial courses for no credits to begin, or whether you can immediately begin your for-credit curriculum.

The tests, frankly, are simple if you are prepared. In regard to the essay challenge, we always recommend that students write at least two practice essays of about 300 words to get in a writing groove. These essays should be revised and edited at home. Here are a couple of examples of the sort of essay questions tendered: What family member or historical figure influenced you, and why? What is your career goal, and why? When given the test essay, you want to demonstrate that you can write reasonably well while organizing your thoughts/ideas in a coherent way.

If you do your homework, you'll get that second chance. The road less traveled is sometimes paved with gold.

CHAPTER 11

TRANSFERRING

Oops, Let's Do It Again!

If you've flipped pages to find this chapter, perhaps you had better hold steady. You're probably contemplating a major move, one that some experts feel could define/shape the course of your future. Perhaps you're holding that hard-earned associate's degree in your hand. Or it's a semester away in your game plan. If so, congratulations! On the other hand, maybe you've just begun your college journey or are further along the way, but something doesn't feel right. You're in the wrong place. You know that much. The problem could be academic, social, or financial. Maybe you're simply homesick or you don't like the weather, your roommate, the dorms, or the food. Or maybe, suddenly, you have a master plan and you want to veer left or right—to a new major, to a more prestigious or demanding school, or maybe, even, to a less stressful environment. You're not alone; according to some reports, nearly one of every five students considers transferring at least once during his or her college years.

Would it be advantageous to leave, or would it be a mistake? Maybe you'll stand pat, but this chapter will offer you a perspective, some facts, and a compass. There are a multitude of questions that evolve around transferring: grades, space, researching schools, the community college factor, those transcript reviews, and the almighty question of whether you would lose credits and time. What follows is a how, when, and why tutorial of transfer advice and answers.

THE MISMATCH: IN PERSPECTIVE

"I want to transfer!"

We hear it more often than we would like. Our guess is that the student transfer figures in the United States each fall might be in the 100,000-plus range, not counting any spring (midyear) numbers. Amazingly, that estimate doesn't just refer to community college graduates anticipating their two-year degrees. That's just part of the equation. Students are transferring for a myriad of other reasons: academic, social, financial, and beyond. There's been, to put it mildly, "a mismatch"!

When many experts talk about transfers, the common reasons they identify might make you smile. You'll read about things such as majors (of course), quality of life, the weather, romance, roommates, the dorms, professors, the "accessibility" of buildings, security on campus, the taste of food, the need for spiritual enlightenment, political consciousness, finding your identity, and general "incompatibility." You almost get the sense that someone is going to complain that there are no orchard or apple trees on Campus Walk.

TRANSFERRING 101: THE PROS AND THE CONS

Black Excel has not done a scientific study/analysis of all the students we have helped who have sought transfer advice and direction over the years. But we've got a sense of what's happening. Some students we have worked with have made wonderful moves; others (wisely) have stood pat. It's not a good idea to be "jumping" between colleges without a purpose or a plan. That's counterproductive. But if you have a handle on what you're doing and why, a change could mean all the difference in the world. We've seen students lose their way at their first college, make a switch, and then report back to us with honors grades, a career road map, and enrollment in a campus club or two, while enthusiastically also saying that they've decided to pledge. Talk about turnarounds!

Okay, let's see if you fit into one of the six common categories of transfers we generally see:

Category 1: Expectant Community College Graduates

These students are looking to successfully transfer to a four-year college after graduating from a community college. It's a very sizable group when you consider that more than half of our 1.5 million students enrolled in college are studying at both public and private two-year community schools.

Many, anticipating getting their associate degrees, are thinking about the next step and their four-year degree options. Questions abound: What school to apply to? What major? What do I have to do to transfer most—if not all—of my college credits?

If you fall into this category, you probably want to know how to navigate a workable transfer. You want the rules—on deadlines, how many credits you must complete to meet college's "residency" requirements (30 credits?), how much aid is available, and how to garner it. You are looking for a happy, amendable crossover.

Category 2: Students in Academic Trouble

Whether at a two- or four-year college, these students are in a quandary. They have not performed well academically. In some cases, the transition from high school created a kind of "culture shock." A student wasn't ready, whether emotionally or in terms of preparedness. Perhaps the work was too hard, the pace too quick, and the student (while not knowing what to expect) had poor study habits and couldn't focus or keep up.

On occasion we've talked to students who have been there. Some, "on probation," had been given a reprieve. But imagine this typical warning: "If your semester grade point average is less than 2.0 during two consecutive semesters on probation, you will be academically suspended." That could unsettle you, to say the least. And still others, barely passing, had simply settled into a malaise. "I'm walking a tightrope," they might confess. That's when they begin to talk of transferring, the hope of a makeover.

Well, sometimes the students in this category get that makeover. And recover.

Category 3: I'm Doing Great: Why Can't I Go to Spelman?

There are students who are doing fine, if not exceptionally well. They are "stars" in class and suddenly believe they want to step up. Why should they stay at Compton Junior College when they should be at Spelman? Or Boston College? That's their attitude. Their question: "Can I cash in my chips and get a college upgrade?" Sometimes such students don't mind if they lose a few credits— or even a semester—when transferring.

Category 4: Another World

There are students who have suddenly discovered that "other world"—that alternate universe they sometimes didn't know was there. Perhaps they were invited to an AKA or Delta party and suddenly found themselves on a campus that looked like Eden. Some colleges are visually gorgeous. At Cornell you'll find gorges, places where you'll actually be able to see chiseled rocks and waterfalls. At Wellesley there's beautiful Lake Waban, tennis courts, dorms with dining halls, and you could easily feel like you're at a country club. The point is that very often we are not at places with saunas, Olympic-size indoor pools, or rows of computers that are readily available. While at historically black Clark-Atlanta, for example, you might suddenly become aware of the University of Georgia—with its bigger library, better dorms, tastier food, a school with extras you couldn't visualize or imagine. Sure, it's that grass-is-greener syndrome. But it's real when (perhaps) you're young, impressionable, or not wise enough to put all the factors into perspective. You want to get where you think there are advantages.

Category 5: I Am at a Highly Selective School, and I'm in over My Head

Sometimes a student (not saying the work is too rigorous or the academic climate too intense) wants a permanent breather. Although admitted to school A or Z, highly ranked and due all praise, happiness and peace of mind are far removed. Now you want to progress at a pace suitable to your needs; hence you ponder that transfer.

Category 6: Reapplication: Let's Do It Again!

These students have dropped out, taken a leave, and are ready to return—preferably to their old school. They've been away a semester, a year, or longer. Grades may or may not have been a factor. The reason could've been money, the need to work, to support a family, or any of hundreds of other personal, health, or financial reasons. The pivotal question: How do I reapply?

TYPES OF TRANSFER

Aside from the upgrade from a two-year community college to a four-year college, there are three other primary kinds of transfer: the 4-to-2 transfer, the 4-to-2-to-4 transfer, and the 4-to-4-to-4 leave.

The 4-to-2 Transfer

Sometimes students will transfer from a four-year school to a two-year school ("4-2 transferring"). The reason could be academic, financial, or personal (Mom is sick, maybe, and you want to be closer to home). Often the maneuver is a good idea and/or the beginning of that "makeover."

The 4-to-2-to-4 Transfer

Sometimes students will transfer from a four-year school, head to a community college for a period of time, and then return to their eventual alma mater ("4-2-4" transferring). We've counseled students who've waved their bachelor degrees in the air after successfully completing a 4-2-4 maneuver.

The 4-to-4-to-4 Leave

Little is said about the "4-4-4" leave. A student takes a leave from an expensive, often prestigious school to return to a state or neighborhood college for a period of time. Usually it's one year. It's a method of saving a bundle of tuition money if there's financial difficulty.

The key here is to explain your situation to the institution where you are enrolled. You want to get prior approval for a "leave" (family problems, perhaps?) and an eventual acceptance of transfer credits when you return to your "home" school. Of course, generally colleges are not agreeable to giving you a leave of absence to spend your cash elsewhere and then, with open arms, also grant you the necessary transfer credits.

Note that Black Excel doesn't recommend this maneuver as a money-saving strategy. The students we know who have successfully take the 4-4-4 step usually had an "emergency" of some kind. A potential problem here: some colleges will not accept credits from other colleges, particularly one with a lesser reputation for rigor or excellence.

TRANSFERRING 101: KEYS TO MAKING YOUR DECISION

The first question to ask yourself is: Do I have a goal? If you are thinking about transferring, there should be some rhyme or reason to your plan. The transfer should take you to higher ground. When you arrive at your next school you should be better off in some way. If it's just a "feel good" switch, you may have gone backward, lost credits and time, and perhaps even hurt your graduate or professional school chances. Dear student, your transfer should be like a strategic move in a chess game. You should be near "checkmate," or in a clearly advantageous position after you make that move.

Here are some things to consider before deciding to make a transfer:

When you should transfer:

- You have received or are anticipating an associate degree. You're ready for the next step.
- When the transfer is equivalent to your going from a Volkswagen to a Benz and you can take the wheel.
- When you are failing and can't recover. You need a "makeover."
- When you have been placed on probation, and your transcript looks like damaged goods and repair seems improbable.
- You are absolutely miserable, for whatever reason.
- Your life's goals/priorities have changed. Now you want to be a nurse, an engineer, a poet, and your college has no gateway to get you there.
- You've done your homework. Your target school is a place where you'll thrive.
- You're not challenged, and you can't endure one, two, or three more years feeling like you're in high school.

When you shouldn't transfer:

- Freshman blues. You're lonely. The cafeteria food stinks. You don't like your roommate.
- You're doing fine (grades, major) and the transfer is a step down.
- You're doing fine, and you're past the two-year mark. You're an arm's length away from your bachelor's degree. Generally, we say "fix" whatever the real or imagined problem is, at the graduate level.
- If the transfer college is going to feel like the Albert Einstein Institute or *Sesame Street;* stand pat. Can you excel at a school where the average student needs one to two hours to complete daily course study/assignments and you will need double that? Or you need one hour, and they need three or four?
- You don't have a plan. Your transfer should take you closer to definable goals.

- Your boyfriend or girlfriend is at Southern Cal and you're in New York, or vice versa. If it's meant to be, it's meant to be. Stay.
- The problem or displeasure might be in your head.

TRANSFER POLICIES

When consulting a school's catalog, read its section on transfers and credits to learn the school's transfer policies. Here are some of the variables you may encounter:

High School Transfers:

At some colleges, your high school transcript must be presented. Often it depends on how many college credits you have completed.

Grades

Generally, the lowest course grade acceptable for transfer is a C. Some state schools, however, will sometimes accept C–and D grades if the transfer student is from a school in their "system." California State University at Fresno, the University of Nevada at Las Vegas, and SUNY at Stony Brook are examples. Some privates, too, will accept an occasional lower passing grade after an overall record review. Bradley, Michigan State, and Temple University will accept a C– under certain circumstances.

Specific Programs

Sometimes specific programs within a college might have separate transfer requirements, including a need for course prerequisites. Typically, majors such as nursing, occupational therapy, education, pharmacy, dental hygiene, and social work come to mind. At James Madison University (VA), nursing applicants need to complete a supplemental application and an interview.

Competitive Schools

At most of the competitive schools—or schools where there are special or technical majors— you need GPAs substantially higher than 2.0 to get admitted. Schools such as Haverford, the University of Pennsylvania, Johns Hopkins, Vassar, Carnegie Mellon, and Northeastern, for example, suggest that a minimum 3.0 is necessary for transfer consideration. You'll probably need even higher scores to be competitive.

Music, Drama, and Other Applicants

Generally, if you are a music or a drama applicant, an audition will be required. Sometimes, if you are an art transfer, a slide presentation or portfolio must be presented. At Morgan State, an audition is required for music applicants. At SUNY Purchase, auditions are necessary for dance and drama applicants. At the University of Southern California, special applications are required of cinema/TV program applicants.

Remedial Courses

Usually remedial or developmental courses are not transferable.

Liberal Arts Transfers

If you are considering a transfer to a liberal arts college, many, most, or none of your technical courses might be transferable. Those specialized credits in electronics, marketing, and medical technology might miss the mark. In some articulation and/or informal (unwritten) agreements, "troublesome" credits might be granted to be used as electives. Pray.

Transferable Courses

More often than not, courses such as Psychology, Art History, Philosophy, Biology, and Comparative and English literature are like money in the bank. They're transferable.

Pass/Fail Courses

If you are contemplating a transfer, Pass/Fail courses should be avoided.

Apply/Entry Dates

Some programs have specific apply/entry dates. Get it right, early on.

Transfer Slots

Often the number of available transfer slots is dependent on "available spaces." The question of whether you're smart enough, or whether you are academically qualified, might be of secondary consideration.

Campus Housing

Often it's difficult for a transferring student to get on-campus housing. Inquire early.

Intercampus Transfers

Intercampus transfers (between subsidiary schools of the same university) are easier.

Transfer Credits

Usually, colleges have a limit on how much transfer credit you can be granted. The following examples show how widely they vary, depending on the college: Haverford, 64; University of Massachusetts at Amherst, 75; North Carolina Central, 60; Johnson C. Smith University (NC), 64; Sarah Lawrence College (NY), 60; Xavier University of Louisiana, 98.

Residency Requirement

Usually, colleges have a transfer residency requirement—that is, the number credits you must complete on campus to earn a degree. Examples at the bachelor's level: Connecticut College, 64 credits (two years); University of Miami, 45 (one and a half years), Delaware State, 30 (one year); Ringling School of Art and Design, 45 (one and a half years); Tuskegee University, 30 (one year); Virginia Polytechnic Institute, 30 (one year); North Carolina A&T University, 36 (one and a half years).

Programs at Public Colleges

Some programs within public colleges might be limited to state residents. For example, the engineering program at San Jose State University is reserved for residents, so you can't even consider transferring unless you've established state residency.

Letter of Good Standing

Sometimes the new school wants a letter of good standing from your former school.

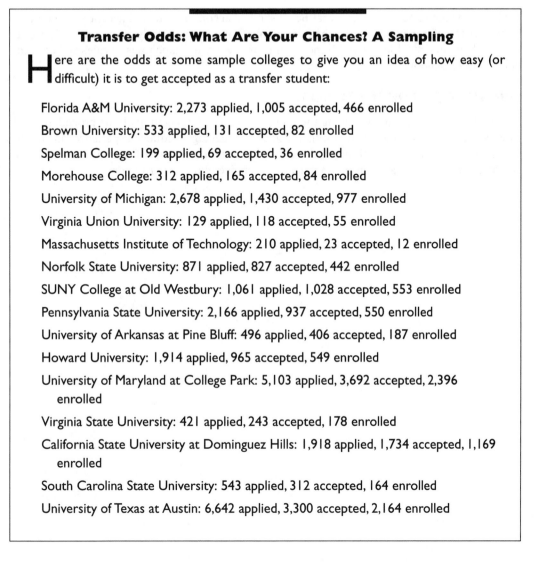

Transfer Odds: What Are Your Chances? A Sampling

Here are the odds at some sample colleges to give you an idea of how easy (or difficult) it is to get accepted as a transfer student:

Florida A&M University: 2,273 applied, 1,005 accepted, 466 enrolled

Brown University: 533 applied, 131 accepted, 82 enrolled

Spelman College: 199 applied, 69 accepted, 36 enrolled

Morehouse College: 312 applied, 165 accepted, 84 enrolled

University of Michigan: 2,678 applied, 1,430 accepted, 977 enrolled

Virginia Union University: 129 applied, 118 accepted, 55 enrolled

Massachusetts Institute of Technology: 210 applied, 23 accepted, 12 enrolled

Norfolk State University: 871 applied, 827 accepted, 442 enrolled

SUNY College at Old Westbury: 1,061 applied, 1,028 accepted, 553 enrolled

Pennsylvania State University: 2,166 applied, 937 accepted, 550 enrolled

University of Arkansas at Pine Bluff: 496 applied, 406 accepted, 187 enrolled

Howard University: 1,914 applied, 965 accepted, 549 enrolled

University of Maryland at College Park: 5,103 applied, 3,692 accepted, 2,396 enrolled

Virginia State University: 421 applied, 243 accepted, 178 enrolled

California State University at Dominguez Hills: 1,918 applied, 1,734 accepted, 1,169 enrolled

South Carolina State University: 543 applied, 312 accepted, 164 enrolled

University of Texas at Austin: 6,642 applied, 3,300 accepted, 2,164 enrolled

FAFSA Form

Generally, when transferring, the FAFSA form must again be completed. It's still the yardstick of how much financial aid you will get. Note, too, that schools often make their financial aid decision after you also fill out their money forms.

Articulation Agreements

Some community colleges have what are known as articulation agreements with other schools. Nassau Community College in New York—highly respected and a school with a reputation for high standards—has articulation agreements with more than 30 colleges, including prestigious private schools such as New York University and Cornell University, as well as sterling state institutions such as SUNY at Binghamton. In simplest terms, the agreement says, "I'll take your

graduating student, acknowledge what he or she has accomplished, and accept your credits."
Inquire. A transfer may be simpler than you think. Some states, clearly, want a smooth transition for their students. Florida and Illinois, for example, try to shape transfer rules and connections between schools.

REMEMBER THE ULTIMATE GOAL

As you debate transferring, weighing the pros and cons and navigating all the procedures and
paperwork, keep your mind on your ultimate goals: a meaningful college experience, an enriching academic program that will prepare you for a career and life, and, of course, a degree at the
end of the day. If you stay focused on those, your choice will be the right one.

PART TWO

THE GET-THE-MONEY GUIDE

Financial Aid, Loans, and Scholarships

CHAPTER 12

FINANCIAL AID

Rules, Myths, and Misconceptions

O nce you've struggled up the long hill to getting accepted to the college (or colleges) of your choice, you are confronted with the next challenging leg of the journey: getting the money to go. The first step in this leg is understanding the "big picture" of financial aid.

THE ALL-IMPORTANT FAFSA

The FAFSA (Free Application for Federal Student Aid) is where the financial aid battle begins. Request and fill out the FAFSA as close to the beginning of the year as possible to be eligible for the key aid programs, including federal Pell grants, Stafford and Perkins loans, SEOG (Supplemental Educational Opportunity Grants), state and public school aid, federal work-study, and more. These federal programs are how most of our people manage to pay for college. In fact, more than 75% of the billions of dollars annually spent on higher education comes from Uncle Sam.

The FAFSA is also the instrument that determines the amount of money you and your parents are theoretically able to pay for college. The FAFSA people will calculate the figures you supply on your form and come up with an EFC or *expected family contribution*. That figure is what you will be expected to pay for college as an out-of-pocket expense.

How Is the EFC Determined?

The expected contribution is reached through a formula called FM or *federal methodology*. This process is often called the "needs analysis." The what-you-must-pay finding is based on a review of your family's assets and income. To complete the FAFSA, you must supply personal financial information, including the following:

- A W-2 tax form (to establish earning for the previous year)
- Your adjusted gross income from your federal and state tax returns
- Checking/savings/CD account information
- Real-estate holdings
- Securities held (including stocks and bonds)
- Dividend income
- Social Security benefits (if applicable)
- Aid to dependent children benefits (if applicable)
- Child support/alimony payments

Although your tax returns are due April 15 of each year, you should complete the returns as early as possible. Then pull the income figures from your return and enter them on your FAFSA, no matter when you actually send the hard copy of the return to the IRS—in that way you can send in your FAFSA as early as possible (see deadlines below). If you didn't file taxes for some reason, simply follow the FAFSA instructions on the form—there will be an alternate way to supply income information.

There are certain things that will have no impact on your FAFSA: home ownership and equity; retirement/pension funds; and annuities.

Playing Smart

Here are some tips that will help you get the most out of the FAFSA:

- If the student's parents are divorced or separated, list only the custodial parent's financial information on the FAFSA. Do not mention the other parent's income or contributions, expect when asked for alimony/child support payments.
- Avoid student/parent information confusion. The FAFSA gathers facts on both parents and students on certain pages of the form. Don't make the mistake of inputting data on the wrong side of the form.
- Don't forget to list your college selections. In section G of the form you can list up to six colleges that you want to receive your EFC findings. Note that you must enter each school's numeric Title IV code. For example:

    UC Berkeley: 001312

    New York University: 002765

    Howard University: 001448

- The codes, unfortunately, are not listed in the FAFSA booklet and application package. You can get the codes from any high school or college financial aid officer. You can also get them off the web at www.ed.gov/offices/OPE/t4_codes.html.
- Accept any aid offered. On the FAFSA form, there's a question that asks what kind of aid you'll accept, including work-study. Always check the "yes" box to all such questions.
- If any answer requires a zero, input a zero; don't leave the space empty—that could lead to a computer error message.
- Be honest. You may be called for verification and all figures you've supplied on the FAFSA must match those of your actual financial documents.
- Always file a FAFSA, even if you think you make too much money to qualify for a federal aid program. The FAFSA is important for other possible financial benefits, including certain loans such as unsubsidized Stafford loans, and "merit" financial awards that colleges will supply only if the FAFSA has been forwarded.
- Don't forget to sign the form!

When Should You Send the FAFSA?

Send the FAFSA as early as possible after January 1. The reason? The early bird gets the financial aid worm, (i.e., the *money*). Remember, you want the financial aid officer at your selected college to look at your needs when the pool of money is overflowing, or at least stacked high. After all, more than 9 million FAFSA forms are filed annually—and believe us when we say that filing sooner is better than later.

Colleges have different aid deadlines at which time your data and materials must be submitted, even though the FAFSA's official due date is May 1. Be sure to check the deadline at your selected school. Here are some sample deadlines to give you an idea of the range (these dates are subject to change; always check directly with the college for the latest due dates):

- Howard: April 1
- Yale: February 1
- Tulane: January 15
- Smith: February 1
- Florida State University: March 1
- Lincoln University: Rolling

If you are somehow left pushing that FAFSA deadline, not the college deadline, you should get a certificate of mailing from the U.S. Postal Service as proof that you beat the deadline. But, if at all possible, don't let this happen to you.

If you are on the Web, you can apply electronically. It's the fastest way to do it. Just go to www.fafsa.ed.gov. Your form will be transmitted in seconds to the U.S. Department of Education, and you're done.

The SAR (Student Aid Report)

After you've sent in your FAFSA and your EFC is calculated, a green form is forwarded to you with the amount you are expected to pay stated. This form is called the SAR or *Student Aid Report*. Your SAR also will list the size of your Pell grant, if you're eligible. The SAR is returned to you in approximately four or five weeks. When you get it, carefully read and check the form, line by line. If you see the word "blank" on certain lines, it means that you have not answered all the required questions. If you must, fill in the blanks and return the form to the processor ASAP. Expect about a three-week turnaround. If there is an asterisk next to your EFC, you have been selected for verification.

Whether there are "blanks" or not, always check items 83 to 94 to ensure that your listed colleges are correct. If the form is correct and complete, you should file it. Although it is automatically forwarded to your selected schools, your school may ask you for it at some future date.

BEYOND THE FAFSA: OTHER FORMS

We've heard students and parents say "Enough's enough" when they discover that many colleges also request that you fill out additional forms.

The CSS

The most common of these is a CSS (College Scholarship Service) form. This form is sometimes referred to as "the profile." The form is designed to take an even closer look at your assets and ability to pay. These forms use an IM or *international methodology* that leaves a college with more latitude to review your total financial situation than using the FAFSA.

About 800 private colleges, including many top-ranked colleges with higher price tags, ask for this form, which was created in 1995. Schools asking for this form include Colgate, Northwestern, Boston University, DePauw, Stanford, Emory, Smith, and Duke.

The CSS is even more nerve-racking than the FAFSA. For example, the CSS requires you to declare the value of and your equity in your home. Many parents see this as a negative, since it implies that financial aid officers are considering whether you can get extra funds for college by borrowing against the value of your home. On the upside, there is a section of the CSS where you can actually "cry poor" by spelling out your special circumstances: another child in college, medical bills, the loss of a job, projected future expenses that are unavoidable, or whatever you can think of.

The CSS is completed in two steps.

Step 1: You must get and fill out the initial profile registration form. Here you'll be asked to fill out basic information, including a list of schools you desire your eventual report to be forwarded to.

Step 2: After about three weeks you'll receive your customized CSS financial aid application. There will be many questions you must answer, including some that are required from the specific colleges you listed. There may also be supplemental forms applicable to your specific profile. One such form, for instance, is a Divorced/Separated Parents Statement. Where is that noncustodial parent, and how much is he or she worth? There's also a Business/Farm Supplement that must be filled out if you or your parents own a business. They will also want to know if your parents have a retirement account.

To obtain the registration form, you can write to:

The College Scholarship Service

255 Phillips Boulevard

Ewing, NJ 08628

Or get a copy of the form from their web site: www.collegeboard.com. The initial form costs $5.00, and there's a charge of $14.95 to forward your data to each individual college you select. Using a credit card, you can fax or call in the information.

Your School's Own Financial Forms

There are colleges that have chosen to use their own form to back up the FAFSA review. Usually there forms are generated by the school's financial aid offices and can be just as thorough as the CSS. Schools such as Harvard, Spelman, Amherst, and the University of Maryland at College Park fall into this category.

State Aid Forms

Instead of a CSS or other form, many states require a state-generated form to accompany the FAFSA. For example, in Kentucky they require a KFAF (Kentucky Financial Aid Form), in California, an SAAC (Student Aid Application for California). Other states, including North Carolina, Pennsylvania, and Florida, also require a state form for state schools.

THE FINANCIAL AID PACKAGE

Brace yourself. After the colleges look at your expected family contribution, your financial aid officer (FAO) will create a financial aid package for you. This happens after, of course, you've received an offer for admission. Now's the pivotal moment. What will your bill look like, and how will the college shape the package? Beyond the honor of being accepted to the university, this is probably the most important moment in the process.

The FAO will look at your EFC and that will dictate the parameters of what can and cannot be done, at least at this first stage. Your EFC will give the reviewer a snapshot of what your family's assets amount to and what your ability to pay is.

Sample Package

Let's say the college you picked has tuition, room, board, and related fees that total $10,500. Let's also say that the FAO decides, based on your EFC, that you and your family can pay $2,000. The FAO will then create a package that might look like this:

Pell grant	$2,500
State grant	$1,000
Stafford loan	$3,000
College grant	$1,000
Federal work-study	$1,000
Total	$8,500

That total represents the amount that you don't have to pay up front. This sort of package is called "meeting your need." Why? Because the cost to enroll at the college is $10,500, and the total of your package and your EFC meets that $10,500 cost. In other words:

Tuition due = $10,500

The package = $8,500 + your EFC ($2,000) = $10,500

Now, if you are lucky enough to win a $2,000 scholarship, does that mean that your entire tuition will be covered with no out-of-pocket expenses? Sorry. The FAO will take that scholarship into consideration and subtract $2,000 from your package—for instance, perhaps $1,000 of your college grant and another $1,000 of your Stafford loan. But the scholarship is still a good thing; it will leave you with a smaller loan to repay. Even if you win more scholarships, the $2,000 EFC is probably etched in stone.

"Gapping": When the College Doesn't Meet Your Need

In the financial aid package just presented, a package was created that met the entire financial need to enter college. Let's suppose, however, that the college was only able to provide you with $8,000 instead of $8,500, leaving you with a $500 gap. Now, even though the experts said you can afford to pay $2,000, you are being asked to pay $2,500 because the college cannot meet your need. Folks, it's important to know that at least 65% of the time, colleges do not have the resources to meet your total need, usually because they've already pushed their in-house grant and federal loan limits to the edge. This is especially true with colleges that have small endowments and limited funds.

Should you beg, borrow, or steal the extra $500 to afford the college? Well, that's up to you. But remember, when there's gapping, you have three options: (1) try to get a package adjustment; (2) consider the option of an unsubsidized loan (see chapter 13 on loans and debt); and (3) compare award letters from all the colleges you've been accepted to, to see if there is another desirable college that can meet your need.

ADDITIONAL TRICKS OF THE TRADE

There are many inside tricks to getting a better financial aid package. Here are a couple that promise a good chance of success.

Getting Independent Student Status

One of the most frequently asked questions that students and parents ask is "How do I get independent student status?" If you are designated an "independent student" after all, the colleges and federal government have to base the EFC on the *student's* financial situation and assets only. Most students, of course, have limited or no resources. This means that a student who is lucky enough to get such a designation might be able to get a nearly "free ride."

We've heard some call this the "disown your child" approach. Well, we should all dream! Years ago, there were loopholes you could use to make such a maneuver; no more. If you are attempting to get "independent" status today, some of the following factors need to be in play:

1. In the award year, you are at least 24 years old.
2. You are an orphan or a ward of the state.
3. You are a graduate or professional student.
4. You are in the Armed Forces of the United States.
5. You are married.
6. You have legal dependents other than your spouse.
7. There are unusual circumstances that must be documented by an FAO or other school administrator.

If you fall into this category, you would not be listed on a parents' tax return as a dependent, you would have your own address, and your own income, and your high school presumably would already know about your special circumstances.

If you truly are an independent student, you have an advantage. But a parent cannot simply say, "I am not responsible—my kid has his own room, so it's the state's problem!"

Establish Residence to Reduce State Tuition

Getting state residence is often pivotal because a resident accepted to a public institution gets greatly reduced tuition. Sometimes the total is less than a third of the total asked of out-of-staters. For example:

Florida A&M University

In-state tuition: $1,800

Out-of-state: more than $5,000

University of Maryland at College Park

In-state tuition: $4,939

Out-of-state: $11,827

Temple University

In-state tuition: $5,300

Out-of-state: $10,000

So obviously, solving the riddle of establishing state residence can save you thousands of dollars over your college career. The question of how to do it is complicated by the fact that each of the 50 states has different legal guidelines for meeting residency requirements.

CHAPTER 13

LOANS AND DEBT

There's an old saying that the only things you can be sure about in this life are death and taxes. Well, if you're thinking about going to college—or are already enrolled and heading toward a degree—the odds are very, very high that you can add "college debt" to that list. The fact is that most students—of any color—are going to be saddled with debt when their college experience is over. For African American students the odds are also high that, whether you're poor or middle-class, the debt will be considerable.

In a recent edition of the *Journal of Blacks in Higher Education (JBHE)*, it was estimated that "by the year 2000, Americans will be borrowing $50 billion in student loans." And just about every award package we see at Black Excel has a federal financial aid component, usually a Stafford or a Perkins loan (more about those later in this chapter). The sad part is that we can't afford to say "No." To decline means you've got to take a rain check (not a good idea) or you could be forfeiting your future. Theodore Cross, writing in *JBHE*, really put it all in perspective: "In 1993 the average white family had a positive net worth of $45,740. The net worth of the average black family was only $4,418. You don't have to be a mathematician to see what this means. One way or another, we've got to borrow."

As college costs continue to rise, more and more of the expense is being passed on to us, the consumer. Fees at many of our HBCUs rose more than 30% between the years 1992 and 1997. In fact, five schools doubled their tuition and fees over this period. Count Morehouse, Spelman, Tougaloo, Clark-Atlanta, and Fisk among this group. Howard, Tuskegee, and Johnson C. Smith, trailing, all had raises of over 37%. The *JBHE* headline to this bad news was "Black Colleges Still Offer Tuition Bargains but Their Edge Is Slipping Away." HBCUs must find a means to compete, as federal aid and support during these changing times, are never fully guaranteed. That said, several of them (e.g., Spelman College) still make the annual "best buy" lists created by *Money* and other magazines.

Of course, the HBCUs are not alone. Across the board we're given an overview of how both large state (public) and private universities are all raising their comprehensive fees and tuition. From Harvard to the University of Maryland to Ohio State, the trend appears to signal that your pocketbook is going to be considerably lightened. During the 1992 to 1997 period, the *JBHE* sample listing of 37 mainstream schools notes that the average increase of fees over the period was more than 39%. The University of Missouri (60.04%) and Rice University (62.78%) topped the public and private university lists respectively. In any case, it's clear that the phenomenon of escalating tuition is not only "a black thing."

The *U.S. News* "Most Debt" College List

Look at the 1999 *U.S. News College Edition's* list of colleges that left the most debt with recent graduates:

- Carnegie Mellon University (PA): $23,770
- Florida State University: $20,904
- Fisk University (TN): $20,000*
- Wesleyan University (CT): $16,958
- Dillard University (LA): $21,000*
- University of Pennsylvania: $19,149
- University of Rochester (NY): $18,900.
- California State University at Dominguez Hills: $23,000
- Massachusetts Institute of Technology: $22,625
- St. Augustine's College (NC): $21,000*

*HBCUs

The *U.S. News* "Least Debt" College List

Now here are the 1999 *U.S. News College Edition's* list of colleges that left the least debt with recent graduates.:

- CUNY—Baruch College (NY): $6,200
- Bowie State University (MD): $6.500*
- Alcorn State University (MS): $3,326*
- Eastern Illinois University: $4,651
- University of Illinois at Chicago: $10,000
- Georgia Institute of Technology: $11,500
- North Carolina State University at Raleigh: $11,700
- University of Texas at Austin: $12,000
- University of Wisconsin at Milwaukee: $9,945
- Louisiana Tech University: $9,723

*HBCUs

THE LOAN OPTION

Fortunately, despite the fact that tuitions are up and financing an education is an ever more daunting affair, money should never be a reason *not* to pursue your higher education. Aside from the other financial-aid instruments discussed in previous chapters (i.e., merit-based awards, grants, and work-study), a variety of loan options are available to help you finance your education. Federally funded loans do, of course, need to be paid back, as opposed to grants and scholarships, but you don't have to begin paying them back until you've graduated (or left college for a long period of time). In fact, you usually don't have to start repaying these loans until you've been out of school for six months. Furthermore, these loans usually are available at relatively low interest rates—as opposed to typical commercial bank loans.

A Few Basic Tips

Before you start considering the basic loan program available, here are some rules to keep in mind:

1. Never borrow more than you need to.
2. Always consult with the financial aid officer at the school first. Ask if any institutional loan programs are available.

3. Complete and forward that FAFSA form. We'll say this till we're blue. And forward it early on.
4. Remember that Stafford and PLUS loans usually offer very competitive rates. And there are low-interest-rate caps.
5. Consider the home equity loan option.

Now here are the primary loan programs available to students.

The Subsidized Stafford Loan

The subsidized Stafford loan, which is offered by banks and other lending institutions but subsidized by the federal government, is usually the first option. These need-based loans are currently available at an interest rate of about 8% (it is adjusted annually but will not exceed 8.25%). A Stafford loan is usually a pivotal part of the financial aid package your college creates for you, although the loan cannot exceed $23,000 for your undergraduate education. The government pays the interest here, and the principal (your monthly payments without interest) is deferred until six months after your graduation. You are given up to 10 years to repay the loan in its entirety. You can apply for a Stafford loan at your local bank or lending institution.

- More information: call the U.S. Department of Education at (800) 433-3243, or check out their web site at www.ed.gov/prog_info/SFA/StudentGuide.

The Unsubsidized Stafford Loan

This is a low-cost loan, your backup choice if you are unable to qualify for the more desired need-based subsidized Stafford loan. Here the interest begins to accumulate as soon as the loan is disbursed, but the principal is deferred until six months after graduation (or dropping out). Usually your payment period is 10 years. This loan is specifically for the student, and will be in his or her name. There are no credit restrictions.

- More information: call the U.S. Department of Education at (800) 433-3243, or check out their web site at www.ed.gov/prog_info/SFA/StudentGuide.

Federal Perkins Loans

These low-interest loans (5% rate) are administered through the financial aid office of your selected college. They are supposed to help to offset the college expenses of "exceptionally needy" students. Generally, the Perkins loan is used as a supplement to your Stafford loan. The yearly maximum for undergraduate students is $3,000; the lifetime maximum for undergraduates is $15,000, although exceptions are made in extreme circumstances. The repayment period begins nine months after leaving school or graduating. You are given 10 years to repay the loan in its entirety.

- More information: Check with the college of your choice for more information.

The PLUS Loan

This loan is targeted to parents of college students. You can borrow the actual cost of your child's education, minus whatever the college grants you as part of the financial aid package. The parent cannot have any loan delinquencies of more than 90 days. The repayment time is

10 years. Your child can have a Stafford loan at the same time. If you are interested in this loan, ask your child's financial aid administrator for a Direct PLUS (Parental Loans for Undergraduate Students) Loan Application and Promissory Note.

- More information: Again, call the U.S. Department of Education at (800) 433-3243, or check their web site at www.ed.gov/prog_info/SFA/StudentGuide.

PRIVATE LOAN ALTERNATIVES: ONLY IF YOU'VE GOTTA GO THERE!

Note that the following loans (other than your home equity mortgage or loan option, perhaps) are your backups, and for good reason. You want the lowest interest rates and repayment plan available, and these are tied either to Treasury bill, prime, or commercial paper rates.

At present, rates are "attractive." But you never know when—and if—the market or economy may take a turn for the worse. If you make some calls, for example, you'll discover that some rates are adjusted quarterly. You'll discover, too, that in a "worse thing happens" scenario, some of these loans actually have caps as high as 18%.

Finally, for those considering such loans, you probably would be wise to contact one of the three major credit agencies to ascertain your "creditworthiness." You can reach TRW at (800) 392-1122 (our first choice), or Trans Union (212) 779-7200, or Equifax (800) 685-1111.

TERI (The Education Resources Institute)

The TERI loan covers the cost of your education minus the financial aid your selected college offers. The minimum you can get is $2,000. You'll need a good credit history and that ability to repay. Parents can cosign. You can get repayment plans of up to 25 years. You can reach TERI by mail at 330 Stuart Street, #500, Boston, MA 02176, or by phone at (800) 255-8374.

EXCEL (Nellie Mae) Loan

The Excel loan covers the cost of your education minus the financial aid your selected college offers. The minimum you can borrow is $2,000. You and/or your parents must have a good credit history, plus the ability to repay. Parents can cosign. It's a 20-year-repayment plan. The fee is about 5% of the loan. You can make contact via mail at 50 Brainbridge Hill Park, #300, Brainbridge, MA 02184-1763, or call (800) 634-9308.

Sallie Mae Signature Loan

The Sallie Mae Signature loan covers the cost of your education minus the financial aid your selected college offers. Note that most students apply with a creditworthy cosigner. Payments begin six months after graduation, with a 15-year maximum term. Contact Sallie Mae at (800) 695-3317.

Sallie Mae "Smart Loan"

This is a tip to students who are, or who will be paying off student loans. You can get a consolidated loan, combining all your loans (Stafford, PLUS, Perkins, and so forth) through Sallie Mae. Here's a sample example of what is possible. If your your monthly payment is $365 or so, a Smart loan can reduce that monthly payment to about $206. For more information call Sallie Mae at (800) 524-9100.

Plato Loan (from Student Support Services)

This loan is targeted to students, with parents able to cosign. You can borrow up to $25,000. The minimum you can borrow is $1,500. You and your parents must have a good credit history, an income of at least $15,000 annually, and the ability to repay. The Plato has a 15-year payment plan. Principal is deferred. The annual fee is about 4% of the loan. For more information call (800) 767-5626.

Extra Credit Loan (sponsored by the College Board)

This loan will cover all costs, minus any financial aid the college offers for four years of study. You must have good credit and the ability to repay. You can stretch your repayment to 15 years. The College Board also has an "extra time loan," which allows you to borrow for one year at a time, with deferment of principal to after the student graduates. This loan has a maximum term of 10 years. The contact number is (800) 874-9390.

The Knight College Resource Group Loans

These loans are similar to some already mentioned here. They cover the cost of your education minus the amount the college awards you for financial aid. Again, a good credit history and the ability to repay are essential. The term is usually for 15 years. The contact number is (800) 225-6783.

Home Equity Loan or Line of Credit

If you or your parents own a home, a second mortgage or home equity line of credit is often considered the best way to go. Generally, the interest on either of these two loan options is tax-deductible. With a line of credit you'll have a checkbook, allowing you to write checks (to whatever limit you've been given) step by step, semester by semester. This way, you've got flexibility.

AND YOU'D BETTER READ THIS . . .

Our position is that pressed with few options, you always take the Stafford loan or whatever loans you must take to get to the next step. If you don't have the funds and you've negotiated with the college and the financial aid people to the best of your ability, it's best to not stand still.

The thing is not to panic and understand that it's better to take the money and get that piece of paper, one way or the other. If you look at any of the loan payback charts, you quickly realize that you can pay back the loan once you have that degree and a modest salary. If you look at some of the repayment charts that are in some of financial aid books, you can see that repayment will be tough, will be a pain, but it's not beyond manageable.

Here's a sample chart (with us just rounding out numbers to give you a general idea of what looms ahead in regard to your eventual repayment responsibility). If you want exact totals, you'd better grab your calculator.

Usually the loans you take out are repaid on a 15-year repayment plan.

Some Repayment Figures

Note that we are citing interest rates that are in the 7% and 8% range. Inquire about probable rates and projections when you discuss your loan with your loan source.

- If you have borrowed $15,000 at 7%, your monthly payment will be about $140 per month. At 8%, about $150.

- If you have borrowed $20,000 at 7%, your monthly payment will be about $185 per month. At 8%, about $200.
- If you have borrowed $30,000 at 7%, your monthly payment will be about $275 per month. At 8%, about $295.

Keep in mind that these figures are not exact, and are simply presented to give you an idea of the hit you're going to take. The pivotal question here is this: Will your degree and the expense be worth the investment? We believe that the unequivocal answer is "Yes."

Your Degree Is Worth Money

That degree will matter and will have economic value. Factor in the other values it offers—greater knowledge, the sharpening of your critical thinking and skills, perhaps a more interesting set of social contacts—and you're ahead of the game. Frankly, we've seen so many first-generation students parlay their degrees into enriching lives and careers that the final expense seems to be only a secondary concern.

The Payback in Perspective?

The question of whether you will be able to repay your loan is admittedly a pressing (and nerve-racking) one. But just think of all the black students and graduates who have preceded you. You are not the first student who will take this journey, sigh over the bills, and agonize over the monthly payments. But looking at this burden in any other way than a rite of passage is a mistake. Your children are going to travel the same road, as will your grandchildren. And theirs.

And take this small comfort: students of all colors and creeds are borrowing at an unprecedented rate. You are not alone.

PAY AS YOU GO?

Yes, some of our folks see dollar signs and probable debt, and back away. They see any loan as an albatross. They decide that it's smarter to defer college enrollment to go to work. They'll save their tuition, perhaps work and study part-time. We call this strategy the "pay as you go" method. These students often take seven or eight years to get that B.A. or B.S. degree. In fact, many of these students often take that amount of time to get that associate, two-year degree. At the end, they owe little or nothing.

We are not disparaging students who, because of their particular situations, must work and/or go to school part-time. But the student who understands how finance works will take the loans if they are available. He or she will have a graduate degree and a career in process long before the "pay as you go" student enters the race. Frankly, we know students who are in law, medical, and other graduate or professional schools and are still increasing their outstanding loan debt. What do they know? To use "other people's money"—that is, the loans—to eventually maximize their advantage. One way or another, that piece of paper is going to pay off.

Play to win. Be prudent, be careful, and don't fear going into debt.

CHAPTER 14

SCHOLARSHIPS

(or, Make Somebody Else Pay!)

The scholarship list you'll find in this section of the book is our latest and best. Although no list can be all-inclusive, Black Excel's is probably the most comprehensive collection of scholarships for African American students you'll find. We have attempted to include all the major sources as well as many that are not well known. You're going to see countless possibilities that will apply to you, wherever you live and whatever college you apply to. But before we get to the scholarships, let's cover some things you need to know about your scholarship search.

GETTING STARTED: TEN THINGS TO CONSIDER BEFORE YOU BEGIN YOUR SCHOLARSHIP SEARCH

Here are 10 fundamentals of scholarship searching:

1. The money will not come to you. You've got to go and get it!

2. The "get the money" process is similar to the process you use when applying to colleges. It's hard work. You send for applications (guidelines) and follow instructions. You're likely to be asked to supply grades, test scores, recommendations, and perhaps write an essay. You must sell yourself by clearly presenting your potential, leadership, and school and community contributions.

3. Generally, no matter what you do, the money won't materialize in 10, 30, or 60 days. In nine of 10 cases, the review process takes months. It's never too early to get started. Ideally, you should begin looking in the fall of your junior year in high school. One potential quick fix: we advise students to contact their local sorority or fraternity chapters, because often there are community "honors" affairs where checks are handed out, usually in the $250 to $1,000 range. Sometimes you can luck out on short notice. But again, you've got to sell yourself with a package for review: grades, an essay, even an interview.

4. Aside from private scholarships, the federal government provides well over $50 billion in aid, grants, and scholarships! A lot of this is in response to your *demonstrated need,* based on an analysis of your submission of a FAFSA (Free Application for Federal Student Aid) form. Depending on how your FAFSA looks, you may be eligible for one or more of the following:

   Federal Pell grants: These grants are the largest administered by the U.S. government and are usually targeted to about 5 million-plus lower-income families. Remember that you automatically apply when you fill out the FAFSA.

Supplemental Educational Opportunity Grants (SEOG): These grants are also government-sponsored. They are, however, administered by the individual colleges, and are generally targeted to students who (after Pell awards) still have unmet need. Again, that FAFSA form has to be on file.

State aid: These awards, incentives, and special-money giveaways are usually targeted to students who decide to study at schools in their home states. If "home," you might be offered lower or reduced tuition compared to what out-of-state students must pay. This is generally true if you pick a state-supported (not private) school. Also, extras such as New York's Tuition Assistance Program (TAP)—added funds—are available to students who have need and maintain residence. Note that states award millions in need-based and merit awards. Consult our listing of state commissions of higher education (appendix E) for contact numbers.

Federal Stafford loans: These loans are administered by commercial lenders, are based on need, and are guaranteed and subsidized by the federal government. They are relatively low-interest, and it's usually where we must go to complete college. The principal and interest don't have to be repaid (in monthly installments) until six months after you graduate. For an explanatory guide and more information call (800) 4-FED-AID.

Perkins loans: These federal loans are administrated by individual colleges and are based (theoretically) on "exceptional need." These loans help students close their "need" gaps. Like the Stafford, payments on these lower-interest loans do not have to start until after graduation (in this case, nine months after).

Work-study: These are jobs that are subsidized by the federal government and that are offered by your college. You'll have a salary. Sometimes these jobs are career- or community-service-oriented. Often they are what you might call "fill-ins"—that is, a job working in the cafeteria or bookstore. For many students of color that minimum wage has been a lifesaver.

5. Scholarships from private foundations, religious groups, civic organizations, corporations, unions, and academic and talent competitions account for only a very small percentage of the money (about $2.5 billion) annually disbursed to students.

6. When you apply to and get accepted by a specific college (Spelman, Yale, Hampton, Syracuse, wherever), that's where and when you're likely to get your best scholarship/grant offer, particularly if you're a strong applicant they want. The gift will be part of your financial aid package.

7. Many students/parents initiate their get-the-money try prior to entering college or early during freshman year. They then give up after a halfhearted effort to win an award. The prevailing attitude seems to be that it's a one-shot deal. Nothing can be further from the truth. Scholarships are available throughout your college years, and often the odds of your getting one will depend on incoming grades and achievements as you proceed toward your degree. If you look closely, you'll notice that many scholarships are not year-specific. Others are targeted to sophomores, juniors, and to-be seniors after they've had an opportunity to be tested "under fire." A sound strategy is to always keep an iron in the fire if you feel you're a worthy candidate.

8. Is the idea of a full-tuition, all-expenses-paid "free ride" for real? Yes, for that rare super student. Marianne Ragins, the author of *Winning Scholarships for College,* went on to Florida A&M after aggressively applying for as many scholarships as she could. Very

organized, and using a tracking system and file folders, she won more than $400,000 in funds. Money due: nothing. Benjamin Kaplan went on to Harvard after winning more than $90,000, according to a story in one college magazine. Again, the key was a stellar academic and achievement record combined with lots of aggressiveness. After applying everywhere, and entering three dozen contests, Benjamin had his money. If you're a student with a strong record, apply, apply, apply.

9. Visit your college adviser! One pivotal stop has to be with your high school grade adviser. He or she should have a database of scholarship possibilities and resources available—not only books, lists, and Internet sources to explore, but also the useful track records/awards of former students who have applied somewhere and won money. If you're a good student, your adviser should be able to direct you to possible "matches" to consider. Of course, check all office postings/announcements for scholarships and competitions.

10. Use shortcuts! Often we hear this: "My college adviser says not to buy any scholarship list, not from any organization—that I can go to the library and get the information for free!" Some students, unfortunately, take this to heart. You should go the library and search for "gems." But it would take the most motivated student an inordinate amount of time and energy to create a list as long and as thoroughly researched as ours for example. A Black Excel offering, a book such as Berry Beckham's *Black Guide of Scholarships* (Madison House, 1998), or Cynthia and Phillip McKee's book *Cash for College* (to name just a few useful and legitimate sources) are time-savers.

BLACK EXCEL'S GUIDE TO GETTING SCHOLARSHIPS AND GRANTS

You're reading this because you want to get the money. You want a scholarship, a grant, whatever it takes to make things easier on your pocketbook. Of course, you've heard the bad news—that tuition is rising faster than inflation, that college is going to take a ferocious bite out of you, that there's going to be a money drain. You don't want to wake up facing a $20,000, $10,000, $5,000, or even a $2,500 bill (we wish!) for a single year, let alone for four or more. You're thinking that this could be the ultimate hardship. When the figures arrive—your financial aid package—will you be left in shell shock?

Will a bargain-basement school be the only answer? Or a two-year school (often said to be a lifesaver), while you save and count your pennies? And finally, will you have to forgo your plans? Perhaps find a job, and go to school part-time while working?

Well, you should take a deep breath and just relax. Every black student and family with dreams of getting a B.A., B.S., M.A., Ph.D., professional, or other degree will take this journey. Indeed, achievers before you got through it, didn't they—the periods of stress and anxiety aside? It's a rite of passage. It's just your turn. The fact that you've gotten to this crossroads is a mighty achievement. After all, the studies and those revealing figures are in: that degree is going to pay off! Even if costs keep escalating, and a college education continues to feel unaffordable.

The truth is that awareness helps. And this scholarship section (with the financial aid chapter) will ease many of your worries. Whether you're headed to Hampton University, our college by the sea, your state school, or even that unheralded college a subway ride away, you're college-bound!

What follows is a hands-on tutorial that is going make your scholarship journey as easy as A, B, C. If you just follow the easy-to-follow steps presented, you're going to optimize your chances of getting a scholarship.

Some key points: we can't guarantee you an award. Your record, your GPA, and what you have achieved (e.g., leadership, academics, and talent) are the keys. And remember: it takes hours to fine-tune an application, telling your story, often with that personalized essay. Only you can do that.

At the end of this chapter we're going to present the profiles of two Ron Brown scholars to give you an idea of what super scholarship winners look like.

YOUR SCHOLARSHIP GET-THE-MONEY TUTORIAL

Here are the seven steps to nailing that scholarship.

Step One: Get Ready

Taking a quick look through our 350-plus scholarship list (chapter 15) is not the way to go. You need a full day (or two) to tackle it. We suggest a Saturday or a Sunday. You also need a clear table; family and caring friends to assist, and a winning, can't-lose attitude.

Other things you'll need: pens and pencils, about 75 first-class stamps, and the same number of 10-inch business envelopes (we highly recommend that you send a stamped, self-addressed envelope with all your letters for quicker returns; of course, this would double the necessary stamps purchased). A typewriter or word processor/printer to type letters is a must. Also, you'll need a notebook to keep records, a calendar to keep track of dates, and a box or file folder to collect incoming mail alphabetically. As applications, brochures, flyers, and corresponding guidelines and instructions arrive, you'll need people to help you read, discuss, and sort material. This is a family affair!

Step Two: Draft Your Letters

You will need *one* letter that asks the scholarship group or college for information and the necessary application guidelines and rules. You can use the following format or something similar (review, also, our personalized sample). After your master copy is ready, make about 80 copies for mailing:

This kind of informal inquiry will usually be sufficient at this stage. Clerks are stuffing envelopes and returning the necessary materials. If, however, you would prefer a more personalized approach, here's an

---

[First letter sample (informal)]

[Date]

[Company/college name here]
[Address]

To Whom It May Concern:

Please send me all available information about your scholarships and/or grants. I would also like to receive an application, catalog, flyers, and any other resource material you think would be useful to a minority student.

Thank you.

Sincerely,
[Sign your name]
[Print your name]
[Your address]

actual letter that a Black Excel student (and scholarship winner) used. Add your own particulars/data and follow the addressing method presented above.

Step Three: Review the List

With your letters and envelopes beside you, begin the process of reviewing page one of our 350-plus scholarship list. When you spot a scholarship that interests you, circle it. When you finish the page, fill in the blanks of your letter forms and then address your envelopes. Relax for a while. Then go to the next page and repeat the process. Take your time. This is going to take a while.

Many students make the tactical mistake of focusing in on one scholarship category. For example, if they are interested in or majoring in accounting, they'll ask: "Do you have any accounting scholarships?" Then they narrow their search. A better strategy would be to target all scholarships that are "general" and specify only academic excellence, leadership, and community service in whatever field/major.

Our experience has been that those interested in areas such as engineering, to name just one category, are very competitive in most nonspecific application pools. Yes, pursue the money in your chosen field, but note all get-the-money opportunities and the bigger picture.

Step Four: Stuff and Stamp

After you have targeted 50 to 80-plus or so scholarship possibilities, stuff and stamp your envelopes. Try to mail all the letters at one time. Log your mailings in your notebook.

Step Five: The Waiting Game

Wait several weeks for packages/applications to arrive. In the meantime, the following material should be readied:

Your Essay: The essay or essays that you wrote for your college applications should be held in a "ready" folder.

Many of the scholarship groups will ask for an essay touching on themes you have already written or thought about, and hopefully (perhaps with a little reshaping), you can recycle your work. Typical essay questions are:

- What person in your personal life or in history has had the greatest influence on you? Why?
- What are your future goals, and what do you think your eventual impact on society will be?

[Second letter sample (personalized)]

To Whom It May Concern:

My Name is Theresa Strong, and this coming September I will be a senior at Forest Hills High School. My SAT score is 1100, I am in the top 7% of my class, and my academic average is 91.50 (equivalent to a 3.7 GPA). I would like to get information and an application concerning your scholarship program.

Sincerely,

Teresa Strong
[Address]

*Teresa actually used this letter, and received lots of material.

Your Résumé: The résumé we suggested you create to attach to your college applications should be ready. Why not display your achievements, goals, GPA, special awards, and extracurricular activities? If you don't sell yourself, who will?

Recommendations: You might need a teacher recommendation or two. Use copies of the ones you've already collected, or simply ask those who have already praised your academic abilities, leadership, and special talents to do a rewrite (as necessary) of their prior recommendation or recommendations.

Step Six: Sorting through Responses

In about two weeks you'll begin to receive applications, brochures, and letters of instruction. And you'll continue to receive a steady flow of materials during the weeks that follow. Be prepared to read and sort through it all.

Here's a sample of what to expect:

Optimist International Essay Contest: A four-page flyer explaining the general rules, judging, and scoring. The student is advised to forward the essay to a local Optimist Club.

United Methodist Scholarship Program: A four-page folder explaining eligibility requirements, the application procedure, lists of scholarships and loans, and directions on how to apply.

American Legion High School Oratorical Contest: Another four-page folder explaining the contest, regulations, information about the judges and tabulators, and how to apply.

Sometimes you'll simply receive a postcard with a box checked. It might say something like:

- "We consider American students who are within one year of completing their studies in a baccalaureate degree program."
- "If you meet the above qualifications, we would be happy to send you an application for your sophomore year."
- "Please write again between September 15 and November 30 for an application."

Often everything will be in order—your instructions, the actual application, and lots of written encouragement. Don't be surprised, and don't get discouraged. Scholarship winners face rough times, get knocked down, get up, and keep going.

And remember, no matter how good a list is, you're going to get that inevitable return envelope saying MOVED, NOT FORWARDABLE, or FORWARDING ORDER EXPIRED. Don't blink. Be persistent. Stay organized.

One student we worked with, now in law school, used a tracking system that began with her writing on each and every envelope she received. Some of her actual notes:

- *Do not qualify.*
- *Deadline Jan. 30.*
- *Due Nov. 25. No time.*
- *Done. Answered 10/1.*
- *Financial aid info.*
- *Call local Elk lodge.*
- *Essay due April 10.*
- *Apply in Sept.*
- *Summer program in Mass.*
- *They want $90 fee?*

- *Only for Louisiana!*
- *Bingo, this looks good.*
- *Done. Feb. 12.*

Step Seven: Apply

When you fill out the applications and provide whatever is required (essays, résumé, etc.), remember your mission: everything should highlight your smarts, leadership ability, character, and how unique and special you are. "If you have it, flaunt it," we say. If a newspaper has done a story on you, forward it. If that audio- or videotape you produced is supreme, let the world see it.

APPLICATION TIPS

Many students are going to be too lazy to follow through. They are going to handle their effort in a sloppy manner. As in the college application process, you do not concede anything to your competitors. Remember: to the reviewer, most scholarship packages look the same. If you can, make lighting strike. Put that winner's stamp on your effort. And beat those deadlines by a week or more.

Dressing Your Application?

Always forward an error-free application, with no misspellings or obvious erasures or use of Wite-Out. Type on cotton-fiber white paper (at least 20% bond). Never use erasable bond; it smudges. Use a black, new ribbon, of course. Exotic or italic typefaces are a no-no. Remember to keep copies of everything.

Who Beats the Scholarship Odds?

When scholarship committees look at applications, their "discovery" formula probably looks something like this (with all categories in the "good" to "superior" range):

SAT + GPA + SPECIAL ACHIEVEMENTS + WORK + TALENTS + CHARACTER and POTENTIAL = WINNING SCHOLARSHIP CANDIDATE.

Let's assume that your hypothetical competition is a guy named John Brown. Let's suppose that his SAT score is 50 points higher than yours and that his GPA is also better. You don't concede. You try to create a presentation that stirs some feeling and hopefully rivets the reviewers. The students with the highest numbers don't always win these awards.

Whether John Brown or any student has a better GPA and SAT score than yours can't be your concern. You must think about you, and selling yourself. It's the college application process all over again. Try to show that (all things considered) you are the best candidate. Against our fictional John Brown, your final formula should look like this:

SAT (it's lower, but you're competitive)

GPA (it's lower, but you're competitive)

special achievements (you're great to extraordinary)

potential (you're great to extraordinary)

work (you're great to extraordinary)

talents (you're great to extraordinary)

Indeed, your objective must be to always impress, to put your persona and story in its best possible form at all times. Do that, and you'll have maximum impact (your goal), whether you win or lose.

Whom Would You Select?

The first scholarship candidate writes: "I was a dance instructor, and taught dance to eleven-year-olds."

The second scholarship candidate writes: "I was a dance instructor, and taught dance to eleven-year-olds. My goal wasn't simply to teach technique, but to instill a sense of culture, camaraderie, teamwork, a work ethic, and responsibility to my impressible students. Perfecting our steps, rotations, and routines were lots of fun, but I was on a higher mission. Several of my students began to achieve at school after our dance classes began."

I like candidate number two. The key is to make the language sing your story.

SCHOLARSHIP BASICS AND AID

Nearly everybody seems to think that if a college says that a family must pay $2,000 for a year's tuition and then you win a $2,000 scholarship, you are home free. Nothing can be further from the truth.

This is how the process actually works: After you fill out your FAFSA form (you must read chapter 12 on financial aid for essential information), the American Testing Service calculates what they call a EFC (expected family contribution) figure. That's a projected estimate of what you (and your family) theoretically can afford to pay (out-of-pocket cash) for college. That figure is sent to all the colleges you apply to. For this discussion, we're using a $2,000 figure. Well, each college gets this "fair" estimate and will use that figure to arrive at what they actually want from you.

Once that $2,000 (or whatever figure) is reached, the college will create a package for you. In chapter 12 on financial aid, we give you a comprehensive review of this process. In the simplified form here, this is what happens. The college will attempt to meet their cost (let's say it's $10,000 for you to attend) by making up the shortage. You'll be asked for the $2,000, and the college will give you a grant, loans, federal (Pell) and state funds, and work-study to reach that $10,000 total due. In short, the college will get you the necessary $8,000 so you can attend. This is called "meeting your need." Note that some "poorer" colleges cannot meet your total need. This, for our folks, often creates a major problem. Imagine that the FAFSA formula says you have the capability to pay $2,000, but the college can't make up the balance. How do you beg or borrow to make up the necessary balance?

Okay, in the above scenario, let's say you suddenly win a $2,000 scholarship. Well, the college would still want $2,000 from you. The school would simply reduce the amount (perhaps) of your grant or loan by $2,000. Got it?

Now the good news! In the case study just presented, the student/family will have less of a loan ($2,000) to pay back in the future if the college reduces its initial loan offer. If the college reduces the work-study part of the package, the student will have more free time to study or do other things. Do note, too, that some colleges will reduce a portion of your "free money"—their grant, when recalculating your package after a scholarship is awarded. If that happens, politely talk to the FAO at your chosen college about this.

If a loan reduction is possible, that's what you would want. Reducing a grant is not helping you, not immediately nor in the future.

The real deal? Generally, you would actually have to win one very lucrative or several substantial scholarships to impact on what the FAFSA formula says you and your family can/must pay. When your scholarship totals begin to exceed the loan, grant, and work-study portions of your "package," that's when the amount due begins to decrease or (congratulations!) disappear.

Be forewarned: Only substantial scholarship money/awards can significantly reduce the amount the FAFSA people calculate that you can afford to pay.

SCHOLARSHIP FAQS

Q: If not from scholarships, where do most of our children get their aid?

From the Pell grant program, a federal student-aid program that disburses about $5.5 billion to students each year. Other pivotal money sources include Supplemental Educational Opportunity Grants (SEOG), Stafford loans, Perkins and PLUS loans, and work-study programs. Go to chapter 12 on financial aid for more information about this.

Q: What are merit scholarships, and how do they work?

Many colleges (with the exception of the Ivies and a few very selective colleges) are offering scholarships to "super" students based simply on their academic ability and talents, regardless of financial need. Whether you're rich, middle-class, or poor is not a factor. The award is based on "merit" and not any formula (from the FAFSA form).

Often these "incentives" to attract you also include a room in an honors or scholars dorm, perks such as season tickets to basketball games, and more.

Q: What are National Merit scholarships?

Usually in the 11th grade, students nationwide take the PSAT (Preliminary Scholastic Aptitude Test). This test is also often referred to as the PSAT/NMSQT or National Merit Scholarship Qualifying Test. Score well, and colleges across the country will send you publicity and recruitment letters and brochures. Your academic profile appears (at first look) to meet their minimum standards. They want you to take a look and perhaps apply.

If you achieve an exceptional score (often in the top 1%, depending on the competition in your state) you will qualify for consideration as a National Merit scholar. If you prevail after the initial screenings you'll be tagged a "semifinalist" or a "finalist." The awards, at various levels to National Merit scholar, will range from $1,000 to more than $8,000 and will be sponsored by both colleges and corporations.

Students of color taking the PSAT will also be simultaneously eligible for awards from the National Achievement Scholarship Program for Outstanding Negro Students.

Extra information about the National Merit scholarships can be obtained by contacting the National Merit Scholarship Corporation at One Rotary Center, 1560 Sherman Avenue, Evanston, IL 60201. Phone: (708) 866-5100.

Q: What are ROTC scholarships, and how do they work?

Some colleges have military (Reserve Officers Training Corps) training at their campuses. This money (more than $130 million) is doled out by the federal government to students who meet stiff academic, leadership, and physical standards. The awards are for both full- and part-time activity, usually with a monthly stipend. But your child must agree to meeting an active-duty obligation after graduation, of sometimes as many as three years.

A student exceptional enough to get an "accept" from one of our five military colleges, can get a fully-paid, tuition-free ride. The schools: the U.S. Naval Academy at Annapolis (MD), the Air Force Academy in Colorado Springs, the U.S. Military Academy at West Point (NY), the U.S. Merchant Marine Academy at Kings Point (NY), and the U.S. Coast Guard Academy at New London (CT).

Of course, this is serious business: early reveille, rigorous basic training and regimen, and—if there is a war or other crisis—the possibility of getting a call.

Q: Should you use a computer service to find scholarships?

Well, we have talked to students/parents who have used scholarship services. Most have been, frankly, disappointed. We have never heard a rave review or endorsement. Most services charge $40 to $120 to "match you" with five to 25 sources. These are sources that theoretically you can apply to. One sour point is that none of the services we have seen was created specifically with our needs in mind. We're a footnote, if that.

We suggest that students who are considering using a computer service—we have no doubt that some are legitimate—go to Mark Kantrowitz's web site (check out appendix B about the Internet) to read about scams. Usually these are services that "guarantee" you money. Nobody can guarantee you money before they even look at your record. Also, beware of services that say they'll "do the work for you." That's unlikely, if not impossible. Only you have the necessary time and information to pitch your case.

Here's a quote pulled from the promotional flyer of one computer service. We're skeptical. This service says it's one of "the best." It then explains that "the best is also one of the most expensive. Your cost is $94.00. $19.00 sent to us for application and brochure and $75.00 sent to the data bank with your application." Nothing really is spelled out. What do you get? It's unclear. Well, if you're going to use a service, you should at least be impressed with its promotional material. In this case, we weren't.

Finally, remember that you do have access to free scholarship databases on the Internet. Read appendix B before you decide what you want to do. And always call the Better Business Bureau in your community to check out any selected computer service you are considering.

Q: Do millions of dollars of scholarship funds go unclaimed each year?

Our unequivocal answer is "No," not if you are talking about money you can get. Each year, nearly every student is searching for money, buying books, going to libraries, asking grade advisers about sources. This chase by a million-plus students and their parents finds just about everything. Sources that are offering scholarships are not in hiding.

Most scholarships that go unclaimed are specifically employment-related. The John Doe Company might have a scholarship or two for the senior child of an employee. Maybe a B+ average is required, or a 1100-plus SAT score. In many cases, no child qualifies within a given year; hence, no money is distributed. Also, there are scholarships available that have requirements that are so specific (often scientific or research-related) that candidates (in any given year) are rare. Is there a student who, for example, is doing work on Einstein's Theory of Relativity? You got the idea?

RON BROWN SCHOLARS

The Ron Brown scholar program has among the most lucrative awards available. These profiles of two recent recipients were presented in the *Ron Brown Scholar Program Newsletter* for October 1997. Think about how you'll need to tell your story to compete with students such as these for scholarship money.

Angela Ledbetter of Historically Black Xavier University of Louisiana

Angela Ledbetter, preparing to embark on her second year at Louisiana's Xavier University, has had no trouble combining academic and extracurricular success. She completed her freshman year with a 4.0 in the university's rigorous biochemistry program, an accomplishment befitting the 1997 valedictorian of Detroit's Cass Tech High School. Ledbetter was one of only 15 students in the Detroit public schools to graduate with a 4.0.

During her freshman year, Angela quickly immersed herself in the frantic world of college life. She became a member of the National Society of Black Engineers and the Biomedical Honors Corps, organizations that have nurtured her scientific pursuits. However, she has not limited her interests to the scientific. Angela has been plunging into the world of student politics. She was elected vice president of Xavier's freshman class and acted as campaign manager for a classmate. When she wasn't passing out campaign literature or studying the symmetry of some intriguing virus, Angela was a volunteer at Armstrong, Inc., an organization that assists homeless families.

Ledbetter, who hopes to open a homeless shelter someday where "homeless people can build their lives," used the Armstrong experience to learn firsthand what running a shelter entails. Angela also organized visits to and planned activities for the Ronald McDonald House, ran a canned-food drive, and participated in the cleanup of a nursing home. She even served as a tutor at the university for students in academic difficulty.

This summer Angela focused on gaining valuable career skills by working at Arbor Drugs, a Detroit drugstore where she serves as pharmacy technician. She also volunteered four hours each week in the Department of Ambulatory Surgery at Detroit's Henry Ford Hospital. From mid-July until the end of August, Angela worked with a federal agency that offers advisory assistance to individuals who would like to start their own business.

Angela has kept her plate full for the summer and is eager to return to New Orleans to begin what is bound to be another incredibly successful year.

Kelly Cross of Princeton University

As a student leader at Princeton University, Kelly Cross continues to place himself in the leadership role he assumed in high school. Now, however, the role isn't nearly as simple as it was in Beckley, West Virginia, and the stakes are higher.

Kelly began his explorations of student leadership in tenth grade, when he was elected sophomore class president at Woodrow Wilson High School. That year he was president of a class of more than 500 students. He served as president the two remaining years, and, in 1997 he delivered the commencement address to the members of his class.

Student government wasn't the only activity that piqued Kelly's interest. He was also deeply committed to community issues. Watching so many of his junior high school friends whom he was certain would go to college drop out of high school and pursue jobs beneath their capabilities, Kelly decided that something needed to be done. Thus he created a peer tutoring system at his high school intended to give academic and social support to fellow students whose loss of hope was driving them to irreparably damage their futures.

In high school, Kelly had the golden touch. However, when he arrived on the campus of Princeton University in the fall of 1997, he realized that getting involved with student government there would require more than people skills. After attending an information session about running for student government, Kelly decided to run for the position of class senator, a post reserved for two students per class. Through a combination of networking and hard campaign work, Kelly gained the momentum needed to push him to victory.

Serving as a class senator has been no easy task. Kelly was frequently barraged by questions from students regarding student government policy and action. "Being able to deal with so many different questions from such varied people has been a learning experience for me," Kelly says.

In addition to his work with the student government, Kelly, along with three classmates, chartered a campus branch of the NAACP. "We noticed a lack of activism among the black students on campus regarding issues we considered very important, such as the assault on affirmative action or the stagnant number of African Americans being admitted to the university. This organization was created with the intent of providing a strong voice for students to express concern over issues relevant to their lives." Last year was focused on building a membership and visions for the organization, while the next academic year will focus on finding a solution to various campus problems.

With so much going on, Kelly is eager to return to Princeton this fall to finish the work he started. Having long been interested in the effect of the past on the present, Kelly plans to major in history. He is interested in a future in the Foreign Service.

CHAPTER 15

SCHOLARSHIP SOURCES

Here is our selected list of money sources. Most of these are straight scholarships; also included in this list are awards, prizes, and internships that can help you get the money you need to pay for college. Many of the sources are targeted to particular fields, and all have their own specific requirements for applying and receiving scholarships. To get started, check the information below, including the targeted fields and the keys to getting the money, and then just forward a short note to any of the scholarship sources that seem applicable. Ask for an application per the instructions in the previous chapter. Good luck!

Academy of Television Arts and Sciences

5220 Lankershim Boulevard
N. Hollywood, CA 91601-3109
(818) 754-2830

Fields: Interest in the television industry
Amount: $1,600 for an eight-week internship
The keys:
- This is the Academy's internship program, taught by professionals in the television field.

ADHA Institute for Oral Health Scholarship

444 North Michigan Avenue, Suite 3400
Chicago, IL 60611-3461
(312) 440-8900

Fields: Dental hygiene majors
Amount: $1,500
The keys:
- Students must be in a dental hygiene program, preferably with a 3.0 or more GPA and financial need.
- Deadline: March 31.

AF ROTC

Office of Public Affairs
Maxwell AFB, AL 36112
(205) 262-7233 or (205) 953-1110

Fields: ROTC program; also, ROTC nurse program available
Amount: Stipends for exchange time
The keys:
- Write or call for specifics.

African Methodist Episcopal Zion Church

1200 Windermere Drive
Pittsburgh, PA 15218
(412) 242-5842

Fields: General
Amount: Varies
The keys:
- This organization has more than 1 million members, over 2,500 churches, and offers scholarships galore to its college-bound members.

AGC Education and Research Foundation

c/o Director of Programs
1957 E Street, N.W.
Washington, DC 20006
(202) 393-2040

Fields: Civil engineering and construction majors
Amount: Varies
The keys:
■ Write for details.

Agnes Jones Jackson Scholarship

NAACP Education Division
4805 Mount Hope Drive
Baltimore, MD 21215-2397
(301) 358-8900

Fields: General
Amount: $1,500 (you can reapply)
The keys:
■ Active youth members eligible.
■ Must have GPA of at least 2.5.
■ Write in January.
■ Deadline: April 30.

Alexander and Maude Haeden Scholarships

Youth Foundation, Inc.
30 West 44th Street
New York, NY 10036

Fields: General
Amount: Varies; more than 90 scholarships
The keys:
■ Must write for details.

Alpha Kappa Alpha Sorority, Inc.

5656 South Stony Island Avenue
Chicago, IL 60637
(312) 684-1282

Fields: General
Amount: Varies
The keys:
■ Academic and leadership grants.
■ Contact your local AKA chapter (more than 820 with over 121,00 members) for details.

Alpha Phi Alpha Fraternity, Inc.

2313 St. Paul Street
Baltimore, MD 21218-5234
(410) 554-0054

Fields: General
Amount: Varies
The keys:
■ There are more than 650 student and alumni chapters. Locate the one closest to you for scholarship possibilities and information. Call for guidance.

American Association of Law Libraries

1100 Central Trust Tower
P.O. Box 5300
Cincinnati, OH 45202
(513) 977-3000

Fields: Law-related major or interest
Amount: Varies
The keys:
■ Must be a college junior or senior with need, and who is interested in law librarianship.
■ Write for details.

American Association of Medical Assistants Endowments

20 North Wacker Drive, #1575
Chicago, IL 60606
(312) 899-1500

Fields: Health-related interest or major
Amount: Varies
The keys:
■ This scholarship is awarded to students who submit the best essays on why they are interested in becoming medical assistants.

American Baptist Black Caucus

c/o St. John Missionary Baptist Church
34 West Pleasant Street
Springfield, OH 45506
(513) 323-4401

Fields: General
Amount: Varies

The keys:
- Write for information.

American Bar Foundation

c/o Summer Research and Social Science for Minority Fellowships
750 North Lake Shore Drive
Chicago, IL 60611

Fields: Law-related majors
Amount: $3,500 stipend
The keys:
- Ten-week fellowships during the summer.
- For students who are beyond their sophomore year with at least a 3.0 GPA and considering a social science career.
- Deadline: March 1.

American Chemical Society Scholars Program

Department of Minority Affairs
1155 16th Street, N.W.
Washington, DC 20036

Fields: Chemical and biochemical science majors
Amount: To $2,500; more than 200 scholarships available
The keys:
- Scholarships for outstanding students majoring in the noted areas.
- Deadline: February 15.

American Congress of Rehabilitation Medicine

122 South Michigan Avenue, Suite 1300
Chicago, IL 60603
(312) 922-9368

Fields: Health-related or general
Amount: Varies
The keys:
- This contest is open to undergraduates who write the best essays related to physical medicine or rehabilitation. Essays cannot be longer than 3,000 words.
- Deadline: May 1.

American Dental Hygienists' Association

444 North Michigan Avenue, Suite 3400
Chicago, IL 60611
(312) 664-3327

Fields: Dental hygiene
Amount: Up to $1,500
The keys:
- Must be enrolled in dental hygiene certificate or degree program.
- At least a 3.0 GPA.
- Deadline: June 1.

American Express Travel Scholarship

c/o Scholarship Manager
1101 King Street, Suite 200
Alexandria, VA 22314-2187

Fields: Must be enrolled in travel or tourism program
Amount: $2,500
The keys:
- Student can be in a community or four-year college.
- An essay must predict the industry's future.
- Deadline: submit during the summer.

American Fund for Dental Health

211 East Chicago Avenue, #820
Chicago, IL 60611
(312) 787-6270

Fields: Dental laboratory majors
Amount: Varies
The keys:
- Must be entering or enrolled in a dental technology field.
- A good academic record and financial need are required.
- Deadline: June 1.

American Geological Institute

Minority Participation Program
c/o Director, AGI Minority
4220 King Street
Alexandria, VA 22302-1507
(703) 379-2480

American Geological Institute
(continued)

Fields: Geoscience majors (geology, geophysics, marine sciences, and earth-science education)
Amount: From $500 to $10,000 for 30 to 50 scholarships; renewable
The keys:
- Good SAT or ACT scores.
- Résumé.
- Three letters of recommendation.
- Must plan to become a geoscientist.
- Deadline: February 1.

American Institute of Certified Public Accountants (AICPA)

1211 Avenue of the Americas
New York, NY 10036
(212) 596-6200 or 6270

Fields: Accounting majors
Amount: Up to $5,000; renewable. More than 350 scholarships available
The keys:
- Must be achieving minority accounting major with more than 30 credits completed.
- Write for details.
- Deadline: July 1.

American Medical Technologists

710 Higgins Road
Park Ridge, IL 60068
(312) 823-5169

Fields: Medical assistant and technology majors
Amount: Varies
The keys:
- Scholarships for students planning to enroll in medical assistant or medical technology programs.
- Deadline: April 1.

American Physical Therapy Association

1111 North Fairfax Street
Alexandria, VA 22314
(703) 684-2782

Fields: Physical therapy majors
Amount: Varies

The keys:
- For outstanding students of physical therapy in the last year of study in an APTA degree program.
- Deadline: December 1.

American Society of Women Accountants

c/o Executive Director
35 East Wacker Drive, Suite 2250
Chicago, IL 60601
(312) 726-9030

Fields: Accounting majors
Amount: Varies
The keys:
- This scholarship is intended to increase opportunities for women in accounting.
- There are more than 130 chapters nationwide.
- Deadline: inquire.

APS Minorities Scholarship Program

The American Physical Society
One Physics Ellipse
College Park, MD 20740-3844
(301) 209-3200

Fields: Physics
Amount: $2,000; renewable
The keys:
- For seniors, freshmen, and sophomore physics majors.
- Standardized test scores and references necessary.
- Deadline: March 15.

Armco Minorities Engineering Scholarships

c/o Armco Insurance Group
703 Curtis Street
Middletown, OH 45043
(513) 425-5293

Fields: Engineering majors; also insurance and risk management scholarships available for business majors
Amount: $2,000

The keys:
- For students who intend to enroll in engineering programs.
- Must have strong academic records, be in the top third of their class, and reside in a community where an Armco office is located.
- Deadline: write for information.

Army ROTC Quality Enrichment Program (QEP)

Gold Quest Center
Army ROTC
P.O. Box 1688
Ellicott City, MD 21043
(800) 872-7682

Fields: General
Amount: To $8,000
The keys:
- Student must attend an HBCU.
- Deadline: December 1.

Army ROTC Quality Enrichment Program (QEP)

Department of the Army
U.S. Army Cadet Command
Attn.: ATTC-PS
Fort Monroe, VA 23651-5000
(202) 325-0184

Fields: General
Amount: $5,000 to $12,000
The keys:
- For HBCU enrollment in ROTC with future commitment for service.
- Deadline: November 15.

Asantewaa

P.O. Box 432
Glenwood, IL 60425

Fields: General
Amount: Up to $2,000
The keys:
- For single mothers.
- Looking for demonstrated self-motivation, goals, community concern, and financial need.

- Awards banquet.
- Deadline: February 2. Write for details.

ASCAP Scholarship and Awards

ASCAP Building
1 Lincoln Plaza
New York, NY 10023
(212) 595-3050

Fields: Talent in writing music
Amount: Varies; 15 scholarships available
The keys:
- Student must write an original composition.
- Deadline: Ongoing.

Association of Official Analytical Chemists, International

2200 Wilson Boulevard, Suite 400
Arlington, VA 22201-3301

Fields: Chemistry, dental, medical, nursing, and related majors
Amount: $1,000
The keys:
- These scholarships are targeted to juniors for their senior year.
- Deadline: ongoing.

Associated Male Choruses of America Scholarship Fund

c/o Coordinator
P.O. Box 482
New Ulm, MN 56073

Fields: General
Amount: $300
The keys:
- Scholarship is for male vocal students looking to further their training during college.
- Deadline: February 1.

AT&T Scholarship and Summer Programs

101 Crawfords Corner Road
Holmdel, NJ 07733-3030
(908) 949-3728

AT&T Scholarship and Summer Programs *(continued)*

Fields: General
Amount: Up to full tuition
The keys:
- Write for brochure.

Avon Products Foundation, Inc.

c/o President
9 West 57th Street
New York, NY 10019
(212) 546-6732

Fields: General
Amount: Varies
The keys:
- Student must be the child of a current Avon employee or a high school senior who resides near an Avon location.
- Deadline: November 2.

Bank of America Achievement Awards Program

c/o Corporate Community Development
P.O. Box 37000
San Francisco, CA 94137

Fields: General
Amount: Varies; 320 scholarships available
The keys:
- For students in California only.
- Each high school picks its Student Achievement Award winner. This group competes for regional recognition.
- High school counselors must get details from noted address.

Baptist General Convention of Texas

(Texas Black Scholarships)
511 North Akard, Suite 1013
Dallas, TX 75201-3355
(214) 741-1991

Fields: General
Amount: $800; renewable

The keys:
- Scholarships are for members of the Baptist Church, who reside in Texas.
- Student should be recommended by a teacher or a minister.
- At least a B GPA, good character, and an interview.
- Deadline: ongoing.

Barbara Deming Memorial Artist Grants

c/o Money for Women
P.O. Box 40-1043
Brooklyn, NY 11240

Fields: Arts interest
Amount: To $1,000; 20 available
The keys:
- Scholarships are for feminists active in the arts, creating work that speaks to social justice, peace, and the condition of society.
- Write for details; no calls.

Beneficial Foundation Scholarship

c/o Scholarship Chairman
200 Beneficial Center
Peapack, NJ 07977

Fields: General
Amount: $100 to $1,000
The keys:
- Parents must be employees of Beneficial Finance.
- For freshman.
- Deadline: April 1.

Black Filmmakers Grants Programs

3617 Montclair Street
Los Angeles, CA 90018
(310) 201-9579

Fields: For student filmmakers
Amount: Varies
The keys:
- Scholarships to filmmakers working in 16mm or 3/4" video.
- Write for submission instructions.

Boston Area Black Alumni Association

c/o District of Columbia Public Schools
Division of Student Services
4501 Lee Street, N.E.
Washington, DC 20019
(202) 724-4934

Fields: General
Amount: N/A
The keys:
- Scholarship will be awarded to a student enrolling in one of the colleges in the Boston metropolitan area.

Boston Chapter of Links, Inc.

46 Brockton Street
Mattapan, MA 02126

Fields: General
Amount: $1,000
The keys:
- For students in the Boston area who are doing well academically, and have financial need.
- Write to Links for scholarship details.

Bright Futures Scholarship Program and Minority Teachers Scholarship Program

(888) 827-2004 toll-free for information

Fields: General
Amount: Varies; up to fully-paid tuition
The keys:
- State-sponsored program for Florida residents only.
- For high-achieving Florida high school seniors with a minimum 3.0 GPA.
- Some awards for economically disadvantaged students.
- Applications available from guidance counselors.

Burger King Company

Fields: General
Amount: $200 monthly to a $2,000 stipend
The keys:
- For students who are Burger King employees, working for more than 3 months.
- Contact supervisor for details.

Business and Professional Women Foundation

2012 Massachusetts Avenue, N.W.
Washington, DC 20036
(202) 293-1200

Fields: Engineering major
Amount: Varies
The keys:
- Must be a junior or a senior, enrolled in a school of engineering.
- Deadline: May 1.

Business Reporting Intern Program

c/o The Dow Jones Newspaper Fund
P.O. Box 300
Princeton, NJ 08543-0300

Fields: Journalism
Amount: Up to $1,000
The keys:
- Various scholarships available. Some, for juniors and sophomores, include paid summer internships to train as a newspaper reporter.
- Deadline: November 15. Must write for details.

Carats, Inc.

6236 North 15th Street
Philadelphia, PA 19141
(212) 424-2212

Fields: General
Amount: Varies
The keys:
- Write for details.

Carole Simpson Scholarship

Radio and Television News Directors
   Foundation
1000 Connecticut Avenue, N.W., Suite 615
Washington, DC 20036
(202) 737-8657

Fields: Broadcast journalism major
Amount: $2,000

Carole Simpson Scholarship
(continued)

The keys:
- Must be undergraduate majoring in broadcast journalism.
- Must submit VHS tape showcasing your reporting and producing skills.
- Deadline: March 2.

Catholic Negro Scholarships Fund

73 Chestnut Street
Springfield, MA 01103

Fields: General
Amount: Varies
The keys:
- For Catholic students pursuing a college degree who have need.
- Write for information.
- Deadline: Ongoing.

Central Intelligence Agency

Undergraduate Scholars Program
c/o Students Program Office
P.O. Box 1925
Washington, DC 20015
(703) 874-4465

Fields: Business, accounting, economics, engineering, languages, graphic design, cartography, computer science, and more
Amount: Tuition assistance and a four-year salary
The keys:
- Looking for minority students with demonstrated academic achievement, leadership qualities, good character, and goals.
- Make contact in August.
- Deadline: Ongoing.

Charles Drew Memorial Scholarship

c/o Omega Psi Phi Fraternity
2714 Georgia Avenue, N.W.
Washington, DC 20001
(202) 667-7158

Fields: General
Amount: $300
The keys:
- For students who have successfully completed their freshman year with a B or more average.
- Deadline: March 31.

Chi Eta Phi Sorority, Inc.

3029 Thirteenth Street, N.W.
Washington, DC 20009
(202) 232-3858

Fields: Nursing majors
Amount: Varies
The keys:
- Nursing-related sorority.
- Locate your local chapter (more than 60 undergraduate and graduate chapters, with more than 6,000 members) for scholarship possibilities and information.

Chicago Association of Black Journalists

P.O. Box 297
St. Peter, MN 56082
(507) 931-1682

Fields: Journalism majors
Amount: Varies
The keys:
- For juniors and seniors who are studying broadcast journalism at a college in Chicago.
- Deadline: April 30.

Clare Boothe Luce Scholarships in Science and Engineering

c/o Henry Luce Foundation, Inc.
111 West 50th Street
New York, NY 10020
(212) 489-7700

Fields: Science, math, and engineering
Amount: Varies
The keys:
- Targeted to encourage women to enter scientific fields.

Club Managers Association of America Scholarships

7615 Winterberry Place
P.O. Box 34482
Bethesda, MD 20817

Fields: General
Amount: $1,000
The keys:
- Scholarships to students who have successfully completed their freshman year and are interested in becoming club managers.
- An essay and need are important.
- Deadline: May 1.

Coca-Cola Scholars Foundation, Inc.

One Buckhead Plaza, Suite 10000
3060 Peachtree Road
Atlanta, GA 30305
(404) 237-1300

Fields: All fields
Amount: More than 100 $4,000 scholarships; 50 $20,000 scholarships
The keys:
- Scholarships for four years.
- Must be a U.S. citizen.

Commission for Racial Justice

Special Higher Education Program
c/o Coordinator
United Church of Christ
700 Prospect Avenue
Cleveland, OH 44115-1100
(216) 736-3786

Fields: General
Amount: From $200 to $2,000
The keys:
- Preference is given to students who are members of the United Church of Christ and who uphold the commission's goals.
- You must express how those goals relate to your life aspirations.
- Need matters.
- Deadline: August 1.

Creole Ethnic Association Fund and Scholarship

P.O. Box 2666
Church Street Station
New York, NY 10008

Fields: General
Amount: $1,000; 5 available
The keys:
- These are annual genealogy, language, and culture research awards.
- A five-year generations genealogical chart must be completed.
- Deadline: June 30.
- Only write for details; no calls.

Cultural Society, Inc.

P.O. Box 1374
Bridgeview, IL 60455
(312) 434-6665

Fields: General
Amount: From $2,600 to $16,000
The keys:
- For enrolling students or undergraduates who are of the Muslim faith.
- Write for application information.

Culturally Diverse Undergraduate Fellowship Program

c/o Environmental Protection Agency
(Sciences Research Division)
Mail Stop 8723R
401 M Street, S.W.
Washington, DC 20460
(202) 260-5283

Fields: Science, math, or engineering
Amount: Full-tuition, summer internships, and monthly stipends
The keys:
- You must be enrolled at an HBCU, have at least a 3.0 GPA, present a goal statement, and apply two years before you graduate.
- Deadline: December 17.
- More information is available at www.epa.gov\ncerqa.

Delta Sigma Theta Sorority

1707 New Hampshire Avenue, N.W.
Washington, DC 20009
(202) 483-5460 or (202) 986-2400

Fields: General
Amount: To $2,000
The keys:
- Scholarships for academically achieving students and leaders.
- More than 850 chapters with more than 185,000 members. Contact your local chapter.
- Deadline: Varies.

Dr. Martin Luther King Jr. Memorial Scholarships

c/o Educational and Cultural Fund of the Electrical Industry
158-11 Jewel Avenue
Flushing, NY 11365

Fields: General
Amount: $2,000
The keys:
- For high school graduates with strong leadership skills, SAT scores, GPA, recommendations, and interview.
- Write for application and instructions.

The Drifters, Inc.

10 Chelsea Court
Neptune, NJ 07753
(908) 774-2724

Fields: General
Amount: Varies
The keys:
- Write for scholarship information.

Ed Bradley Scholarship

Radio and Television New Directors
  Foundation
1000 Connecticut Avenue, N.W., Suite 615
Washington, DC 20036
(202) 737-8657

Fields: Broadcast journalism
Amount: $5,000
The keys:
- For undergraduates majoring in broadcast journalism.
- Must present a VHS tape to showcase your reporting and producing skills.
- Deadline: March 2.

Elk's "Most Valuable Student" Scholarship/Leadership Award

Grand Lodge BPO Elks
Office of the Grand Secretary
2750 Lakeview Drive
Chicago, IL 60614
(312) 477-2750

Fields: General
Amount: 500 $1,000 to $5,000 scholarships; renewable; more than 1,500 one-time awards of $800 to seniors
The keys:
- Scholarships for academic achievement, leadership, character, community and school service, and need.
- Deadline: usually in January.
- Contact noted or local lodge for application information.

Engineering Scholarship Program for Minority Community College Graduates

c/o Scholarship Service of the College Board
45 Columbus Avenue
New York, NY 10019
(212) 713-8000

Fields: Engineering track with physics, chemistry, and calculus completed
Amount: Varies
The keys:
- Scholarships for students graduating from community colleges. Also, students with more than 60 credits completed who plan to transfer to a four-year school with an engineering program.
- A 3.0 or higher GPA is desired.

Episcopal Commission for Black Ministries

c/o Episcopal Church
815 Second Avenue
New York, NY 10017
(212) 867-8400

Fields: General
Amount: Varies
The keys:
- Write for scholarship information.

Eta Phi Beta Sorority, Inc.

16815 James Couzens
Detroit, MI 43235
(313) 862-0600

Fields: General
Amount: Varies
The keys:
- Scholarships available for qualified students. Write for scholarship and chapter locations.

Executive Women International Scholarship Program

c/o Director of Administration
Spring Run Executive Plaza
965 East 4800 South, Suite 1
Salt Lake City, UT 84117

Fields: Business majors
Amount: $100 to $10,000
The keys:
- Student must be pursuing a career in business.
- Scholarships rewarded across the nation based on GPA, leadership qualities, work, character, recommendations, and an interview.
- Send an SASE for local EWI chapters.

Federation of Masons of the World and Federation of Eastern Stars

P.O Box 1296
Austin, TX 78767
(512) 477-5380

Fields: General

Amount: Varies
The keys:
- Fraternal group that has donated thousands to disadvantaged students and the children of its members.
- Write for scholarship information.

Foundation for Economic Education

c/o Freedom Essay Contest
30 South Broadway
Irvington-on-Hudson
New York, NY 10533

Fields: General
Amount: $500 to $1,500
The keys:
- For undergraduates; this is a writing and/or screenplay contest.
- Fewer than 3,000 words necessary.
- Deadline: January 15.

Fukunaga Scholarship Foundation

900 Fort Street Mall, Suite 500
P.O. Box 2788
Honolulu, HI 96893
(808) 521-6511

Fields: Business administration
Amount: $6,000 to $8000
The keys:
- Based on achievement and an interest in pursuing business major and need.
- Deadline: March 15.

Gannet Foundation Scholarships

c/o Administrator
Lincoln Tower
Rochester, NY 14604
(716) 262-3315

Fields: Journalism, news, broadcasting
Amount: Varies
The keys:
- For outstanding student pursuing a career in journalism or related areas.

George E. Johnson Foundation and Education Fund

Johnson Products Co., Inc.
c/o Administrator,
8522 South Lafayette Avenue
Chicago, IL 60620-1301
(312) 483-4100

Fields: Business, chemistry, engineering, physics, prelaw, predentistry
Amount: Varies, but more than 63 available
The keys:
- Achieving college student with need.
- Deadline: Ongoing.

George M. Brooker Collegiate Scholarship for Minorities

c/o Institute of Management Foundation
430 North Michigan Avenue
Chicago, IL 60611-8775

Fields: Real estate or related majors
Amount: $1,000
The keys:
- Must be in or entering a real-estate program, with an eye to a career in the field.
- At least 3.0 GPA within major.
- Deadline: March 15.

Glamour's Top Ten College Competition

c/o Glamour Magazine
350 Madison Avenue
New York, NY 10017
(800) 244-4526

Fields: General
Amount: $1,000; 10 available
The keys:
- Scholarships for 10 female college students. Should demonstrate superior leadership skills, have initiated volunteer and campus activities, and be achieving academically.
- Deadline: January 31.

Golden State Minority Scholarships

1999 West Adams Boulevard
Los Angeles, CA 90016
(800) 666-4763

Fields: Business, economics, life insurance, and related majors
Amount: Varies
The keys:
- Scholarships for outstanding students at the junior and senior levels.
- A minimum 3.0 GPA necessary.
- Only students/residents of Houston, California, and Detroit are eligible.
- Write for varying deadlines.

Guideposts Youth Writing Contest

c/o Guideposts Magazine
16 East 34th Street
New York, NY 10016
(212) 251-8100

Fields: General
Amount: $1,000 to $6,000 scholarships; 10 available
The keys:
- Students must write a first-person essay about an inspirational experience, preferably spiritual.
- Deadline: November 15.

Hallie Q. Brown Scholarship Fund

c/o National Association of Colored Women's Clubs, Inc.
5808 16th Street, N.W.
Washington, DC 20011
(202) 726-2044

Fields: General
Amount: Up to $1,000
The keys:
- Must be nominated by an NACWC member.
- Must be a U.S. citizen and have financial need.
- Offered biannually in even-numbered years.
- Deadline: March 31.

Hampton University

Hampton, VA 23668
(804) 727-5328 or (800) 624-3328

Fields: General and specific majors; from biology to mass media and more
Amount: Varies; nearly 50% of students receive grants or scholarships from college
The keys:
- All students who are accepted are considered for awards and assistance.
- Hampton, one of the most highly endowed HBCUs, has a lot of big-business and corporate-sponsored aid support.
- Competition is intense for the best awards.
- Deadline: March 15.
- FAFSA deadline: March 31.

The Harry S. Truman Scholarship Foundation

712 Jackson Place, N.W.
Washington, DC 20006
(202) 395-4831
Web site: www.truman.gov

Fields: General
Amount: $3,000 senior year, to $30,000 toward postgraduate study
The keys:
- Very prestigious award.
- You must be nominated by college as a junior with outstanding leadership potential and communication skills.
- You must intend to pursue a career in government or public service.
- 75 Truman scholars will be picked.
- Inquire at your college.

Health Science Collegiate Program

Navy Medical Programs
NRD Atlanta
2400 Herodian Way, Suite 400
Smyrna, GA 30080
(800) 282-1783

Fields: Pharmacy majors
Amount: $1,200 monthly stipend and benefits for active duty
The keys:
- Opportunities for students within 24 months of graduation from programs in pharmacy.
- Deadline: Ongoing.

The Herbert Lehman Fund

c/o Scholarships for African American Students
99 Hudson Street, Suite 1600
New York, NY 10013
(212) 219-1900

Fields: General
Amount: $1,400
The keys:
- Must be entering a college where African Americans are underrepresented.
- Write for application between November 1 and April 1.
- Deadline: April 15.

Horace Mann Scholarships

P.O. Box 20490
Springfield, IL 62798
Web contact: www.horaceman.com

Fields: General
Amount: $1,000 to $20,000
The keys:
- For children of public employees with outstanding records.
- Deadline: February 28.

I Have a Dream Foundation

330 Seventh Avenue
New York, NY 10001
(212) 293-5480

Fields: For younger students
Amount: Varies
The keys:
- You've seen this story on TV. Scholarships offered to entire junior high school classes!
- Write for details.

Improved and Benevolent Protective Order of Elks of the World

P.O. Box 159
Winston-Salem, NC 27986
(919) 358-7661

Fields: General
Amount: Varies
The keys:
- Largest fraternal organization in the world, awarding more than $2.5 million in scholarships to youth of all races.
- Write for information.

Indiana Minority Teacher Scholarships

c/o Student Assistance Commission
964 North Pennsylvania Street
Indianapolis, IN 46204
(317) 232-2350

Fields: Education majors
Amount: $1,000
The keys:
- Students must agree to teach in the state for at least two years.
- Write for details/information.

INROADS/Internships for African American Students

1221 Locust Street
St. Louis, MO 63103
(314) 341-7488

Fields: Business, communications, and engineering majors
Amount: Varies by internship
The keys:
- Must be a resident of Pittsburgh County.
- Deadline: January 31.

Intel Science Talent Search*

Science Service
1719 N Street, N.W.
Washington, DC 20036
(202) 785-2255
*Formerly Westinghouse Talent Search. Intel is the nation's oldest and most highly regarded scholarship and science competition.

Field: Varies, but must be original research project recognized by a national jury of scientists
Amount: The top 10 finalists receive totals from $100,000 (the winner) to $20,000; 300 semifinalists receive $5,000 each, as well as computers
The keys:
- An original research project that is impressive to a jury of esteemed scientists. Some past winners have gone on to become Nobel Laureates.
- A completed entry form signed by a teacher or adviser.
- A high school transcript.
- Call for official entry rules and forms; e-mail webmaster@sciserv.org, or visit http://www.sciserv.org/request.htm.
- Deadline: December 1.

International Benevolent Society, Inc.

837 Fifth Avenue
P.O. Box 1276
Columbus, GA 31902
(706) 322-5671

Fields: General
Amount: Varies
The keys:
- The society has more than 165 chapters in 11 states.
- Annual scholarships to members of the order.
- Write for scholarship and chapter information.

Iota Phi Lambda Sorority

503 Patterson Street
Tuskegee, AL 36088
(205) 727-5201 or
811 East 116 Street
Los Angeles, CA 90059

Fields: General and business majors
Amount: Varies
The keys:
- Scholarships to qualified students, including those with an interest in business.
- Write for information and chapter locations.

The Ivies

P.O. Box 1502A, Yale Station
New Haven, CT 06502

Fields: All majors
Amount: Varies
The keys:
- This is a resource group that helps students seeking admission and aid at the Ivy League schools: Harvard, Yale, Princeton, Cornell, Columbia, Penn, and Dartmouth.
- Write for information.

J. Victor Herd Memorial Scholarship

c/o Center for Insurance Education
Howard University
Washington, DC 20059
(202) 636-5118

Fields: A concentration of courses in insurance
Amount: Full tuition for junior and senior years
The keys:
- The school is looking for academic excellence and superior leadership qualities.

Jack and Jill America Foundation

P.O. Drawer 3689
Chattanooga, TN 37404
(615) 622-4476

Fields: General
Amount: Varies
The keys:
- Scholarships are available.
- Write for information and chapter lists.

Jackie Robinson Foundation Program

3 West 35th Street
New York, NY 10001-2202
(212) 290-8600

Fields: General
Amount: Varies
The keys:
- For high school seniors demonstrating academic achievement, leadership skills, and need.
- Deadline: April 1.

Kappa Alpha Psi Fraternity, Inc.

2320-24 North Broad Street
Philadelphia, PA 19132-4590
(215) 228-7184

Fields: General
Amount: Varies
The keys:
- There are nearly 700 chapters in the United States.
- Locate the one closest to you for scholarship possibilities and information.
- Call for assistance.

Kodak Minority Academic Scholarships

Eastern Kodak Company
343 State Street
Rochester, NY 14650
(716) 724-3127

Fields: General
Amount: Varies
The keys:
- Write for details.

Last Dollar Undergraduate Assistance Program

c/o Virginia State Council of Higher Education
James Monroe Building
101 North Fourteenth Street
Richmond, VA 23219
(804) 786-1690

Fields: General
Amount: $200 to $1,600; renewable
The keys:
- Must be a resident of the state of Virginia, enrolled in a public college.
- Deadline: June 1.

Lee Elder Scholarship Fund

1725 K Street, N.W., Suite 1112
Washington, DC 20006

Fields: General
Amount: Varies
The keys:
- For students with academic achievement, career goals, and need.

Links, Inc. (Scholarship Program)

P.O. Box 2343
Attn: Laura Rycraw
Orange, CA 92669-0343 or
1200 Massachusetts Avenue
Washington, DC 20005
(202) 842-8686

Fields: General majors
Amount: Varies
The keys:
- More than 240 chapters with more than 8,000 members.
- Find the one closest to you for scholarship possibilities and information.

Lutheran Brotherhood Senior College Scholarships

c/o Scholarships
625 4th Avenue South
Minneapolis, MN 55415
(800) 328-7168 or (612) 340-8028

Fields: General
Amount: To $2,000; more than 800 available
The keys:
- For students who are Lutheran or who attend a Lutheran college.

Lutheran Church Women Scholarship

c/o Lutheran Church Women
2900 Queen Lane
Philadelphia, PA 19144
(215) 848-3418

Fields: General
Amount: To $1,500
The keys:
- Female students must be members of the Lutheran Church of America.
- Deadline: February 1.

Mary McLeod Bethune Scholarship Challenge Grant

Florida Department of Education
1344 Florida Education Center
Tallahassee, FL 32399-0400
(904) 487-0049

Fields: General
Amount: $3,000; renewable for four years
The keys:
- For Florida residents enrolled at the following HBCUs: Florida A&M, Florida Memorial, Edward Waters, and Bethune-Cookman College.
- Write for details and deadline dates.

Maryland State Scholarship Board

2100 Guilford Avenue
Baltimore, MD 21218
(410) 974-5350

Fields: Education majors
Amount: Varies
The keys:
- Future teachers; must agree to work in a "critical shortage" area for one year.
- Write or call for details.

Maxwell House Coffee Minority Scholarship

250 North Street
White Plains, NY 10625
(914) 335-2500

Fields: General
Amount: $3,000
The keys:
- Students must be headed to an HBCU.
- Graduates from New York, Chicago, Detroit, St. Louis, Newark, and Baltimore are eligible.
- Write for more information.

Michael Jackson Scholarship for the Performing Arts

c/o United Negro College Fund
8260 Willow Oaks
Corporate Drive
P.O. Box 10444
Fairfax, VA 22031-4511
Main office: (212) 326-1258

Fields: Performing arts
Amount: Varies
The keys:
- Student must be enrolled in a UNCF college with good grades (2.5+ GPA) and need.
- Contact the financial aid office at your school.

Microsoft Corporation

National Minority Technical Scholarships
One Microsoft Way
Redmond, WA 98052-8303
e-mail: scholar@microsoft.com

Fields: Computer science, engineering, and
related disciplines
Amount: $1,000; 10 available
The keys:
■ Must have interest in the PC/software industry
and be an outstanding student (sophomore or
junior) with a 3.0 GPA or higher.
■ Deadline: February 26.

Minority Scholarships

c/o American Architectural Foundation
Director AIA/AAF Scholarship Program
1735 New York Avenue, N.W.
Washington, DC 20006
(202) 626-7511
Web site: www.alaonline.com

Fields: Architecture
Amount: Varies
The keys:
■ For high school seniors and community
college students entering four-year degree
programs at schools of architecture.
■ Deadline: January 15.

Minority Scholarships

American Institute of Certified Public
Accountants
1211 Avenue of the Americas
New York, NY 10036-8775
(212) 575-7641

Fields: Accounting major
Amount: More than 700 renewable scholarships
in the $500 to $2,000 range
The keys:
■ Must have completed 30 credits with a 3.0
GPA.
■ Deadline: July 1.

The Music Assistance Fund/American Symphony Orchestra League

1158 15th Street., N.W., Suite 800
Washington, DC 20005-1704
(212) 580-8700

Fields: For those seeking symphony orchestra
careers
Amount: Up to $3,500
The keys:
■ Scholarships are based on live auditions. You
should demonstrate outstanding skill and
promise. Your goal: to play in a symphony
orchestra.
■ Deadline: December: 15.

NAACP ACT-SO (Afro-Academic, Cultural, Technological, and Scientific) Olympics

c/o NAACP Los Angeles Chapter
3910 Martin Luther King Jr. Boulevard,
Suite 202
Los Angeles, CA 90008
(213) 296-2630

Fields: Talent in humanities, sciences, or visual
and performing arts
Amount: Varies
The keys:
■ This is a nationwide academic and talent com-
petition.
■ Contact high school adviser.
■ Deadline: March 31; April 26 to submit
projects.
■ Write for ACT-SO, Olympics of the Mind
history and competition rules.

NAACP Honeywell Engineering Scholarships

c/o Director of Education
4805 Mount Hope Drive
Baltimore, MD 21215
(301) 358-8900

NAACP Honeywell Engineering Scholarships (continued)

Fields: Engineering majors
Amount: $4,000
The keys:
- For engineering students with a 3.0 GPA or higher.
- Scholarships are targeted for students at Howard, Hampton, Georgia Tech, Tuskegee, Florida A&M, MIT, and several other schools. Inquire.
- Deadline: April 30.

The NAACP Willems Scholarship Education Division

4805 Mount Hope Drive
Baltimore, MD 21215-1704
(301) 358-8900

Fields: Chemistry, physics, math, and computer sciences
Amount: $2,000; must reapply
The keys:
- Must be a U.S. citizen with a 3.0 GPA or B average.
- Preference to NAACP members.
- Deadline: April 30.

NABA National Scholarship

c/o National Association of Black Accountants, Inc.
7249-A Hanover Parkway
Greenbelt, MD 20770
(202) 543-6656

Fields: General business, including accounting and finance
Amount: $500 to $6,000
The keys:
- Must be NABA member with a GPA of 2.5 or higher.
- Twelve credits in accounting should be completed by the end of the spring semester in which you apply.
- Deadline: January 31.

National Achievement Scholarship Program for Outstanding Negro Students

One American Plaza
1560 Sherman Avenue
Evanston, IL 60201

Fields: General
Amount: $2,000 to $8,000 annually; 700 available
The keys:
- This is a major, prestigious award based on your score on the PSAT test.
- Merit scholars qualify here.
- Your grade adviser will inform you of test dates.

National Action Council for Minorities in Engineering, Inc. Scholarship Programs

3 West 35th Street
New York, NY 10001-2264
(212) 279-2626, ext. 218

Fields: Engineering majors
Amount: Varies
The keys:
- Said to be the largest source of minority engineering scholarships.
- NACME aims to increase the number of minority engineers.
- Deadline: on going.

National Alliance for Excellence

Merit Competition for High School and College Students
Scholarship Foundation of America
55 Highway 35, Suite 5
Red Bank, NJ 07701
(908) 747-0028

Fields: Excellence in performing or visual arts
Amount: $1,000 and higher; 50 available
The keys:
- You must write for an application and send an SASE.
- You must have performing or art talent, including a good academic record.
- Deadline: Ongoing.

National Association for Sickle Cell Disease, Inc.

4221 Wilshire Boulevard, Suite 360
Los Angeles, CA 90010-3503
(213) 936-7205

Fields: General
Amount: Varies
The keys:
- Based on essay submitted.

National Association of Black Journalists

c/o College Attendees Program
University of Maryland
Taliaferro Building, Suite 3100
College Park, MD 20742
(301) 405-8500

Fields: Journalism
Amount: $2,500; 10 available
The keys:
- For minority students majoring in Journalism.
- A writing sample and extras must be submitted.
- Deadline: March 10.

National Association of Black Journalists Scholarships

c/o Scholarship Coordinator
P.O. Box 17212
Washington, DC 20041
(703) 648-1283

Fields: An interest in writing/journalism.
Amount: $2,500
The keys:
- Scholarships for promise in journalism.
- Deadline: fall.

National Association of Black Sales Professionals

P.O. Box 5303
River Forest, IL 60305
(708) 445-1010

Fields: General
Amount: Varies
The keys:
- NABSP scholarships are for achieving students who are promising sales professionals.

National Association of Letter Carriers Scholarships

100 Indiana Ave., N.W.
Washington, DC 20001
(202) 393-4695

Fields: General
Amount: $800; 15 available
The keys:
For freshman children of those in the organization.

National Association of Plumbing, Heating, Cooling Contractors

Educational Foundation Scholarship
P.O. Box 6808
Falls Church, VA 22040
(703) 237-8100

Fields: Construction-related fields
Amount: $3,000
The keys:
- Seniors and/or freshmen must be sponsored by an NAPHCC member.
- Finalists will be asked to present transcripts and recommendations.
- Deadline: April 1.

National Association of Realtors

430 North Michigan Avenue
Chicago, IL 60611
(312) 329-8296

Fields: Related majors
Amount: $500 to $1,500
The keys:
- Scholarships for students interested in a career in real estate.
- Deadlines: the 15th of April, October, and December.

National Basketball Association (NBA) Scholarships

645 Fifth Avenue
New York, NY 10022
(212) 826-7000

Fields: Education majors
Amount: $2,500; 10 available
The keys:
- For high school seniors who are college-bound, intend to become educators, and live in a community with an NBA team.
- Grades, an essay, and recommendations are necessary.
- Deadline: February 15.

National Black Caucus of Local Elected Officials

1301 Pennsylvania Ave, 6th Floor
Washington, DC 20004
(202) 626-3120

Fields: General
Amount: Varies
The keys:
- Contact the National Black Caucus and your local elected officials for assistance.

National Black Lawyers Association

1225 11th Street, N.W.
Washington, DC 20001
(202) 583-1281

Fields: General
Amount: Varies
The keys:
- Write for scholarship information.

National Black M.B.A. Association

180 North Michigan Avenue, Suite 1820
Chicago, IL 60601
(312) 236-2622

Fields: Business majors
Amount: Varies

The keys:
- More than 24 chapters and more than 2,000 members across the United States. Locate the chapter closest to you for scholarship possibilities and information.
- Call or write for guidance.

National Black Nurses Association, Inc.

1511 K Street, N.W.
Washington, DC 20005

Fields: Nursing major
Amount: Up to $2,000
The keys:
- Must be in a nursing program, and a member of NBNA.
- Good scholastic record important, with involvement with nursing and community activities a plus.
- Deadline: April 15.

National Black Police Association (NBPA) Scholarship

3251 Mount Pleasant Street, N.W.
Washington, D.C. 20010-2103
(202) 986-2070

Fields: General
Amount: $500
The keys:
- For a freshman studying at a community college.
- Student must be in the top three-fifths of the class with at least a 2.5 GPA.
- This group is looking for depth of character, a service orientation, and an interest in law or law enforcement.
- Deadline: June 1.

National Civilian Community Corps Program

Recruitment Division
1100 Vermont Avenue, N.W. 11th Floor
Washington, DC 20525
(800) 94-ACORTS

Fields: General
Amount: Varies
The keys:
- Write for details.

National Coalition of 100 Black Women

50 Rockefeller Plaza, Concourse Level,
    Room 46
New York, NY 10020
(212) 974-6140

Fields: General
Amount: Varies
The keys:
- Write for scholarship information.

National Federation of Music Clubs Competitions and Awards

1336 North Delaware Street
Indianapolis, IN 46202
(317) 638-4003

Fields: Music
Amount: Up to $10,000
The keys:
- You must send $1 and an SASE, requesting a list of over 100 scholarships and awards in the music area.
- Auditions are required.
- Deadline: varies.

National Federation of Press Women, Inc.

P.O. Box 99
1105 Main Street
Blue Springs, MO 64015
(816) 229-1666

Fields: Women journalism majors
Amount: Varies
The keys:
- Must be a junior or a senior majoring in journalism.
- Deadline: February 1.

National Foster Parent Association

c/o Scholarship Chair
Information and Services Office
Houston, TX 77024
(713) 467-1850

Fields: General
Amount: Determined by trust fund
The keys:
- Scholarship is for foster and adopted children affiliated with NFPA.
- Deadline: March 1.

National Foundation for the Advancement of the Arts

3915 Biscayne Boulevard
Miami, FL 33137
(305) 377-1140

Fields: Dance, theater, music, art, film, or writing
Amount: Varies
The keys:
- Must be a high school senior with talent in one of the areas listed.
- Deadline: April 15 or October 1.

National Foundation for the Advancement of the Arts (Talent Search)

c/o NFAA
800 Brickell Avenue, Suite 500
Miami, FL 33131
(800) 970-2787

Fields: N.A.
Amount: $100 to $3,000
The keys:
- This is a talent competition for scholarships.
- Submit an audiotape or videotape.
- More than 300 scholarships available.

National Honor Society

c/o National Assoc. of Secondary School
    Principals (NASSP)
1902 Association Drive
Reston, VA 20191-1537
(703) 860-0200

National Honor Society (continued)

Fields: General
Amount: 150 $1,000 awards; one $10,000 national award
The keys:
- Must be a National Honor Society member with an excellent academic and extracurricular record.
- School principals nominate two students from each school.
- Deadline: December 15.

National Pan-Hellenic Council, Inc.

Suite 30, IMU
Bloomington, IN 27405
(812) 855-8820

Fields: General
Amount: Varies
The keys:
- This is the coordinating agency for eight major historically black sororities/fraternities with more than 1.5 million members. It's your gateway to finding numbers and addresses to those groups and their scholarships.
- Write for information.

National Presbyterian College Scholarship

c/o Presbyterian Church (USA)
100 Witherspoon Street
Louisville, KY 40202-1396

Fields: General
Amount: $500 to $1,400
The keys:
- Must be Presbyterian Church member headed to a Presbyterian-related university.
- Students must have over a 3.0 GPA, submit SAT/ACT scores, and have need.
- Deadline: December 1.
- Also national loan program ($200 to $2,000). Inquire.

National Press Photographers Foundation, Inc.

c/o Director
4029 N.E. 204th Street
Seattle, WA 98155
(919) 383-7246

Fields: Photography
Amount: Varies
The keys:
- Must show aptitude for photography and intend to pursue it as a career.
- Write for information.
- Deadline: February 1.

National Scholarship Trust Fund

4615 Forbes Avenue
Pittsburgh, PA 15213
(412) 621-6941

Fields: Graphic arts majors
Amount: From $500 to $1,000
The keys:
- A wide range of art/graphic arts scholarships available.
- Candidates must aim to pursue a career in graphic arts.
- Academic record/extracurricular activities a factor.
- Deadline: March 1.

National Security Agency

c/o Undergraduate Training Program
Attn.: M322 (UTP)
Fort Meade, MD 20755-6000
(800) 962-9398

Fields: Computer and electrical engineering, math, science, or language majors
Amount: Full tuition with other benefits
The keys:
- This government organization is looking for strong students (3.0 GPAs and higher), who are willing to work summers at the NSA.
- Write for application and details.

National Society of Professional Engineers

Scholarships Education Foundation
2029 K Street, N.W.
Washington, DC 20006
(202) 463-2300

Fields: Engineering majors
Amount: $1,000; more than 150 available
The keys:
- Very high SATs required, including a math score in the 600 range.
- Deadline: September 1.

National Sorority of Phi Delta Kappa, Inc.

8233 South King Drive
Chicago, IL 69615
(312) 783-7379

Fields: General
Amount: Varies
The keys:
- Sorority of more than 5,000 members. More than $50,000 in scholarships awarded.
- Write for scholarship information and chapter locations.

National Space Club

655 15th Street, N.W., #300
Washington, DC 20005
(202) 639-4210

Fields: Aerospace science majors
Amount: Varies
The keys:
- For students who plan to pursue a career in aerospace or related technologies.
- Deadline: January 1.

National Student Nurses Association Foundation

555 West 57th Street
New York, NY 10019
(212) 581-2215

Fields: Nursing majors

Amount: Varies
The keys:
- Must be enrolled in a program leading to a nursing degree.
- Excellent grades, community service, and need.
- Deadline: February 1.
- Send an SASE envelope with 55 cent postage for information.

National Urban League Scholarship

c/o GRANDMET Scholarship
120 Wall Street
New York, NY 10005
(212) 310-9000

Fields: General
Amount: $1,000; 15 available
The keys:
- Scholarships are for minority high school and college students who are achieving academically.
- Deadline: April 26.

National Urban League Scholarships (Duracell)

120 Wall Street
New York, NY 10005
(212) 310-9000

Fields: Business, engineering
Amount: $10,000 and internship during junior and senior years
The keys:
- Interest in business fields and engineering.
- Sophomores ranking in the top 25% of their class.

Navy Recruiting Command

Code 314
4015 Wilson Boulevard
Arlington, VA 22203
1-800-USA-NAVY

Fields: ROTC programs: part- and full-time
Amount: Stipends for a commitment to serve for varying times
The keys:
- Write or call for specifics.

NCR Foundation Minority Scholarship Program

c/o College Relations Manager
NCR Corporation
1700 South Patterson Boulevard
Dayton, OH 45479
(513) 445-1337

Fields: Business, engineering, computer science, accounting, or a related major
Amount: $5,000; renewable for three years
The keys:
- This, the Paul Laurence Dunbar Memorial Scholarship, is for achieving students.

Negro Educationa\l Emergency Drive

2003 Law and Finance Building
429 Fourth Avenue
Pittsburgh, PA 15219
(412) 566-2760

Fields: General
Amount: $100 to $500
The keys:
- For high school students who are accepted to college and who might be considered "average" achievers with need.
- Write for details/application.

New York Philharmonic Music Fund and Scholarship Program

Avery Fisher Hall
Broadway and 65th Street
New York, NY 10023
(212) 580-8700

Fields: Music
Amount: Varies
The keys:
- Music/talent scholarships are available.

The New York Times College Scholarship Program

R&R Education Consultants
Columbia University Station
P.O. Box 250861
New York, NY 10025-1507

Fields: General
Amount: $15,000; renewable to four years; four available
The keys:
- For college-bound high school students who are enrolled in New York City schools.
- High achievement necessary, as well as a commitment to make significant contributions to society and "overcome barriers."
- No restriction on college choice.
- Deadline: November 2. Write for details.

Nuclear Energy Training Program

c/o Oak Ridge Associated Universities
P.O. Box 117
Oak Ridge, TN 37831
(615) 576-3428
Fields: General
Amount: Varies
The keys:
- Seven HBCUs are involved; write for details.

Omega Psi Phi Fraternity, Inc.

c/o International Headquarters
2714 Georgia Avenue, N.W.
Washington, DC 20001
(202) 667-7158

Fields: General
Amount: $500 to $1,000
The keys:
- Locate chapter nearest you for details (more than 660 nationwide).
- For members and nonmembers.

Orville Redenbacher's Second Start Scholarships

P.O. Box 39101
Chicago, IL 60639

Fields: General majors
Amount: Varies
The keys:
- Scholarships for students 30 and over just beginning studies.
- Write for guidelines.

Pacific Gas and Electric Company

77 Beale Street, Room F-1500
San Francisco, CA 94106
(415) 972-1338

Fields: General majors
Amount: $1,000
The keys:

- For students accepted to college who have overcome despite cultural, economic, or other disadvantages.
- The student must reside near a PGEC Service area.
- Contact your adviser.
- Deadline: November 15.

Paul Douglas Teaching Scholarship Program

U.S. Department of Education
Seventh and D Streets, S.W.
Washington, DC 20202-5447
(202) 732-4507

Fields: Education
Amount: $5,000; renewable
The keys:

- Must be enrolled in state-supported teaching program.
- This is a nationwide scholarship program, involving all 50 states.
- You must teach at least two years in the target state for each year's award.

Pepsi-Cola's Summer Internship Program

c/o College Recruiting Manager
Pepsi-Cola Company
Somers, NY 10589
(914) 767-7434

Fields: General; business a plus
Amount: $2,000 (for interns)
The keys:

- Scholarships and internships for sophomores.
- African-Americans students interested in finance, sales, and related areas.

Phi Beta Sigma Fraternity

145 Kennedy Street. N.W.
Washington, DC 20011
(202) 726-5424

Fields: General
Amount: Varies
The keys:

- Scholarships for qualified students.
- Write for instructions and chapter information.

Presidential Scholars Award Committee

Florida A&M University
P.O. Box 599
Tallahassee, FL 32307
(800) 599-3796

Fields: General and specific science majors
Amount: $1,000 to full tuition (many available)
The keys:

- Scholarships are awarded by committee selection.
- Outstanding students only, with academic and leadership achievement.
- Looking for National Achievement and National Merit Scholars.
- Deadline: April 1.
- Your admissions application puts you in the running.

PUSH for Excellence College-Bound Program

Excel Scholarship Committee
Operation PUSH Headquarters
930 East 50th Street
Chicago, IL 60615

Fields: General
Amount: Varies
The keys:

- Write to PUSH for Excellence instructions.

Radio Technical Commission for Aeronautics

(William Jackson Award)
1717 H Street, N.W.
Washington, DC 20006

Fields: Interest in aviation or telecommunications
Amount: Varies
The keys:
- Essay required to win scholarship.

Ralph McGill Scholarship Fund

c/o The Atlanta Constitution
P.O. Box 4689
Atlanta, GA 30302
(404) 526-5526

Fields: Newspaper journalism
Amount: Varies
The keys:
- For juniors and seniors from the South who are interested in newspaper work and have maintained at least a 3.0 GPA.
- Application deadline: May 1.

Ron Brown Scholars Program

The Jordan Building
1160 Pepsi Place, Suite 110-B
Charlottesville, VA 22901
(804) 964-1588

Fields: All fields, with a goal of service to others with impact
Amount: $10,000 per year to $40,000
The keys:
- Academic excellence; excellent leadership potential; service to others; need.
- Twenty scholars selected annually.
- Deadline: January 9.

The Roothbert Fund

360 Park Avenue South, 15th Floor
New York, NY 10010
(212) 679-2030

Fields: Education

Amount: $1,200; 56 available
The keys:
- Scholarships are for students with character and strong spiritual values, and who hope to become teachers.
- Must be residents of New York City, Washington, D.C., Philadelphia, or Providence.
- Deadline: March 1.

The Roy Wilkins Scholarship

NAACP Education Division
4805 Mount Hope Drive
Baltimore, MD 21215-3297
(301) 358-8900

Fields: General
Amount: $1,000
The keys:
- Must be an entering freshman with a 2.5 GPA or better.
- Preference to NAACP members.
- Write for information. Enclose a self-addressed, stamped envelope.
- Deadline: April 30.

Sachs Foundation Professional Award

c/o United Bank Tower
90 South Cascade Avenue
Colorado Springs, CO 80903
(719) 633-2353

Fields: General
Amount: $3,000; more than 40 scholarships available
The keys:
- For African Americans in Colorado with a minimum GPA of 3.4.
- Deadline: March 1.

Scholarships for Children of Military Personnel

Scamp Scholarship Fund
c/o Coordinator
136 South Fuller Avenue
Los Angeles, CA 90036
(213) 934-2288

Fields: General
Amount: $3,500
The keys:
- Parent must be a veteran.
- Deadline: April 1.

Scholastic, Inc.

Scholastic Art or Writing Awards
555 Broadway
New York, NY 10012
(800) 631-1586

Fields: Interest in art or writing
Amount: $100 to $5,000
The keys:
- An art and writing competition for students in high school.
- Write for submission guidelines. Enclose an SASE.

Scholastic Visual Awards Scholarships

(Portfolio Entry Form)
555 Broadway
New York, NY 10012
(800) 631-1586

Fields: Art and photography majors
Amount: $1,000 to $5,000
The keys:
- A portfolio must be presented displaying outstanding talent in either art or photography.
- Write for portfolio form and dates for submission.

School for Field Studies

376 Hale Street
Beverly, MA 01915
(508) 927-7777

Fields: Related majors and research interest
Amount: Varies
The keys:
- Scholarships for high school students and undergraduates who want to be involved with research/scientific expeditions and environmental concerns.

Selena Brown Book Scholarship

c/o National Association Of Black Social
  Workers Scholarship Committee
8436 West McNichols Street
Detroit, MI 48221

Fields: General
Amount: Varies
The keys:
- Must be an active NABSW member. At least a 2.5 GPA is desirable, with a service profile and an interest in doing research in the black community.
- Deadline: January 1.

Shell Oil Companies Competition

Two Shell Plaza
P.O. Box 2099
Houston, Texas 77001
(715) 241-4511

Fields: Business and technical majors
Amount: Varies; more than 50 available
The keys:
- Scholarships are for those pursuing a career in business or technology.
- Deadline: Ongoing.

Sigma Gamma Rho Sorority, Inc.

840 East 87th Street
Chicago, IL 60619
(312) 873-9000

Fields: General
Amount: Varies
The keys:
- Scholarships for academic and social achievement.
- Locate the closest local chapter (more than 400, with more than 72,000 members) for scholarship possibilities and details.

Snap Technologies Scholarship Essay Contest

Snap Technologies, Inc.
161 Townsend Street, #333
San Francisco, CA 94107

Fields: Technology majors
Amount: Varies
The keys:
- Must e-mail for instructions:
  scholarships@snapweb.com.

Soroptimist International

c/o Soroptimist Foundation
2 Penn Center Plaza, Suite 1000
Philadelphia, PA 19102
(215) 732-0512

Fields: General
Amount: $1,250; 54 available
The keys:
- These scholarships are directed at students who show superior leadership, as well as service to their schools and communities.
- Deadline: December 15.

Stanley E. Jackson Scholarship

Foundation for Exceptional Children
1920 Association Drive
Baltimore, MD 21215-3297
(703) 620-1054

Fields: General
Amount: $500
The keys:
- For disabled minority students. Financial need.

State Farm Companies Foundation

One State Farm Plaza
Bloomington, IL 61701
(309) 766-2039

Fields: Business, math, prelaw, or computer science majors
Amount: Varies

The keys:
- Must be a junior or a senior with an exceptional academic record.
- You must be nominated by a dean or a department head.
- Deadline: February 28.

The Sutton Education Scholarship

c/o NAACP Education Division
4805 Mount Hope Drive
Baltimore, MD 21215-3297
(301) 358-8900

Fields: Education
Amount: $1,000; you can reapply for second year
The keys:
- Preference given to NAACP members.
- 2.5 GPA desirable.
- Deadline: April 30.

Thurgood Marshall Scholarship Fund

100 Park Avenue, 10th Floor
New York, NY 10017
(212) 878-2220

Fields: General
Amount: $4,000 (renewable)
The keys:
- For students enrolling at historically black colleges.
- 3.0+ GPA desirable, with an SAT score over 1000.

The Tillie Golub-Schwartz Memorial Scholarship

c/o Scholarship Committee
Golub Corporation
P.O. 1074
Schenectady, NY 12301

Fields: General major
Amount: $2,000 for each of four years
The keys:
- Minority student must show a commitment to improving humanity and the world.
- Write for information.

Tuskegee Airmen Scholarship Fund

c/o Tuskegee Airmen, Inc.
P.O. Box 19063
Chicago, IL 60619-0063
(773) 224-0776

Fields: Aviation or related aeronautics f
ields
Amount: Varies
The keys:
■ Write for guidelines.

United Federation of Teachers (UFT)

c/o Scholarship Fund
260 Park Avenue South
New York, NY 10010
(212) 777-7500

Fields: General
Amount: $1,000
The keys:
■ Students must be graduates of a New York
City high school with an interest in pursuing
an education career.
■ Applications can be obtained at all New York
City high schools.

United Negro College Fund

8260 Willow Oaks
Corporate Drive
Fairfax, VA 22031
(800) 331-2244

Fields: General and specific majors
Amount: Varies
The keys:
■ Scholarships are awarded to students enrolled
in 41 member HBCU schools.
■ Write for scholarship information and instruc-
tions.
■ Deadline: Varies.

Veterans Service Officer

100 South Lawrence Street
Montgomery, AL 36104
(205) 832-4950, ext. 392 or 393

Fields: General
Amount: Varies
The keys:
■ For dependents of veterans.
■ Write or call for details and instructions.

Virginia State Council of Higher Education

c/o Scholarships
James Monroe Building
101 North 14th Street
Richmond, VA 23219
(804) 225-2141

Fields: Education
Amount: Varies
The keys:
■ Student must be in the top 10% of his or her
high school graduating class and be enrolled in
a teacher education program.
■ Write for information.

Wal-Mart Competitive Edge Scholarships

Wal-Mart Stores
702 S.W. Eighth Street
Bentonville, AR 72716
(800) 966-6546
Web site: www.wal-mart.com/compedge

Fields: Must be a manufacturing, industry, or
technology major attending or planning to
attend one of 140 colleges; you must write for
a list
Amount: About 250 students each year win
$5,000 stipends; they are renewable
The keys:
■ Over 1100 on SAT with at least a 3.5 GPA.
■ Must be a high school graduating senior, or in
college.
■ Deadline: March 1.

Westinghouse Electric Corporation

Bertha Lamme-Westinghouse
  Scholarships
Society of Women Engineers
345 East 47th Street, Room 305
New York, NY 10017
(212) 509-9577

Fields: Engineering major
Amount: $1,000
The keys:
- For female high school senior; must write essay on why she is entering the engineering field.
- Character and teacher references and good academic record necessary.
- Deadline: May 15.

William Randolph Hearst Foundation

Senate Youth Program
90 New Montgomery Street, #1212
San Francisco, CA 94105
(800) 841-7048

Fields: General
Amount: Varies
The keys:
- Award includes scholarship and week's trip to Senate.
- For students holding elective offices in school.

William Randolph Hearst Foundation

90 New Montgomery Street, #1212
San Francisco, CA 94105
(415) 543-4057

Fields: Journalism majors
Amount: Varies
The keys:
- Hearst Scholarships are awarded at more than 90 participating colleges.
- Write for information and deadlines.

Wisconsin Minority Student Grant Program

c/o Higher Education Aids Board
P.O. 7885
Madison, WI 53707-7885
(608) 267-2206

Fields: Government majors
Amount: Varies
The keys:
- For students who have attended a summer institute, are interested in a career in government, and have completed their junior year.
- Write for details.

Woodrow Wilson National Minority Access Foundation

c/o Director
CN 5281
Princeton, NJ 08543
(609) 924-4666

Fields: Public policy or international affairs
Amount: Varies
The keys:
- For a student seeking a career in government related areas.
- Deadline: Inquire.

World Institute of Black Communications, Inc.

10 Columbus Circle
New York, NY 10019
(212) 586-1771

Fields: Advertising
Amount: $1,000 to $2,000
The keys:
- For students who have been in the internship program of the American Association of Advertising Agencies.
- Write for details.

Xavier University

Palmetto and Pine Streets
New Orleans, LA 70125
(504) 486-7411

Fields: General, science, and arts majors
Amount: Varies to full tuition
The keys:
- Xavier administers and/or participates in many scholarship/grant programs, including ONR Future Scientists, ROUSSEVE Scholars, General Motors, and the UNCF program.
- Deadline: March 1 for admissions application.
- Selections are from the accept pool.

Xerox Corporation

Technical Minority Scholarships
Corporate Employment and College Relations
800 Phillips Road
Webster, NY 15480
(716) 422-7689

Fields: Technical sciences, chemistry, or engineering majors
Amount: Varies to $4,000
The keys:
- Student must be in a technical degree program.
- Academic excellence required.

Zeta Phi Beta Sorority, Inc.

1734 New Hampshire Avenue, N.W.
Washington, DC 20009
(202) 387-3103

Fields: General
Amount: Varies; to $2,500
The keys:
- For academic achievement.
- Contact nearest chapter for details.

PART THREE

THE COLLEGES

CHAPTER 16

TOP COLLEGES FOR AFRICAN AMERICAN STUDENTS

H ere are profiles of more than 100 top colleges for black students. The profiles are organized by state and include a mix of private and public schools, as well as both historically black colleges and predominantly white colleges and universities.

Remember that our tuition figures (and sometimes room and board costs) are based on recent numbers provided by the colleges. The numbers generally do not reflect the final "price tag." College aid packages include grants, work-study, and/or scholarships that reduce your cost. It's essential to contact the individual schools for real ballpark figures.

The handshake icons represent historically black colleges.

ALABAMA A&M UNIVERSITY	Director of Admissions P.O. Box 908 Normal, AL 35762 (256) 851-5245 Web site: www.aamu.edu	**Application deadline:** July 15 **1999–2000 Tuition:** $2,076 (residents); room and board, $2,930

ALABAMA

College Ranking

Alabama A&M is a large, academically sound historically black university.

The Campus

At Alabama A&M University, the famous Wilson Building overlooks everything. The "rolling" 1,201-acre campus—"The Hill"—is located in the Appalachian foothills of northern Alabama and sits on green lawns. You can actually drive from this state-supported school and be in downtown Huntsville within minutes. At AAMU, at the main 200-acre campus, you have five undergraduate schools to choose from: the Schools of Arts and Sciences; Education; Business; Engineering and Technology; and Agricultural and Environmental Sciences. There are 55 buildings on campus, including 12 residences and two "vibrant living" Learning Centers. The West and Foster complexes have apartment-style suites, aerobics rooms, banquet halls, and computer labs. The regular dorms include Hopkins Hall for men and Thomas Hall for women. More than 3,000 students can be accommodated on campus.

At AAMU you'll also find a state-of-the-art Telecommunications Center. Also, there's the J. F. Drake Memorial Learning Library, with more than 400,000 volumes. In the James Wilson Building (a historic landmark) you will find the "State Black Archives," Research Center, and Museum. A recent photographic exhibit presented there was "Black Women Against the Odds." More than 500 computer workstations are at locations about the campus. Students hang out at "The Quad" or visit the LRC Auditorium to see films such as *Do the Right Thing* or *Waiting to Exhale.* Bibb Graves Auditorium is the spot for large affairs such as the Student Convocation.

According to the AAMU Challenge Council Campaign, things are looking up. It says: "The State of Alabama has recently allotted AAMU $1 million toward its endowment over a 15-year period." Okay?

Campus Life

At AAMU there are more than 100 clubs, organizations, and special-interest groups. The major fraternities and sororities as well as the Pan-Hellenic Council are on campus. There's an annual *Stepshow* at Elmore Gymnasium. There's a Baptist Student Union, NAACP, Toastmaster International, Nigerian Student Association, Circle K Club, Chemistry Club, Masonic Club, Islamic and Christian organizations, University Choir, Gospel Choir, Pershing Rifles (male/female), AAMU Jazz Band, and University Players (Mainstage and Stage II). Also, the "La Sophistication" Models and Rare Elegance Modeling Troupes present annual fashion "extravaganzas." Important events include Miss Maroon and White Pageant, Greek Organization Initiation Week, Annual Christmas Musical, and Women's and Men's Week.

At AAMU the NCAA Division I Bulldogs have some strong teams. Louis Crew Stadium is a $10-million-plus complex with 21,000 seats. You can go to the "Magic City Classic" and see your team play (perhaps) Alabama State in football. Also, you can enjoy the Maroonettes and the Marching "Maroon and White" Band. You've got, too, intramural sports. The school's gym has 7,000 seats, an Olympic-size pool, and a health education complex.

Academic Realities

Freshmen are required to take "Survival Skills for University Skills." To make the coveted Honor Roll you must have a 3.3 grade-point average or higher. Stars? Dr. Arthur J. Bond, the dean of the School of Engineering and Technology, is called the "father" of the National Society of Black Engineers (NSBE). Indeed, the school has forged strong relationships with some of Huntsville's and the nation's top industries—the U.S. Army, Motorola, NASA, and Boeing. The school brags that 85% of its premed students enroll in medical schools across the country.

Getting In

The acceptance rate is 64%, and the average ACT score is 17. In a recent year 1,916 applied and 1,227 were accepted. Nearly 67% of the students are from Alabama, with the balance from 38 states and several foreign countries. There are approximately 3,500 full-time students. The most popular majors are Business, Education (about 22% each), Engineering (14%), and Biology (7%).

**TUSKEGEE
UNIVERSITY**

Old Administration Building,
Suite 101
Tuskegee, AL 36088
(334) 727-8500
Web site: www.tusk.edu

Financial aid deadline: As
soon as possible after January
1. Tuskegee requires the CSS
profile and FAFSA.
Application deadline: April 15.
Applications will be considered up to four weeks before
registration.
Early decision deadline:
March 15
1999–2000 tuition: $9,762;
room and board, $4,946

College Ranking

This school, the only one designated a National Historic Landmark by the U.S. Congress, was
founded by Booker T. Washington in 1881. It's the home of the legendary "Tuskegee Airmen"
and it's one of only two colleges today funded by NASA to develop a technology to grow food
in space during future space missions.

This liberal arts and science college talks about "building the values that strengthen America" while providing "educational programs of exceptional quality." Tuskegee's high rank,
strength, and reputation, are based on the continued impact and contributions of its graduates
nationwide. Tuskegee is the number-one producer of African American aerospace science engineers in the nation. Tuskegee has also graduated more black generals than any other historically
black college. If you're interested in becoming a vet, it's the place to be. This is the only black
institution to offer a doctor of veterinary medicine. It has graduated more than 70% of the vets
of color in this country.

The award-winning novelist, Ralph Ellison, is a Tuskegee alumnus. The television and movie
entertainer Keenan Ivory Wayans also is a graduate.

The Campus

Tuskegee is in Macon County, Alabama, about 40 miles from Montgomery, the capital. In 1882,
Dr. Washington purchased an abandoned 100-acre plantation that's now the nucleus of the present campus, covering more than 5,000 acres. The central location has more than 150 buildings,
including the various colleges and residence halls.

Most of the structures are either of "modern" or "historic" architecture, generally surrounded
by lawns and trees. There's Band Cottage, the oldest building on campus (1889); the Old
Administrative Building (which students built themselves), Tompkins Hall; and the Daniel
"Chappie" James Convocation Arena, which is dedicated to the first African American four-star
general, himself a graduate of Tuskegee. The Kellogg Conference Center has 108 lodging
suites, a 300-seat amphitheater, 20 meeting rooms, and a fitness center. "The Oaks" is the former home of Dr. Washington (1899) and a visitors' favorite. Another centerpiece on campus is
the Booker T. Washington Monument.

TU comprises five colleges: the College of Business, Organization, and Management; the
College of Liberal Arts and Education; the College of Engineering, Architecture, and Physical
Sciences; the College of Agricultural, Environmental, and Natural Sciences; and the College of
Veterinary Medicine, Nursing, and Allied Health. The colleges offer 41 degrees in varying
majors.

The residence halls are said to be "living and learning" environments. For our women, there's the Charles E. White, Frederick Douglass, Olivia Davidson, and other halls. Men's residences include James Hall, Sage, and other living locations. In the larger settings you'll find kitchens, utility rooms, washers and dryers, and study areas with Internet access. TU usually places about 2,000 students (about 67% of the student body) in these resident halls or apartments. For higher-achieving students there are Honor Houses.

In the University Chapel you'll find the "Singing Glass Windows," which have "Negro lyrics from spirituals" inscribed. In the George Washington Carver Museum you can see "Black Wings," which chronicles the training of the Tuskegee Airmen.

Campus Life

At TU you'll find more than 100 clubs and organizations. There are honor societies, student government, the *Campus Digest* (the student newspaper), a drama club, a concert band and other ensembles, city/state clubs, religious groups, and the Tuskegee University Choir, which has performed at the White House and Radio City Music Hall. All the national sororities and fraternities, including Delta Sigma Theta and Alpha Kappa Alpha, are on campus. About 10% of the students are in Greek-letter fraternities or sororities.

Important events on campus include Founder's Day, the annual Homecoming Parade (with Miss Tuskegee), the MTU Spring Pageant, the Campus All-Star Challenge Tournament (debating), and convocation/graduation.

The intramural sports program provides students (about 10%) an opportunity to participate in organized athletics: volleyball, tennis, slow-pitch softball, and tag football.

The Golden Tigers (school nickname) have basketball, football, and other competing teams. The basketball team, for example, plays Morehouse, Alabama A&M, Savannah State, and Clark-Atlanta. The court here is located at the 5,000-seat James Center Arena. Behind Warren Logan Hall (where you'll find the gymnasium and swimming pool) is the 10,000-seat football stadium and baseball fields. When the shouting begins, the marching band will begin its steps.

Academic Realities

Although about 71% of the students—nearly 90% from public schools—are from out of state, most are from the South. These students are from more than 40 states and 34 foreign countries.

The most popular majors are Engineering (18%), Biology (8%), and Business and Computer Science (each about 5%). Beyond the major, students must complete a core curriculum, including courses in the humanities, political science, English, math, history, and natural sciences.

There's a wide range of courses, with "intensity" and "stress" levels varying from pleasant to very difficult. In the Department of Sociology, for example, you might begin with Introduction to Sociology, go to Race and Culture, and eventually take Statistics and have to think about probability and empirical problems. Many of the courses require a bit of hard study.

About 500 bachelor's degrees are awarded annually. Within the year, about a quarter of the graduates are in professional or graduate schools. For example, Tuskegee students who have selected medicine as their career goal have gone on to pursue their M.D.'s at medical schools such as Howard, the University of Chicago, Johns Hopkins, Case Western Reserve, Morehouse, and Meharry.

During Career Day, hundreds of recruiters appear on campus, including representations from IBM, Ford Motor, General Electric, Polaroid, Dow Chemical, Lucent Technologies, and AT&T. Internships and cooperative educational opportunities are available.

Getting In

Tuskegee accepts about 64% of the students who apply, with about 66% of the enrollees having graduated in the top 25% of their high school graduating class. The school is generally looking for students who have taken the college preparatory route. For example, for engineering majors—the largest entering group—the admission team would like to see a transcript that includes courses such as Physics, Trigonometry, Chemistry, and Computer Science.

Most students who apply take the ACT, although SAT scores also are acceptable. The average ACT score is about 21, and the SAT is in the 900-plus range.

Although a complete application review is the rule—there's a close look at your essay, for example—Tuskegee's analysis is that students who have scored composite scores of at least 1,000 and ACTs of 24, with a GPA of at least 2.5 (on a 4.0 scale), tend "to be more successful in completing their freshman-level courses than those who score lower."

Note that the average GPA of entering students is about 2.7. In a recent year approximately 3,460 students applied and 2,220 were accepted; 95% were African American.

Families are encouraged to visit the campus.

CALIFORNIA

CALIFORNIA INSTITUTE OF TECHNOLOGY

1200 East California Boulevard
Pasadena, CA 91125
(626) 959-6341
Web site: www.caltech.edu

Financial aid deadline: January 15
Application deadline: January 1
Early decision deadline: November 1
1999–2000 tuition: $19,476; room and board, $6,000

College Ranking

CalTech, as it's called, is one of the most highly ranked and academically challenging schools in the nation. It is known primarily for its strong programs in the sciences, especially computer science and engineering, and the school features state-of-the-art facilities on campus and beyond.

The Campus

CalTech, in Pasadena about 12 miles northeast of Los Angeles, is on 124 acres of land. There are 103 buildings, including residences. CalTech students use six physics labs on campus. Also, there's the Karman Laboratory of Fluid Mechanics and Jet Propulsion. They also boast the Mount Palomar and Owens Valley telescopes, the Caltech Submillimeter Observatory, and the Jet Propulsion Laboratory, an internationally famous facility that CalTech operates for NASA. You get the idea.

Campus Life

The central focus at CalTech is academics, with long hours of study and challenging courses the norm. Nonscientific endeavors might include trips to CalTech Y, part of the student center. There you can use the exercise facilities, listen to notable speakers (Nikki Giovanna has read her poetry), chat in meeting rooms, or plan your trip to the cultural mecca of downtown Los Angeles.

Although there are varsity sports (e.g., basketball, swimming, tennis, and fencing), there is no football team. Intramural sports include badminton, racquetball, table tennis, tennis, water polo, and volleyball.

Note that there are seven undergraduate residences, with one or two of our folks living at each location.

Academic Realities

The new president is David Baltimore, a cowinner of the Nobel Prize for medicine. His faculty includes members of the National Academy of Science, National Academy of Engineering, Academy of Arts and Sciences, and other Nobel Prize winners. The coursework is extremely challenging and focused; the teaching ratio is three students to one instructor in the classroom. The most popular majors are Engineering (48%), Physical Sciences (30%), Biology (13%), and Mathematics (6%).

Getting In

In 1996 and 1997 CalTech had two African American entering freshmen each year. When you look at the enrollment percentages of students of color accepted to the nation's highest-ranked institutions, this school always has the lowest admissions statistics across the nation in regard to us. We're lucky if we're 1% of the student body. We understand that CalTech is demanding and is looking for what one guidebook calls (as a positive), "student body intelligence." Still, if we're graduating from Harvard and Princeton and Amherst at high rates (and 97% of the freshman at MIT return after the freshman year, with African Americans totaling 6% of the class), what does that say? Is admissions simply about sky-high SATs (and CalTech has the highest in the nation)? In the spring 1997 issue of the *Journal of Blacks in Higher Education* it was noted, "at CalTech, only 5 of 882 students, or 0.6 percent, are black." But stay tuned. For the class of 1999, 587 AAs applied and 162 were accepted. Encouraging? Note that there's now a new associate dean and director for minority student affairs, and the university claims that "support for minority affairs has been increased."

At CalTech the acceptance rate is about 23%, with about 60% of the students arriving from out of state. As is predictable at these "tech" schools, the male/female ratio is 3 to 1. In a recent year 2,389 applied and 540 were accepted. There are about 900 full-time students, with African Americans still at 1%.

And for readers who don't know what "quantum physics" is, you better turn to the next profile.

STANFORD UNIVERSITY

Dean of Undergraduate Admissions
Old Union, Second Floor
Stanford, CA 94305
(415) 723-2091
Web site: www.stanford.edu

Financial aid deadline: February 15. The FAFSA and CSS profile are required.
Application deadline: December 15
Early decision deadline: November 1
1999–2000 tuition: $23,058; room and board, $7,881

College Ranking

"Stanford is the Harvard of the West!" is an often-heard quote, which may actually do a disservice to the particular strengths of this school. This prestigious school in the the San Francisco Bay Area is a choice pick. It's a school where a faculty member might be a Nobel Laureate, a Pulitzer Prize winner, or a MacArthur Fellow. And it's west of the Mississippi.

The Campus

The campus is beautiful, covering more than 8,180 acres under a heavenly sun and sometimes palm trees. Even when it rains, it's refreshing. You'll see strollers, joggers, and bikers everywhere. Landmarks include the Lawrence Frost Amphitheater, with its dazzling display of flowers, in a setting designed for university ceremonies and the performing arts. There's the Thomas Welton Art Gallery, and the Rodin Sculpture Garden, where you can see the work of the famous artist. That $4.7 billion endowment *is working*.

The Stanford Medical Center is "one of the best." The Bechtel International Center (a hub for U.S. and foreign students) is like a United Nations when folks gather. The Green, Turman, and Meyer Libraries hold more than 6.3 million volumes. When not studying in the dorms or the libraries, students congregate at Tressider, the student union, or the Coffeehouse. The Stanford Shopping Center is on more than 70 acres with 140-plus stores, restaurants, and other services. *All on campus!*

Some say that Stanford is a vacationer's delight. Westward, there are the foothills of the Santa Cruz Mountains and the beaches of the Pacific Ocean. Nearby, there's Yosemite National Park, where you can hike and camp. Travel a while to the east, and it's the Sierra Nevada or Lake Tahoe, for skiing. And a few miles south, there's the legendary Silicon Valley, the home of the computer and the high-tech industry. If this is not enough, there are the neighboring cities of Palo Alto and Menlo Park, with all the movie houses, theater companies, shops, and restaurants you will ever need.

Freshmen must live on campus, where there's a "lot of diversity" and even theme houses. Many of us stay in Ujamaa for support and camaraderie. There are more than 80 residences on campus, including Florence Moore Hall, Lagunila Court, Kimball Hall, Stern Hall, and the Greek-letter "Row Houses." The "old" Governor's Corner complex—with units such as East, Potter, and Robinson—was built in the 1980s. Still, we see lots of style: oak fixtures, kitchenettes, leather sofas in the lounges. At every location there is air conditioning and dining halls. And the views from some locations take you to the foothills or some other pleasant site.

Campus Life

There are more than 500 clubs, organizations, and special-interest groups at Stanford. For us, there's the Black Students' Union, and the Black Recruitment Orientation Committee (BROC). These groups acquaint new students of color to Stanford while "developing a sense of family." Also, there's the Committee on Black Performing Arts (CBPA) and the African American Fraternal and Sororal Association (AAFSA). Under AAFSA you'll interact with Alpha Kappa Alpha (Xi Beta chapter), Kappa Alpha Psi (Lambda Nu chapter), Delta Sigma Theta (Omicron Chi chapter), and the other black Greek-letter organizations on campus. The school newspapers: *Stanford Daily* and *Stanford Report*. An important campus event is Founder's Day.

The "Cardinals" have made history in several varsity sports, including basketball. This school has won more national championships than any other major college. It has won Olympic medals, had football upsets, and nearly everybody agrees that the "athletics are outstanding."

The women always field strong swimming and volleyball units. Intramural and club sports are also very big here. You can play volleyball, badminton, racquetball, and cricket, and participate in judo, rugby, and more.

Academic Realities

Unlike most colleges, Stanford uses a "three-headed quarter system," one student reminds us. Counting the summer sessions, it's as if "the shop never closes." And in a sense, it doesn't. At times it can feel like you're on a speeding train. *Hold the handrail.*

You'll be in an intellectual environment with smart, motivated, and achieving students. One academic building on campus is sometimes called "the physics tank." Some of the courses in the preprofessional tracks will severely test you—courses in the sciences, engineering, and high-tech areas, for example. Of course, the humanities and the social sciences, also are popular.

A recent graduating class had 367 students majoring in Biology (21.6%), 206 students in Economics (12.2%), 104 in English (6.1%), 108 in Psychology (6.4%), and 79 in Computer Science (4.7%).

If you're in a popular introductory class you might find 200 students around you. Generally, however, a freshman class holds 20 to 80 students. As you go along, the ratio of student to teacher can be a comfortable 10 to 1.

To graduate, you must take a number of required courses. There's Writing and Critical Thinking and a one-year foreign-language sequence as well as American, world, and gender offerings. Degree in hand, you'll have taken (including the requirements of your major), courses in the applied and natural sciences, the humanities, and math. But it's like a melting pot, because you can dip and dab from more than sixty departments and interdisciplinary programs. And some of these courses can be pulled from Stanford's African and Afro American Studies Departments. For example, you can take an Afro American Literature course, or one called Race and Ethnicity in the American Experience.

Getting In

The question is, How? The admissions people hint at what's important. You should spend time "discovering who you are." You should be able to demonstrate "how you contribute to the life of your high school and community." You should know what the important influences on your life are and what questions "remain unanswered." At every crossroads, you should have taken the most challenging path. And if that's not enough, Stanford accepts have taken the most difficult courses and have received an A, not once, not twice, but consistently.

Stanford only accepts about 13% of its applicants. The numbers are daunting. In a recent year, 18,888 students applied and 2,500 were accepted. These students have an average 1440 SAT score. Of the high school graduates, 86.6% graduated in the top 10% of their classes. More than 96% of the students were in the top 25%. Of 1,335 transfers, only 127 students were accepted—that is, only 10%. About 30% of the entering freshman class arrive from private schools.

UNIVERSITY OF CALIFORNIA AT BERKELEY

110 Sproul Hall
Berkeley, CA 94201
(510) 642-3175
Web site: www.berkeley.edu

Financial aid deadline:
  March 2. FAFSA required
Application deadline: November 30
Early decision deadline:
  November 30
1999–2000 tuition: $3,628
  (state residents); $10,174
  (nonresidents); room and
  board, $8,122

College Ranking

The University of California at Berkeley is considered one of the world's leading intellectual centers. This school is consistently one of the highest-ranked public universities in the country. The faculty here is star-studded. The team includes 8 Nobel Laureates, 3 Pulitzer Prize winners, 14 MacArthur Fellows, a Poet Laureate emeritus of the United States, 140 Guggenheim Fellows, 198 members of the American Academy of Arts and Sciences, and 121 members of the National Academy of Science. And that's only part of the equation.

When you look at a map of UC at Berkeley, you wonder if students need scooters to get around. The overview is awesome—the blocks, twists, and turns remind you of a maze. When the chancellor, Robert M. Merdahl, says, "Berkeley is currently engaged in a capital campaign to raise $1.1 billion," you are not surprised. This is a major institution, a school that's competing against the most richly endowed private universities in the United States.

Berkeley says there are 10 reasons to consider its school: (1) world-class faculty; (2) world-class students, with generally about 200 National Merit scholars; (3) diversity and variety (you'll find students from every cultural and geographical background); (4) Berkeley and the Bay Area: bookstores, coffeehouses, artists and performers, and more; (5) undergraduate education comes first; (6) 350 organizations and endless opportunities, (7) more than 100 undergraduate majors; (8) top-notch facilities; (9) marketable degree (based on its reputation!); and (10) low cost and high value.

The Campus

The school, about 10 miles east of San Francisco, is on 1,332 acres of land. There are more than 100 buildings, including residences. Along Centennial Drive you can see eucalyptus trees. At other locations you'll spot live oaks and Romanesque landscaping. Sather Tower, commonly called "Campanile," is probably the school's best-known landmark. This tower rises 307 feet, has an observation deck, and its bells ring at 7:50 A.M. each day, at noon, and at 6 P.M. The oldest landmark is Founder's Rock, which is at the corner of Hearst Avenue and Gayley Road. At Barrows Hall you'll find the African American Studies Department. Among other points of interest are California Hall (the chancellor's office), Sproul Hall (admissions), the King Student Union, Berkeley Art Museum (there are 11 galleries), Durham Studio Theater, Botanical Garden, Black Recruitment and Retention Center, Heart Museum of Anthropology (with its art, artifacts, and archaeological samples), Ludwig's Fountain, and Lawrence Hall of Science (with its astronomy, computer, and biology exhibits). The main library, Doe, has more than 8 million volumes.

About 2.2 % of the African American students (26 to 28) reside in a black theme house in the Unit #1 Residence. Some other groups have similar arrangements. Overall, there are seven residence complexes for students, some accommodating nearly 850 students. All the residences have dining and recreational rooms as well as social programs. Most locations have courtyards, and a few have fireplaces. Clark Kerr Campus is a Spanish-style complex with computer facilities. Foothill is a "rustic housing complex" that offers a view of courtyards, trees, and the bay. Bowles is an all-male residence. Stern, which is carpeted, is all-female. About 25% of the students reside on campus.

Campus Life

At Berkeley there are more than 300 clubs, organizations, and special-interest groups. All the major black fraternities and sororities are on campus: Omega Psi Phi, Alpha Phi Alpha, Iota Phi Theta, Delta Sigma Theta, Sigma Gamma Pho, and Alpha Kappa Alpha, to name a few. Also, there's the Berkeley African Students Association, Muslim Student Association, Black Business Association, NAACP, Students for Hip-Hop, Black Prelaw Society, National Association of Black Accountants, Pan African Student Union, National Council for Negro Women, Black Engineering and Science Association, Black Environmental Design Students, and more targeted to us.

Other groups include the Cal Chess Club, Premedical Society, Cal Literary Arts Magazine, Diversity Video Project, UC Jazz Ensemble, Circle K International, Marching Band, KALX radio, Debate Team, and Cal Corps (a volunteer program). There are Army, Navy, and Air Force ROTC units.

UC at Berkeley (the "Bears") is a PAC 10 Conference school. It's won conference and national championships. There are men and women's intercollegiate sports. If you wish, you can head to California Memorial Stadium (seating 76,000 people) for the annual football game with #1 rival Stanford. If you are interested in intramural sports, you can walk down Ellsworth Street to the Recreational Sports Facility. Note that Berkeley has four gymnasiums, four swimming facilities, three weight rooms, a martial arts room, and two 400-meter tracks. You can find, too, tennis, handball, racquetball, and squash courts.

Academic Realities

The students at Berkeley are very bright overachievers, some say. They are all top students who will approach the work with vigor. Undoubtedly, the climate at this school will be intense in regard to academics. Expect an academic environment similar to those at the highly ranked private colleges.

About 82% graduate after six years. Support services include a Student Learning Center, an Academic Achievement Division, and a Black Recruitment and Retention Center. At Berkeley there are five undergraduate colleges: the Colleges of Chemistry, Engineering, Environmental Design, Letters and Sciences, and Natural Resources. There are also two schools: the Walter A. Hass School of Business (you can't enter until your junior year), and the School of Optometry, which you can't enter until your senior year or unless you already have a college degree. With the boundaries mentioned, you have thousands of courses to choose from, and well as over 100 majors available to you. The most popular majors are: Biology (9%), Economics (7%), Computer Science, Psychology, and English (about 6% each).

Getting In

The acceptance rate at Berkeley is about 31%. In a recent year 30,044 applied and 8,448 were accepted. An estimated 3,812 students enrolled. There are nearly 21,000 full-time students.

Most students are from California (more than 85%). The rest arrive from every state in the country and more than 100 foreign countries. The average GPA was 3.87. The middle 50% of entering students had verbal SATs of between 600 to 710. The math middle scores were between 630 to 740. Note that in a past *Journal of Blacks in Higher Education,* it was indicated that blacks had SAT scores more than 250 points lower than "others" while gaining admission. It should be noted that after Proposition 209 (the anti-affirmative action initiative passed in 1998), there appeared to be a black "brain drain." We felt unwelcome, and there was a 8.2% dip in applications to the school (1997 to 1998). In recent news releases the school claims that there's been an increase in black applicants due to "strong recruitment and a more comprehensive application review." We'll see.

| **UNIVERSITY OF CALIFORNIA AT LOS ANGELES** | 405 Hilgard Avenue
Los Angeles, CA 90095
(310) 825-3101
Web site: www.ucla.edu | **Financial aid deadline:** March 1
Application deadline: November 30
1999–2000 tuition: $3,698 (state residents); $13,502 (nonresidents); room and board, $7,692 |

College Ranking

Want to see Beverly Hills, take a ride to Bel Air, break into Hollywood, perhaps get a darker tan on the beaches of Santa Monica? Well, do we have a university for you! UCLA, the University of California at Los Angeles, is a highly ranked public school with lots of prestige and clout. It consistently ranks among the best national universities in the country.

The Campus

Stretching over 419 acres in the "urban" Westwood section of Los Angeles—Hollywood and the Sunset Strip are not far away—the UCLA campus is described by most as "beautiful." There are 272 buildings, including residences. Strolling, you'll see Romanesque and Tudor Gothic styles of architecture as well as modern structures. Botanical gardens are everywhere, with the sun (almost always) overhead. There are 13 "official" libraries, with more than 7 million volumes. Powell Library, the main undergraduate study stop, has several reading rooms. Ackerman Union, the student center on campus, is a gathering place where you can find fast-food outlets (Taco Bell, Panda Express). On South Campus you'll find the School of Engineering and facilities for the sciences. On North Campus you'll find the humanities resources. Bruin Walk (the main pedestrian path) leads to the East Side, where all the dorms are located. Students live in residences with names such as the new Sunset Village, and high-rise settings like Rieber and Dykstra. There are also theme houses.

Campus Life

UCLA, with nearly 24,000 undergraduate students, is the "epitome of diversity," according to many students. There are Asians (39% of the body count), Hispanics (14%), and African Americans (6%). This last total translates to about 1,400 black students, more than you find at most colleges. Also, this school has spawned a "who's who" of black achievers: Kareem Abdul Jabbar (one of the greatest basketball players of all time), Arthur Ashe (the first Black tennis player to win at Wimbledon), Ralph Bunche (a Nobel Peace Prize winner and UN diplomat), and Thomas Bradley (the first black mayor of Los Angeles) among many others.

At UCLA there are more than 350 clubs, organizations, and special-interest groups. It's a very long and exciting list. Outlets that might be of particular interest to us include: the African Student Union, Black Greek-Letter Council, African Art Ensemble, Black Prelaw Society, African Women's Collective, Black Hypertension Project, Black Caucus, African Activists' Association, Black Business Association, Black Prehealth Organization, and Black Latino AIDS Project. All the black fraternities and sororities are active here. They include Alpha Phi Alpha, Phi Beta Sigma, Alpha Kappa Alpha, Sigma Gamma Rho, Delta Sigma Theta, and Zeta Phi Beta.

Sports at UCLA "is god," one student says. The Bruins have won more than 84 championships in a variety of intercollegiate competitions. Its basketball teams are legendary, and football is also very, very popular. Other winners include victories in track and field, women's softball, golf, swimming, men's gymnastics, and volleyball. In intramural sports, large numbers of students participate. Beyond the usual club sports, you can surf and water-ski.

Academic Realities

At UCLA there are five undergraduate colleges: Letters and Science; Engineering and Applied Science; Arts and Architecture; Nursing; and Theater and Film. Within these schools there are more than 112 degree programs, and more than 3,000 courses available to you. The most popular majors are Psychology (11%), Economics (10%), and Political Science, Sociology, and English (8% each). There is also a major in Afro American Studies. Students, while pursuing their majors, must meet some "broad general education" requirements, including taking English Composition, and core courses in the humanities and sciences (social, physical, and life).

Getting In

At UCLA the acceptance rate is about 36%. In a recent year 29,302 applied and 10,642 were accepted. Only about 3% of the students who arrive are from out of state. Still, more than 65 foreign countries are represented on campus. The average SAT score is 1240 to 1260. Black students should be cautioned that California's Proposition 209 and the affirmative action controversy, are still playing themselves out. Black enrollment at UCLA has dropped precipitously over the past year as a result.

COLORADO

U.S. AIR FORCE ACADEMY

HQ USAFA/RRS 200
USAF Academy, Colorado
   Springs, CO 80840-5025
(719) 472-2520
Web site: www.usafa.of.mil

Financial aid deadline: Not
  applicable
Application deadline: January
  3 for the fall
Early decision deadline: Not
  applicable
1999–2000 tuition: Tuition and
  room and board are free

College Ranking

The academy is world-renowned.

The Campus

The Air Force Academy is one of Colorado's top tourist attractions. The campus is on 18,000 acres in the foothills of the Rocky Mountains. In the cadet area there's the 150-foot-high Cadet Chapel, with 17 aluminum spires. The buildings in this area are of contemporary architecture. From campus you can see the famous 14,000-foot Pikes Peak.

At the Academy every dorm, laboratory, and classroom is connected by a "local network." You can easily reach the multimedia education area, where there are research laboratories. You are beside Colorado Springs, and its metropolitan population of more than 300,000.

Still, students will not be stationary, and sometimes will travel to air force bases around the world for training. Cadets will eventually fly in helicopters, a T-43 jet navigator trainer, and other planes. The basics will be learned on the ground. There's an Academy library, an outstanding planetarium, and great athletic facilities.

Campus Life

Like the other military academies, expect a nonstop, dawn-to-dusk regimen. At the Air Force Academy you'll be sent to boot camp training (BTC). You'll be subjected to obstacle courses and "intense physical, emotional, and mental challenges" in the Rocky Mountains, where the Academy is located. After your orientation you'll be accepted into the "Cadet Wing," which means you're accepted into the fraternity of cadets.

At the Academy all cadets march to breakfast at Mitchell Hall after doing "details" (e.g., laundry and cleaning) at about 6:00 A.M. Breakfast is served at 7:00 A.M., but "fourth classmen" (the new students) must serve upperclassmen first. Then the the fourth classmen must eat at attention, staring straight ahead without speaking. There's a "strict ritual" for all incoming cadets in almost all areas.

Academic Realities

The top majors are: Engineering (29%), History (10%), and Behavioral Sciences, Biology, and Management (about 9% each). Every cadet graduates with a bachelor of science degree and a commission as a second lieutenant. It's a five-year commitment to service for your country. The good news is that the entire program, including tuition and fees, is free.

In class there's rigorous coursework that includes courses such as Chemistry, Engineering, Mathematics, and Computer Science. That's 15 to 21 credits a semester, including classes in Military Arts and Sciences, which cover areas of study that include leadership and military history. Some of this study will be done in the new Consolidated Education Training facility. All this study/activity is done with cadets assigned to "squadrons." You basically sleep, eat, and plan with these comrades (about 110 of them) on a continuous daily basis. Yes, you must always greet all upperclassmen, including women, by name and rank. Don't forget to salute. When in Terrazo, the Academy courtyard, freshmen must run to wherever they're headed.

Getting In

The acceptance rate at the Air Force Academy is about 15%. In a recent year 9,602 students applied and 1,485 were accepted. The average SAT score was in the 1230 to 1260 range, with the lowest quarter of students scoring 1210 or lower. Generally, there are about 5,000 full-time cadets, with a men-to-women ratio of about 84 to 16. African Americans make up about 5% of the student body.

Students who are interested in the Air Force Academy should call or write for specific application instructions and details. At the USAF, for example, you must get nominated by a member of Congress and pass a very intense academic, character, and personality review.

CONNECTICUT

| WESLEYAN UNIVERSITY | High Street
Middletown, CT 06459-0260
(860) 685-3000
Web site: www.wesleyan.edu | **Financial aid deadline:** January 15
Application deadline (priority): January 1
1999–2000 tuition: $25,120; room and board, $7,440 |

"A small college with university resources."
— a description of Wesleyan from their promotional material

College Ranking

Wesleyan University is one of the premier colleges in the United States. It's a school that garners strong respect and a high ranking no matter what poll you look at, and it sits alongside schools such as Amherst, Haverford, Smith, Bowdoin, Wellesley, and Bryn Mawr.

Wesleyan is a school that takes pride in its reputation for academic excellence as well as its revered image as a place of "diversity." It's no wonder that educators and students alike sometimes refer to this institution as "Diversity University." That nickname hints at the worthiness of the school's mission.

The Campus

When you first arrive at Wesleyan, you're surprised that the actual school—its space—seems diminutive when you consider its reputation. For some reason you expect to see acres upon acres of land, with buildings and dormitories stretching for miles. But that's not the case. Wesleyan is a small New England school, in a small town with a population of about 45,000. Still, Hartford and New Haven are relatively close by car (15 to 20 miles). In each place you'll find substantial black communities. Wes students (more than 90% from out of state), also can head to Yale, UConn, or Trinity College, all about a half hour away. Wadsworth Falls and the beautiful countryside are also nearby.

Wesleyan has a campus of ivy-covered brownstones and other buildings that have a stately look. The architecture varies, from the modern Center of the Arts to the sometimes older dorms (now renovated) that were built in the 1960s. One college guide correctly points out that the imagery leaves you with an overall impression of "Main Street, U.S.A."

These 120 acres have resources that are equivalent to some of the larger universities. At Wesleyan there's a Science Tower, an observatory with one of the largest telescopes in Connecticut, and an athletic center. There's Mocon, the main dining hall, and two smaller cafeterias, a famous Art Galley, Olin and three other libraries, and a computer center and other labs (some open 24 hours a day).

Clark Hall is four stories high and is exclusively for first-year students. It's across the street from the Science Center and just a few steps from Olin Library. The halls of Clark are coed, with two resident advisers per floor. They are assigned to supervise 38 students. On each floor there are double and triple rooms, always with three hall bathrooms—one coed, and two specially for either men or women.

West College, just another of many residences, is on Foss Hill and is near the center of the campus. It's for students who are interested in living in a "multiracial, multicultural community." Here you'll find Wesleyan's only student-run café, in a setting that allows for weekly theatrical, musical, educational, and other forums. Enjoy the dorm's beautiful courtyard, play pool, or simply play tunes on the available piano. For African Americans interested in theme houses, there's the Women of Color House (343 High Street) or Malcolm X House (227 Pine Street), the latter founded in 1969 to celebrate and affirm the "African Diaspora." Ten spaces are usually reserved for first-year students.

Campus Life

In recent years there's been a "new students of color orientation" for arriving students. This is a helpful "multifaceted" presentation given by upperclassmen that covers all the necessary topics: resources, the surrounding community, how to study, partying and recreation, majors, and more from a black perspective.

There are more than 250 clubs and organizations on campus. As an African American you have many options and/or avenues you can explore. There's the African Studies Center, with its W. E. B. Du Bois Library on the second floor. There's *Ankh,* the black student newspaper. There's Ujamaa, a student group, and "Little Ujamaa," the mentoring group for black teenagers. If you can sing, go look up the Students of Color A Cappella Group. If you can dance, there's the Women of Color Dance Troupe.

Although most guides say the Greek-letter life is almost nonexistent at Wes, there's the Pi Alpha chapter of Delta Sigma Theta. The sisters share connections with the "sisterhood" at Yale, Southern Connecticut State, and the University of New Haven. Last, if you want to volunteer, you can join Big Brothers/Big Sisters, counsel at the Ingersoll Youth Shelter, or assist at the Church of the Holy Trinity.

And there's more to do on the Wesleyan campus. You'll find a drama/teacher group, a radio station, and student-run newspapers. You've also got aikido (martial arts), chess, Bad Sam (a sketch comedy group), Cross Street Tutorial, volleyball, Philosophy Majors (a club), and religious and cultural clubs galore.

There are, too, many intercollegiate sports clubs. At Wes you can pick your "delight" or your "poison", as one student put it.

Protests? Of course. Recently there have been several small protests because an African American professor wasn't granted tenure. Students are asking for the "hiring and retention of more faculty of color."

Academic Realities

Imagine the best debate you've ever had; then imagine an environment where that kind of dialogue is continuous, intense, and always available. At some colleges you might advance by studying by rote, memorizing things. But here you're encouraged to think, to create. The "scholar-teachers" (affordable because of Wesleyan's high endowment) are accessible.

Classes are generally small, and you're intellectually challenged. Your viewpoint and ideas are valuable. Of course, in this environment there are many "hot" courses as well as "hot" professors. One example was a Toni Morrison class a few years back. Everybody wanted to take that class. English, along with Political Science/Government, and History are very popular majors.

Art, art history, and education also attract a lot of attention. As in the past, courses such as Biology and Chemistry are tough, as well as those in any of the preprofessional tracks such as law or medicine. Last, there's an African Studies major. With any major, you can take courses such as The Harlem Renaissance, Jazz Dance, or the Anthropology of African Americans.

If you've been "chosen," you'll probably rise to the occasion. The school's freshman retention rate is a high 92%, and at the sophomore level it's even higher. And yes, there are self-designed majors, cooperative education, internships, and accelerated degree possibilities.

Getting In

In a January 1999 news release, it was noted that applications to Wesleyan (more than 6,000) had set an all-time record. It's a very popular school, with more than 2,700 students in residence from over 48 states and 32 foreign countries. But it's not an easy admit. The acceptance rate is about 33%, with the usual freshman class projected to be about 715 students. When you factor in the fact that 42% of this total applied early decision, and that 215 valedictorians and salutatorians are in this grouping, you can see that getting in is no cakewalk. You must be academically capable. For example, Wesleyan reports that of the class of 2002, more than 70% of the admitted students took Calculus, and that 74% took a triad of courses including Biology, Chemistry, and Physics. Be forewarned: be prepared. Usually more than 200 National Merit scholar semifinalists are on campus at any given time.

African Americans make up about 8% of the student body. Although recent median SAT scores for Wesleyan students were 686 (verbal) and 679 (math)—with the average ACT score 29.1—we can be "in the ballpark" with scores that are much lower. Be on the college preparatory track, and present exemplary support material: leadership quality, special talents, services to your high school and/or community. Note that 54% of the students applying are from public schools. Indeed, if you think you might be a "fit" at Wesleyan, apply.

YALE UNIVERSITY

Office of Undergraduate
  Admission
P.O. Box 208234
New Haven, CT 06620-8234
(203) 432-9300
Web site: www.yale.edu

Financial aid deadline:
  February 1
Application deadline: December 31 (fall)
Early decision deadline:
  November 1; for the class of 2003, Yale accepted 526 of its early-decision applicants, or about 40% of the class
1999–2000 tuition: $24,500

"The faculty at Yale includes scholars, artists, and scientists who have contributed greatly to our understanding of the world; and who continue to lead us into the twenty-first century."

—from the *Yale University Viewbook*

College Ranking

Many years ago at my first job, I met a new coworker who said "Yale" when he was asked where he'd completed his undergraduate work. Suddenly every head at the lunch table turned, and studied the young black face. It was if somebody had whispered the formula for the cure for cancer. Everybody wanted to hear his story. Was he brilliant? How had he made it? Where was he headed?

Today, the word "Yale" still causes a reaction. It's a university that is more than highly regarded; it is one of the nation's academic shrines, with a reputation that invokes awe. The list of eminent/achieving graduates includes Nobel and

> "**Y**ale undergraduates in the engineering department taught the *Columbia* shuttle crew to run a zero gravity experiment. In tribute, the payload commander waved a Yale banner on TV."
>
> —FROM THE *Yale University Viewbook*

Pulitzer Prize winners, CEOs, and other movers and shakers. Our last two U.S. presidents (Bush and Clinton) are alumni. A few Yalies of color include Supreme Court justice Clarence Thomas, his nemesis Anita Hill, and the neurosurgeon Dr. Benjamin Carson. In the entertainment field, there's actress Angela Bassett of *Waiting to Exhale* fame. Since its founding in 1701, Yale has been one of the most famous schools in the world.

The Campus

When you look at the architecture, the campus of Yale has a "Gothic air." Beyond the arched doorways and vines, however, you'll also see a mix of contemporary structures. Located in urban New Haven, Connecticut, this Ivy League New England school covers more than 200 acres. On campus there are more than 220 buildings, including the 12 residential colleges (living quarters) that will be pivotal to your quality of life. Sometimes Yale is called a "campus school" because of surrounding New Haven. "The Haven" is not considered as desirable as Boston or Cambridge. Black communities reside nearby, and that's a point of concern for many. The telling phrase is, "It's not safe." But, of course, many of us say "it's all right" with a wink.

Generally, Yale's facilities are state-of-the-art, and within those ivy-covered walls you'll find teaching excellence, scholarship, and research components that rival and/or surpass the best at most other schools. From the air you can see that the campus is divided into what appears to be dozens of large city blocks. On the ground you get the sense of a classic grassy, college landscape.

At Yale you've got the second largest library system in the nation, with 21 branches and more than 10.8 million volumes. On campus you can visit the Sterling Memorial Library, between Elm and Wall Streets on the central campus. With its Gothic tower, this building looks like an ancient cathedral. It's the home of the Yale University African Collection and the Fortunoff Video Archives for Holocaust Testimonies. At the Rare Book and Manuscript Library you can peruse the James Weldon Johnson Collection. There you'll find representative manuscripts by Richard Wright *(Native Son),* Jean Toomer *(Cane),* and Zora Neale Hurston *(Their Eyes Are Watching God),* to name a few of our literary giants. You'll find, too, hundreds of photographs by Carl Van Vecten, including some of Alvin Ailey, Paul Robeson, Margaret Walker, and others.

Other key spots include the University Art Gallery, a planetarium, the Peabody Museum of Natural History, the Whitney Humanities Center, the March Botanical Gardens, and the top of East Rock, where you can picnic.

Freshmen are randomly assigned to one of 12 residential colleges. Ten are located on "Old Campus," on grassy quadrangles that cover about two acres of land. As one student ably puts it, "Calhoun is a planet, and Morse is a planet, and so it goes." He's naming the residences. Some of the others are Pierson, Branford, Dwight, and Trumbull. "The Yale way," he says, winking, "is modeled after Oxford University." He's on point. Yale's students (about 400 in each location) live in buildings that usually have a Gothic air and exterior. In fact, in some places you'll even find some medieval halls, arched windows, and vaulted ceilings.

Yale's idea is to create a "microcosm of the larger community within each college" while reflecting the diversity of the larger student population. The goal is to promote "integration and inclusiveness," not a house that can be said to have a "jock, artsy, or nerd" personality. Each college has assigned "masters," dean, and SAC (Social Action Committee). This group coordinates and supervises residence activities. There'll be lectures, discussions, and a calendar of events. Poets will read, musicians will play, guest speakers will appear. Some colleges have established annual traditions—Morse, for example, has a Casino Night, while Pierson sponsors a Halloween Dance.

Your "planet" will also have a library, TV lounges, computer terminals, and study space. There'll be rooms for meetings, music rehearsals, and photography work (Davenport has a darkroom). Other recreational outlets include tables for Ping-Pong, pool, and board games. At Silliman you'll find a small theater; at Calhoun, a sauna. At other locations are pottery and art studios, and even weight rooms. Not only are kitchens available, but also each college has a dining hall, serving anything from "hot dogs to shrimp Creole."

Most students will reside in bedrooms that open into suites. These rooms usually have high ceilings, oak panels, and sometimes a fireplace. Outside there will be a courtyard, rows of benches, and perhaps a swing. You can play Frisbee, slap a volleyball, or simply study under the trees.

Until you graduate, you'll live, eat, and socialize with those in "your home." During freshman year, however, you'll live on Old Campus (a tradition), in a section that is often called "the 19th-century quadrangle." Theoretically you'll bond there with other new Yalies before you get your eventual assignment beginning with your sophomore year.

Campus Life

For black students the pivotal place on campus is the African American Cultural Center. The center is the home or meeting place of more than 25 different resident groups. Some include: the Black Student Alliance at Yale (BSAY), Shades (a multicultural a cappella group), Children's Mentorship Program, *Akili* (a black magazine), Caribbean Club, Black Church at Yale (interdenominational worship in the black tradition), Black Women's Caucus, Heritage Theater Ensemble and Hekah Theater Productions, Urban Improvement Corps (one-on-one tutoring to New Haven youth), Black Pride Union, African Student Alliance, National Society of Black Engineers, Premed African American and Latino Society, Yale Black Political Forum, and the Alliance for Cultural Evolution.

You'll also find the Alpha Phi Alpha fraternity (Zeta chapter), Delta Sigma Theta (Pi Alpha chapter), Kappa Alpha Psi fraternity (Nu Gamma chapter), Omega Psi Phi fraternity (Epsilon Iota Iota chapter), and the Zeta Phi Beta sorority.

Some of these groups have invited speakers to Yale that have included Amiri Baraka, Sister Souljah, Branford Marsalis, the Hudlin brothers (film), and Marian Wright Edelman.

The center also serves as a home to New Haven community groups such as the Coalition of 100 Black Women, the Larry Ferrell Dance Ensemble, and the Paul Higgins African Drumming Troupe.

More than 300 other clubs, organizations, and special-interest groups also serve students. There are, too, performances galore. The New Haven Symphony Orchestra will visit, or you can sit in on the Duke Ellington Fellowship Concert. Student and professional drama groups appear (recently students saw *The Hobbit* and *Life Is but a Dream*). One lecture was called "Ethics and the Impeachment Process."

You can join Habitat for Humanity, one of 14 a cappella groups (e.g., the Whiffenpoofs, Whim-n-Rhythm), student government, write for the *Yale Herald* or *Yale Daily News,* audition for the Yale Repertory Theater, volunteer for a community-service organization, play chess, dance, sing in a glee club, be a cheerleader, swim, or find one of many other outlets to keep you occupied when your head is not in a book. And, of course, there's the very popular Yale Political Union, where you can go to hear "all sides" debate in the Oxford and Cambridge tradition.

Yale has its varsity teams, and the Yale-Harvard football encounter—"The Game"—is a biggie. This Bulldog-Crimson event is an occasion for shout-outs, parties, and lots of celebration and fun between the students of color of both schools. Also popular at Yale are basketball, tennis, track, soccer, swimming, golf, hockey, and the crew groups. In most cases there are men's and women's teams. The women's fencing squad, for example, usually does well.

Intramural sports are also very popular, with large numbers of students competing, especially when there are events/competitions between the residential colleges.

Academic Realities

Students say that the coursework is very challenging, and that you'll find "intellectual stimulation" and "academic rigor" at Yale. In fact, some say that Yale is one of the "toughest schools in the Ivy League" in regard to study and coursework.

Generally, students take four or five courses a semester. There are no specific core or class requirements, but all students must meet distribution rules. You must take at least two courses each from four categories: the humanities, social sciences, languages and literature, and math/sciences. Still, you'll have lots of latitude. Yale offers more than 2,000 courses to pick and choose from. Last, you must demonstrate proficiency in a foreign language.

You do not need to declare a major until your junior year (with engineering and the sciences being the exceptions). At that time you'll have more than 70 options available to you, including an African American Studies journey, if you wish. Along the way, all students can take courses such as Jazz Studies, From West Africa to Black America, The Civil War and Reconstruction, or African American Literature from 1920 to the Present.

As you proceed, your classes are usually conducted in either lecture, seminar, or tutorial formats. Classes vary in size, from a dozen students to hundreds if it's a popular introductory class. Sometimes a presenter can be a Nobel or Pulitzer Prize winner, a MacArthur fellow, or some other esteemed person.

During the first two weeks of each semester you can "shop" for courses that you might eventually select to take. You can visit or sit in as many courses as you wish. Finally, after making your personal evaluations, you can register for the courses you feel are to your liking and that serve your need.

Recently, the most popular majors have been Biology and History (both 11%), Economics (10%), Political Science (9%), and English (8%). Broken down into general categories, 41% of the students major in the arts and humanities, 33% in the social sciences, 25% in the biological and physical sciences, and 1% in other arts and sciences.

One sour note is that several years ago Yale abandoned the very helpful PROP (week-long preregistration and orientation program for minority students) program. We would arrive, be familiarized with Yale resources, including the cultural centers, and be made to feel at home. We would sit in on lectures, enjoy "jams" and parties, and even be assigned a freshman counselor.

Then, with the University of California's Board of Regents vote to abolish affirmative action, there seemed to be a we-can't-allow-self-segregation stand, probably based on legal considerations. The protests by the Coalition for Diversity were impassioned but futile. It was a "major setback," many black upper-class students who had experienced PROP felt. The old welcome had been pivotal to their selection of Yale.

One freshman program that is still popular and available is called FOOT (freshman outdoor orientation trips). It allows new students to "make new friends." It's a six-day backpacking and camping trip to the Catskills and Adirondack Mountains. At least 20% of the incoming students are said to participate.

Another program is called OIS (the orientation of international students). Here, the school sets up a program that helps "familiarize international students with American academic and social customs."

Getting In

Yale graduates are "expected to become leaders" is a quote we often hear. So no, don't imply or infer that you are just another Joe or Jane intent on an invite. When you start to shape your application, *make it matter.* If you're holding an ace, you want to play it. You had better, because the competition is not going to fade. Some students from other cultures have actually heard that four-letter word, "Yale" when they were in the cradle. You want to make another gigantic effort here. After all, if it's a leaders' pool, that's where you want to be.

Yale (with about 5,320 full-time undergraduates) is a reach for most students. Admissions competition is like a war, with the acceptance rate at about 18% in a recent year. About 12,500 students applied, and 2,144 were accepted. In a *Journal of Blacks in Higher Education* survey it was noted that there were about 1,320 black applicants in the class discussed here. Exactly 104 of us enrolled (7.9%).

> Two recent Yale essay questions were:
> 1. Write an essay about an activity or interest that has been particularly meaningful to you. One page.
> 2. Write about something that we might not learn [about you] from the rest of your application. One page.

More than 90% of all entering students graduated in the top 10th of their high school class. Their median SAT scores were about 1435, with the lowest quarter of scores below 1340. If you are not daunted by the odds, you can be competitive if you are "in the ballpark." Do apply. Historically, we have sometimes scored hundreds of points lower on those SATs and other tests. Your total package should simply demonstrate that you "can hang" academically and that you are an asset. No score is etched in granite, but an 1150 SAT is the workable minimum. Be informed: the statistics say we are graduating in very high percentages and going on to excel.

Note that in a recent year, students arrived from every state and more than 50 foreign countries. Of the American students, 53% arrived from public schools and 47% came from private, parochial, and other schools.

DISTRICT OF COLUMBIA

GEORGETOWN UNIVERSITY

Office of Undergraduate
  Admissions
103 White-Gravenor
37th and O Streets, N.W.
Washington, DC 20057-1002
(202) 687-3600
Web site:
  www.georgetown.edu

Financial Aid deadline:
  February 1; a CSS profile is
  required
Application Deadline: January 1
Early decision deadline:
  November 1
1999–2000 tuition: $23,088;
  room and board, $8,693

College Ranking

Georgetown is highly regarded. It sits in the capital, about 10 minutes from the White House by car. It's probably best known as home of the Hoyas of basketball fame, but the school's fine academic reputation is built on its prestigious business, government, and international studies programs. Undoubtedly its proximity to government and political power has shaped the school and its mission.

The Campus

When you first arrive at the gatehouse leading to the campus of Georgetown, you'll marvel at the Gothic buildings. This Jesuit university was founded in 1789, and it is one of the oldest colleges in the United States. The college is on more than 110 acres of land, with more than 60 buildings including residences.

On the main campus you can see the Observatory (the third observatory built in this country), a historic landmark, as well as more modern buildings. Stately Healy Hall looks like it was transported from England. Nearby is the quad, a grassy knoll where students congregate, study, and sometimes throw Frisbees. Lauinger Library has a state-of-the-art glow. Dedicated to "all Georgetown students who have lost their lives in war," the library serves more than 5,000 visitors daily. It holds some of the 1.4 volumes located at various libraries around campus. At the Thomas and Dorothy Leavey Center there is always lots of activity. It's a multipurpose complex, with a Student Activities Building that includes a 450-seat cafeteria, student pub, Georgetown Café, Hoyas Restaurant, and fast-food eateries. There is also a conference center with a grand ballroom, and a guest house with 146 luxurious rooms. Georgetown also has a planetarium, a learning center, radio and TV stations, and more.

The White House is 10 minutes away, and the District of Columbia is considered an extended classroom. There you've got the Kennedy Center for the Performing Arts, the Smithsonian, the National Gallery, the Folger Shakespeare Library, the Library of Congress, embassies, and museums, all close enough to take advantage of. Bikers and joggers can enjoy the C&O Canal near campus. You can paddle a boat on the Tidal Basin.

Georgetown is said by some students to have an "Old World charm." On a bus ride you'll see stately brownstones, cobblestone streets, an upscale community with restaurants, art galleries, and fashionable shops. Not far from campus—go to Wisconsin Avenue and M Street—you'll find theaters, restaurants, shops, and bars, all crowded. In September there's a nearby street festival for Adams-Morgan Day, with music and dancing. You'll find vendors of all kinds (food, trinkets, books, CDs).

The residences are within walking distance of classrooms. At New South you'll find freshmen and one of the school's cafeterias. At Village C, built in 1986, there's an East and a West Wing, again for freshmen, who live in double occupancy rooms. The only high-rise on campus is the Harbin residence. At LXR Hall you'll find wall-to-wall carpeting and full Internet capacity in each room in the only cluster of single rooms on campus. Village A is a series of town houses with private balconies. From some windows you can see the Washington Monument, the Kennedy Center, and even the Potomac River.

Campus Life

"The Black House" (with its *Kaleidoscope* newsletter) is a center for living, club meetings, and social events. Black organizations on campus include the Black Students' Alliance (BSA), NAACP (which sponsors events such as the recent Martin Luther King Jr. celebration at Gaston Hall), Black Movements Dance Theater, Umoja, African Society of Georgetown, Black Theater Ensemble, Caribbean Culture Club, Gospel Choir, and a Muslim Students' Association. *The Blackboard* (a literary magazine) is published by students of color.

At Georgetown there are no formal Greek-letter organizations on campus. Look hard and you can find the Kappa Alpha Phis (Kappi Chi chapter). It's a partnership of brothers from American, Catholic, George Washington, and Georgetown Universities.

The Leadership in Education About Diversity (LEAD) program works to "raise awareness of prejudices in order to promote open interaction between people of all backgrounds." There are also "diversity ambassadors," who include students and faculty who aim to "build an inclusive community."

The consensus seems to be that Georgetown is a "politically conservative campus." One student of color says, "it's not a blacker-than-thou atmosphere. We're aspiring leaders and businessmen and -women. We're aware but very focused on the final payoff." More than 60% of the students head to the private or public sector—often the corporate world—while others head to medical, law, business, and other professional and graduate schools.

Serving all students, the campus organization that coordinates student activities at Georgetown is the Student Activity Council. Other groups include Georgetown Jazz, Concert Choir, Mock Trial and Law Team, and Community Action Coalition (volunteers who work in homeless shelters, in schools, and elsewhere). Also, there are many language clubs, the Senior Class Committee, theater groups (Mask and Bauble, Friday Afternoon), Campus Ministries, political clubs, student government, a chess club, a cappella groups (the Grace Notes, the Chimes), the Senior Class Committee, and more.

Important campus events include Homecoming in October, the Crew Team Ball, a Casino Night, and a Diplomatic Ball (said to be "super posh") sponsored by the School of Business. Also, there's an All-Day Fair on Copley Lawn.

The Hoyas—the basketball team—are very popular here. This is the school of retired legendary coach John Thompson and current Knicks center Patrick Ewing. Usually the team is competitive in the yearly NCAA postseason tournament. The football squad also has its loyal fans, and students can almost become fanatical during games involving their teams. The track teams also have won titles. Besides other varsity sports, students are also getting involved with intramural sports. Yes, students often head to the Yates Recreational Complex. It's been called "one of the most sophisticated and contemporary sports complexes in the country." It's four levels high, covers more than 142,000 square feet, and has facilities for basketball, weight and exercise workouts, and swimming (a 25-meter, 8-lane pool). Also, there are two tracks, and courts for squash, racquetball, badminton, handball, and tennis.

The new MCI Center offers a Metro connection to all Hoyas games.

Academic Realities

At Georgetown you will be hitting the books, with lots of study required. You select your school and major immediately. Each program has its own course/core requirements. Most of the programs (there are 28 academic departments) are highly structured, with little room to maneuver in regard to taking electives. The business and nursing tracks are often said to be "the most restrictive." For most programs you must take courses in theology, English, philosophy, and history as well as a foreign language. If you are a majoring in the tough areas of physics, biology, or chemistry, you are exempt from some social science requirements.

In the School of Business Administration you'll get an international flavor to your studies. In the College of Arts and Sciences, you can select majors in many areas, including the humanities, the sciences, history, and more. In the School of Languages and Linguistics you can study one of 14 languages. And you are encouraged to spend at least a semester abroad improving your skills. The School of Nursing is heavy on "theory and practice" but aims at giving you a well-rounded liberal arts grounding.

Generally you must take 40 courses, or five a semester to graduate on time (four years). About half of the classes will have about 20 students or so, with larger lecture courses going as high as about 60 per lecture hall. An average class size might be 25 to 30 students.

The most popular majors are: Business (22%), International Studies (19%), Political Science (9%), Economics and English (about 8% each).

Getting In

The acceptance rate for the class of 2002 was 23%. Exactly 13,416 applied, 3,147 were accepted, and 1,491 (a 47% yield) enrolled. At last count, the full-time undergraduate body was about 5,920. Approximately 6% of these students were black.

Getting in is not easy. You must apply to one of the undergraduate schools, each with its own admissions standard/requirements. There's the very popular (and competitive) Edmund A. Walsh School of Foreign Service. The school is the oldest and largest school of international studies in the nation. The College of Arts and Sciences has a variety of strong and varied programs, including a very strong premed program.

All the schools are looking for perceptive and very capable students (who have handled a tough college prep track courseload), and who have strong records of high school and/or community service. Relevant summer work is always a plus. A recent Georgetown class included 111 class presidents, 200 students who were on the debate team, 194 who were news editors, 227 who were involved with dramatics, 175 who were involved with model UN groups, and many who were involved with varsity sports. For example, about 100 students were members of swimming teams in high school.

To get in, students must not only present their SAT scores, but also take three SAT II College Board tests, including the one in writing. You can select the subject areas of the other two. Of course, there's the obligatory essay—make it good—and one teacher recommendation. Note, too, that each student is interviewed by a member of the Alumni Admissions Committee that has members in every state. If you apply for early decision, you are not obliged to enroll if you're accepted, unlike at other schools.

Most of Georgetown's students are from the Middle Atlantic states, so applicants from other areas usually will get a good (if not sympathetic) look in application reviews. Here's an actual geographical sampling: New York (229 students), New Jersey (135), Maryland (108), California (109), Florida (66), Massachusetts (81), Virginia (61), Texas (42), Illinois (59), Pennsylvania (75), and District of Columbia (13). Students arrive from 50 states, and 128 foreign countries.

The admissions team includes an admissions officer, a dean, a faculty member, and at least one student.

HOWARD UNIVERSITY

2400 6th Street, N.W.
Washington, DC 20059
(202) 806-2752 or 2755
Web site: www.howard.edu

Financial aid deadline:
April 4; submit FAFSA as
soon as possible after
January 1
Application deadline:
February 2 for the fall
semester
Early decision deadline:
November 1
1999–2000 tuition: $9,330;
room and board, $5,350

"Howard is a place where students can find role models: economists, scientists, mathematicians, professors of language, and history and philosophy scholars of all kinds. That can be an eye-opening experience!"

—one faculty member, the College of Arts and Sciences

College Ranking

In years past, Howard University was often referred to as the "black Harvard." This eminent, multifaceted historically black college was our undisputed best, and we could point to legacies such as former Supreme Court justice Thurgood Marshall and a virtual army of graduates (doctors, lawyers, businessmen, entertainers, and other role models) to prove it. The novelist, Toni Morrison, is an alum. And the actress and dancer Debbie Allen. Andrew Young, a former U.S. ambassador and major. Jessye Norman, our opera star. The former governor of Virginia Douglas Wilder. Ralph Bunche, the first African American Nobel laureate. Vernon Jordon, a former head of the NAACP. Philosopher Alain Locke, who taught at Howard for more than 40 years, was the first African American Rhodes scholar. You get the idea.

Today some people think that this grand old school (the largest among historically black colleges) has lost some of its luster. The younger kids seem to be talking more about Spelman, Morehouse, Florida A&M, and Hampton. But Howard still is a formidable force, and the ratings are not forever etched in stone. H. Patrick Swygert, Howard's goal-oriented and energetic president, has our "ancient gem" once again flexing its muscles.

In 1995 *Money* magazine named Howard University as one of the "three best" educational values among U.S. colleges. In the *Black Enterprise* rankings of the "top 50 Colleges for African Americans," Howard is in the 5th position.

> Lesli Ferrell says, "I attended UCLA as an undergrad, got satisfactory grades, majored in something 'interesting' (read not relevant to the job market), and found my way into corporate America through a Bank of America training program." She continues with an interesting story but ends by saying, "I went to Howard to RECHARGE my battery." There she mentored and was mentored, ran for office, and attended hundreds of social activities. On graduation day she writes, "I stood next to more African American lawyers, teachers, doctors, anthropologists, psychologists, etc., than most people will ever see in a lifetime."

The Campus

Howard University's "universe" covers more than 241 acres at four college campuses. There's the Divinity School, the Howard Law Center near Rock Creek in northeastern Washington, and the Beltville campus in Maryland. The main undergraduate campus, however, is in central Washington, D.C., and covers 89 acres. At this urban location you'll find the Blackburn Student Center, classrooms, dorms, administrative offices, and the Founders Library, with its 2.2 million volumes. The library is also the home of the Howard University Museum, where we exhibit art and interpret artifacts. And if you take a stroll on campus, you'll see (on display) the creations of many of our artistic "masters," including work by Romare Bearden, Elizabeth Catlett, and Jacob Lawrence.

At Howard you can settle in a dormitory, but there are lots of renovations taking place. There's some housing "restructuring" going on, to be sure. The freshman residence hall for women is Tubman Quadrangle, which houses five dorms. Three are called Baldwin, Frazier, and Wheatley, after our heroes. The Crandell and Truth residences are undergoing redesign. At Tubman you've got a ResNet computer lab and a courtyard for relaxing.

The men have Drew Hall, and a coed residence is the Howard Plaza Towers. To many, Cook Hall, a sophomores' dorm, is generally described as the "best." There's air conditioning, lounges, a weight room, and a super-size television. Frankly, Howard's housing can accommodate only about half of its students. There are "satellite dormitories," such as Carver Hall (men) and Meridian Hill Hall (coed), that all are within 10 blocks of the campus and utilize shuttle buses. Note that the general area around Howard has been described as a "poor neighborhood," with the usual inner-city problems.

Campus Life

It's often said that Howard is a "party school," a "fashion show," and that there's a lot happening. One student calls the environment "a social and cultural heaven." You will have something to do. And yes, it's true, the Alpha Kappa Alpha sorority was founded at Howard in 1908. Now they're all here: Delta Sigma Theta, Alpha Phi Alpha, Sigma Gamma Rho, Phi Beta Sigma, and others. On a sunny day you may see them "stepping" in "The Yard," situated in the middle of the campus. There is "socializing," to put it mildly.

On campus there are more than 150 student clubs and organizations. You can write for the student newspaper, *The Hilltop,* or work at the school's radio or television station. A show called *Spotlight* was an Emmy-nominated TV effort. Big campus events are Opening Convocation, Charter Day, Spring Festival, and Homecoming, where the marching band, "The Thunderdome," always rallies the crowd. In sports, the Howard Bisons (basketball, football) are always a major sports and social attraction.

There's a Gospel choir, African Cultural Ensemble, Pan-African association, chess club, and intramural sports (bowling, tennis, touch football, handball) to keep you occupied. Off campus you'll have access to the capital, and the Georgetown and Adams Morgan communities. You'll find malls, concerts, museums, restaurants, clubs, the John F. Kennedy Center for the Performing Arts, even the Library of Congress. For older students, the popular nightspots are The Mirage, Ritz, and Chapter Three. And it's all just a car or bus ride away.

Academic Realities

Howard will take you on whatever journey you want to travel. Carla Peterman, who picked Howard over Rutgers and Yale, was named a 1999 Rhodes Scholar. She participated in Howard's exchange program and studied for a semester at Duke (besides Duke, Howard has exchange programs with Harvard, Smith, Stanford, Tufts, the University of California at Berkeley, and several other schools). Other students we have talked to have gotten their degrees while on "cruise control." Still, it's interesting to note that graduates in general go on to enter graduate and professional schools—those of law, medicine, dentistry, and business—at very impressive rates.

In classes with motivated, career-minded students, Howard will get you ready. Prepare, however, to perhaps sit in classrooms that might contain 150 to 200 students in introductory classes. At upper-division levels, the numbers decrease considerably, and you might have 20 students in a class. Along the way, you will be challenged. Core requirements include courses in math, English, speech, and the physical sciences, as well as African American history. Popular majors include Journalism, Accounting, Nursing, Psychology, Biology, Radio/Television, and Management (Marketing). All this in a setting where professors are considered "friendly" and most helpful.

Getting In

In a recent year, 4,850 students applied to all the undergraduate divisions and 2,802 were accepted. Generally, Howard appears to be accepting those capable students who have been taking college preparatory courses and doing well. The acceptance rate for applying students is about 58%. The mean SAT composite is 1,019. Note, however, that the admissions requirements vary among the 10 undergraduate schools. For example, the review of students hoping to enter the Arts and Sciences, Engineering, Education, or Art Schools (a portfolio is necessary), will all be looked at differently. About a quarter of the students score below 820 on their SATs. If you're looking at an engineering run, obviously that won't open the door. The total picture is important. Your high school record, recommendations, leadership qualities, school and community service, potential, and alumni relationships are pivotal.

Howard's admissions numbers say it's a "melting pot." Nearly 80% of the students are from out of state, including foreign students from more than 100 countries.

FLORIDA

**BETHUNE-
COOKMAN
COLLEGE**

640 Dr. Mary McLeod
   Bethune Boulevard
Daytona Beach, FL 32114
(800) 448-0228
Web site:
   www.bethune.cookman.edu

Financial aid deadline:
   March 3
Application deadline: July 30
1999–2000 tuition: $8,560;
   room and board, $5,270

"Enter to learn, depart to serve!"

   —Founder's motto

College Ranking

BCC is a career-oriented liberal arts institution that maintains a close association with the United Methodist Church. It is the sixth-largest of the 41-member United Negro College Fund colleges with about 2,500 full-time students enrolled.

The Campus

Students say that at Bethune-Cookman College, you'll have good weather year-round. Located near Daytona Beach in Florida (and a relatively short ride from Orlando and Disney World), this school is on 62 parklike acres of land. Including nine residence halls (four male and five female halls housing nearly 1,800 students), there are 33 buildings. One National Historic Site on campus is the home of Dr. Mary McLeod Bethune, the college's founder.

   On campus you'll find the Charles C. Parlin Student Center, where students congregate and dine "with family." In Cookman Hall there's the office of the Cultural Affairs Program. The Mary McLeod Bethune Fine Arts Center is the home of the Office of Humanities, the Journalism Program, and an art gallery and studio. In Harrison Rhodes Hall you'll find the offices of the Social Sciences Division as well as classrooms.

Campus Life

On campus, nine fraternities and sororities play a big role. You've got them all, from Alpha Kappa Alpha to Zeta Phi Beta. Congratulations are due to Natasha Curry, a soror, and Miss Bethune-Cookman College, 1998–1999. Other groups (there are about 50) include the Thurgood Marshall Society, Gospel choir, drama and dance groups, NAACP, Haitian Club, National Council of Negro Women, Marching Wildcats, *Voice* (school newspaper), and other special-interest and cultural organizations. Career Day and Founder's Day are big events.

   Varsity sports also are popular. There's football at Municipal Stadium (19,000 seats), basketball at Moore Gymnasium, baseball at Jackie Robinson Ballpark, and other intercollegiate teams. Intramural sports also are available. You have tennis and racquetball courts, a weight room, and a gym at your disposal.

Academic Realities

In a typical year about 280 bachelor's degrees are awarded. Students can select majors from 39 areas while pursuing a course of study in one of six academic divisions—Humanities,

Education, Business, Nursing, Science/Math, and Social Sciences. The most popular majors are: Business (23%), Education (21%), Criminal Justice (11%), Nursing (9%), and Psychology (7%). In a recent year, a sample of the enrollment of student majors looked like this: Business Administration (390 students), Accounting (113), Elementary Education (278), Nursing (162), Mass Communications (139), Psychology (106), and Criminal Justice (252). BCC has combined 3-2 engineering programs with Florida A&M, University of Florida, and Tuskegee University.

Getting In

About 72% of the students who apply are accepted. It's a school for students who "want to further their intellectual and social development." Key admission factors are "character and personality." The average SAT is about 900. The approximate entering GPA is about 2.25. As part of the admissions process, you're asked to present one letter of recommendation. Note, too, that BCC usually enrolls about 100 transfers each year. In a recent year 250 applied, 195 were accepted, and 109 enrolled.

About 70% of the students are Floridians, with 20% of the "others" representing 38 states. The international students (5%) arrive from foreign countries, including Caribbean islands.

FLORIDA A&M UNIVERSITY	Suite 112, Foote-Hilyer Administration Tallahassee, FL 32307 (904) 599-3796 Web site: www.famu.edu	**Financial aid deadline:** April 1 (fall); submit FAFSA as soon after January 1 as possible **Application deadline:** May 15 **Early decision deadline:** February 1 **1999–2000 tuition:** $1,800 (state residents); $5,300 (nonresidents); room and board, $3,173

College Ranking

The values that are clearly identified in FAMU's mission statement are: "Equality, equity, excellence, and enhancement." That's a telling hint as to why *Time/Princeton Review* named this university the "College of the Year" in its 1998 magazine edition. This college has been ascending under the tutelage of Dr. Frederick Humphries, who has personally recruited outstanding students as if he were coaching a championship basketball team.

Since 1992, this state-supported school has been vying with Harvard for the distinction of enrolling the most National Achievement scholars. In 1992 and 1995 FAMU prevailed, with Harvard winning in the interim. At Black Excel we knew that was a sign. Few seemed to notice. In 1999 *Black Enterprise* ranked FAMU third behind Spelman and Morehouse as one of the nation's "Top 50 Colleges for African Americans."

The Campus

Florida A&M is in the city of Tallahassee (population 200,000) and is one of 10 schools in the state university's system. It is about eight blocks from the Capitol Complex, with malls a short drive away. This 419-acre campus (can you find some shade?) is visually appealing. The campus is on the highest of seven city hills, is about 22 miles from the Gulf of Mexico, and is not too far from several parks, some with lakes. On campus you'll walk under ancient oaks, enjoy the beautiful flowers and grass, and undoubtedly stop at "The Set," a main hangout near the Student Union.

FAMU's campus has 111 buildings, including the student residences. The Carnegie Center is the home of the Black Achievers, off the main quad. The "Tech Buildings" include the College of Engineering and Computer Systems Department. The Student Union is in the heart of the campus. There you'll find bowling lanes, a billiards room, and offices for groups such as the Student Government Association. The Teleconference Center, built in 1994, is described as their "hi-tech link to the world." Coleman Memorial Library has more than 400,000 volumes, and also has a fully equipped photography laboratory and television studio. At the University Commons you'll find the student cafeteria.

Most students live in the traditional residence halls, designed for double occupancy, with air conditioning, shared bathrooms, and desks. The Paddyfote houses men in sections A and B, and women in C and D. All-women's dorms include the Cropper—a step away from classes—Diamond, McGuinn, Truth, and Wheatley residences. For students who are married or have extra funds, there are the apartments at Polkinghorne Village and the Palmetto Street Complex. There you'll get suites with carpeting and bedrooms for four-student groupings.

About 89% of the FAMU student body is black, with about a 7% white total.

Campus Life

You can get some "southern hospitality" at more than 130 clubs and organizations on campus. Popular events include Homecoming, which always features a fashion show, and the Coronation of the Queen (Miss FAMU). Other popular events are Greek Week (some of the frats have their own houses), and Harambee. *Famuan,* the school newspaper, is published once a week.

If you wish, you can get involved with the NAACP, Pan-African Cultural Club, Golden Bridge Mentor Program, Images Modeling Troupe, the FAMU Gospel Choir (which released its first album in 1985), dance and drama clubs, or the school's radio station (WAMF-FM). More than 34% of FAMU students participate in intramural sports. And for this school's spirited Rattler football games—in 25,000-seat Brag Stadium—there's always The Marching 100, FAMU's 300-plus high-stepping band, which has won the Sousa Foundation's prestigious Sudler Trophy for performance. ABC and CBS have called this group "The Nation's Number One Band."

Florida A&M offers both Navy and Army ROTC.

Academic Realities

The average SAT score at FAMU is about 1036, with enrollment increasing as well as the number of baccalaureates awarded each year (1,524). FAMU has now overtaken Howard as the leader in this area. Obviously, admission to some programs is highly selective (e.g., Engineering and Business). The students at the different schools sometimes sound like they are studying at different colleges. FAMU stress and competitive levels vary, depending on your major. Still, the overall environment is a nurturing one, not one of tension or dread.

That said, look to be trained to compete. In the School of Business and Industry's "Bull and Bear" lounge you can find students in business suits and ties studying. Nearby, an electronic ticker displays the latest stock figures. Academically, the Schools of Business, Engineering, and Pharmacy are said to be the toughest. You'll find those professional tracks to medicine, dentistry, and law.

In the School of Arts and Sciences (with more than 50 majors available), FAMU offers many options. Here's a recent sample of enrolled students: Computer Sciences (291), Criminal Justice (248), English (103), Political Science (246), Psychology (267), Social Work (76), French (3), Molecular Biology (9), Business Economics (256), Chemistry (63), Theater (27), and African American Studies (18).

You can also get certification in Education, which is the selected major of about 13% of the students. You can study, too, Journalism, Fine Arts, Drama, and Music.

> **"W**hat my instructors did really well at A&M was to teach me about professional life. They graded us tough and acted like bosses. Out on the job, I kept saying, 'My goodness, they told us this!' I was prepared." —PAMELA DAVIS, AN FAMU GRADUATE AND PRESENTLY A PUBLIC RELATIONS ASSISTANT AT CNN.

Getting In

FAMU's acceptance rate is 61%. In a recent year, 4,850 applied and 2,905 were accepted. Ideally, the school is looking for SATs of about 1010 and ACTs of at least 21. The average GPA of arriving students is about 2.5 (on a 4.0 scale). Still, you can get in with lower test scores and grades. Dr. Humphries has noted that at least 30% of the school's slots will be held for students who "ordinarily would not qualify" (but who are still above average), because that's part of the mission of our schools—to reach out, to lay down a path. Apply when you can "bring to the university other important attributes or special talents" that might not be reflected in your transcript.

Remember that 77% of the students (about 9,300) at FAMU are "homegrown" Floridians. Still, this school attracts a sizable number of students (about 23%) from Georgia, Illinois, Michigan, Alabama, and Texas. States with lesser totals (but very notable numbers) are South Carolina, New York, California, Maryland, Pennsylvania, and Ohio. Also, more than 100 students are from foreign countries, including Nigeria, Haiti, China, the Bahamas, and Bermuda.

Be aware that very large numbers of transfer students apply to Florida A&M. In one recent year more than 440 of such students enrolled.

GEORGIA

CLARK-ATLANTA UNIVERSITY

223 James P. Brawley Drive, S.W.
Atlanta, GA 30314-4389
(404) 880-8018
Web site: www.cau.edu

Financial aid deadline:
April 15 (priority); CSS form necessary (the telephone number of the financial aid office is 404/880-8000)

Application deadline:
March 31

1999–2000 tuition: $8,830; room and board, $5,170

"I'll find a way or make one!"

—Clark-Atlanta motto.

College Ranking

The 1988 merger of Clark College and Atlanta University (CAU) signaled good things for the future, including an enhanced reputation for everybody involved. As a member of the Atlanta University Center Consortium (with Spelman, Morehouse, Morris Brown, the Theological Center, and Morehouse School of Medicine), more press and attention were inevitable. Today we see more Clark-Atlanta stickers than ever before. Not only does it offer bachelor degrees, but it offers many graduate and doctoral programs as well. CAU is ranked first in the nation in granting Ph.D.'s to African Americans.

The Campus

Clark-Atlanta University is a private college about a mile southwest of Atlanta. Located on 113 acres of urban land, the university boasts 30 buildings, including residences. Many of CAU's buildings are shared with the consortium of schools, including a state-of-the-art Science and Technology Research Center and the Woodruff Library (with more than 750,000 volumes). Buildings are both stately and modern, and there are even a few tree-lined quadrangles. A nice location on campus is the Pedestrian Promenade (and courtyard) which was created for the Olympic Games in 1996. If a student is looking for a luxurious campus with physical amenities such as a huge gymnasium, Olympic-size swimming pools, and state-of-the-art nautical equipment, CAU doesn't have them. It does have a 5,000-seat stadium with weight rooms, office space, sky boxes, and concession areas. In 1996, the stadium served as a field hockey arena for the Olympic competitors.

Campus Life

CAU students feel the "elitism" of their Spelman and Morehouse brothers and sisters, who are sometimes said to have an "air of snobbery" about them. It's about "their tradition," one senior says sadly. Ironically, the schools are all within walking distance of each other, there is often cross-registration, and students of the consortium all go to the same events and use many of the same facilities. Still, that "feeling" is everywhere. The pecking order seems to be Spelman and Morehouse, with Clark-Atlanta being "okay," and Morris Brown tailgating.

There are more than 60 clubs, organizations, and special-interest groups on campus. Some that might be of particular interest include the NAACP, *Panther* (student newspaper), Campus Ministry, WCLK-FM (the campus radio station), theater/drama and dance groups, the Student Government Association, a choir, a jazz ensemble, and a marching band. All the major "eight" fraternities and sororities are represented at CAU and are very active. Popular school events include Homecoming, Alumni Weekend, United Negro College Fund Drive, Consolidation Day, Spring Arts Festival, and Commencement.

CAU is a NCAA Division II varsity school and a member of the Southern Intercollegiate Athletic Conference (SIAC). There's the usual assortment of school teams. Students have access to a gym, weight-lifting room, pool, and tennis and basketball courts. School colors are red, black, and gray.

Beyond the campus are the expressways and skyscrapers of Atlanta. Students can enjoy Six Flags Amusement Park, Underground Atlanta, Stone Mountain Park, Omni (the professional basketball arena), Martin Luther King Jr. Center, museums, restaurants, theaters, and more.

CAU distinguished alumni include educator Marva Collins (founder and director of the Westside Preparatory School) and poet James Weldon Johnson.

Academic Realities

Students can study in one of several schools, including the Schools of Arts and Sciences, Business, and Education. There are programs in business, communications, education, the health professions, engineering, computer science, biological sciences, social sciences, and more. The most popular major categories for students are: Business (24%), Education (16%), Communications (14), Psychology (9), Social Sciences and History (8%), Biological and Life Sciences (5%), Math (4%), Computer Science (3%), and the Visual and Performing Arts (3%). Preprofessional tracks are available in law, medicine, engineering, dentistry, pharmacy, and seminary studies. There's an African American Studies program. At CAU there are more than 200 full-time faculty members. In a recent graduating class, 528 bachelor's degrees were awarded.

One interesting study-abroad program that Clark-Atlanta offers is a four-week program for credit that is run by professor James D. McJinkins. The trip is to Kingston, Jamaica, and you have to write a fifteen-page research paper for six credit hours at the University of the West Indies.

CAU has 3-2 year engineering degree affiliations with Georgia Tech, North Carolina A&T, Boston University, and other schools.

Many students say the school "goes easy" on students the first semester (and year) and that graduate students sometimes teach your first sequence of courses. Students who are in technical tracks, taking courses such as Biology or Chemistry, find the going more difficult. Also, it is not unusual to find Morehouse or Spelman students sitting next to you, due to overcrowding at their schools. Note, too, that CAU has a wider range of course selections than its companion schools. If problems arise and you need remedial help, there's the Student Support Service.

We've heard that there is a high attrition rate at Clark-Atlanta after the freshman and sophomore years, often due to "financial difficulties"—that proverbial lack of money. Only about 51% of the students graduate in six years.

Getting In

Getting into CAU has been described by some as only "minimally difficult." Clark-Atlanta accepts about 69% of its applicants. In a recent year 6,576 applied and 4,449 were accepted. Eventually 1,223 students decided to enroll. About 60% of the students were from out of state, arriving from more than 45 states and approximately 64 foreign countries. Many students are from the South, but sizable numbers arrive from New York City, Detroit, Miami, Chicago, and Los Angeles. There are generally about 4,500 undergraduate students on campus, with women (70%) more than doubling the count of men. The average SAT score is about 900. The most important factor here is your secondary school record (a 2.5 GPA or higher is desirable).

EMORY UNIVERSITY

Boisfeuillet Jones Center
Atlanta, GA 30322
(800) 727-6036
Web site: www.emory.edu

Financial aid deadline: February 15; either the FAFSA or the CSS profile are required
Application deadline: January 15
Early decision deadline: November 1
1999–2000 tuition: $23,130; room and board, $7,650

College Ranking

Emory University is one of the highest-ranked colleges in the nation. With an endowment that now is more than $4 billion (the sixth largest in the nation), the sky could be the limit. Some experts, however, do say that it's often a "second choice" to students looking to the Ivy League and other prestigious schools. Right now it looks like these students are in a "win-win" situation.

Note, also, that in a recent edition of the *Journal of Blacks in Higher Education* it was pointed out that Emory had the highest percentage of black students enrolled among elite universities, 10.3%, more than any of the top 25 nationally ranked colleges or universities.

The Campus

When you arrive at Emory, you will probably stand on North Decatur Road and enter through the Hopkins-Haywood Gate, the main entrance. You'll get a suburban, picture-postcard view— of flowers in bloom, green lawns, shrubbery. Walking on those pathways and hills, you'll discover a 631-acre campus (it's about six miles from downtown Atlanta) that will be memorable. Another plus is Lullwater Park, which adjoins the campus. You can stroll on walking trails, birdwatch, and even hold hands (perhaps) at a small lake. In Atlanta you'll find a myriad of attractions: malls, museums, restaurants, cinemas, whatever your heart desires.

At Emory there are 116 buildings, including residence halls. They are generally impressive, colorful, sometimes with grand and marble facades, with overhanging trees that seem to be everywhere. Of course, you'll see Emory College (the liberal arts nucleus of the university). A definite stop will be at the Woodruff Library, Emory's largest. It's the one you head to for serious study—and a little quiet time. Candler Library is the smaller, more popular location, where both studying and socializing take place. The Emory libraries (five altogether) have more than 2.4 million volumes.

The Michael C. Carlos Museum is said to have one of the largest collections of Sub-Saharan African Art in the United States. There's Carlos Hall, with computer labs that connect to the campus and the "global networks." More than 1,200 students use the computers daily. The "Quadrangle"—where students often congregate—is at the academic core of Emory's campus, where you'll find educational outlets for many of the 50 majors available to you. Another popular gathering spot is the area around Cox Hall, with its clock tower. If you wish, you can march to the Glenn Memorial Chapel, where the annual Baccalaureate Ceremony is held. You can pose for a camera shot where South African archbishop Desmond Tutu once spoke at commencement.

The first-year residence halls include single-sex and coed dormitories, on-campus apartments, fraternity and sorority housing, and theme houses. Some of the dorms (all with air conditioning, TV lounges, and movable furniture) include Dobbs, Longstreet, McTyeire, and the Means and Thomas residences (both in "The Complex"). Also, there is Turman North, which is comprised of four residences and a spacious lawn for socializing and studying. The similar Turman East has an outdoor amphitheater and deli. And yes, there is a Black Student Alliance House, an upper-class, coed residence where our folks often select to reside.

Campus Life

Alpha Phi Alpha usually hosts an annual "Stepshow" for sickle-cell anemia research. This event attracts about 1,000 students each year, with other Greek-letter blacks arriving to participate from neighboring Georgia colleges.

There are more than 200 clubs, organizations, and special-interest groups on campus. Blacks look to their black fraternities and sororities for support. Here you'll find Delta Sigma Theta, Alpha Kappa Alpha, Omega Psi Phi, Kappa Alpha Psi, and Alpha Phi Alpha, not to mention the Black Student Alliance, The Fire This Time, and Ngambika.

The student online newspaper is called *The Wheel*. Others include *The Fever, The Fire,* and *The Spoke.* Some of the clubs/art groups are the Emory Dance Company (regularly playing to capacity houses), Music at Emory, the Indian Cultural Exchange, Sailing Club, Habitat for Humanity, EV News, International Association, and chess, photography, debate, film, and art outlets for students. There's also a jazz band, an orchestra, radio and TV stations, the Student Government Association, and College and Media Councils. At the Carter Center you can fight "hunger, poverty, and oppression" through collaborative initiatives.

Important campus events also include the Heritage Ball and the Festival of the Nine Lives.

Last, there are more than 40 intramural sports and/or events for students, and a 3,000-seat gym with four basketball courts, an Olympic-size pool, Nautilus weight rooms, and squash, tennis, and racquetball courts. There's also a 400-meter track and soccer field with a 2,000-seat capacity.

Note that Emory does not sponsor varsity football.

On campus, you can use an EmoryCard, a multipurpose card that that serves as "a token" to the library and eateries. It can serve as your "meal ticket" while you deduct payments from your meal plan. Note that the Dobbs University Center is where most students eat. It's open 24 hours a day, and you can get standard cafeteria food, including pizza, deli sandwiches, and Burger King food, to mention just a few possibilities.

Academic Realities

The academic climate is said to be "serious." Usually the introductory classes will range from 25 to 200 students, with one lecture hall able to seat 250. At upper levels, classes can be as small as six to 12 students. Most students are premed, with many being Biology and Chemistry majors. These courses are often described as "difficult" and "stressful." The most popular majors are Biology, Psychology, Business, Nursing, and English.

There are comprehensive and "rigorous" (some say) liberal arts distribution requirements that are necessary beyond any major. You must take courses in six necessary categories, including courses that fall under the titles of Tools of Learning, the Individual and Society, and Aesthetics and Values.

There's an African American Studies major. Courses that you might find of interest (available to all majors) include: Jazz: Its Evolution and Essence, Race and Ethnic Relations, Dynamics of the Black Community, and African American Literature to 1900 (and the follow-up course, covering the period after 1900). The noted Nobel Laureate Wole Soyinka, is a professor with the Black Studies Institute.

About 1,500 bachelor's degrees are awarded annually.

Getting In

Admission to Emory is very competitive, with the school looking for students who have taken the most challenging high school courses and have done exceptionally well. We're talking about courses such as Physics, Chemistry, and Biology at honors or advance placement levels. Your "demonstrated interest in attending Emory is carefully noted and factored into admissions decisions."

At Emory the acceptance rate is about 44%. In a recent year approximately 9,780 applied and 4,500 were accepted. More than 86% of the students graduated in the top 10% of their high school class. The median SAT score is about 1345. About 10% of the arriving students are African American.

Most Emory undergraduate students (6,316) are from the South, although 48 states are represented, including large contingents of students from the Middle Atlantic and northeastern states. Students also arrive from 105 foreign countries.

About 65% of the students are from public schools.

GEORGIA INSTITUTE OF TECHNOLOGY	225 North Avenue Atlanta, GA 30332-0320 (404) 894-4154 Web site: www.gatech.edu	**Financial aid deadline:** March 1 (for school's form) **Application deadline:** January 15 **1999–2000 tuition:** $3,108 (state residents); $10,350 (nonresidents); room and board, $5,700

College Ranking

Georgia Tech, as it's often called, is one of the most highly regarded colleges in the South. *U.S. News & World Report* ranks the school among the "Best National Universities," and it is one of the finest technical institutions in America. If you're interested in being a scientist or an engineer, you should take a close look.

The Campus

Georgia Tech is in downtown Atlanta. A state-supported urban institution, it is located on 350 acres. The school has 170 buildings, including residences. The campus has a new look. Tech was one of the colleges that hosted the 1996 Summer Olympic Games, and it benefited from necessary renovations and the reconstruction of facilities across campus. Some say the campus "is self-contained." The Georgia Tech Library and Information Center has 2.7 million volumes. A gathering spot is the Georgia Tech Student Center, where you'll get everything: 12 bowling lanes, 14 billiard tables, pinball and video games, a theater, the Buzz By Snack Bar, a cafeteria, credit union, and ballroom. At the Robert Frost Center for the Arts (where 1992 vice-presidential debates were held) you'll see theatrical performances. And yes, there are tree-lined walks, and you'll see azalea blossoms in the spring.

More than 70% of the students at Georgia Tech live in modern dormitories as a result of the Olympics. There are lots of suitelike rooms with kitchens, even language halls where you can experience other cultures. After all, 21% of the students arrive from 106 different countries.

Campus Life

There are more than 200 clubs, organizations, and special-interest groups on campus. Cultural and social outlets that might be of particular interest to us include African American Association, African American Student Union (AASU), Caribbean Student Association, National Society of Black Engineers, Big Brothers/Big Sisters, and Techwood Tutorial Program. All the major "eight" fraternities and sororities are on campus. Alpha Phi Alpha has sponsored a Miss Black and Gold Scholarship pageant. AASU puts on a Valentine's Day Jazz Set and an annual

Step Show. Heritage Bounded is a lecture series. Off campus there's the city's Underground, with its theaters, shops, and cultural attractions.

Georgia Tech's basketball teams have set the country ablaze. In 1990 the football team won a collegiate national championship. Varsity sports at all levels are popular. Intramural sports are popular. More than 5,000 students get involved.

If you visit the campus, take a picture of the beautiful Kessler Campanile (the water-spouting fountain in front of the 300-seat amphitheater). The fountain's four speakers sometimes belt out the "Ramblin' Wreck" Georgia Tech fight song.

Academic Realities

There are five undergraduate schools: the School of Engineering, School of Sciences, School of Architecture, School of Computing, and there's the Ivan Allen College of Management, Policy, and International Affairs. The faculty here is considered one of the best in the nation. National Merit Scholars abound, and the student body usually has one of the highest SAT averages in the nation. You can get your B.S. in any of 31 degree areas. The journey will be rigorous and the degree marketable, to say the least.

The academics here are both intense and competitive. For example, whatever your career destination, freshman year is likely to see you tackling courses such as Physics, Calculus, and Chemistry. It's sometimes said to be "overwhelming," with students beside you who are very, very capable academically. During the early going there are some difficult "weed-out" courses that nudge some students to transfer to a business management track. You will study long and hard. Generally, African American students, especially those from poorer school districts, begin with the helpful and rigorous Challenge Program, which takes place in a five-week academic boot camp in the summer. The stats say we have successfully run the obstacle course when we arrive in the fall, sometimes outstandingly so. The success of this program has brought the school national attention.

Students are required to take some liberal arts courses. You complete 18 credits in the humanities and the same total in the social sciences. The Tech co-op allows students to not only "master the classroom techniques, but get some practical experience." This is called the "Cooperative Plan." There are about 19 *Fortune* 500 corporations and high-tech industries in Atlanta that actively recruit using these programs.

Support services for African Americans include the Office of Diversity Issues and Programs, Office of Minority Education Department (OMED), the university-wide Freshman Experience Program, and Challenge.

Getting In

At Georgia Tech the acceptance rate is about 61%. In a recent year 7,676 applied and 4,702 were accepted. The SAT average was about 1320. Out of approximately 8,800 students, 9% were African American. Nearly 40% of the students were from out of state. Here, your high school record is pivotal. You must be able to show that you have been able to handle a demanding courseload (Chemistry, Physics, and similar courses). Also, your test scores have to be "in the ballpark." Note that a quarter of the entering students score less than 1230, and undoubtedly some scores in the 1100 range are considered.

MOREHOUSE COLLEGE

830 Westview Drive, S.W.
Atlanta, GA 30314
(800) 851-1254
Web site:
www.morehouse.edu

Application deadline:
February 15
Financial aid deadline: April
14; recommendation: submit
as soon as possible after January 1; FAFSA, CSS profile,
and a school form required
1999–2000 tuition: $9,668;
room and board, $5,976

"There is an air of expectancy at Morehouse College. It is expected that the student who enters here will do well. It is also expected that once a man bears the insignia of a Morehouse graduate he will do exceptionally well. We expect nothing less . . ."

—the charge of the graduating class of 1961, Dr. Benjamin E. Mays, president, 1940–1967

College Ranking

Morehouse College is one of the most competitive and highly selective historically black colleges. The school is a member of the Atlanta University Center Consortium, the largest private educational consortium with a predominantly black enrollment in the world. The six-college group includes Spelman College, Clark-Atlanta University, Morris Brown College, the Theological Center, and Morehouse School of Medicine.

Morehouse has an endowment of more than $50 million, placing it third behind Spelman and Hampton among black colleges. The school was founded in 1867, and distinguished graduates include Dr. Martin Luther King Jr., Spike Lee, Julian Bond, Olympic gold medalist Edwin Moses, and college presidents Samuel DuBois of Dillard and David Satcher of Meharry Medical School. In 1994 Nima A. Warfield, a Morehouse senior, became the first Rhodes Scholar from a historically black college.

The Campus

Morehouse is a private liberal arts college about three miles from downtown Atlanta. It is on 61 metropolitan acres, and there are 35 buildings, including residences. You'll find modern and Colonial-style buildings. On a stroll, you'll pass Gloster Hall, which is the main administrative building. The Kilgore Center (a recreation center with pool tables, Ping-Pong, etc.) has a dorm wing. Overhead is a tower, and inside you'll also find the President's Dining Room, guest quarters, a student lounge, and a snack bar. At Hope Hall there is a post office in the basement, and biology labs. The Chemistry and Biology Departments are in the Nabrit, Mapp, and McBay Buildings. There is a computer center, Woodruff Library, and the Martin Luther King Jr. International Chapel. Also, there's a Frederick Douglass Commons (a student center) and the Walter R. Chivers Dining Hall. At Archer Hall there is a gym, and a swimming pool that was ready for the 1996 Olympics. Just a couple of years ago the campus dormitories were upgraded with air conditioning. Residences include Samuel T. Graves Hall (190 students), Benjamin Mays Hall (with a central lounge, and a dining hall for 360 students), as well as W .E. B. Du Bois, Howard Thurman, and Charles D. Hubert Halls. At Franklin L. Forbes Hall there are 169 beds.

Campus Life

Be aware that Spelman women are only a step away and are an integral part of the social/dating/classroom scene at Morehouse. The social scene is lively, to say the least. Each Morehouse freshman is paired with a Spelman sister. At the start, you've got a "friend and adjustment buddy." Remember that coed classes are common, and the total social fabric is "just about shared" at parties, sports events, and the sister/brother Greek-letter scene.

At Morehouse there are about 70 clubs, organizations, and special-interest groups. All the major "eight" fraternities and sororities (counting Spelman) are on campus and very active. Other outlets that might be of particular interest include National Student Council for Africa (NSCA), NAACP, Gospel Theater Ensemble, Morehouse Mathletes Club, Nation of Islam Student Association, Frederick Douglass Tutorial Institute, Morehouse Business Association, Black Men for the Education of Sexism, Morehouse Powerlifting Tigers, National Society of Black Engineers, National Association of Black Accountants, Southern Christian Leadership Conference, Tae-Kwon-Do Club, Young Business World Association, a radio/TV station, a chess club, literary and newspaper *(Maroon Tiger)* publications, music groups, a marching band, preprofessional clubs, a debating team, and choral groups. The Glee Club performed at President Clinton's 1992 inauguration.

On Western Drive you'll find tennis and basketball courts. Also, there's the Archer Hall Recreation and Fitness Center. ROTC is available. Last, there's the world of nearby Atlanta. You'll find the Underground Mall, restaurants, clubs, and a nightlife that is easily accessible.

Morehouse is a member of the NCAA (Division II), with basketball, football, track (including cross-country), and tennis teams. Howard University is a perennial rival.

"The House," as Morehouse is sometimes called, is known for its "mystique." If you and your parent attend the precollege annual "Prospective Student Seminar," you'll get a chance to learn about the school's legacy and mission. The administration, faculty, and students will talk about "keys" such as "character," "scholarship," and "leadership." Once enrolled, there'll be a New Student Orientation Program (NSOP) for new students and their families. A recent session was called "Affirming Excellence Through Transformation." You'll be taken on a campus tour, given financial aid workshops, and more.

Your first day on campus, upperclassmen escort freshmen to Sales Chapel Hall, where you'll hear about those "accomplished" graduates like Dr. Martin Luther King Jr. and former Morehouse president Benjamin Mays. During Freshmen Week, new students must dress in white shirts, slacks, and tie. The freshmen are then grilled in question-and-answer sessions in hallways by upperclassmen. New students are required to know about the history and tradition of Morehouse and are given a booklet for review. After "induction," students are treated to a day at the Six Flags Amusement Park in Atlanta. "Spirit Night," a Morehouse rallying event, usually occurs within the first week of the academic year. You are inspired with speeches about the meaning/tradition of becoming a "Morehouse man."

Academic Realities

The hardest courses at Morehouse are said to be in the biology (premed) and the math/science tracks. The general consensus seems to be that student difficulty arises when students are not astute enough to balance their academics (study/homework) with recreational activities. To be sure, there is an endless calendar of cultural and social events: Greek-letter affairs and parties, to name two things. You must focus. The problem is more one of using study time wisely than of confronting academic "pressure." There is strong competition. All your classmates are capable and achievers. The most popular majors include Business, Psychology, Engineering, Biology, Political Science, and English. There are more than 36 majors available, including African Studies and African American Studies.

Note that there are premed, prelaw, and predentistry tracks. Computer literacy is required for Mathematics, Accounting, Engineering, Finance, and Management majors. There is a Phi Beta Kappa chapter (the oldest national academic honor society) on campus. All Morehouse students are part of the Atlanta University Center Consortium, and can cross-register for classes at Spelman, Clark-Atlanta, and Morris Brown.

To those who are interested, Morehouse runs a cooperative 3-2 engineering program with Georgia Tech and a 3-2 architecture program with Michigan State. You attend Morehouse for the first three years and the professional school for the final two. You then receive two degrees.

There is a Morehouse Academic Scholarship Program (MASP) for incoming freshmen. These awards are for "high academic ability." Contact admissions for extra information.

A commendable percent (10%) go on to medical school (totals shift yearly, but Morehouse usually has one of the most successful postgraduate placement records of the historically black colleges), more than 9% to law school, 9% into M.B.A. programs, 7% into engineering, and another 10% into other graduate areas. Morehouse graduates obviously are held in high regard and have little difficulty gaining admission to some of the premier colleges in the United States.

At a recent Baccalaureate Commencement, more than 10,000 showed up. Oprah Winfrey spoke, and Dr. Lerone Bennett Jr., the executive editor of *Ebony*, gave the commencement speech. A total of 451 B.A. and B.S. degrees were awarded.

Getting In

The acceptance rate at Morehouse is about 69%. In a recent year about 2,706 students applied and 1,869 were accepted. Students arrive from approximately 40 states and 12 foreign countries. The average SAT score is about 1045. More than 82% of the students are from out of state. The undergraduate body count is usually about 3,000 full-time students.

Morehouse is looking for future leaders (don't forget this when you're putting your application together), and the admissions team will try to admit the best students in their application pool, all factors considered. An academic average in the 85 and above range is desirable. A key factor will be your GPA, because that will signal your academic ability/drive. If you are in honors or top classes taking courses such as Physics and Chemistry, you are going to look very appealing to the admissions people. Enrollment in top/gifted high schools, or in special senior-year programs connected with colleges, will be a major plus. Your SAT or ACT score also will be very important. SATs above 1000 combined will place you in excellent position.

MORRIS BROWN COLLEGE

Director of Admissions
643 Martin Luther King Jr.
Drive, N.E.
Atlanta, GA 30314
(404) 220-0378
Web site:
www.morrisbrown.com

Application deadline: Rolling
Financial aid deadline: Rolling
1999–2000 tuition: $8,210;
room and board, $4,750

College Ranking

Morris Brown College is a private, liberal arts college with a strong nurturing atmosphere for "need a second chance" students.

The Campus

Morris Brown is a member of the Atlanta University Center Consortium, including Spelman, Morehouse, and Clark-Atlanta University. The school is a short walk from the other schools and is on 18 acres of land about a mile from downtown Atlanta. On campus there are 13 buildings, including five student residences. About 45% of the students reside on campus.

On campus, a gathering place is the Hickman Student Center, with its focus on telecommunications. There you'll find a computer lab and conference rooms. At the W. E. B. Du Bois Center you'll find "global studies" and a concern for issues that relate to the world. The idea is that Africa, Asia, Europe, and South America are next door. Other points of interest are the Robert W. Woodruff Library (which is shared by all AUCC students), the Art Gallery at Jordon Hall, the CyberLab, the Learning Resource Center (LRC), Herndon Home Museum, and the Morris Brown Research Institute (MBRI).

Campus Life

There are 102 clubs, organizations, and special-interest groups on campus. All the major and local fraternities and sororities are on campus and are very active. There's the Pan-Hellenic Council, International Student Organization, Drama League, a glee club, orchestra, and the Florida Club, Pre-Alumni Council, drill team, pep band, and marching band.

The Wolverines participate in 10 NCAA Division II intercollegiate sports, including football, basketball, track and field, and tennis. There are men's clubs in soccer and baseball.

Academic Realities

Morris Brown is the alma mater of James Allen McPherson, now a professor of English at the University of Iowa, and a Pulitzer Prize winner for his short-story collection.

If there's a college theme here, it's that you deserve a "second chance." The intent is to serve the needs of students who may be educationally handicapped and considered by some to be "high risks" but who nevertheless have potential, talents, and abilities. Programs are offered through the Divisions of Education and Psychology, Natural Science and Mathematics, Social Science, and Humanities. Incoming students have more than 40 areas of study available to them. There are premedicine, pharmacy, and dentistry tracks. Each student must take a computer course. The most popular majors are Business (25%), Education (19%), Health and Social Sciences (8% each), Computer Sciences (6%), and Biology and Psychology (about 5% each). Students can cross-register with schools in the other Atlanta University schools.

Getting In

The acceptance rate at Morris Brown is 66%. In a recent year 2,882 students applied, 1,811 were accepted, and 589 enrolled. The average SAT has been in the 860–870 range. The ACT average has been about 17. The most important admissions factor is your secondary school record. Most of the incoming freshmen are from the Southeast, with 51% out-of-staters. International students (about 180 are on campus) arrive from the Bahamas, Canada, Jamaica, Ethiopia, and Nigeria.

SPELMAN COLLEGE

350 Spelman Lane
Atlanta, GA 30314
(404) 681-3643; (800) 932-2411
Web site: www.spelman.edu

Financial aid deadline: submit all aid forms as soon after January 1 as possible
Application deadline: February 1
Early decision deadline: November 15 for "academically outstanding" students
1999–2000 tuition: $10,715; room and board, $6,730

"At Spelman, we enjoyed the beauty of the arts—music, dance, and drama—and we heard the most distinguished scholars and theologians of our time. . . . They lit a fire in our souls for success and challenged us to aim beyond our circumstances, to be a credit to our people, our nation, our world."

—Dr. Audrey Forbes Manley, speaking at her 1998 inaugural as the eighth President of Spelman College, her alma mater

College Ranking

The Spelman mystique continues to soar. It seems that practically every young black woman we meet wants to go there, and with good reason. This school was recently ranked first in a *Black Enterprise* rating of the "Top 50 Colleges for African Americans." Of course, nobody was surprised. Several years before, *U.S. News & World Report* ranked the school first, calling it the "Best Liberal Arts College" in the Southern Region. In 1998 *Money* magazine said Spelman was one of the "best college buys," placing it fifth in desirability. A few years before, Spelman made the Templeton Honor Roll for "Character-Building Colleges." Getting continuous praise, it's no wonder Spelman was recently bestowed a Phi Beta Kappa charter.

And this is the place—under the brilliant tutelage of former president Dr. Johnetta Cole—that received a $20 million donation from Bill Cosby in 1988, the largest ever from an individual to a historically black college. Spelman's endowment (more than $156 million) is now only second to Howard's among schools of color.

The Campus

Spelman's oval-shaped, 32-acre campus is attractive. There is a nicely manicured lawn with occasional magnolia trees and flowers. Even with circling gates, this parklike setting (three miles from downtown Atlanta) has a postcard look. It's a small area that has 29 buildings, counting the dorms, department, administrative, and other structures. The space accommodates more than 1,150 students—the "Sisterhood"—and is part of the nearby consortium of schools that include Morehouse, Clark-Atlanta, and Morris Brown College.

On campus you'll find that most of the buildings are clustered in the center space, while the dorms seem to circle the outskirts of the structures. Spelman has the feel of a small school but with all the amenities of a larger school. It's a short stroll to the International Affairs, Writing, and Camille Olivia Hanks Cosby Academic Centers. With 4,500 feet of exhibition space, there's the Spelman College Fine Art Museum and the AUC Student Crisis Center, where you can sit in on tutorials and study skills workshops. Also, you'll find music studios, science and language labs, a nursery school, and a media-training outlet. For a photo opportunity stand in front of the Sisters Chapel, with its pillared columns. Helpful, too, is the Woodruff Library of the Atlanta University Center (shared by all the schools in the consortium), with more than 830,000 volumes available, including archival materials in the Countee Cullen Memorial Collection.

The 11 dorms are generally described as "adequate." The relatively new Living and Learning Center II and the Howard Harreld residences are generally called "the best." Although it is said that the Laura Spelman House has "historic charm," many consider it "ancient." McViCar, another dorm that seems to be unpopular, is over an infirmary. A key plus, whatever the accolades or complaints here, is that that each dorm has many study rooms, including computers.

Most students eat at the Manley Student Center when using their meal-plan tickets. Popular fast-food spots on campus include The Grill (for burgers), or Subway, for sandwiches. Off campus there's Mick's for popular American food dishes. Upper-class women, by the way, usually opt to live off campus (not nearby) in one of the nicer residential neighborhoods about 15 miles away.

Campus Life

Greek-letter life plays a very important part of life on this campus, with more than 15% of the students joining Delta Sigma Theta, Alpha Kappa Alpha, or one of the other sororities. These sorors, as well as more than 25% of the "Sisterhood," eventually get involved with some kind of community service, often in the "poor" West End neighborhood that surrounds Spelman.

The social life at Spelman is generally described as "good" to "great." Though it's a single-sex school, the Morehouse, Clark-Atlanta, and Morris Brown men are never too far away. There's a Spelman-Morehouse Chorus, the Spelman-Morehouse Players, and an ongoing "connective" air in regard to cultural, entertainment, and Greek-letter events. You'll see everybody at a "Jambalaya: A Season of Discovery," a modern jazz and dance/ theater performance, for example. In 1997, students were saying "party like it's 1999!" and you can if you're so inclined.

Excurricular activities are in abundance. You can write for *Spotlight,* the school newspaper, *Reflections,* the yearbook, or joint the AST African Sisterhood, women who are very involved culturally. Of course, Spelman has its traditional "Homecoming" and "Founder's Day." Throw in the debate team, jazz band, Student Government Association, the bowling lanes, tennis courts, gym, and perhaps a Howard vs. Morehouse sports event and you've got more than enough to keep you involved (other than with the books).

Academic Realities

Spelman offers a well-rounded, top-notch liberal arts education. You'll find a nurturing, yet a very challenging environment. You will be called on to use your critical and analytical thinking, to be sure. And you'll be expected to express yourself with confidence while writing with substance and skill. But you won't feel, for example, the kind of academic tension or daily pressure you might feel if you were at a school such as Johns Hopkins, to name just one of the dozen or so schools that will give you "mental whiplash." Test and study pressure will be closer to what you'll generally find at some of the better state and private colleges and universities. "You'll be able to take a breath," one Spelman junior says, who's hoping to get into law school. Still, at any given time, 10 National Merit scholars might be on campus, with perhaps more than 50 high school valedictorians. At Spelman, many of the majors are designed to lead to professional careers. You've got prelaw, premed, and business tracks, as well as an assortment of other roads (engineering, the sciences) that can take you just about anywhere you want to go. The core curriculum will polish your skills and leave you well rounded and ready. Note that most classes are small (20 to 35 students), with nurturing if needed and individual attention a real possibility.

Spelman is part of the 12-School Exchange and, if you wish, you can take a semester at Vassar, Wellesley, Smith, Mount Holyoke, or several other colleges in the exchange. Spelman has 3-2 engineering programs with Georgia Tech, North Carolina A&T, Auburn, Columbia, Boston College, and several other schools. You get a B.S. from Spelman and a Bachelor of Engineering from the participating school.

Spelman has a Spelman–Bryn Mawr Summer Mathematics Program, which is a joint venture established by the Mathematics Departments of the two schools. It's a "summer research experience" at a specified location. Spelman also has a Women in Science and an Engineering Scholars Program (WISE), where students can work with the professional staff at NASA centers during the summers. The school's goal is to increase the number of minorities with Ph.D.'s in the science and engineering fields. The school has a joint enrollment program for honor students enrolled in the Atlanta public high schools. You apply in your 11th year, and if accepted into the program you can take courses at the first-year level at Spelman. These courses, if passed, can be used for credit at the school or at another college.

Getting In

Spelman is undoubtedly the most competitive historically black college in regard to getting an accept. During the 1990s, the college's acceptance rate has, at times, been as low as 32%. At present its acceptance rate is in the 48% range, but that increase doesn't begin to tell the real story. Spelman's pool of applicants is now stronger than ever. Today many students realize that the school is a "premier" selection and don't apply. We've heard dozens of students say something akin to, "It's like applying to Yale. I don't have a chance."

This stronger pool of students is highly recruited by the prestigious Ivy League, the Seven Sisters Schools (e.g., Smith), and highly ranked institutions such as Emory and Stanford. In short, Spelman is actually competing against many of the top schools to get its "yield"—that is, students who, after considering their options, decide to become Spelmanites. Yes, it's always an impressive, talented, and academically capable incoming freshman (women) class.

Most students arriving at Spelman are from southern states, Washington, D.C., New York, New Jersey, or California.

At the Spelman web site you can download your admissions application.

ILLINOIS

NORTHWESTERN UNIVERSITY

1801 Hinman Avenue
Evanston, IL 60204-3060
(847) 491-7271
Web site: www.nwu.edu

Financial aid deadline: February 15; quarter system
Application deadline: January 1; quarter system
Early decision deadline: November 1
Other deadlines: schedule music auditions by November 15
1999–2000 tuition: $23,496; room and board, $7,114

College Ranking

In recent years Northwestern, with its emphasis on liberals arts and career development, has been ranked among the top 10 universities in the nation. Several of its six undergraduate schools have outstanding reputations: the Medill School of Journalism, the School of Speech, and the School of Music all garner national accolades. Also of merit are the McCormick School of Engineering and Applied Sciences, the School of Education and Social Policy, and the College of Arts and Sciences (CAS). At times Northwestern has been called "the Ivy of the Midwest."

The Campus

Sitting on the shore of Lake Michigan, Northwestern University's Evanston campus is often called "beautiful." It's about twelve miles away from Chicago, the nation's third-largest city. In the summer you can cycle, rollerblade, or study on the beach.

About 176 buildings, including residences, stretch over NU's 231 acres. If you bring your camera, you can create an album of postcards: lovely trees, flowers, courtyards, pathways, Gothic and cathedral-like architecture. University Hall, the home of the College of Arts and Sciences' English Department, is the oldest building on campus (1869). NU's libraries have more than 3.6 million volumes. The spacious Deering Library, with its elegant arched windows and high ceilings, is the home of special collections. McCormick's main engineering building—often referred to as "Tech"—is one of the largest academic structures in the world. It covers more than 750,000 square feet and is filled with offices, classrooms, laboratories, and research facilities. A gathering place is the Norris University Center, where you can find the offices of student organizations. In the basement of Annie May Swift Hall is WNUR-FM (89.3), the "largest student-run station in the country."

Another popular spot is the Pick-Staiger Concert Hall. There students can enjoy one or more of more than 400 musical performances annually. Depending on your mood, you can journey from "Mozart to Duke Ellington." At the Weinberg College of Arts and Sciences you'll find art studios and science labs.

Students can select regular dorms, either single-sex or larger coed structures with suites that open up into common living rooms. You can also opt to live in one of 11 residential colleges (living quarters). These are usually thematic residences that might accommodate those in the

Fine and Performing Arts (Jones), Communications (CRC), Commerce and Industry (Thomas G. Ayers), or Humanities (Chapin). Finally, there are fraternity and sorority houses.

Freshman usually live on the North Campus, where you can find "more energy and excitement," says one sophomore. From the South Campus, where more upper-class students choose to stay, you can see the lake from some windows.

Campus Life

Many cultural events take place at Black House, which is a gathering place for many groups of color. For Members Only (FMO) is the pivotal group on campus, coordinating many affairs, forums, lectures, and entertainment events. Other groups include the Northwestern Society of Black Engineers, Black Law Students' Association, Blacks in Communications, African American Student Affairs, African American Music Alliance, Muslim Cultural Student Association, Black Student Alliance, Black Greek Council, and (often involved) the Northwestern University Black Alumni Association (NUBAA).

Besides the usual socializing, black fraternities and sororities play a role. The Zeta Phi Beta sorority has helped feed the homeless at the Carter Temple on Chicago's South Side. The Alpha Kappa Alpha sisters have mentored seventh- and eighth-graders at the Jordan Community Center. The Alpha Phi Alpha fraternity has been involved with the Coe Pops basketball and tutoring program. Sigma Gamma Rho and Delta Sigma Theta also have impressed us.

Some typical events that have been sponsored over recent years by black groups include:

- Northwestern Homecoming Bash Youth Gospel Explosion Performance by NAYO dance ensemble
- MUNTU Dance Troupe performance "A Celebration of Gospel" featuring the Northwestern Community Ensemble and Second Baptist Church of Evanston
- "Delta Expo," an exposition by black-owned companies
- "Ritualism I: Myth, Magic, and Metamorphosis," an exhibit by black artists
- *The Colored Museum* a play; also *Divine Days* a play adapted from the work of former Northwestern professor and novelist Leon Forrest
- Lecture by Tony Brown, host of *Tony Brown's Journal* (PBS)
- Lecture by Susan Taylor, editor of *Essence* magazine
- Lecture by Earvin "Magic" Johnson, basketball superstar
- Lecture by W. Deen Muhammad, American Muslim leader
- Lecture, "Destroying the White Mind in the Black Student" by Dr. Khallid Muhammad
- Lecture, "The Impact of African Americans in Film" by Ossie Davis

Other NU clubs, organizations, and special-interest groups also are available. At last count, more than 200 options were available to students. There are performing arts and a cappella groups, the *Daily Northwestern* newspaper, *Syllabus* (the yearbook), drama and dance clubs, radio and TV stations, the Northwestern Volunteer Network (you can work with a social agency in Chicago), political and religious outlets, and more. Important events include the Dance Marathon, which is said to be the "second-largest philanthropy event held by a college in the nation." There's the Waa-MuShow, a comedy musical review, and Armadillo Day, where students dress up in "silly clothing."

Northwestern is a Big Ten school that has ascended in sports. The football Wildcats, after "being doormats forever," became the Big Ten champions in 1995 and went to the Rose Bowl in 1996. That run was like a fairytale. The next year, applications to the school skyrocketed.

NU's athletic facilities are top-notch. NU, after all, has 17 varsity teams. Ryan Field, with the help of $20 million, was upgraded for gridiron games. There's also the Nicolet Football and Conference Center. Inside SPAC are the Norris Aquatics Center and the Henry Crown Sports Pavilion. Enjoy an Olympic-size swimming pool, and basketball and racquetball courts as well as fitness rooms and a private beach on the lake. NU's intramural program also is solid.

Last, Chicago and its delights are only a 20-minute car or subway ride away. There's the Art Institute of Chicago, the Alder Planetarium, the Shedd Aquarium, famous museums and concert halls (go hear the renowned Chicago Symphony Orchestra), restaurants, and Michigan Avenue for shopping.

Academic Realities

NU academics are said to be "rigorous," with the quarter system probably exacerbating the study and workload. Also, some professors use "the curve" method of awarding grades, which means that a limited number of A's and B's might be available in any specific class. At times, then, you are forced to compete against the impressive minds of your classmates. Some students are said to receive their first C's at NU.

A major NU component is its academic-career development orientation. As you proceed, you will get to intern and learn in a hands-on manner. For example, students in the Medill School of Journalism have more than 80 study/work options available to them during a "media tech quarter." They can spend time getting real experience at one of dozens of newspapers or television stations nationwide. Students at the McCormick School of Engineering and Applied Sciences will get a chance to work with professional engineers. In every school there are opportunities to interact with industry, often on practical projects. Within the above "keep it real" framework, students in all disciplines must pursue core requirements that encourage a very wide range of study. A dance major might sit in on an economics or a statistics class. That engineering prodigy might study the art masters.

For very talented students there are a several honors and special programs. As a student in the Integrated Science Program (ISP) you can complete your bachelor's degree in three years, or opt for a master's in four. The Honors Program in Medical Education (HPME) is your direct key to the Northwestern School of Medicine after three years of undergraduate work. There's a program called Mathematical Methods in Social Sciences (MMSS), where math is integrated into courses that ordinarily might not emphasize numbers.

For about 138 students there's the Northwestern University Minority Engineering Opportunity Program (MEOP). This is an intense four-week summer program that has a graduation rate twice the national average for minority engineering students. The enrollees are exposed to the different fields of engineering, with the aim of sharpening academic skills before the first day of school.

In a recent year about 1,028 students were enrolled in the Weinberg College of Arts and Sciences, the school with the largest enrollment. The counts for the other schools are:

- 351—McCormick School of Engineering and Applied Sciences
- 195—School of Speech
- 179—Medill School of Journalism
- 113—School of Music
- 28—School of Education and Social Policy

The most popular majors at NU are Engineering (13%), Economics (9%), Journalism (7%), Biology and Psychology (5% each).

Note that an African American Studies major is available. You can take courses such as

The Art of Toni Morrison, the Harlem Renaissance, and Black Families in Literature, to name just a few here.

In recent years NU has set up a "Task Force on Underrepresented Minorities" and come up with two reports that provide an "analysis of the undergraduate admission experience with African American and Hispanic students during the last decade." The school wants to intensify its recruitment efforts, not only in the Greater Chicago area but also "beyond its traditional midwestern student base." Indeed, NU is facing heightened competition from other top-ranked schools for the very capable students it is seeking. In the past few years NU has been having difficulty increasing its black accept rates. Several strategic moves are being considered, including a Black Cultural Center.

We'll keep an eye open. Of course, some say that NU is a "conservative" campus, where "self-segregation is the rule rather than the exception." If you're looking for a very supportive and nurturing atmosphere as an African American student, NU might not be the place.

Getting In

The acceptance rate at Northwestern is 29%. In a recent year about 16,680 applied, with 4,909 being accepted. More than 96% of these students graduated in the top quarter of their high school class. The median SAT was about 1360, with the ACT score about 30. Get "in the ballpark" with your SAT (the 1100-and-up range), then make a strong a case for yourself in all other categories. Your high school record, essay, and recommendations should say you're a "fit." Although a little over 6% of the student body is black, there are indications (see the Task Force note above) that NU would like a higher percentage. More than 76% of the student body is from out of state.

NU's students arrive from 50 states. A recent geographical breakdown looks like this:

Midwest: 923 students—from states such as Illinois, Michigan, and Minnesota

Middle Atlantic: 277 students—from states such as Pennsylvania, New York, Maryland, and the District of Columbia

West: 261 students—from states such as California and Oregon

South: 180 students—from states such as Virginia, North Carolina, Georgia, and Tennessee

Southwest: 103 students—from states such as Texas

New England: 72 students—from states such as Maine, Connecticut, Massachusetts, and Rhode Island

Students also arrive from 43 foreign countries.

UNIVERSITY OF CHICAGO	5801 South Ellis Avenue Chicago, IL 60637 (773) 702-8650 Web site: www.uchicago.edu	**Financial aid deadline:** January 15 **Application deadline:** May 14 **1999–2000 tuition:** $24,234; room and board, $7,970

College Ranking

The University of Chicago is one of the most highly regarded and selective academic institutions in the nation. This school is the home of Nobel Laureates and some of the country's best students, and is often mentioned in the same breath as the Ivies.

The Campus

The university is on a 180-acre campus in the integrated community of Hyde Park on the South Side, and is surrounded by "eclectic" neighborhoods on three sides and Lake Michigan on the fourth. The campus is tree-lined, self-contained, and a marvel of fabulous architecture. Here you'll walk along the main quads and see Gothic buildings with gargoyles. The modern buildings, too, are noteworthy, with creations by Wright, Saarinen, and Mies van der Rohe. In the Science Quadrangle you'll note the John Crerar Library and Kersten Physics Teaching Center. During orientation you'll hear a lecture at the "grand old" Rockefeller Chapel. Coffee shops are everywhere.

Campus Life

Clubs and organizations that might be of special interest to our students include first and foremost, the Organization of Black Students. It's the main African American group on campus. Recently it sponsored its first "Hip-Hop Show." It's also had recent Poetry Nights and invited novelist John Edgar Wideman to lecture. A recent old-movie series included showings of *Carmen Jones, Stormy Weather, Purple Rain,* and *The Wiz* (all black musicals). OBS calls itself a "support group" and "cultural outlet." Still, it appears that our students spend most of their time studying. There are no Greek-letter black students here.

There's a University Jazz Ensemble, WHPK 88.5 FM, the campus radio station, and Model United Nations (MUNUC), the largest organization on campus. Also, there are theater groups, the Second City Comedy Club, the University Chorus, and about 200 other groups available to you. Of course, Chicago is considered a jazz and blues center. Besides the Chicago Symphony you'll find clubs, restaurants, and other cultural and social outlets.

At UC there're men's and women's intercollegiate sports. But no, you won't hear a lot about "the Maroons." UC is a member of the academically-minded University Athletic Association, with schools such as New York University and Johns Hopkins. Students do participate in more than 21 intramural sports, including billiards, touch football, and ultimate Frisbee. Some say part of the UC sports cheer is, "Wars, x-squared, y-squared." Wow!

Academic Realities

There are five school divisions: New Collegiate, Humanities, Biological Sciences, Physical Sciences, and Social Science. In all, you'll discover distinguished professors. There are Nobel Prize winners who sometimes teach, as well as "other stars." All students pursue a major, their "concentration," only after they complete a "common core." In the old days, students essentially had to read from "the great books" list. Today students must complete 15 courses, and it's a substantial workload. Within the "core" framework you must take courses in the humanities, mathematical sciences, natural and social sciences, and civilization. The most popular majors are Economics (20%), Biology (14%), English (9%), Political Science and Psychology (6% each).

Getting In

The acceptance rate at UC is about 61%. Only a select group applies, you see, and the school must make its "yield" numbers. Many of their great accepts (one in three) select to go elsewhere. Still, the SAT average is extremely high: approximately 1300. To get in, excellent grade and test scores are essential. The school lists the high school record, class rank, your essay, and recommendations as being very important. In a 1997 survey by the *Journal of Blacks in Higher Education,* 475 African Americans applied and only 182 were accepted. That's 38.3%, less than the school's average, which signals that getting an accept won't be easy. A little over 4% of the full-time student body (about 3,650 students) are students of color.

UNIVERSITY OF ILLINOIS AT URBANA-CHAMPAIGN	177 Henry Administration Building 506 South Wright Street Urbana, IL 61801 (217) 333-0302 Web site: www.uluc.edu	**Financial aid deadline:** March 15 **Application deadline:** January 1 **1999–2000 tuition:** $4,746 (state residents); $11,838 (nonresidents); room and board, $5,560

College Ranking

Here is another of the top-ranked public universities. The University of Illinois at Urbana-Champaign is known for its world-class faculty and wide array of academic choices. Robert L. Johnson, the founder of Black Entertainment Television (BET), is a graduate. That should send a signal.

The Campus

The University of Illinois at Urbana-Champaign is *big*. There are about 26,000 full-time undergraduates, 1,470 acres, and more than 200 buildings. This midwestern school is also surrounded by cornfields and farms. Still, it's parklike on campus, with trees, walkways, and Gothic and Georgian buildings. You can see the majesty of the Engineering Quad and the Chemical and Life Sciences structures.

Campus Life

This state-supported school, with more than 150 undergraduate majors, is also diverse. Approximately 7% of the student body is African American. Some say that the small town of Urbana offers "little in regard to social opportunities." But hey, you've got the personalities of 26 dorms to compensate. With study carrels where you live, access to "Plato" (the university's computer network), and coffee shops (Espresso Royale), you'll adjust to your "corny" surroundings.

Note, too, that there are separate Black Orientation and Black Homecoming Days. And believe it or not, each year we have our own commencement exercises at Foellinger Hall.

There are 700 clubs, organizations, and special-interest groups on campus. Some that might be of particular interest to us include the Central Black Student Union (the umbrella local for many groups), CBSU Buddy Program, African Cultural Center, Black Chorus, Omnivov Dance Troupe, National Society of Black Engineers, *Griot* (the black newspaper), and WBLM (the black radio station). All the major "eight" fraternities and sororities are also on campus, and they are active.

Finally, U of I is a Big Ten school, with a sports program that will keep you screaming. The "Fighting Illini" football team will get a rallying cry. A perennial conference power, the basketball team has a huge following. With a swimming pool and all kinds of "play" courts, the Physical Education Complex (IMPE) is always full. There're also a Sports Wellness Center and an array of intramural sports available.

Academic Realities

U of I is composed of eight colleges: Liberal Arts and Sciences, Communications, Fine and Applied Arts, Agriculture, Business, Education, Engineering, and Applied Life Sciences. Each school has its own admissions and course requirements. Several of the schools, such as the one teaching engineering, have top reputations. Even though U of I boasts a prestigious faculty, the teacher-to-student ratio is 20 to 1 or higher. Classes can run from 20 students to nearly 1,000 (for introductory courses). The undergrad library is one of 39 on campus (more than 9 million volumes are available). There are more books here than at every other college except Harvard and Yale.

The most popular majors are Engineering (18%), Business (14%), Biology (9%), Psychology (7%), and English (6%). There is an African American Studies program. Also there are Summer Bridge and Transition programs.

Getting In

The acceptance rate at U of I is 68%. In a recent year 18,140 applied and 12,373 were accepted. The average ACT score was about 27. Out-of-state arrivals were at about 8%. Generally, African American students arrive from Chicago and the surrounding areas. Approximately half the students reside on campus.

LOUISIANA

DILLARD UNIVERSITY

2601 Gentilly Boulevard
New Orleans, LA 70122-9985
(504) 286-4670
Web site: www.dillard.edu

Application deadline: rolling
1999–2000 tuition: $8,900;
   room and board, $4,600

"Ex fide, fortis" (From confidence, courage)

    —Dillard's motto

College Ranking

In a recent *U.S. News & World Report* ranking, Dillard was accorded a "second tier" rating for a southern liberal arts school. Such a rank was particularly impressive because DU was accorded the highest "academic reputation score" in its grouping, which included 26 schools. More interesting is that its academic ranking (a 3.4 score) was better than all but three schools in the first tier. This appears to indicate that DU is academically sound—that the students are capable and achieving. In the meantime, the president is talking about "recruiting national scholars."

The Campus

Dillard University is a private, liberal arts college in New Orleans (pop. 497,000) and is on 48 acres of land. Some have described the campus as one of "America's most loveliest," with its well-kept lawns, ancient oak trees, and generally "inviting" landscape. Students say they have state-of-the-art classrooms and laboratories, and seem pleased with the setting. Still, new president Michael L. Lomax (1997) has embarked on an "aggressive renovation plan." Williams Hall, which faces the Avenue of the Oaks, already has the fresh look of a home for students. On campus, there are 21 buildings, including residences. Look for improvements across campus. Affiliated with the United Methodist Church and the United Negro College Fund, Dillard is about a mile's drive from the city. The Will W. Alexander Library holds 144,000 volumes.

Campus Life

There are dozens of clubs, organizations, and special-interest groups on campus. There are eight fraternities and sororities on campus (from Alpha Phi Alpha to Delta Sigma Theta to Zeta Beta Sigma), and they are all very active. The University Theater recently performed the play *El Hajj Malik*. The Dillard University Concert Choir and Female Quartet are entertaining. Also, there's a gospel choir, band, radio station, yearbook group, the NAACP, honor societies (Alpha Chi, Beta Kappa Chi), Pan-Hellenic Council, GSA, and many other student outlets. Some campus clubs include E. Franklin Frazier (Sociology), Kenneth B. Clack (Psychology), Criminal Justice, Modern Dance, Karate, Premed, Computer Science, and Circle K. A lecture series has brought folks such as the Reverend Jesse Jackson, the late poet Gwendolyn Brooks, Lani Guinier, and Amiri Baraka to campus. Army ROTC is available.

On a sunny day you will see students on the terrace of Karney Hall, or headed to Lawless Memorial Chapel. They might mention that a scene from the movie *Double Jeopardy* was shot on campus and that they saw Tommy Lee Jones. Or you might hear about the legacy of the Camphor Hall residence and how a student began the "Society for the Advancement of African American Males." This group now impacts on more than 400 elementary school students in the nearby community.

Dillard (with its Blue Devil mascot) has intercollegiate basketball, cross-country track, and tennis teams for both men and women. For intramural activity there are basketball, aerobics, flag football, swimming, volleyball, and weight training. The school has a gymnasium, sports hall, tennis courts, and a swimming pool.

Academic Realities

Dillard has six academic divisions: Business, Education, Humanities, Nursing, Natural Sciences, and Social Sciences. Within those boundaries, students can pursue one of 36 undergraduate majors. The most popular majors are Business, Preengineering, and Mass Communications. If they wish, students can travel on prelaw, medicine, pharmacy, dentistry, veterinary science, or optometry tracks.

One group on campus that is getting a lot of attention is the Mazda Scholars. These are students who have been given foundation scholarships to study in Dillard's Japanese Studies Program. Students who plan on majoring in biology, chemistry, and nursing, must meet higher admission standards. Music applicants must audition. There are about 84 black faculty members, with 36 nonblacks. The teacher-to-student ratio in class is about 1 to 15.

Alumni include former U.N. ambassador Andrew Young and Smith College President Ruth Simmons.

Getting In

The acceptance rate at Dillard is about 79%. In a recent year 1,400 applied, 1,257 were accepted, and 433 enrolled. The average SAT score was approximately 900. The ACT average: 19. About 50% of the students scored between 700 and 899 on their SAT test. More than 16% scored over 1,000. Of the enrolling students, about 53% were from out of state and the Southeast. A small number of arriving international students were from Nigeria, Ghana, Spain, Greece, South Africa, or Canada.

GRAMBLING STATE UNIVERSITY

100 Main Street
Grambling, LA 71245
(318) 247-3811
Web site: www.gram.edu

Application deadline:
July 1
1999–2000 tuition: $4,602
(state residents), $9,952
(nonresidents); room and
board, $2,636

"Not only do we have an outstanding marching band and athletics program, but also the university is the fifth-largest producer of African American undergraduates in the country."

—Neari F. Warner, vice president of academic affairs

College Ranking

Grambling, the university "where everybody is somebody," is generally best known for its legendary football teams (more than 400 victories) and its former coach, Eddie Robinson. The GSU Tiger Marching Band is also world-renowned and has appeared on TV and performed at the Astrodome, the Silverdome, and the Sugar and Rose Bowls. But Grambling also offers a fine education in a classic black college setting.

The Campus

The university is in Grambling, Louisiana (population 6,000). This state-supported school is on 383 acres of land, has 67 buildings including residences, and is about 60 miles from Shreveport. GSU has five undergraduate schools: the Colleges of Education, Sciences and Technology, Business, Liberal Arts, and Nursing. On campus you'll find the Comprehensive Counseling Center, Martin Luther King Justice Center, Audio Video and TV Center, a library with more than 273,000 volumes, a museum, and an Afro American Study Center, and well as the Favrot Student Union, which is a "unifying force for an entire campus." About 30% of the woman live in single-sex residences, while 24% of the men do so. The others reside off-campus. About 20% of the students have cars.

Campus Life

Besides its outstanding varsity sports program, including basketball and football—there's a 25,000-seat stadium—GSU has a world of clubs, organizations, and special-interest groups to keep students occupied. All the major sororities and fraternities (count 11) are on campus, and all are very active. For example, there are Delta Sigma Theta and Alpha Kappa Alpha sororities, as well as the Alpha Phi Alpha fraternity (Delta Sigma chapter).

Also, there's the Great Books Symposium, Student Government Association, Black Dynasty, Black Stone (prelaw society), Circle K International, Criminal Justice Club, Tiger Pep Squad, Baptist Student Union, Voices of Faith, Ladies of Essence, Project Rescue, Association of Black Psychologists, Biology Club, Pan-Hellenic Council, Student Athletic Committee, Powerlifting Team, cheerleaders, orchestra, choir, yearbook, radio (KGRM 91.5 FM) and TV, Little Theater Guild, Men's Dormitory Council, and *Gramblinite* (school newspaper). Army, Air Force, and Navy ROTC also are available. Important days on campus include Founder's Day, Class Reunion, and Homecoming.

Academic Realities

The most popular majors are Business, Criminal Justice, Nursing, and Biology. You're also got prelaw, medicine, veterinary science, dentistry, and engineering tracks. You'll find, too, cooperative programs in just about all categories. An audition or portfolios are necessary for art, dance, music, or drama applicants.

The Earl Lester Cole Honors College (created in 1990) is a key GSU program. Its goal is to develop leaders and "scholars for service." Bright, academically capable students with strong test scores and grades are encouraged to apply for the freshman honors sequence (FHS). They take special and interdisciplinary courses and seminars that result in "distinction." Most of these students are awarded presidential scholarships from a variety of sources.

Getting In

GSU accepts about 76% of the students who apply. In a recent year 5,696 students applied and 3,726 were accepted. The freshman class was approximately 2,630 students. Full-time student enrollment is usually about 6,830. Approximately 41% of students arrive from about 42 states. International students come from approximately 10 countries, including Nigeria, those in the West Indies, Japan, and Mexico. In a recent year more than 300 transfer students were accepted, with 295 enrolling. The U.S. Department of Education ranks GSU as having one of the lowest in-state and out-of-state tuition and room and board rates.

GSU says that students should score "630 or above" on the SAT test. About 80% of the students who take the ACT score between 12 and 17. No essay is required. Student orientations are in May and June of each year.

| **XAVIER UNIVERSITY OF NEW ORLEANS** | 7325 Palmetto Street
New Orleans, LA 70125
(504) 486-7411
Web site: www.xula.edu | **Application deadline:** March 1
Financial aid deadline: May 1
for FAFSA and school's form;
apply much earlier.
1999–2000 tuition: $8,700;
room and board, $5,100 |

College Ranking

"We *beat* Harvard!" That's what President Ronald Brown of liberal arts Xavier University in New Orleans can say. In recent years this Catholic historically black college, defying the odds, has placed more students of color into medical schools than the most prestigious colleges in the nation, including Harvard. Xavier is also breaking records by producing more pharmacists than any other school, as well as graduating future dentists and sizable numbers of other health professionals annually. Xavier has been designated a "Model Institution for Excellence" by the National Science Foundation. Xavier lead the nation in African American physics graduates from 1995 to 1997, averaging 14 a year. Its Debate Team has won the HBCU National Tournament (1998–1999) for its skills.

The Campus

Xavier University is a small private university, on a 29-acre campus in New Orleans (population 497,000). Affiliated with the Roman Catholic Church, this college is about two miles from the downtown area and has 34 buildings, including residences. A central location on campus is the grassy quad and its paths. Strolling from that spot, you'll pass the Norman C. Francis Academic/Science Complex. There's also Xavier South, a multistory office building that has a food court. There you'll find the Mardi Gras Café and a Pizza Hut. The Library/Resource Center (with 122,000 volumes) and the new Living/Learning Center are important locations. The Student Center has the University Dining Hall and cafeteria, auditorium, and meeting rooms. Peter Claver Hall and the House of Studies are women's dorms. St. Michael's Hall is one men's residence. Students also reside in the six-story Katherine Drexel Building, and the Fountainbleau Apartments.

Campus Life

There are many clubs, organizations, and special-interest groups on campus. Some that might be of particular interest to us include the NAACP, A.W.A.R.E., Gold Star Dance Team, National Society of Engineers, Chess Club, National Association of Black Journalists, Pure Genius Poetry Club, International Students Organization, Concert Choir, Symphonic Band, Opera Workshop, Jazz Ensemble, University Chorus, National Society of Black Chemists and Engineers, Prepharmacy Student Association, MAX, Big Brothers/Big Sisters, Campus Ministry Gospel Choir, Nubian Expressions, Yearbook *(Xavierite), Herald* (student newspaper), and African-American Studies Club. All the "eight" major black fraternities and sororities are at Xavier and are very active. Alpha Kappa Alpha (Epsilon Tau chapter) recently won first prize stepping in the annual Xavier University Springfest Greek Show.

Remember, too, that this college town is the home of the Mardi Gras, restaurants, shops, theaters, and more. Two eateries that students cite as being good are the Bennachin's African Restaurant and Palmer's Jamaican Restaurant.

Xavier, a member of the Gulf Coast Athletic Conference (NAIA), has varsity men and women's "Gold Rush" basketball teams. Each year the men play in the Morehouse Hoops Classic. The school has tennis and cross-country teams. Also, there's a Xavier-Black Rugby Team and the Black Magic Volleyball Team. Note that Xavier usually offers about 40 athletic scholarships.

Academic Realities

The key here is not that it's hard or competitive but that there are nurturing and support services. There are no shortcuts from study or the rigor of some courses, but there's a lot of "hands-on caring," as one student puts it.

At Xavier there is a preprofessional emphasis. You can go prelaw, medicine, pharmacy, dentistry, optometry, veterinary science, or theology. All this is available through the College of Arts and Sciences. About 52% of the students are on preprofessional tracks. The most popular majors are Biology, Psychology, and Chemistry. The breakdown of student interest areas by category looks like this: natural sciences (74%), social sciences and education (11%), business (7%), arts and humanities (5%), and other (3%). You can take double majors, and there are honors programs. Xavier also has a 3-1 year medical and dental arrangement with Louisiana State, and 3-2 programs in engineering with the University of Maryland and Tulane University. Cooperative work/study programs are available in art, business, humanities, and the social and behavioral sciences. Many graduates have gotten jobs at companies such as AT&T, Bell Labs, Champion International, AETNA, and IBM.

At many colleges the idea is to weed out some students in certain majors. The goal is to create an inclusive, elite group. Xavier goes in the opposition direction. The school wants you to make it. High standards never secondary, the attitude is to provide intensive tutoring, positive reinforcement, and support. Specially-created workbooks are used to show you the way in the sciences, for example. The goal is to make you do science—to make you really see and feel what happens in regard to an equation or work in a laboratory. You are taught not to analyze by rote. Early on, you are asked to attack the actual tests (barriers, some say) that society places in our way. At Xavier, the Medical College Admissions Test (MCAT) and Graduate Record Exam (GRE), to name two, are not surprises. At test time you are as ready as you can be.

At this school, student-faculty relationships and interactions are strong. A pivotal force at Xavier is chemistry professor J. W. Carmichael (the premedical adviser), who has been named a National Professor of the Year by the Council for the Advance and Support of Education. John Scott, an art professor and Xavier graduate, is a MacArthur Foundation fellowship winner.

Support groups include the Office of Career Services, the Office of Student Services, and the Office of Student Programs.

Getting In

Xavier continues to make national headlines about its success with African American students. One *New York Times* story led the cheer: "Tiny Black College Takes High Road in Sciences" was the headline. Indeed, about 44% of Xavier graduates immediately go on to professional or graduate schools. As more of our folks discover the school, expect getting in to become tougher. School reports note that "the student count has raised more than 50% during the past 15 years."

In a recent year, 2,724 students applied and 2,492 were accepted. That's an acceptance rate of about 92%. Eventually 743 students enrolled. Of this total, about half were from New

---

For the sixth straight year, historically black Xavier has placed more African Americans (95) into medical school than any other college or university in the United States. Rounding out the list in 1998 was Howard (43), Morehouse (35), Spelman (34), Harvard (32), University of Michigan (22), University of North Carolina (21), City University of NY (20), Yale (18), and Hampton (18). Over the years, Xavier graduates have been accepted into a long list of medical schools, including those at Harvard, Northwestern, Emory, Baylor, Meharry, and Tulane.

Early on, Xavier targets some promising students at the junior high school level, and then nurtures and oversees their development through their college years. This wise "hands-holding" and mentoring is the result of the fine work of a small group of science and math instructors. They developed the Xavier strategy over a period of about 15 years. Foundation and corporate grants (e.g., from the Howard Hughes Medical Institute and the Health Careers Opportunity Program) were pivotal.

Before some students reach Xavier, they become part of the Summer Science Academy. Their development begins with four summer enrichment programs that bring students up to speed and sharpen their abilities. Indeed, if Xavier targets you, be prepared for constant homework, daily quizzes, and constant and repeated grading. As backup, successful Xavier students serve as mentors and group leaders. If you are absent from class or study, you get a call. Parents are factored in for orientation, consultation, and support.

Orleans. The rest of the students arrive from 40 states. The majority of students are from the Southeast. The main feeders are Chicago, Los Angeles, Houston, Memphis, Atlanta, St. Louis, and New York City. There is also heavy representation from Alabama, Mississippi, Texas, and Tennessee. About 3% of the arriving students are from 20 foreign countries. About 31% of the approximately 2,900 full-time students reside on campus.

You're in a receptive situation here. Still, the secondary school record is important, and test scores are a factor. The average GPA is about 3.0 on a college preparatory track. More than 60% of the students graduated in the top 25% of their high school class. The average SAT score is over 1000. The average ACT is 21. Also, although an essay is not required, it is considered. Of course, you should use it if you feel that you've got to make a case for yourself. If you're an art or a music applicant, a portfolio or an audition may be necessary.

International students arrive from the Bahamas, Ghana, India, Nigeria, and Vietnam.

MARYLAND

**JOHNS HOPKINS
UNIVERSITY**

3400 North Charles Street
Baltimore, MD 21218
(410) 516-8171
Web Site:www.jhu.edu

Financial aid deadline:
    March 15
Application deadline: January 1
Early decision deadline:
    November 15
1999–2000 tuition: $23,660;
    room and board, $7,870

College Ranking

A top-rated university with an especially prestigious premed program. "If you want to be a doctor," one black student tells us, "you go to Johns Hopkins!" A graduate headed to the medical school at Temple, he's proof enough. Indeed, the statistics say that this school can booster your chances of getting that M.D. if you can handle the "very rigorous" study load. The students here, after all, are exceptionally bright, focused, and do create an "academically intense" environment. With world-renowned faculty and researchers everywhere, thinking and studying are continuous. Gertrude Stein and Woodrow Wilson were graduates.

The Campus

Johns Hopkins is in Baltimore. Sitting on a 140-acre Hamate campus, with 33 buildings including residences, the school is about three miles from the downtown Inner Harbor area. The school is near the Baltimore Art Museum and Wyman Park. A "hop and a skip away" is your "major" urban setting. On campus you've got lawns and tree-lined quadrangles. There are modern and Georgian structures (lots of red brick). The two "go to" libraries are always full. There's the four-level Milton S. Eisenhower Library, which is underground. Across the quad is the "Hut" or Hutzler, which has lots of reading rooms. There are, of course, many science buildings, with laboratories and research stations spread across campus. All the liberal arts classes and "action," however, are centered in Gilman Hall. The oldest building on campus, it has "serpentine hallways" and a bell tower.

Campus Life

All freshman and sophomores must reside in residence halls. They generally move off campus into university-owned apartments for their junior and senior years. There are about 90 clubs, organizations, and special-interest groups on campus. There's a Black Student Union (with *Perspectives*, a newsletter), the NAACP, and Hopkins Organization of Minority Engineers. Helpful, too, is the Office of Multicultural Affairs. Most of the major black fraternities and sororities are on campus: Omega Psi Phi, Alpha Psi Alpha, Delta Sigma Theta, and Alpha Kappa Alpha, to name a few. Poet Nikki Giovanni and the educator and author Dr. Jawanza Kunjufu have lectured on campus. A gathering spot (with study carrels) is the "BSU Room," in Memorial Residence Two.

Johns Hopkins has varsity sports teams, but students admit that "they aren't that good." The lacrosse team, however, has won national championships. The baseball team is also said to be respectable. Intramural sports are popular.

Academic Realities

There are four undergraduate schools, including the Schools of Arts and Sciences and Engineering. If you're pursuing a B.A. major, you must take 30 credits outside your major. The informal "core" is aimed at giving students a wide range of knowledge/experience. Those studying engineering, for example, also are expected to become "well-rounded." Those B.S. candidates must take a grouping of humanities and arts-related courses. At Johns Hopkins the most popular majors are: Engineering (25%), Biology (15%), International Relations (9%), and Political Science and Economics (7% each). Note that about a third of Hopkins graduates get an accept to medical school, and a quarter to law school. Many others pursue other higher degrees, including the Ph.D.

Getting In

The acceptance rate at Johns Hopkins is about 40%. In a recent year 8,453 applied and 3,448 were accepted. The average SAT score was about 1350 to 1360. A quarter of students scored below 1290. Of 3,884 full-time students, 8% were African American. Most students are from the East Coast, with Maryland (13%), New York, New Jersey, and Connecticut being key states. Nearly 6% of the students are from foreign countries.

MORGAN STATE UNIVERSITY

1700 East Cold Spring Lane
Baltimore, MD 21251
(800) 332-6674; (419) 319-3000
Web site: www.morgan.edu

Financial aid deadline:
April 15 priority date; apply much sooner
Application deadline:
April 15, with notification on a rolling basis; December 15 is the deadline for the spring semester
1999–2000 tuition: $1,937 (state residents); $4,729 (nonresidents); room and board, $5,256

"Applications for admission have risen dramatically, placing Morgan among the top ten public campuses nationally in terms of receiving applications from African American students."

—Earl S. Richardson, president of Morgan State University

College Ranking

Morgan State is one of about 15 historically black colleges that has good name recognition around the country. The school, which was founded in 1867, could cite its credentials, as one student puts it, "in any academic showdown." Not only does it rank fourth among all colleges and universities in the country in producing black graduates who went on to get their Ph.D.'s, but it also can boast a backlog of more than 70 Fulbright Scholars since 1960. Spread over 140 acres in northeastern Baltimore, the school is the home of one of the nation's top 10 future employment markets, according to a major study. To be sure, Morgan State is a major resource for the African American community.

The engineering program at Morgan State is "rated one of the best in the United States." Thanks are due to Engene DeLoatch, who arrived from Howard in 1984 to cofound a program that includes electrical, civil, and industrial engineering. A renowned educator and now dean of engineering at MSU, DeLoatch is responsible for producing a cadre of well over 500 engineers. The last we heard, DeLoatch was a panelist at the National Institute in Science Education affair and was also present at the annual Black Engineer of the Year awards. Today more than 40 corporations provide intern and cooperative work experiences for MSU engineering students.

The Campus

You can reach the campus, in Baltimore, off Cold Spring Lane and Hillen Road. The scenery is of stately buildings surrounded by manicured lawns and lovely trees. The area has a suburban feel, and a residential neighborhood surrounds the campus. Welcome Bridge divides the campus into two sections. On-campus you'll pass the statue of Frederick Douglass that stands in front of Holmes Hall, which is the university's most widely recognized landmark. The building, which contains offices, has a tower with a clock. There's the Benjamin Banneker Communications Center (a telecommunications outlet), and Truth Hall, which serves as the main administrative building. The McKeldin Center (student union) has 10 conference rooms for lectures and banquets. Inside, you'll find the Parham Ballroom. The Morris A. Soper Library has more than 600,000 volumes. Another gathering place is the Carl Murphy Fine Arts Center. Academic spots include the Clarence M. Mitchell Jr. Engineering Building, and the Science Complex, which is the oldest building on campus. The Booker T. Washington Service Center and the Talmadge Hill Field House, also are important locations.

There are a number of residential halls and a coeducational apartment complex. Female residences include the Harper-Tubman Residence and Blout Towers. Baldwin is a four-story male residence with recently remodeled rooms. The one "mixed" building, eight stories high, accommodates more than 600 students, including freshmen. Other housing units include the Argonne Complex (with suites) and Cummings. Rawings Hall has a dining hall that serves the entire campus. Some students choose to rent off-campus at locations in nearby Dutch Village, Berkeley Square, and Kingston Gates.

Campus Life

Students say that the social life and related activities at Morgan State are good, but that there is "little feeling of tradition" on a day-to-day basis. The aura of being a "Morgan man or woman" doesn't seem to be part of the equation. One upper classman suggested that "maybe it's because so many students commute." In any case, major Morgan events include Homecoming (with a Golden Bears football game) and an "I Love Morgan Day." Many students like to chat or hang out near "The Bridge"—being seen, socializing. Also, you can go to parties that are "jumping." The Greeks (seven fraternities, six sororities) play a major role on campus.

Students often head to the McKelden Center, headquarters to more than 80 student organizations. Groups that might be of particular interest to students include: the Morgan State Choir, which is considered "one of the nation's most prestigious university choral ensembles," with more than 125 voices. The choir has toured the Bahamas and Europe. There's the "Magnificent Marching Machine" Band, with 100-plus players. There's Kuumba (a tutoring and mentoring program), Umoja Student Affairs Council, SASY (a big sister/little sister group), JAHOD (mentoring for high school females), MSU Symphonic Band, and Jazz Combo and Ensemble. The campus radio station is WEAA-FM (88.9). There is also a television production studio, a yearbook *(The Promethean),* and a school newspaper *(The Spokesman).*

On-campus entertainers have included Stevie Wonder, Danny Glover, Gregory Hines, Whoopi Goldberg, and Jesse Jackson, and there has also been an "Evening with Bill Cosby." Morgan's track teams (both male and female) are strong and notable, and still compete at the Penn Relays and in international competition. The football team is said to be "very bad," although the marching band is a joy to watch. Basketball (including the Lady Bears team) is popular. There is a volleyball team, and a wrestling squad that has won championships. Howard is the school's main rival in sports. Also on campus is Hughes Stadium, a gymnasium, and handball, racquetball, and tennis courts.

When students are not on campus or at nearby parties, they visit Inner Harbor in the city, where there are shops and restaurants. At Pier Six is a 2,000-seat concert pavilion, and the Great Blacks Wax Museum is a student favorite. There is also the Baltimore Museum of Art, and great jazz clubs such as Ethel's Place. Washington, D.C., is just 40 miles away. Prominent alumni include Earl G. Graves, publisher of *Black Enterprise;* Kweisi Mfume, president of the NAACP; Zora Neale Hurston, novelist; Wilson Goode, a mayor of Philadelphia; and Darren J. Mitchell, a U.S. congressman.

> Hugh Watts, Class of 1991, loves his school. He says, "Morgan State University has an excellent chemistry and engineering program. The School of Business has been named after one of its own, Earl Graves, publisher of *Black Enterprise* magazine." As an insider's tip for new students he says, perhaps tongue in cheek, "Kiss up to all faculty!"

Academic Realities

The Morgan State students rarely mention any type of academic pressure. The rough ride appears to be for students who are pursuing a major in Engineering, Biology, Chemistry, or in advanced mathematical courses. The majority of students (whether in liberal arts, business, education, or social service) appear to be faced simply with the question of buckling down and doing the work. Students with academic deficiencies or poor study habits will probably have some rocky times. Without a doubt—and this seems to be a near consensus—students who are not focused and get involved in the social/partying merry-go-round will generally have problems.

Morgan offers preprofessional programs in business, law, medicine, dentistry, and pharmacy. Indeed, the school has more than 62 majors to choose from, including Music, Fine Arts, Theater and Telecommunications. There are schools of the Arts and Sciences, Education and Urban Studies, and Engineering, as well as Business. The most popular majors are Business (22%), Engineering (11%), Psychology and Social Work (9% each), and Education (8%). Morgan State has a plethora of majors a student can pursue. MSU is a comprehensive institution, with a pre-professional mission. For every 10 freshmen at Morgan, approximately four will not return for sophomore year. Fewer than half of those remaining will graduate. Although financial considerations are sometimes a factor for those dropping out, others just don't make the emotional and intellectual transition required. Tutoring is available for all courses, as well as counseling/career assistance at the Learning Resource Center.

For those who can handle it, there are cooperative education plans with colleges such as Coppin, Towson, and the University of Maryland, and cross-registration with Loyola. Opportunities abound. A major plus, of course, is its city of Baltimore location. Students can serve internships in almost all areas, and there are countless opportunities for cooperative work/study and mentorships. Students regularly get aboard at AT&T Laboratories; Smith, Kline, & French Pharmaceuticals; the National Cancer Institute; Baltimore Union Memorial Hospital; the Goddard Space Flight Facility; and schools, museums, and social work agencies. Washington, D.C. also is a resource for students. Graduates go on to work at Honeywell, Allied Bendix, IBM, and other leading corporations. Some graduates gain admission to selective professional schools of medicine and law. While on campus some students serve as research assistants. Those interested in Army ROTC can serve as cadets while at MSU.

Getting In

Once a relatively easy task, gaining acceptance to Morgan State has become increasingly difficult because of an unprecedented number of applications. Morgan now accepts about 55% of its applicants. This pattern will continue, with entrance difficulty increasing as the school continues to pick and choose selectively. Of 4,721 recent applicants, Morgan accepted 2,601. There are approximately 4,480 full-time undergraduates. Since Morgan is a state school, Maryland residents (67%) are accepted more readily than out-of-staters. The key feeder states in a recent year were New York (626 students), New Jersey (368), and Pennsylvania (238). Other important states were Virginia (110), the District of Columbia (105), California (62), and Connecticut (59). Students with high grades and SATs are eligible for scholarship money. For example, if you have a combined SAT of above 1000 (with a B average) you could be eligible for a full Morgan State scholarship. There are also partial scholarships available for students with SATs in the 900s. Morgan does not require any particular distribution of high school courses, and either SAT or ACT scores are acceptable. Morgan also does not require an interview, but you can request one (on-campus only) if you wish.

| **UNIVERSITY OF MARYLAND AT COLLEGE PARK** | Mitchell Building
College Park, MD 20742
(301) 314-8385
(800) 422-5867
Web site: www.umd.edu | **Financial aid deadline:** February 15 (priority)
Application deadline:
February 15; *note: aid and housing are affected by when you apply*
1999–2000 tuition: $4,939 (state residents); $11,827 (nonresidents); room and board, $6,076 |

College Ranking

The University of Maryland is generally considered a top school, ranked behind the first tier of academic giants but steadily increasing its reputation. In the early 90s a bumper sticker began to appear around campus that said "I'd rather be studying," perhaps a signal that the school was trying to lose its "party school" image. In recent years the Schools of Business and Engineering (graduate level) have been ranked among the nation's top 25 in their disciplines.

In recent *U.S. News & World Report* rankings, UMaryland has been assigned a 3.7 "academic reputation score" (out of a possible 5). This score is the highest in the strong second tier grouping, which includes more than 100 schools and is an indication of this school's obvious accent and mission.

The Campus

This suburban, state-supported school covers more than 1,375 acres. It's one of the largest universities in the United States. It's the "flagship" school in the 11-institution higher-education public school system, with departments and divisions galore. This school is about a half-hour drive from Washington, D.C. On your first visit you'll note the white-pillared buildings, Georgian in style and usually of red brick. These UMCP housing and school units are in quadrangles surrounded by grassy knolls with valleys and lifts. It's "like an immense grabbag," says one student.

There are more than 300 buildings. First, you've got seven libraries, holding more than 3 million volumes. There's the Stamp Student Union, where you can see movies. There, you've also got eateries (Roy Rogers, Taco Bell), a bowling alley, billiards, even a bank. The state-of-the-art computer center is a sight to behold. This school is "wired." There are more than 3,500 PC terminals across the campus. In the planning stage is a new multicultural center as well as recreational and performing arts buildings. The new golf course, with its pro shop and showers, is ready. Imagine, too, the college/classroom locations which are too numerous to list here.

On this campus, most UMaryland students are residents of the state, with large constituents of enrollees from Washington, D.C., Virginia, New York, and New Jersey. The numbers are large. You'll be one of about 32,000 students (with, perhaps, 24,500-plus full- or part-time undergraduates). About 13% of these students are of color. And every day your educational and cultural options will be considerable.

There are both coed and single-sex dorms. Most students reside in either the South Hill or North Hill residential areas. In the North Hill section you'll find the Cambridge, Denton, and Ellicott ("Hellicott") dorms; in the South, the Leonardtown and North and South Hill ("The Suites") dorms.

Campus Life

The black Greek-letter groups are a pivotal part of the social life on campus. Some say that "our thing"—whatever it is on campus—is like a world unto itself. There are parties galore, with a very active social life and nightlife available for those who are interested. For political awareness or entertainment there's the Nyumburu Cultural Center, which is located in the Adele H. Stamp Student Union. There is, too, a Black Student Union, and a group called the Diversity Initiative, which is very active.

For our folks, you can meet and listen to visiting lecturers such as Henry Louis Gates, or sit in on seminars such as "Time Management—How to Pick Classes." At the Hoff Theater you might sit in on the Annual Homecoming Talent Show, a "Comedy Jam," or a Jazz/Poetry Night. In a recent year there was actually "A Look Inside the World of Hip-Hop" conference.

You will have something to do—there are more than 450 clubs and organizations on campus—whether it's listening to *Yester Now,* the black-oriented radio show, or reading *Black Explosion,* one of our newspapers. Finally, Howard University is a popular visiting spot. It's only about a fifteen-minute trip by car from College Park.

You'll be on the edge of your seats. UMCP is a member of NCAA (Division I) in basketball and football and other sports, usually is *very* competitive.

Academic Realities

We have heard stories that you can "cruise" along or be greatly challenged, depending on your major. If you're on the engineering track or into physics, it won't be a cakewalk. There are 14 schools and colleges at UMCP, with a good 300 possible journeys available to you, from Theater to Journalism to Economics majors. The most popular are in Business, Engineering, Biology, Education, Criminal Justice, Political Science/Government, and Science. It's a universe of possibilities, to say the least. And what about African American students? This university usually graduates more blacks students annually than any other of the predominantly white schools.

The overall academic level is not of the "rigorous" type, but if you are a very strong student, there is a university honors program. It has been called one of the best values at a state university. You are routed to special classes and assignments, while being given the elite treatment: better dorms, better award packages. These students can take courses such as "Doctrine and Debate in World Religions" or "Black Women and the Public Eye."

Students with adjustment problems can find support with the Office of Minority Student Education (OMSE). Students can get academic counseling, group workshops, seminars, or advice on time management and test-taking. One continuous complaint is that a lot of introductory courses are crammed with students (50 to 200).

Extras: There are Cooperative Education, internships, Navy and Air Force ROTC, study abroad, and self-designed majors.

Getting In

For Maryland State residents, it's not too difficult. The school must accept 75% of its own students. If you're an out-of-stater, however, you'll get a stringent look. Approximately 65% of all applicants are accepted, with stats for AAs about the same. More than a third of the accepted students were in the top 10% of their high school graduating class, and more than 77% graduated in the top quarter. Note that in 1990 the Maryland State Legislature voted to point the university toward "higher academic" and related standards, including raising the overall average for SATs (a messaging rod for many prestigious schools).

To gain acceptance you should demonstrate academic capability and clear potential. The courses you took and your secondary school record matter first and foremost. College preparatory courses and 2 science labs, are desirable. In regard to your SAT I or ACT scores, you should be in the school's "ballpark" range (see below). Your essay should showcase your writing ability and say what you're about (leadership, goals, and other positives) in some way. Your recommendations also should present/argue your case for admission.

The average SAT score is about 1180 (half score higher, half score lower). The lower quarter of accepted students present scores in the 900 range (and sometimes a bit lower), but are certainly making their cases with the preponderance of presented support material. Keep in mind that the University of Maryland usually graduates more students of color than other predominately white colleges. You've got to look like a "fit," with staying power.

UNIVERSITY OF MARYLAND AT EASTERN SHORE	Director of Admissions and Registrations Bird Hall Princess Anne, MD 21853 (410) 651-2200 Web site: www.umes.edu	**Application deadline:** July 15 **Early decision deadline:** July 15 **1999–2000 tuition:** $3,036 (state residents), $7,646 (nonresidents); room and board, $4,130

College Ranking

This is a historically black public college that's the lesser-known branch of the top-ranked University of Maryland.

The Campus

This multipurpose school, located in the Princess Anne section of the state, is on 540 acres of land. The campus is attractive, with nicely manicured lawns, neatly trimmed trees, and flowers. You enter into a "quad" with walkways that lead to you to the steps of several centrally located buildings. One stately building is J. T. Williams Hall, the location of the main administrative offices. To reach those steps you must pass a line of national flags. You feel like you're headed to the United Nations. A first-time visitor might be surprised at how neat everything looks. Obviously there is some substantial state support—that is, relatively speaking. In terms of ranking, Eastern Shore is the "stepchild" behind the flagship College Park and the Baltimore branch.

Walking on campus, you'll note the Ella Fitzgerald Center for the Performing Arts; Carver Hall (and the Natural Sciences Department); Waters Dining Hall with its splendid white pillars, and Tawes Gym. There's also the Arts and Technology Center, the Art Museum, a college farm, a greenhouse, tennis courts, and a stadium. You'll note, too, several dorms and housing complexes that will remind you of a well-kept, middle-class neighborhood. Eastern Shore has Schools of Arts and Science, Professional Studies, and Agricultural Science.

Campus Life

At Eastern Shore you'll find the major eight black Greek-letter organizations as well as a host of other clubs and special-interest groups. A short list would include the *Hawk Flyer* newspaper, the Black Awareness Movement, Ecumenical Campus Ministry, Phenomenal Women,

NAACP, Students for Progressive Action, For Sisters Only, Students in Free Enterprise, Caribbean International Club, National Student Business League, a choir, drama and dance groups, a radio and TV station, and intramural athletic outlets. If you're inclined, there are swimming, volleyball, bowling, soccer, basketball, and more. Eastern Shore also has intercollegiate teams in basketball, baseball, track and field, and other sports.

Academic Realities

The most popular majors are in Business (17%), Education (16%), and Computer Science and the Health Sciences (about 9% each). Other key majors are in the math/sciences areas as well as in Criminal Justice, Engineering, and in Liberal Arts/Interdisciplinary studies. Options abound. You can proceed by taking courses that will prepare you to enter law, medicine, dentistry, veterinary science, and pharmacy programs. You can obtain education certification in several areas. There's also a music degree (an audition is required for entry). If you are interested in hotel/restaurant management, you can cross-register at nearby Salisbury State. There are also transfer programs (e.g., in engineering and medical technology), that can lead to degrees from the College Park branch.

Getting In

The acceptance rate here is about 75%, including a sizable transfer group (perhaps 15% of all new enrollees). The average SAT score is about 840. The key is your overall application presentation. Remember, too, that there is a summer readiness program for students who might need remedial help. About 55% of the students reside on campus in coed, male only, and female only, residences.

About 75% of the students here are African American, with more than 90% arriving from public schools. Because of state residency requirements, about 75% of the student body is from Maryland. The other 25%, the outsiders, must pay more than double what their fellow students pay. Note that more than 100 students (from more than 40 countries) arrive from places such as Trinidad, Jamaica, Bermuda, Liberia, and elsewhere.

U.S. NAVAL ACADEMY

117 Decatur Road
Annapolis, MD 21402
(410) 267-4361
Web site: www.nadn.navy.mil

Application deadline:
February 1
Tuition and room and board:
It's free for a five-year commitment to the U.S. Navy as an ensign or a Marine second lieutenant

College Ranking

The nation's only naval academy.

The Campus

On "the Yard," the Annapolis campus, you'll have more than 338 acres of land to study and train on. It's all between the south bank of the Severn River and Maryland's state capital, historic Annapolis. There are 25 historic buildings here, including Bancroft Hall, which is the largest dormitory in the United States. All midshipmen live there, and it covers 4.8 miles of hallway.

Campus Life

At Annapolis you'll experience the rigors of life on the high seas and in the classroom. As a "plebe" during your first year, you'll be placed on a relentless schedule of physical conditioning. Some say that's "the toughest year." Later you'll travel in "fleet units" to foreign ports, or train offshore under sail.

There are approximately 4,000 full-time midshipmen, and African Americans make up 7% of the body count. A key support group at Annapolis is the Black Studies Club. Intramural sports and activity are continuous. And finally, there's the annual Army-Navy football game.

Academic Realities

At Annapolis you'll be challenged mentally and physically, no question. It's a very competitive environment. You and your class are "ranked" from day one. The plus, of course, is that you'll graduate as a commissioned officer (with a five-year commitment), and Uncle Sam will pay for everything. And even give you a stipend.

You'll experience "warfare" situations, including Marine Corps tactics, surface and submarine warfare. On ground you will get familiar with the equipment in Rickover Hall: "wind tunnels," tanks, and a nuclear reactor. In class you will have to decide on one of 18 degree disciplines. The core curriculum, however, will entail studies in physics, chemistry, math, science, and engineering as well as "professional military training." You will be, with a computer, "hardwired to the academy network."

Here's a quick snapshot: you're up at 5:30 A.M. There's a fitness workout, then off to four classes up until noon. After "formation" and lunch, there are two more classes. Drill and parade occur several times during the week, and if you're a plebe there's mandatory study in the evening of at least $2\frac{1}{2}$ hours. The most popular majors here are: Engineering (39%), Political Science (11%), Oceanography, History, and Economics (9% each). Note that the male-to-female ratio here is 86 to 14.

Getting In

To apply for the academy you've got to get "nominated" by a member of Congress, the Navy or the Marine Corps, or the vice president or higher. Why make it easy? The Navy has its way. They'll take an equal number of students from varying regions across the country while factoring in all 50 states. The acceptance rate is about 14%. The average SAT scores are high, but a quarter of the admits score less than 1230. To get in you must be physically fit, academically strong, have strong character, and be motivated and an achiever.

MASSACHUSETTS

AMHERST COLLEGE

Wilson Admission Center
P.O. Box 2231
Amherst, MA 01002
Web site: www.amherst.edu

Financial aid deadline: February 15; FAFSA and CSS form necessary
Application deadline: December 31
Early decision deadline: November 15
1999–2000 tuition: $22,680; room and board, $6,560

College Ranking

Amherst is often said to be one of the finest liberals arts colleges in the nation. It is often ranked first in polls of smaller liberal arts schools. In a recent *U.S. News & World Report* rating, Amherst was listed ahead of colleges such as Swarthmore, Williams, Wellesley, and Haverford. And the *Black Enterprise* magazine editors have taken notice: In that magazine's "Top 50 Colleges for African American Students" rankings (there was a heavy emphasis on historically black colleges), Amherst was among the top 10 mainstream schools selected. A major plus is undoubtedly the excellent academic programs and fine teaching you'll discover at Amherst. There are close relationships between students and faculty. This relatively small college offers a very intimate environment to grow, study, and evolve in.

The Campus

Overlooking Holyoke Range and the Pelham Hills, Amherst College is on a hill. Almost every point on the college's 964-acre campus offers a panoramic view. Whether near the academic or residential buildings, athletic fields, bird sanctuary, or biking along a 15-mile trail in the woods, you'll feel at home. The campus space, after all, is relatively small in size. This New England college has about 1,600 students, and the odds are high that you'll recognize just about every face over four years. And no, you won't see many black faces around the picturesque town of Amherst (population 35,000).

College Hall, which was previously a Congregational church, houses the administrative offices of the college. The Johnson Chapel may be the best known and most frequently occupied building on campus. There you'll find the student counseling center. The $17 million Life Sciences Building (1996) is the home of the Biology Department and labs. Converse Hall is a stately pillared building that holds the Office of Financial Aid, Public Affairs, and the registrar. At Converse you'll also find classrooms and the "Red Room," one of the school's busiest lecture halls.

At the "Octagon," which was originally an observatory, there are meeting halls, classrooms, and the Gerald Penny Memorial Black Cultural Center. In Wilson Hall, a brick-red building circled with trees, you can find the Black Studies and Philosophy Departments. Some other key locations are the Robert Frost Library (800,000 volumes), the Mead Art Museum, the Pratt Museum of Natural History (fossils, meteorites), and the Buckley Recital Hall. The hall is used for concerts but also has a music library, pianos, 13 practice rooms, and a recording studio. In the Front Room you can have club meetings, visit snack bars, or play in a game room.

Behind the Front Room are the "social dorms"—the Coolidge, Davis, Stone, Pond, and Crossett houses (there are 30 student residences in all at Amherst). Walking through the arched doorway of the Pratt Dormitory, you'll find rooms for coeds and students at all class levels. Also, you'll find the offices of WAMH, the student radio station. Student publication offices for *The Olio* (the yearbook) and *The Student* (the college newspaper) are also in the building. In the Morrow Dormitory you'll find the "Iso Ward." This is an area inhabited by "thesis-writing seniors in search of quiet and solitude." Last, there is the Charles Drew House, which is "devoted to African American culture," and named after our pioneer in the science of blood preservation.

Campus Life

At Amherst there are about 100 clubs, organizations, and special-interest groups. Also, the dining spot at Valentine Hall appears to be a "socializing" location for the entire student body. "The Quad," too, is a place (a huge grassy knoll) where students can toss a Frisbee or talk.

"Here," one black student says, "you feel that the talk of getting along and diversity is more than lip service." There's a Black Student Union, International Students Club, the College Mountain Bike Team, Amherst Photography Association, Diversity Educators (giving workshops on race relations), Chess Club, Bluestockings (an a cappella group), Glee Club, Ham Radio and Electronics Club, Gospel Choir, WomenSpeak, Tae Kwon Do group, Women of Color, Amherst College Orchestra (with about 50 members), and more. Popular days at Amherst include Casino (you're allowed to gamble for charities for one night), Triathlon, Homecoming Day, and Parents' Weekend.

Amherst competes in more than 25 intercollegiate sports (NCAA Division III), including football, basketball, swimming, ice hockey, tennis, and track. More than 80% of the student body participates in intramural sports. After all, Amherst has 36 tennis and 10 squash courts, Nautilus and weight rooms, and a small golf course.

Do note that fraternities and sororities were abolished at Amherst in 1984.

Academic Realities

Your classmates will all be very capable. Most will have able academic preparation. For example, most students who enroll at Amherst have taken calculus. These students weren't looking to take any shortcuts. Prepare for serious study in generally small classes where the professors will get to know you. Out of 31 departments, you'll have hundreds of courses to choose from.

Even after you select your major, you'll have a lot of choices to make in regard to what direction you want to take. At Amherst it's suggested that you take only four courses a semester. Other than the first-year seminars, to put you in focus and sharpen your critical thinking, there are no core requirements.

The most popular majors are English (20%), Economics (11%), Biology (9%), Psychology (9%), and History (8%). In the senior year, more than 50% of the class selects to undertake writing a thesis under the guidance of a faculty adviser. Of interest here is the fact that you *need only 32 courses* to graduate.

A major plus, too, is that Amherst is part of the Five-College Consortium, and you can take courses at UMass, Hampshire, Smith, or Mount Holyoke. There are buses that will shuttle you among the schools.

Of the entering students at Amherst, 58% are from public schools, 36% from private, and 6% from parochial. The enrollment of African American students is usually in the 7% range. That's about 114 students of color registered at any given time. About 430 students receive their degrees annually.

A key selling point: It's said that about 90% of the students who look to law, medical, or business schools get their acceptance letters.

Getting In

This is a very selective college. The acceptance rate is an astounding 20%, which is the lowest of any of the smaller, prestigious liberal arts colleges. In a recent year, 5,210 applied and only 1,039 were accepted. The median SAT score was about 1410. Note that at least 25% of the enrolling students score below 1330 and that African American students have gained acceptance using the total attack approach we outlined in the first section of this book.

Shape and polish that essay. The associate dean of admissions, Kathy Mayberry, has written that the review team wants to "look beyond test results, grades, and class rank." Remember to distinguish yourself. Also, understand that those two recommendations from teachers can be pivotal. It's essential, also, to take at least three SAT II tests (beyond the regular SAT). The English or writing test is a *must,* and a science or math test is recommended. For the final test, you can select any test area that excites you. Overall, the best advice is to take the most challenging curriculum that you can in high school.

| **BOSTON COLLEGE** | 140 Commonwealth Avenue Chestnut Hill, MA 02167 (617) 552-3100 Web site: www.bc.edu | **Financial aid deadline:** February 1 **Application deadline:** January 15 **Early decision deadline:** November 1 **1999–2000 tuition:** $22,256; room and board, $8,250 |

College Ranking

Boston College is a large Catholic college with a wide array of course choices and well-regarded academics.

The Campus

Boston College is on 240 acres in the affluent area of Chestnut Hill, Massachusetts. Located in a scenic residential neighborhood, the school is only about 6 miles from the major city of Boston. Across campus it's about a 15-minute walk (often with tree-lined quadrangles). If you like jogging, there's actually a miniature reservoir "in the front yard." BC is one of the largest Catholic colleges in the country, and a bit conservative.

For study, there's the O'Neil Library (with more than 1.4 million volumes). There's also the Museum of Art in Devlin Hall, where there are constant exhibitions, lectures, and even tours. At the 600-seat E. Paul Robshan Theater Arts Center, you can see a half a dozen plays that are produced each year. Murray House (the computer center) and Greycliff's Honors House are also notable locations. If you take the T train you can get to the cultural goodies of the city in no time.

Campus Life

There are many clubs, organizations, and special-interest groups on campus, including the Black Student Forum, which sponsors a Black Family Weekend and Kwanzaa dinner. Also, there's the Benjamin E. Mays Mentoring Program, Caribbean Culture Club, Voices of Imani (the Boston College Gospel Choir), NAACP, Swingin' Eagles Stage Band (jazz), A.H.A.N.A. (an umbrella group of minority students), and Umoja and Talented Tenth (support groups for both women and men). Boston College also has a "Screaming Eagles" Marching Band. This group has more than 200 members, including musicians, dancers, cheerleaders, and a color guard. The B.C. Sharps are a female a cappella group. There's also the University Choir.

Remember, this was the home of Doug Flutie. There are 17 varsity teams, with the football and basketball teams generating some excitement. Not too long ago, this team beat Kansas State in the Aloha Bowl. In basketball, it's the Big East and great schools such as Georgetown and Syracuse ahead. The Silvio O. Conti Forum Sports Arena is the main gym on campus. It's gigantic, and can seat the entire student body. For those who want to work up a sweat, there are club teams in aerobics, fencing, figure stating, dance, scuba diving, and swimming.

Academic Realities

There are four undergraduate schools: College of Arts and Sciences, Wallace E. Carroll School of Management, School of Nursing, and School of Education. There are 40 areas of possible study, and you can go from "Art History to Geophysics to Nursing to Political Science." Sweetening the pie is an honors program and the possibility of cross-registering for courses at nearby Tufts, Brandeis, or Boston Universities.

At BC, the most popular majors are Business (29%), English (10%), Education (8%), and Psychology and Communications (7% each). There is a Black Studies Program that includes courses such as Religion in Africa, Race Relations, and Black Woman Writers. Options Through Education is a program that admits "economically disadvantaged" students to campus for a six-week summer orientation (with college support and counseling). The Intercultural Office also has been a help to students needing academic assistance, as well as the Learning to Learn Program.

Getting In

The acceptance rate at BC is about 39%. The average SAT score is about 1270. In a recent year about 16,455 applied and 6,455 were accepted. A total of 2,168 students enrolled. Only about 25% of the students were from Massachusetts. Students arrived from 50 states and 91 foreign countries. There are approximately 9,000 undergraduate students, with about 4% being African American. Here's a partial geographical breakdown of where students arrive from: Massachusetts (3,011), New York (2,902), New Jersey (1,716), California (1,189), Connecticut (1,166), Pennsylvania (750), Florida (481), Illinois (479), Texas (305), and Ohio (301). About 74% of the students reside on campus.

BOSTON UNIVERSITY

121 Bay State Road
Boston, MA 02215
(617) 353-2300
Web site: www.bu.edu

Financial aid deadline: February 15
Application deadline: January 1
Early decision deadline: November 1
1999–2000 tuition: $24,100; room and board, $8,130

College Ranking

Often overshadowed by its prestigious neighbors, Boston University—the largest private university in the country, gives a solid academic experience in a lively urban environment.

The Campus

It's big, and it's part of the cityscape. Boston University is on 132 acres of concrete—a "high-rise picture," some say. It's Gothic buildings with a six-lane highway in the middle. Some tree-lined streets with restaurants and brownstones offer relief (as well as the Charles River on the northern side), but it's not your typical campus. You won't see rows of flowers, quadrangles, or courtyards. There are approximately 15,400 full-time undergraduates. At BU you're not far from what makes college students rant and rave about Boston—the cafés, bookstores, art galleries, theater district, chic shops, museums, and performances by the Boston Symphony Orchestra and Opera Company.

At BU there are 10 undergraduate colleges/schools: the Colleges of Liberal Arts, Engineering, Education, and Basic Studies, and the School of Management, School of Communications, School of the Arts, Sargent College of Allied Health Professions, Metropolitan College, and the School of Hospitality Administration. Adding to this complex of wonders is the $100 million Metcalf Center for Science and Engineering, with its state-of-the-art labs, classrooms, lecture halls, and offices. Here you'll find facilities for math, physics, biology, chemistry, and computer science students. The King Center for Career, Educational, and Counseling Services addresses the "personal, academic, and career-development needs of the university's students." Within the 332 buildings on campus, including 23 libraries with 2.1 million volumes, resources abound.

Campus Life

Clubs and organizations that might be of special interest to African American students include the Office of Multicultural Affairs (OMA), with its Ahana Peer Advising and activities support. For Homecoming Week, OMA hosts an African Cultural Show. Also at BU: UMOJA, the African American Student Association, NAACP, BU on Tap (dance), Model United Nations, Minority Engineers Society, Caribbean Club, Dance Theater Group, Drum Circle, Fusion (jazz/hip-hop dance group), On Broadway (musical theater group), Gospel Choir, Black Seminarians Association, and National Black Society of Engineers. Greeks-letter groups such as Alpha Phi Alpha, Kappa Alpha Psi, and Alpha Kappa Alpha are active. They interact/relate/recruit "citywide" with their counterparts at other Boston colleges. Note that there are more than 350 activity outlets and organizations on campus.

The biggest sport at BU is hockey. The Terriers are an "acclaimed team." The big game is always with its archrival, Boston College. There's also NCAA basketball, swimming, track and field, diving, rowing (crew), and tennis. Intramural activities include table tennis, tennis, volleyball, and even water polo.

Academic Realities

At BU, the most popular majors are: Social Sciences/History (18%), Business (17%), Communications (15%), Engineering (8%), Psychology and Health Sciences (8% each), and Biology (6%). African American Studies is offered as a minor. For special study there's the Minority Research Library, with more than 5,000 books and periodicals that chronicle our lives and struggles. Audio recordings are in the Thurman Room. Read about BU alumni: Edward Brooke, our first U.S. senator, for example.

Getting In

At BU the acceptance rate is about 55%. More than 73% of the students arrive from 50 states and 135 foreign countries. A little over 4% of the students are African American. A negative factor for us may be that BU makes all the "most expensive" lists. With fees, tuition, and room and board, the cost per year easily goes over $30,000 before they consider your aid package. The SAT average is in the 1240 to 1260 range. The ACT range is 25 to 30. The Minority Orientation Program introduces incoming students from "ethnically diverse backgrounds" to the BU community and its abundant resources. The goal is to ensure academic and career success.

HARVARD UNIVERSITY

Byerly Hall
8 Garden Street
Cambridge, MA 02138
(617) 495-1551
Web site: www.harvard.edu

Financial aid deadline: As soon after January 1 as possible; the FAFSA, CSS form, and parental forms are necessary
Application deadline: January 1
Early decision deadline: November 1
1999–2000 tuition: $24,407; room and board, $7,757

College Ranking

Harvard is *Harvard. Prestige. Power.* It's been said that it's the most famous university in the world, the alma mater of world shakers and newsmakers. Here you'll find world-famous scholars and faculty, the world's largest college library, state-of-the-art science and research centers, superb laboratories, a curriculum of more than 3,000 available courses, a galaxy of other resources, and an eventual degree that experts say will open more doors than *any* American Express card. In the rankings game it's no question that Harvard is the undisputed heavyweight champion (although it is sometimes outranked in the *U.S. News & World Report* poll by Princeton and CalTech).

The Campus

More than 350 years old, the 380-acre campus of Ivy Harvard has a distinguished but modern aura to it. Strolling in "the Yard," you'll pass wrought-iron gates, quadrangle courtyards, and many brick-red Colonial buildings. If you had the time, you could count more than 400 buildings on campus, with a sizable number as modern as the Science Center, which is always a point of discussion, if not awe. Still, one black parent we talked to said that she was surprised that students with navy blue blazers and insignia—wearing pennyloafers—were not around every corner. Of course, if she ever visited the Harvard Club in New York, she would feel the "old money" while smiling at the sight of leather sofas, oak desks, and the hanging framed pictures of gentlemen who look like millionaires. Keep in mind that David Rockefeller and U.S. presidents Theodore Roosevelt, Franklin D. Roosevelt, and John F. Kennedy are distinguished alumni. However, the campus has diversified over the years and the student body includes people of color, international students, and students from economically disadvantaged backgrounds, although the sense of privilege and expectation among the student body has not diminished.

Harvard has the highest endowment (more than $3.5 billion) of any college in the United

States. The Massachusetts campus is modeled after England's famous Cambridge University. The college is in the aptly named town of Cambridge, across the Charles River from Boston, and is a center of resources. Beyond Harvard Yard, where the oldest buildings stand, you'll find Lamont Library (there are 96 others). Counting all locations, you have more than 13.5 million volumes at your disposal. Other important locations on campus include Loker Commons (1996), the splendid student center with amenities such as restaurants, coffee shops, and more. The MAC (Malkin Athletic Center) is a modern facility with an Olympic-size pool, exercise equipment, weight and aerobics rooms, and the standard assortment of necessary courts: volleyball, basketball, squash, and racquetball. There are also learning resource centers, a planetarium, art galleries, and a natural history museum.

All first-year students are assigned to 17 living locations in or around Harvard Yard. It's a yearly ritual. The newcomers eat as a unit in the Freshman Union Hall, which has (besides some better-than-average college food) a 100-foot ceiling and chandeliers. For the sophomore year these students are assigned to one of 12 coed houses, each with its own resources—computer terminals, study rooms, library, dining hall, and staffing. These "intellectual communities"—accommodating about 400 students each—are a tradition at Harvard. In the past, each residence had its own personality and/or special interests. Your home was like a college within a college. Today the boundaries are not as set, but each of the houses still has its specific attitudes. Some of the houses have names such as Adams, Eliot, Dudley, Dunster, Quincy, Kirkland, and Cabot.

At Cabot House, students brag about the extras: an exercise and dance room, and a photo lab. At Eliot there is said to be a "preppie" constituent. Airs exist because of passed-on reputations and the lottery. You can apply with "15 of your friends," one student advises. Get your pick, and you could create a setting where there's a strong interest in chess, for example. At the "Radcliffe Quad" you're more than a mile away from the Yard. If you prefer to not be distracted, that could work for you. Some of the older houses have fireplaces and very large, wood-paneled rooms.

Campus Life

You'll have more resources available to you than most students will during their undergraduate years. "There's definitely a sense of a black community at Harvard," a junior in the Black Students Association says. There's the Afro-American Cultural Center, W. E. B. Du Bois Institute, the Black Men's Forum, Black C.A.S.T. (theater group), Association of Black Radcliffe Women, Expressions Dance Group, and a Big Sibling/Little Sibling Program (mentoring). Here's an actual Black Students Association calendar of events for one short period:

March 6: Sexy Saturday Party—Dunster House

March 12: Junior Parents Weekend Reception—Currier House

April 9–11: BSA-Kuumba Gospel Fest

April 15: BMF (Black Men's Forum)—Celebrating Black Women

April 17: BSA—Panel Concerning the Community

April 24–26: Prefrosh Weekend

April 24: Black Cast *Eleganza!*

April 24: Caribbean Club Carnival

April 30: BSA Hip-Hop Music Conference—The Next Level

Last, there's the Institute of Politics (IOP), where students are given a chance to speak with our leaders. Some of the luminaries that black groups have invited to campus include Hugh Price (president of the Urban League), Tony Brown (author and TV personality), and the Pulitzer–Prize winning poet Gwendolyn Brooks.

Harvard doesn't officially allow fraternities or sororities on campus. Still, sisters of color (AKA's/Lambda Upsilon) do venture to schools such as Wellesley and MIT to pledge. And the Rho Nu Chapter of Alpha Phi Alpha has appeared at forums on campus with the Black Students Association. This chapter connects with MIT and Tufts.

In the wider Harvard community there are well over 250 clubs, other organizations, and special-interest groups. Nearly every day of the week you can hear lecturers or see movies. There's a jazz band, a cappella groups, orchestras, choral ensembles, opera, literary magazines, a chess club, student government, and radio and TV outlets. Also, there's *The Crimson* daily and other newspapers. If you're into community service, you can visit the Phillips Brooks House (PBH) for an assignment. You can tutor Roxbury students or serve meals to the homeless.

Important Harvard events include the Harvard-Yale football game, the annual "Head of the Charles" raft race regatta, and hockey encounters at the Bright Hockey Center. Harvard has more than 41 varsity teams, perhaps the most in the nation. Intramural sports in tennis, swimming, sailing, and other sports are popular.

Finally, heading off campus, you can visit the ultimate college town. In Boston you'll find restaurants, clubs, museums, and theaters. Also, there's legendary Harvard Square, with its eateries, clothes, and bookstores, and with its bohemian atmosphere. And if that is not enough, you can head to any of a half-dozen colleges. MIT is Harvard's closest neighbor, with Northeastern, Wellesley, Boston College, and Boston University within short driving distance.

> "For me, being black at Harvard has meant reaching out to other black students here at the college in terms of friendship, support, and advice. I have been extremely active in the Black Men's Forum as president. I have gone to a lot of black parties, and I find myself eating with other black students in the Dining Hall. This means I have attended several lectures and discussions about race, heard a lot of great black music, have had unforgettable conversations at dinner, made lifelong friends and wrestled with the fact of being 'black' in the context of Harvard." —MARK PRICE '98, PRESIDENT BLACK MEN'S FORUM '97–'98

Academic Realities

You'll be in an academic environment where smart students will be flanking you every step of the way. You can't worry about what one Harvard administrator has called "the fallen prince syndrome"—that is, you were the superstar at your high school, but suddenly you feel like you're just a face in the crowd. There will be competition, and you will have to buckle down. But soon you'll realize that you can hang with 470 valedictorians, 360 National Merit scholars, or whoever else might be in your class. The *JBHE* people have set the record straight. At Harvard, we will graduate at a 95% rate, and no claim of "preferential admissions" can negate the fact that we are doing admirably. And, of course, we do have a historic role model: W. E. B. Du Bois (Masters, 1891).

At Harvard there's peer and tutoring support for those who need (at any point along the way) a little hand-holding. You're just a phone call away from one-on-one assistance, whether it's in writing, chemistry, or math. In picking classes, you'll have dozens of options. And you won't have to pick a major from any of 45 departments till after your freshman year. An interesting plus is that there's a one week "shopping period" during each semester when you can simply visit and audit a class to see if you want to later register for it. Also, there's a foreign-language proficiency requirement (passing a skills test) that doesn't seem to present too much of an obstacle. Your mission? You've got to pass only 32 courses, taking a reasonable four per semester.

In lecture and introductory classes the student count can go as high as 800-plus. This sometimes occurs when a Nobel Laureate or star is the teacher/presenter. In 1992, for example, Spike Lee taught a class called Contemporary African American Cinema. There was a rush to enroll. Generally, however, classes usually seat an average of about 20 students.

Although there's a core requirement, the only course that's specifically required is Expository Writing (Expos). Beyond that you have to take eight courses pulled from the humanities, arts and literature, social and natural sciences, foreign cultures, and history. This amounts to 25% of a student's courseload. Still, students say the journey is not a difficult one. You have more than 300 acceptable courses to choose from, which leaves you with a lot of latitude and choices.

At Harvard the most popular majors are Economics (11%), Biology and Political Science (about 9% each), English (8%), and Biochemistry (6%). Of course, there are countless other major/minor possibilities. An added plus is that the African American Studies Department under the guidance of Henry Louis Gates is very strong. You'll undoubtedly go that way for a course or two. "Take Afro American Studies 10 with Cornel West!" is a tip from the Black Students Association.

Of course, in the end you'll be in a win-win situation. More than 400 companies recruit on campus each year, and you will be a very desirable candidate. And to those continuing their education, the prospects are also bright. Very large percentages of Harvard graduates get accepted to medical, law, and business schools.

Getting In

> "The hardest thing about Harvard is getting in!"
>
> —An often-heard, often-repeated quote

In a recent class about 16,600 students applied and about 2,200 were accepted. That's an acceptance rate of about 13%, one of the lowest in the nation. About 8% of the students are African American. In a survey conducted by the research team at the *Journal of Blacks in Higher Education,* 184 black students were accepted to Harvard in 1997 and 132 enrolled. The yield was 71.7%, the highest of any school. In a nutshell, if we get a Harvard accept, the odds are very high that we are heading to Massachusetts.

"Harvard does not admit students by the numbers," says the admissions team. Some students with perfect scores are not admitted, while some students with "modest scores" are. Modest, of course, means very *strong* scores. But for us, they needn't be astronomical. "Energy, initiative, the support of leaders and counselors; and evidence that a student will take advantage of what Harvard offers" is the pivotal message. The read on you should be that you're on the fast track—a likely or potential star. Harvard is *not* interested in ordinary Joe or Jane. You should be taking the most rigorous academic courses and be at the *top of your class.*

Yes, the Harvard student body (about 6,600 full-time undergraduate students) is diverse. About 25% come from the Northeast, about 20% arrive from the Mid-Atlantic and Midwestern regions, and 15% from the West Coast. The smallest groupings are from the South and

Southwest (about 16% combined). Students arrive from all 50 states, the District of Columbia, and more than 118 foreign countries. In a given year, nearly 700 international students might be on campus.

MASSACHUSETTS INSTITUTE OF TECHNOLOGY	77 Massachusetts Avenue Communications Office, Room 4-237 Cambridge, MA 02139 Web site: www.mit.edu	**Financial aid deadline:** February 1 **Application deadline:** January 1 **Early decision deadline:** October 15 **Interview deadline:** December 15 **1999–2000 tuition:** $25,000; room and board, $6,900

College Ranking

MIT is one of the most highly regarded colleges in the world, with a reputation that would make you believe that every student sleeps with a calculator and/or computer chip under his or her pillow. This is the premier science and technology college in the nation and also boasts strong graduate programs in business and government.

The Campus

This urban campus is composed of a series of buildings covering 142 acres of land. There's a West Campus and an East Campus, Kendall Square, and the "infinite corridor," where you'll find the heart of MIT, with lots of classrooms and labs. Some call Lobby 7, in one tall building, the gateway to everything. There you might find a 26-foot-long banner advertising a student play, or a table where you can observe the "world's best paper airplane competition." On the West Campus there's the Student Union and athletic fields. On East Campus you'll see the Public Service Center and "a few patches of green."

There are many MIT libraries, including the Baker, which is in Building 10 and has one of the premier engineering collections in the nation. There you'll find clusters of Athena terminals under the Great Dome, that eye-catching metal and glass ceiling. Other libraries are the Lindgren (earth and planetary sciences), the Lewis (music), and the Dewey (management and social sciences). There are six others, which seem to cover areas from A to Z. Count more than 2.5 million combined volumes in these locations, not to mention more than 2 million microfilm sets and related items. There's also the MIT Museum. Its exhibitions explore the "interplay between art, science, and technology." It's a wonder. On a visit, you can see the world's largest collection of holograms.

MIT has 10 institute houses for undergraduates, and nearly 40 other fraternity, sorority, and independent living quarters that are used by students. Unlike other highly ranked schools (e.g., Cornell, Brown, and Wesleyan), there are no "theme houses" that some might call self-segregated. Black students can generally be found living all over the campus. Still, at New House, a dorm on campus where more of us live and congregate, it's sometimes affectionately called Chocolate City. Telling is how this group of folks now has a web page with the noted name. This is the opening banner: "In the land of Vanilla Villas we all need our . . .Chocolate City!" Of course, when you go to the CC online calendar and scroll through several months of dates to see what's happening, you keep reading this: "Study Night."

The men-to-women ratio on campus is 60:40. About 97% of MIT students live on campus.

Campus Life

In 1994, MIT students placed a replica of a campus police car on the top of the Great Dome.In 1990, MIT students made the incoming college president's office "disappear." They hid it behind a huge bulletin board that had been specially crafted for the occasion. They call the creators of these occasional pranks (only two listed here), "MIT hacks."

Relax, there is a campus life! There's a Black Student Union, which has sponsored events such as Kwanzaa and welcoming affairs for arriving students of color. The National Society of Black Engineers (NSBE) has an outstanding award-winning chapter. Count, also, the Black Mechanical Engineers at MIT. There are black sorority and fraternity chapters, including Delta Sigma Theta, Alpha Kappa Alpha, and Kappa Alpha Psi.

There's a Concert Choir, the MIT Symphony Orchestra, Festival Jazz Ensemble, Shakespeare Ensemble, Student Art Association, the Artists in Residence Program (they invited novelists Toni Morrison and Isabel Allende), clubs that relate to chess, films, automobiles, and more. There are more than 30 music, theater, and dance groups.

MIT's intramural program is probably one of the largest in the country. More than 65% of the students participate in one sport or another. This translates into over 800 intramural teams.

There are 39 varsity teams (24 for men and 15 for women). Football is very popular, as well as ice hockey.

Academic Realities

Look for stress and rigor around the clock. This will be mental and psychological war, to put it mildly. If you are reading this and not blinking, then you are ready. During freshman year, you'll be only able to get pass/fail grades, with F's erased from your official transcript if you hit the wall. Most students agree that you'll set a breathtaking pace in regard to study and assignments. The workload will be "merciless" and then some.

You will inevitably say, that this guy or gal is a genius when you arrive with your bags and meet a few classmates. You'll think they all are potential Nobel Laureates. Perhaps they should be, when you consider some of the MIT core requirements. You'll need a year of physics and calculus, a semester of biology or chemistry, and several sophomore-level science courses with lab. To keep you well rounded there are some required courses in the arts, humanities, and other traditional tracks, and a writing course to take you away from those equations for a while.

The top majors are Engineering (47%), Biology (13%), Computer Science (9%), Mathematics (6%), and Business (5%). Students don't select majors until their sophomore year, but here's a recent MIT breakdown of those who did pick majors: Engineering: 2,062 students; Science: 805; Architecture and Planning: 85; Humanities and Social Sciences: 164; Management: 165.

And yes, there are students who are on premed or prelaw tracks within the above classifications. Note that about 8.7% of MIT students go on to medical school, as well as large numbers who head to law school. In both categories it is a fact that MIT students score exceptionally high—if not the highest—on MCAT (medical) and LSAT (law) exams.

As an MIT student you can cross-register for classes at either Harvard or Wellesley. You have, too, more than 1,000 Athena workstations located about campus—with MITnet—for study, research, and e-mailing.

More than 80% of MIT students eventually do research under the auspices of the Undergraduate Research Opportunities Program (UROP). It's almost a rite of passage, and you can get involved as early as freshman year if you have the time and inclination. This résumé/knowledge enhancing research work, with you as part of the team, is always under the supervision of a distinguished professor, scientist, and maybe even a Nobel Laureate.

Getting In

In a recent year, 7,836 applied and 1,938 were accepted. That's a 25% acceptance rate. Keep in mind, however, that this rate is based on an exceptionally bright application pool. You don't apply to MIT if you don't know about the Bohr Model, Newton's laws, and electrons. The odds are high that a solid number of applicants are applying to Harvard and/or Yale, with Cornell as their "safety" pick.

Students arrive at MIT from 50 states and the District of Columbia. Also, over 108 foreign countries are represented, with the number of international students in the 340 range. Of the 4,326 full-time students enrolled as undergraduates, 225 are African American. Another 125 students of color are enrolled in graduate school. Of the MIT students, 72% are from public schools, 22% from private schools, and 6% from international institutions.

SMITH COLLEGE	7 College Lane Northampton, MA 01063 (413) 584-2700 Web site: www.smith.edu	**Financial aid deadline:** February 1 **Application deadline:** January 15 **Early decision deadline:** January 1 **1999–2000 tuition:** $22,622; room and board, $7,820

College Ranking

Smith College is not only one of the premier women's colleges in the country but also a top 10 national liberal arts institution.

The Campus

Located in the Northhampton section of Massachusetts, Smith College is in the foothills of the Berkshire Mountains, about 90 miles west of Boston. You have 125 acres here. Some say it's a camera's delight, because gardens abound. At Smith there's "Paradise Pond" and the Lyman Plant House. The 105 buildings, including residences, give you a variety of looks. Look one way, and you can marvel at 19th-century architecture. Look elsewhere, and you've traveled to the millennium.

On campus, the impressive Clark Science Center has new computer capabilities and remodeled classrooms. The Center for Foreign Languages and Cultures has digital and audio

> "**S**mith intends to establish the Picker Program in Engineering and Technology, making it the first women's college to offer a program in engineering." —PRESIDENT RUTH SIMMONS AND SMITH TRUSTEES, FEBRUARY, 1999.

equipment for individualized study. School concerts are held in the renovated Sage Hall for the Performing Arts. If you need dance, music, or theater facilities, there's the Mendenhall Center for the Performing Arts. Inside, there's also a television studio. Considered one of the finest college museums in the country is the Smith Museum of Art. Neilson Library has 1.3 million volumes.

Campus Life

Students reside at more than 35 different residences, some accommodating 10 or as many as 100 "Smithies." The students are high achievers, usually highly independent, motivated about "what they want to do," and very competitive. It's a school that places a strong emphasis on women's issues, and often there's a strong feminist vibe. An event that's made major news at Smith has been the recent inauguration of Ruth Simmons, an African American woman, as president. At this point it appears that this leader is following in the tradition of Spelman's legendary Johnetta Cole. Ms. Simmons is accessible, walking about the campus, dialoguing with students, and always available.

There are many clubs and organizations on campus. The Black Student Alliance, however, is the key organization for students of color on campus. BSA sponsors a Black Arts Festival, Kwanzaa, Jazz Night, a big sister/little sister program, a Black Smith Graduation Ceremony, and more. A hangout is Unity House, where you can chat and socialize. Although there are no "official" sororities on campus, students do get involved, participate, and are asked to pledge by groups at other nearby colleges. Visiting lecturers have included Sonia Sanchez (poet and professor), Toni Morrison (Nobel Prize–winning novelist), and Joycelyn Elders (former U.S. surgeon general).

Smith has 14 intercollegiate teams and many intramural clubs on campus. The club sports include badminton, golf, riding, sailing, croquet, fencing, and swimming.

Academic Realities

There's an Afro American Studies major. Important support programs are the Summer Bridge Program, Discovery Weekend, and the Institutional Diversity Office.

Since Smith is a member of the Five-College Consortium, which includes Amherst, Mount Holyoke, Hampshire College, and the University of Massachusetts, its students often take courses at these schools. It's a reciprocal arrangement. Shuttle buses take students to and from these schools daily.

Getting In

The acceptance rate of students applying to Smith is about 56%, with 80% arriving from out of state. There are 2,630 full-time undergraduates. A little over 4% are African Americans. The average SAT score is in the 1260 to 1280 range. Once in, students have their pick of many disciplines. The most popular majors are Political Science (9%), Psychology (9%), English (9%), Biology (6%), and Economics (6%).

TUFTS UNIVERSITY

Medford, MA 02155
(617) 627-3170
Web site: www.tufts.edu

Financial aid deadline:
February 1
Application deadline: January 1
Early decision deadline:
November 1
1999–2000 tuition: $24,751;
room and board, $7,375

College Ranking

Some students say Tufts offers "the best of all worlds." Here you've got the benefits of a liberal arts college with the aura/feel of a large university. If you're taking notes you can list the positives: small classes, bright students, distinguished faculty, global concerns and international students, state-of-the-art facilities, the proximity of Harvard Square and downtown Boston. It adds up to a growing reputation.

The Campus

The 140-acre campus, in Medford, Massachusetts, has Uphill and Downhill sections. There are 167 buildings. Uphill, students enjoy the original red-brick residences and academic buildings. There's the Fletcher School of Law and Diplomacy, the computer center, and the dining halls. Also, it's the location of the quads, green lawns, and a lot of open Frisbee space.

Downhill, you'll find the newly renovated 378-bed South Hall dormitory, chemistry building, and athletic facilities. Also on campus is the Olin Center for Language and Culture. There, students can experience computerized classes. The Aidekman Art Center has a theater in the round. At the Mayer Campus Center is the Rez and the Hotung Café, two popular eating places. One of the theme residences Downhill is the African American House, where about 30 students of color reside.

Campus Life

There are many clubs, organizations, and special-interest and cultural groups on campus. Some of the outlets that might be of special interest to us might include the Pan-African Alliance, Third Day Gospel Choir, and Black Theater Company. Tufts' African American Center is our gathering spot. The Black Student Union is the most involved group. The major fraternities and sororities are active and include: Alpha Kappa Alpha, Delta Sigma Theta, and Kappa Alpha Psi.

Some students say "school spirit is low" at athletic events despite the antics of Jumbo, the school's mascot. The women's and coed sailing teams have won national championships (the Leonard M. Fowle Trophy). The men's soccer and women's lacrosse teams have won ECAC championships. There are 33 varsity teams. Intramural sports include men's crew, sailing, hockey, and football.

Academic Realities

At Tufts there is the College of Liberal Arts and the College of Engineering. One of the Tufts innovations is its Experimental College (Ex College). The college is actually a yearly offering of about 30 courses that introduce students to the world of international citizenship, the media, and more. An added component is the opportunity of students to become involved in an annual international symposium that brings experts together to discuss issues. Last, Ex College aims to help freshmen with their transition into college.

Students taking liberal arts majors must take core requirements in writing, a foreign language, the humanities, arts, social/natural sciences, and math. One non-Western course also must be included. Engineering students must be well rounded. They must take added courses in English, the humanities, and the social sciences. The most popular majors are Biology (12%), International Relations (10%), English (7%), Political Science and Economics (6% each). There are programs in African Studies and New World Studies.

Getting In

At Tufts, the acceptance rate is about 32%. In a recent year 12,291 students applied and 3,899 were accepted. Approximately 73% of the students are from out of state. Besides in-state students (27%), the most students arrive from New York, New Jersey, and California. International students (from 61 countries) are about 7% of the student body. Of 4,723 full-time students, 5% are African American. The average SAT score is in the 1300 to 1320 range. The Academic Resource Center provides peer tutoring and support.

UNIVERSITY OF MASSACHUSETTS AT AMHERST	University Admissions Center Amherst, MA 01003 (413) 545-0222 Web site: www.umass.edu	**Financial aid deadline:** March 1 **Application deadline:** February 1 **Early decision deadline:** November 15 **1999–2000 tuition:** $5,212 (state residents), $13,254 (nonresidents); room and board, $4,790

College Ranking

A large, well-respected public college, even in this college town full of prestigious institutions. Dr. J—Julius Erving of basketball fame—is a graduate. And the singer Natalie Cole.

The Campus

Set on the outskirts of Amherst, Umass is on 1,404 acres. And when you stroll by the pond near the center of campus, you might see a swan or two. Including residences, there are 337 buildings. The school is in the Pioneer Valley and is surrounded by the Berkshire foothills.

On campus there's the Knowles Engineering Building, and the Malcolm X center. You'll see Georgian architecture, Colonial styles, and more modern structures. It's said that UMass has one of the largest dorm systems in the nation, accommodating more than 10,000 students. There are traditional residences and high-rises. Count more than 45 different locations.

Campus Life

Students here will have cultural outlets and academic support. There's a Martin Luther King Jr. Center, the Anna Kowanna Center, an outlet for Caribbean concerns and awareness. Also, there's the Committee for the Collegiate Education of Black and Other Minority Students (CCEBMS), which has impact. The New Africa House is a gathering spot for many groups of color. On campus, all the major eight black fraternities and sororities are active.

At UMass at Amherst, whether you're studying or socializing, there are more than 250 clubs and organizations available to you. Counting men and women's intercollegiate teams, there are about 30. The Mullins indoor sports arena has 10,500 seats. There's a 20,000-seat outdoor stadium, two gyms, and other indoor facilities. You can swim, run, dance, get in a whirlpool, lift weights, or simply take a steam bath. Beyond study, if you wish, you can have a full calendar.

Academic Realities

UMass has nine undergraduate schools, with more than 100 academic majors. Among the schools is the School of Humanities and Fine Arts, the School of Management, and the School of Food and Natural Resources. Many of the programs here are highly regarded. Generally, students are enthusiastic. They must take College Writing, and a core of courses called Social World. You have to take classes from six disciplines: the humanities, literature, the arts, and the social, natural, and behavioral sciences. The most popular majors are Psychology (7%), Nursing, Communications, and Hotel and Restaurant Management (about 5% each). Also, 4% of the students major in Political Science. There is also an African American Studies major.

Getting In

About 73% of the students who apply gain admission, with an average SAT score of about 1100. Approximately 27% of the students arrive from out of state. International students total 3%. Generally, the majority of students—61%—reside on campus.

MICHIGAN

MICHIGAN STATE UNIVERSITY AT EAST LANSING	250 Administration Building East Lansing, MI 48824 (517) 355-8332 Web site: www.msu.edu	**Financial aid deadline:** April 1 **Application deadline:** July 30 **1999–2000 tuition:** $5,174 (state residents); $12,370 (nonresidents); room and board, $4,205

College Ranking:

Located on the outskirts of Detroit, Michigan State is a gigantic, state-supported school with a solid academic reputation.

The Campus

MSU is a parklike, 5,200 acres in size. North of the Red Cedar River, you can stand on tree-lined banks. Elsewhere, you can visit historic landmarks that date back to the Civil War. There are courtyards, walkways, paths, ivy, and 18-hole golf courses. There are more than 30,000 undergraduate students, utilizing more than 432 buildings. Many are modern and state-of-the art. You can study at the MSU main library, enjoy a concert at the Wharton Center for the Performing Arts, or visit the Kresge Art Museum. Generally, the residences get a thumbs up. MSU has the largest dorm capacity of any U.S. university. Nearly half of its enrolled students reside on campus in settings that some students call "little cities." It is not unusual to have a library, lounges, weight rooms, and computer workstations within walking distance of your room.

Campus Life

There are more than 350 clubs, organizations, and special-interest groups here. Look for the Black Student Alliance (BSA), Black Caucus, and Cultural Heritage Rooms. All the major eight black fraternities and sororities are active. A plus is that the school has an atmosphere of diversity, with a good mix of cultural groups. About 90% of the students are from Michigan, and from the Lansing, Detroit, and Grand Rapids areas.

Most know about the Spartans' great football and basketball championship teams (remember Magic Johnson?). MSU has "an attitude" and that accompanying "school spirit" that sometimes reaches fever pitch. If that's not enough, there are intramural sports: swimming, volleyball, whatever you want. Oh, yes, sports is BIG here!

Academic Realities

Academically, the school has a good ranking/reputation. You'll find more than 150 majors here. Some of the most popular include Business Management (16%), Social Sciences and History (12%), Engineering (9%), Communications (8%), and Biology (6%). The academic support services are excellent. There's an Office of Minority Affairs, a Charles Drew Science Enrichment Program, and guidance groups such as Minority Students in Engineering.

Getting In

Something to think about is that Clifton Wharton is the first man of color to become the president of a major university. MSU is in the forefront. With 8% of the student body African American, we're a formidable number.

About 81% of the more than 20,000 students who apply are accepted. The ACT score range is between 21 and 26.

UNIVERSITY OF MICHIGAN AT ANN ARBOR	Office of Undergraduate Admissions 1220 Student Activities Building Ann Arbor, MI 48109-1316 (734) 764-7433 Web site: www.umich.edu	**Financial aid deadline:** February 15 **Application deadline:** February 1 **1999–2000 tuition:** $6,881 (state residents); $20,505 (nonresidents); room and board, $5,614

College Ranking

The University of Michigan is a prestigious, highly regarded public university. Founded in 1817, it was one of the first colleges to wave that public banner. Today, one of those rare leaders in both academics and sports (e.g., Duke), it's a school that garners respect for most of its 18 schools and colleges. If the magazine and book rankings are on target—and we believe they are—this institution sits alongside the powerhouse schools. It's generally mentioned among the top 25 universities. It's among the leading public Ivies.

The Campus

The UMich campus is often said to be "a universe" because of its size. With more than 2,871 acres, 210 buildings and residences, and more than 22,000 full-time undergraduates walking around, you will need a map (and a compass?) when you first arrive. "It'll all look beautiful," says one student, talking about the varying architectural structures. You'll find that classical look, a Gothic flavor, and more modern buildings as you tour. You'll see structures that are ivy-covered, many with crisscrossing quadrangles and lovely pathways. Ride those maize and blue buses that continuously circle the campus and you will be in awe. And maybe worried. You may have to take back-to-back classes on the Central Campus and (a mile away) the North Campus. Is it all too grand, too massive?

Pillared Angell Hall is the home of the College of Literature, Science, and the Arts. Inside there's a $3.8 million microcomputing center as well as auditoriums, classrooms, and offices. In the Alexander G. Museum building you'll find exhibits of dinosaurs and prehistoric life. Also, there's a planetarium and museum shop inside. The Power Center for the Performing Arts has a 1,420-seat theater that is used for dance, drama, concerts, and lectures. The Michigan Union has a Club Restaurant, fast-food operations, retail stores, and conference and meeting halls. Two other important buildings are the Activities and Publications buildings. In the first you'll find radio stations WCBN and WJJX. In the latter there are outlets to create literary magazines, the yearbook, and a daily newspaper.

One popular meeting place is "Diag," which connects the Central Campus at its corners. It's said to be a "center for banners, protests, and social and political demonstrations." Another hangout is Regent's Plaza, where you'll find a 1.5-ton cube that was created by artist Bernard Rosenthal. The cube can spin on its axis when pushed. At UMich there are 23 libraries. The Shapiro Undergraduate Library holds 200,000 volumes, while the Science Library, on the third and fourth floors, is said to be the largest single collection of books relating to the sciences, with 400,000 books. UMich is also the home of the Gerald R. Ford Presidential Library.

Residences are often described as "communities," for socializing and relaxing. "Home" is probably where you're going to make and sustain many of your initial/lifelong friendships. Of course, black students do head to some of the organizations and Greek-letter groups for support, parties, and their welcome. There are about 10 dorms on campus, most with reputations and/or personalities, shaped by rumors and word-of-mouth. Bursley, for example, is on the North Campus and somewhat "isolated." But the dorm is close to where most art and music classes are given, so a lot of the residents are said to be "artsy."

On Central Campus you'll fine the Alice Lloyd Residence. There, in the Umoja Lounge, students give an annual "Bronx Elegance Fashion Show." In the Hill area residences there's Couzens House. There you're find C.A.M.E.O. (the Couzens Active Minority Ethnic Organization). The South Quadrangle is divided into "seven neighborhoods" or houses. One, Ambanta, is for "multicultural residents."

Note that about 96% of the freshmen live in residence halls. These halls are either large, apartment-style structures or turn-of-the-century, homelike dwellings. Most have on-site meal service.

Campus Life

There are more than 700 clubs, organizations, and special-interest groups on campus. There's Habitat for Humanity, glee clubs, University Students Against Cancer, a marching band, a symphony, dance and theater groups, student government, a student newspaper *(Michigan Daily)*, a radio station (WVON), a band, and dozens of other membership options. Special events include Martin Luther King Day, the Holocaust Conference, and Native American Powwow.

The Center for Afro American and African Studies (CAAAS) is important. There are, too, many other black outlets. Our fraternities and sororities are in the house. The Alpha Kappa Alpha (Beta Eta chapter) has been at UMich since 1932. Alpha Phi Alpha (Epsilon chapter) as well as the other major Greek-letter groups are here. The Black Student Union, Office of Multicultural Initiatives, Black Music Student Association, and Black Business Student Association (BBSA) are available. Look to the Labor of Love Fellowship, Black Theater Workshop, and Students of Color at Rackham (SCOR). The University of Michigan Gospel Chorale also is strong. It has a CD out titled "Give You Praise." This group has opened for the Winans, Sounds of Blackness, and toured in Illinois, Wisconsin, Chicago, and elsewhere.

In regard to intramural sports, there's something for everybody. You can get involved from A to Z, from aikido to water polo. UMich has even created a "Drop-in Program," where you can walk on (arrive) and participate in impromptu play in basketball, squash, handball, swimming, racquetball, or any number of other friendly and competitive sports. If you wish, you can also rent equipment for outdoor activities. You can pay for bikes, boats, camping equipment, or (for the winter) toboggans, snowshoes, or cross-country skis.

The Wolverines are football giants (go to the Rose Bowl tapes). Varsity sports in basketball (Big Ten), gymnastics, tennis, track, lacrosse, and wrestling also are there for your enjoyment. There's even a women's ice hockey team.

Academic Realities

You will be in an academically challenging environment, with many academic options/majors available to you. Many programs in the Literature, Sciences, and Arts, and engineering, business, and health-related areas are highly regarded. Prepare to buckle down. One student from New York advises that "the engineering ride is no joke. It's demanding and often stressful."

All students must take an English Composition course, at least one course in the "race and ethnicity" category, courses in "quantitative reasoning," and a language. In addition, 30 credits have to come from outside your major concentration and include courses in the humanities, social and natural sciences, math, and "creative expressions." While doing this you can pull courses from the Afro American and African Studies Department, if you wish. Typical courses might include Origins of Jazz, Survey of Afro-American History, and Comparative Black Art. Also, there are more than 65 other departments that allow you countless selection possibilities.

Although you can find classes with 15 to 20 students, some lecture courses will actually accommodate (and seat) 200 to 500 students. UMich suggests that you find a balance among

Shawn J. Ward graduated from the University of Michigan with a degree in Mechanical Engineering and is working toward his masters in the same discipline at Oakland University in Michigan. He states: "I am a black male, and I feel U of M is a great majority (mainstream) school for minorities. The black population now stands at about 10% of the student body. The school is high on diversity from the top on down. There are ethnicities present from around the world due to the fact that it is an internationally known university. Minority programs are frequently held throughout the year. They are sponsored by the university, as well as other organizations such as Greeks (I am an Omega), Black Student Union, and the Office of Minority Affairs."

Shawn admits that he might be biased because of his alma mater, but feels that "the mainstream schools give students a wake-up call on how the real world LOOKS and operates." He says, "I, myself grew up in an all-black neighborhood as well as attended black public schools. Going to U of M helped me to learn other ethnic backgrounds, how to work with them in class, and the harsh reality of separatism. I feel that this experience prepared me for what I experience now in corporate America."

"large, small, and medium-size classes." But that's easier said than done. Reasonably, most students take four classes a semester while working toward their degree.

There are also academic and honors options for astute, select freshman. Interflex (about 50 students) is a seven-year M.D. program. There's the residential college, where about 600 students live together. These students study in a smaller classroom environment with a lot of personalized attention and "perks," including a specially selected faculty.

The most popular majors are Engineering (18%), Psychology (9%), English (7%), and Biology and Political Science (about 5% each). UMich draws students from all 50 states, the District of Columbia, and more than 115 foreign countries. In a recent class, 37 National Merit finalists enrolled.

At present UMich appears to be very concerned about diversity issues in regard to admissions, the law, and possible future developments. As of this writing, this school (like many others) is facing lawsuits that ultimately will impact on us one way or another. In its published statements the school favors diversity. Its lawyers are arguing that a mixed "environment benefits [all] college students." Still, we have been closely following some of the reports about "problems" and "prejudice" against blacks in regard to the university's School of Medicine. Stay tuned.

Getting In

You must apply directly to one of 13 schools. The largest is the Literature, Sciences, and Arts School. Others include those of Engineering, Nursing, Architecture and Urban Planning, Business, Art and Design, and Music. Here's a recent breakdown of the enrollment numbers of students in several of the University of Michigan undergraduate schools:

- Literature, Science, and Arts—15,114
- Engineering—4,639
- Business—652
- Nursing—520
- Music—649
- Art and Design—551
- Education—283
- Kinesiology—742

The acceptance rate at UMich, about 69%, is among the highest of the schools that are generally ranked in the top 50. In a recent year, about 19,700 students applied and nearly 13,700 were accepted. Eventually 5,325 enrolled. As you'll note, that's less than a 50% yield. For many capable students Michigan is a very wise—if not first-choice—backup selection.

The high acceptance rate is truly not reflective of how hard it is to gain an accept. As a public institution, Michigan has to give priority to its residents. Generally, about 70% of the enrolling students must be from Michigan. Consequently, massive numbers of out-of-state applicants are turned away. Those who are accepted are really put through a very rigorous review. It's not an easy admit. About 68% of the admitted students are in the top 10% of their graduating classes. The average SAT score is in the 1300 range. Usually we are competitive with scores of about 1100 with a strong total package, including strong essays and recommendations. Desirable students have about an average 3.4 and higher GPA, achieved while on a demanding college preparatory track. The college reports that more than 96% of the enrolling students had a GPA of more than 3.0.

Note that we number about 9% of the student body, which translates to more than 2,060 students of color. In a recent graduating class, 321 African Americans received degrees.

MISSOURI

| **WASHINGTON UNIVERSITY IN ST. LOUIS** | Office of Admissions
Campus Box 1089
1 Brookings Drive
St. Louis, MO 63130-4899
(314) 935-6000
Web site: www.wustl.edu | **Financial aid deadline:**
February 15
Application deadline:
January 15
Early decision deadline:
November 15
1999–2000 tuition: $23,634;
room and board, $7,313 |

College Ranking

Washington University is a well-regarded private university, among the top 20 in the nation, with a renowned faculty and top-of-the-line academic programs.

The Campus

Washington University, on 169 acres of land, is in a St. Louis suburb. The campus has its charm, with many of the 101 buildings covered with ivy, stunning arches, and eye-catching gargoyles. Some say it's "architectural splendor." It's hard to disagree after you feast your eyes on the Gothic granite or "Colonial white limestone." And the courtyards are beautiful, with flowers galore. Look at the very huge Olin Library, where many of the school's 3.2 million volumes are. There's also a new natural science building, as well as one for the Psychology Department. The School of Social Sciences is ready. The Lewis Art Center is newly renovated, as are several dorms. The residences have names with personalities (Rubelman, Beaumont, Eliot, Fontbonne). It's a school that has, er, higher aspirations? An Ivy rival?

Campus Life

There are many clubs, organizations, and special-interest groups. Some that might be of special interest to our folks include the Association of Black Students, Black Premed Society, and Shades (an organization of multiracial students). Speakers who have appeared on campus include Cornel West, Toni Morrison, Henry Louis Gates, bell hooks, and Ntozake Shange of "Colored Girls" fame. Indeed, there are things to do. Nearby is Forrest Park, one of the largest in the nation. There, you're close enough to visit the Art and/or History Museums. Or even the St. Louis Zoo.

Academic Realities

WU students are bright, its facilities state-of-the-art, and the social scene is said to be exciting. The faculty is also renowned, and the school's programs are rated top-of-the-line. Nearly 20% of the students are premed, and WU has one of the country's best known medical centers.

At Washington, there are five undergraduate schools: Arts and Sciences, Business, Engineering, Fine Arts, and Architecture. If the students are to be believed, most schools get "rave reviews." Students are challenged, and the work is demanding. A student must take a course in Multicultural and Gender Studies, but also must gain credit in "four distributional categories." The categories include the Humanities, Natural and Behavioral Sciences, History, and Literature. Here the most popular majors are Premed (15%), Engineering (14%), Business (12%), Psychology (10%), and English (6%). These students are serious! Add the luminous faculty (e.g., past poets laureate and Nobel Prize winners), and it's a strong combination. Relatively new here is an African American Studies program.

Getting In

At WU the acceptance rate is about 40%. In a recent year 13,792 applied and 5,546 were accepted. There were approximately 5,200 full-time students, with 6% African Americans, and international students at 7%. The average SAT score is in the 1260 to 1280 range. Note, however, that the admissions team's most important consideration is your high school record and recommendations. Besides that test score, the essay is also pivotal, as well as your extracurricular activities and special talents.

NEW JERSEY

PRINCETON UNIVERSITY	P.O. Box 430 Princeton, NJ 08544 (809) 256-3060 Web site: www.princeton.edu	**Application deadline:** December 31 **Financial aid deadline:** February 1 (suggested), including the school's person financial aid form **Early decision deadline:** December 1 **1999–2000 tuition:** $24,630; room and board, $6,969

"We do make specific efforts to encourage students from minority backgrounds to become aware of what Princeton has to offer . . . and what each of them, as individuals, has to offer Princeton."

> —Princeton Admissions

College Ranking

Princeton University is usually ranked as one of the top five universities in the United States. That group generally includes Harvard, Yale, Stanford, and MIT. It's one of the elite schools, a place where you can find among the faculty a Joyce Carol Oates, a Toni Morrison, as well as other Nobel Prize winners and other stars. Here you've got some of the best programs and departments in the world. Whether you're studying English, engineering, or molecular biology, you're getting a top-notch education, if not the best one available.

The Campus

Princeton has one of the best-looking campuses in the nation. Located in a small New Jersey town, this Ivy League school is on 600 acres, and has 140 buildings, including colleges and residence halls. The architecture is often majestic. The trees, ivy, and landscaping add an aura. There are modern structures, too. Some are by Robert Venturi, a leading American architect.

The look of Nassau Hall is historic, and the University Chapel is ornate. Firestone Library (one of more than 20 on campus) is said to be a "quiet, great study location." More than 5 million volumes are available across campus. Other notable spots include the Amy Award–winning McCarter Theater and the University Art Museum. The Third World Center is a "comfortable, inviting place to read, work, relax, and meet others members of the community." Inside you'll find Liberation Hall (with a seating capacity for 400) and the Paul Robeson reception area. There, you'll also find a fireplace, sofas, and African artwork and artifacts.

The residential colleges all have theaters, dining halls, lounges, game rooms, study carrels, computer clusters, and more. The colleges, which accommodate 450 to 500 students each, are named Butler, Forbes, Mathey, Rockefeller, and Wilson. Upper-class students usually reside in dorms or eat in club dwellings on Prospect Avenue. About 98% of the students reside on campus.

Campus Life

There are more than 200 clubs, organizations, and special-interest groups at Princeton. Some that might be of particular interest to our folks include the Organization of Black Unity, Gospel Ensemble, Minority Business Association, Third World Center Governance Board, Baptist Student Fellowship, Princeton Steel Drum Band, Akwaaba (for those interested in Africa), NAACP, Society of Black Engineers, ONYX (women's discussion group), Imhotep, Concerned Black Men, Culturally Yours (the only one of 12 a cappella groups with "soul"), and the Black Arts Company (with 15 dancers and 10 actors). A recent performance was *B.A.C. at Ya!* The group choreographed Margaret Walker's *For My People.* They've also performed *Colored Girls* (Shange) and *The Colored Museum,* two plays. All the major black Greek-letter groups are on campus, including Alpha Kappa Alpha (Omicron Nu chapter) and Delta Sigma Theta (Rho Epsilon chapter), which sponsors an annual "Tribute to Black Women." Black groups also support an annual Black Solidarity Day Dinner.

The Princeton Tigers usually field competitive basketball teams. You'll enjoy football at 45,000-seat Palmer Stadium. The big games are against Harvard and Yale. Other key teams include tennis, crew, lacrosse, and field hockey. There are 45 intramural teams as well as athletic clubs. On campus is an Olympic-size waterway for sailing and crew teams, a 6,500-seat gymnasium, and an aquatics center.

Academic Realities

Students should expect rigor, and prepare to compete against some of the brightest students in the nation. There's a massive amount of work. If you're a B.A. student, you must take courses in four areas as you pursue your major. The courses include study in art and letters, the social and natural sciences, and history and philosophy. A course in writing is also necessary, as is proficiency in a foreign language. There's a junior paper and a senior thesis. You'll stay busy.

The most popular majors, while studying in one of four undergraduate schools, are Engineering (17%), Biology (12%), History (11%), Economics (10%), and English (8%). An African American Studies program, in Palmer Hall, also is available. Generally about 220 students take courses such as Race, Class, and Intelligence in America or African American Literature. Hello, Ms. Morrison!

Getting In

Like most of the Ivy schools, you're going against "the best of the best." Two pivotal questions will be "Can you handle the Princeton workload?" and "What do you have to offer the school?" Your prior record should show that you've handled the most rigorous college preparatory courses, such as Calculus, Physics, and Chemistry, while sometimes at honors or advance-placement levels.

The acceptance rate at Princeton is about 13%. In a recent year 14,875 students applied and 1,700 were accepted. The SAT average here is in the 1420 to 1430 range, but we can be competitive—and gain an accept—with test scores that are somewhat lower. When applying, you should use the whole-package approach, selling yourself with your essays, recommendations, extracurricular activities in school and the community, as well as your special skills and talents. "Stop the show," as we say, with your presentation. Remember that often this school is looking for "a varied, interesting, and able student body."

At Princeton there are approximately 4,600 students, but the African American body count is a strong 7%. The Affirmative Action Office is in Nassau Hall.

NEW YORK

CITY UNIVERSITY OF NEW YORK (CUNY)

The following five colleges are senior colleges in the City University of New York system, known as CUNY. CUNY has one of the largest community college systems in the country, and CUNY schools are a good option for New York–area students looking to stay close to home, save money, and get a solid education. There have been some controversies over the quality of academics at some of these institutions, but they still offer good value and convenience for many students.

BARUCH COLLEGE OF THE CITY UNIVERSITY OF NEW YORK	17 Lexington Avenue
	New York, NY 10010
	(212) 802-2300
	Web site:
	   www.baruch.cuny.edu
		Financial Aid deadline:
		   March 1
		Application deadline: May 1
		1999–2000 tuition: $3,320
		   (state residents); $6,920
		   (nonresidents); no room or
		   board

College Ranking

A commuter school in the City University of New York system. A good, bargain school for local students looking for an opportunity for a degree.

The Campus

The campus is made up of large buildings scattered throughout the Chelsea section of Manhattan. A gathering/study place here is the Newman Library (more than 270,00 volumes), which has seating for nearly 1,500 folks. The Sidney Mishkin Art Gallery has notable exhibitions. Also, several artistic groups have "in-house" residencies. One is the Jean Cocteau Repertory Theater, another the Alexander Spring Quartet. Interested students should be aware that a 14-story academic complex is being built with classrooms, a theater, recital space, and a television studio.

Campus Life

There are about 100 clubs, organizations, and special-interest groups on campus. There's not a lot of school spirit because most students are traveling, studying, or working when there's free time. Still, there's a gym, weight and exercise rooms, and a pool. Also, the men and women each have five intercollegiate teams.

Academic Realities

During both early and late hours of the day, African Americans (23% of the student body) head to this public school in the fashionable Gramercy Park/Flatiron section of Manhattan. These students are fighting the odds. They commute. They couldn't go away for one reason or another. At Baruch (with its six buildings) the tuition is reasonable, and students want a degree to "step up." Generally, these matriculants are pursuing majors in "specialized areas" such as business (e.g., Accounting, Marketing, or Investments and Securities) or Public Administration. Actuarial Science, Advertising, Journalism, Computer Management, Education, and Music also are among the options.

There are three undergraduate divisions at Baruch: the School of Arts and Sciences, the School of Public Service, and the School of Business. The latter is said to be "the largest business school in the country." The most popular majors are Business (74%), Computer Science (9%), Communications (5%), Psychology (4%), and the Social Sciences (3%). There are about 7,900 full-time students, and 4,750 go part-time (usually while working).

Getting In

In a recent year 4,612 students applied and 2,712 were accepted. That's about 59%. To gain admission, the school is looking for an SAT of about 1000 and/or a GPA of above 80% in academic courses. Note, too, that usually about 1,400 students transfer in yearly. There also are more than 750 full- or part-time faculty.

BROOKLYN COLLEGE OF THE CITY UNIVERSITY OF NEW YORK

2900 Bedford Avenue
Brooklyn, NY 11210
(718) 951-5001
Web site:
   www.brooklyn.cuny.edu

Financial aid deadline:
   March 1
Application deadline: rolling
Early admissions deadline:
   April 15
1999–2000 tuition: $3,393
   (state residents); $6,993
   (nonresidents); no room or
   board

College Ranking

A commuter college in the City University of New York system ideal for local students looking for a solid education at an affordable price.

The Campus

This urban campus, in the Flatbush section of Brooklyn, is on 26 acres, with eight buildings. There are elm trees, walkways, and some ivy-covered walls. There's even a central quadrangle. The main building, with its pillars, is said to be a replica of Independence Hall. There's a six-story student center and an $8.1 million dining facility, with a full-service restaurant.

Campus Life

This school has a Black Solidarity Day celebration, and several of the black Greek-letter organizations are now active. There are more than 100 clubs and special-interest groups on campus. Here you'll experience art exhibits, films, and concerts at the Brooklyn Center for the Performing Arts.

Students have the use of sports facilities including tennis courts, a swimming pool, a soccer field, basketball courts, a track, weight-lifting and exercise locations, and more.

Academic Realities

More than 23% of the students (of approximately 7,600) are African American. They appear to be hardworking, driven, and hoping to cash in "on a brighter future." The are two undergraduate schools; one is the College of Arts and Sciences. It's the home of 31 academic departments, including the Conservatory of Music and the School of Education. Generally, the goal of this college is to train students for business and the professions. You can study business management, accounting, computer science, creative writing (for a B.F.A.), biology, the performing arts, and more. It is said that Brooklyn College students are second in the nation in regard to passing the Certified Public Accountant exam.

Beyond your major, there is a "core" requirement of "two tiers." In one tier you must study cultures and the world. One course is titled People, Power, and Politics. In the other tier you must take courses such as Landmarks of Literature. The most popular majors at Brooklyn College are Education (22%), Business (18%), Psychology (11%), Computer Science (7%), and Health Sciences (5%). Students with more than a 90% average in high school college preparatory courses are eligible for merit scholarships. About 79% of the courses have 20 to 50 students. Note that this is a commuter school with no residences.

Getting In

The acceptance rate at Brooklyn is about 83%. In a recent year 3,762 students applied and 3,117 were accepted. The male-to-female ratio is 40:60. To gain admission, it's suggested that you have an 85% average in college preparatory courses or have an SAT score in the 1100 range. There is a SEEK program (Search for Education, Elevation, and Knowledge). Also, there is a freshman-year college program that helps students with their "transition from high school to college."

| **CITY COLLEGE OF THE CITY UNIVERSITY OF NEW YORK** | 160 Convent Avenue New York, NY 10031 (212) 650-6977 Web site: www.ccny.cuny.edu | **Financial aid deadline:** March 1 **Application deadline:** rolling **1999–2000 tuition:** $3,309 (state residents); $6,909 (nonresidents); no room or board |

College Ranking

This is a school with a legacy, previously called "the Harvard of the proletariat." The old stats are startling: eight Nobel Prize winners, ninth in the country for awarding Ph.D.'s, 11th among colleges in producing "leading business executives" (according to Standard & Poor's). "Now," one student says, "the powers-that-be are looking away, saying there's too much tutoring, too much remedial help, that standards have been set aside." It's a new equation, some argue, a put-down of "new students."

The Campus

At 138th Street, in St. Nicholas Heights in Harlem, you'll say "wow" when you first see City College. On 34 acres of land, you'll see black folks carrying books, chatting, heading to class. More than 36% of the students here are African American, while Hispanics register in at 33%. You'll wonder and perhaps smile as you note the 14 stately-looking buildings.

The campus, certainly, is a resource. The North Academic Building (NAC) covers three city blocks. Inside are 200 classrooms, labs, lecture halls, and a media center. The ultramodern Steinman Hall—Engineering Building stands six stories high and has 40 research and teaching labs. Shepard Hall is ivy-colored and looks like a castle. Aaron Davis Hall is a performing arts center, with 750 seats and a small, experimental theater.

Campus Life

On campus there are more than 100 clubs, organizations, and special-interest groups. These include the National Society of Black Engineers, CCNY Students for Cultural Exchange, Film Club, CCNY Salsa-Mambo Club, Muslim Student Organization, *The Campus* (student newspaper), and several black fraternities and sororities.

Academic Realities

Interestingly, at least one report says that the average age of students now studying for a degree at CCNY is far higher than at other schools. Many of the folks here are fighting heavy odds, many working part-time. At City College today you're looking at your typical inner-city, motivated, striving-to-better-himself-or-herself student. Politically, however, the school and its administrators are being criticized for "lowering standards." To our chagrin, there's talk of "reorganization." Budget cuts have already hurt.

City College meets a lot of our needs. Julie Dash, the writer and producer of the movie *Daughters of the Dust,* is a graduate. So is the famed novelist Walter Mosley. Also, there's Colin Powell, the former chairman of the Joint Chiefs of Staff. In 1998, 15 CCNY engineering students won the National Design Competition of the American Institute of Chemical Engineers. Recently the Debate Society had victories over Harvard, Yale, and Princeton. Over the past decade it's said that 75% of the students applying to medical schools were accepted. CCNY is also said to be ranked 10th nationally in graduating minority engineers.

Once accepted, students enter the College of Arts and Sciences, the School of Architecture, the School of Education, the School of Engineering, or the Sophie Davis School of Biomedical Education (which accepts students into the CUNY School of Medicine). The most popular majors are Engineering (17%), Education (9%), Computer Science and Psychology (7% each), and Biology (5%). There's an African American Studies major.

Getting In

The acceptance rate at City College is about 70%. In a recent year, 3,333 applied and 2,327 were accepted. Usually there are about 6,020 full-time students. About half of that total attend part-time. This is a 100% commuter school without residences. The average SAT score is about 990.

| **HUNTER COLLEGE OF THE CITY UNIVERSITY OF NEW YORK** | 695 Park Avenue
New York, NY 10021
(212) 772-4490
Web site:
    www.hunter.cuny.edu | **Financial aid deadline:**
    March 1
Application deadline: rolling
1999–2000 tuition: $3,328
    (state residents); $6,928
    (nonresidents); no room or
    board |

College Ranking

Hunter College is considered one of the most reputable of New York's City University schools.

The Campus

A public school, it is in the middle of the affluent Upper East Side in Manhattan on three acres. Usually the first thing you'll see as you exit from the subway and head toward the school on Lexington Avenue is a glassed-in walkway that's overhead. That walkway stretches across two streets, connecting two of HC's school buildings. Cars travel beneath. It's an avoid-traffic convenience for students, and one feature of the school's four buildings.

Campus Life

It's a liberal arts college, with six undergraduate schools, and the "cultural mecca" of New York literally "in the yard." Not far away is Broadway and the theater district, Lincoln Center, Central Park, Radio City Music Hall, Bloomingdale's, museums, restaurants, and "a world" more.

Hunter has a student body of about 9,700 students, the majority of whom commute from all locations in New York City. The female-to-male ratio is about 70:30, this institution once having been a single-sex school. About 4% of the students are classified as "international," coming from other countries. About 20% of the students are African American. About 3% reside in campus housing, or in approved apartments in the city.

Hunter has an active intercollegiate sports program, and its basketball team is always exciting and usually a winner. In the basement on campus is a multistory gymnasium that students rave about.

Academic Realities

Those who begin studies can go premed, or major in Urban Planning, Education, Nursing, or other liberal arts or "professional disciplines." A major plus is the in-state low tuition. Popular majors include Psychology (18%), Sociology (11%), English (10%), and Film Studies and Accounting (6% each).

The Brookdale Health Science Center, the smaller branch of the school, is about 50 blocks away. There you'll find the Hunter-Bellevue School of Nursing and a health sciences wing that specializes in training in the fields of gerontology, physical therapy, and community health.

Getting In

The admissions process is selective. Hunter accepts only about 55% of its applicants. In a recent year 6,669 students applied and 3,635 were accepted.

QUEENS COLLEGE OF CITY UNIVERSITY OF NEW YORK	63-30 Kissena Boulevard Flushing, NY 11367 (718) 997-5000 Web site: www.qc.edu	**Application deadline:** January 1 **1999–2000 tuition:** $3,383 (state residents); $6,983 (nonresidents); no room or board

College Ranking

Queens College, a commuter college in the City University of New York system, has long been considered one of the best of the City University schools.

The Campus

Located in Flushing, about 10 miles from Manhattan, QC has the look of a typical campus: self-contained and with quads, some trees, and grass. The students here are from Queens or one of the other four boroughs of New York. With no dorms, it's a commuter school. This school is always a choice for a good student from New York who, for whatever reason, prefers to stay close to home. On 76 acres, the school has only 20 buildings. A central spot is the ultramodern Rosenthal Library which holds more than 712,000 volumes. You'll find one of about 500 IBM Compatible and Apple computers just about everywhere. The Student Union is the most popular hangout.

Campus Life

At Queens there are clubs, organizations, and special-interest groups. Some that might be of particular interest to us include the Black Student Union, SEEK Association, Future Black Lawyers, Caribbean Student Association, National Society of Engineers, Science Organization of Minority Students, and Third World Alliance. Several black Greek-letter organizations are present (e.g., the Alpha Kappa Alpha sorority and the Phi Beta Sigma fraternity), but pledging is not officially endorsed by the college. Oh, well, they'll find you!

Queens has about 16 varsity teams, but it's a great day if "100 students show up"! But there's always the Fitzgerald Gym, which has Nautilus equipment and an Olympic-size pool. Keep in mind that this is a commuter school. Gotta head home!

Academic Realities

At Queens College there are more than 50 majors you can choose from. In introductory classes you might find yourself with 300 fellow students, listening to a lecture. All students, in whatever direction they're headed, must complete about a third of their coursework taking liberal arts and science area requirements (LASAR). Nevertheless, QC has a reputation for "strong programs" in just about all disciplines. The most popular majors are Accounting (16%), Psychology (11%), Sociology (10%), English and Computer Science (6% each). There is a Black Studies program.

Getting In

The QC acceptance rate is about 67%. In a recent year 4,099 applied and 2,759 were accepted. Of about 7,900 students, approximately 10% are African American. The average SAT is about 1100. Approximately 1% of the students are from out of state.

COLUMBIA UNIVERSITY	212 Hamilton Hall New York, NY 10027 (212) 854-2522 Web site: www.columbia.edu	**Financial aid deadline:** February 1 **Application deadline:** January 1 **Early decision deadline:** November 1 **1999–2000 tuition:** $24,974; room and board, $7,732

College Ranking

Columbia University is an Ivy League school in New York City. It is one of the oldest universities in the nation and is usually considered one of the top 10 academic schools in the country.

The Campus

Before you reach Manhattan's Morningside Heights, you'll see the buildings. The gateway to this Ivy League school is at Broadway and 116th Street, and you'll enter the grounds of this 36-acre campus in a bit of awe. On a stroll, you'll notice the architecture. College Walk, a collection of pathways and promenades, takes you to the centerpiece of it all, the enormous stately Low Memorial Library building, an architectural landmark designed by McKim, Mead, and White. There you'll find the main location of one of the largest university library systems in the country (there are more than 6.6 million volumes on campus) as well as the Visitors' Center and administrative offices. If you are just taking a look, you might head downstairs and walk through the maze of corridors. Blink, and you might lose your bearings.

Even it you're a New Yorker, seeing Columbia for the first time is a surprise. Columbia is in uptown Manhattan, parallel to the streets of Harlem. On the streets around the campus you almost get the feeling of being in Greenwich Village. You will pass cafés, shops, bookstores, eateries, newsstands, and students in constant motion. Once on campus you'll feel as though you've been transported to another town. The cityscape gives way to a grassy campus with ivy-colored buildings. The entire landscape is modeled after the Athenian agora.

To the north of Low Memorial Library is Pupin Hall, where pioneering atomic research was conducted. To the east is St. Paul's Chapel, the Sherman Fairchild Center for the Life Sciences, which many students describe as "impressive," the Computer Science Building, and the Morris A. Schapiro Center for Engineering and Physical Science Research. On South Campus is Lerner Hall, which serves as the new student activities center. There's also the Butler Library and the School of Journalism. For eating, you can head to JJ's, in the basement of John Jay Hall, a residence. And if you're lucky, you'll eventually pass theater students rehearsing portions of a play, out in the open. This can happen even if there's a bit of rain. For those who are interested, the 22-acre campus of Columbia-Presbyterian Medical Center is only about two miles away. If you take that stroll, you can overlook the Hudson River.

Campus Life

At Columbia there are many clubs, organizations, and special-interest groups. Some that might be of particular interest to our folks include the Black Student Organization, Caribbean Student Association, Haiti Student Association, Gospel Choir, Charles Drew Premed Society, *Black Heights* (a literary magazine), National Society of Black Engineers, Black Theater Production Association, Sisters (an all-campus feminist group), Charles Hamilton Prelaw Society, and *Columbia Daily Spectator* (the school newspaper). Last, there's the United Minorities Board, which is a coalition of campus minority groups. Each year this group sponsors a Third World Weekend, to orient new students to the school and the community. There is also the Intercultural Resource Center (IRC), which is known as the "Third World house." The IRC sponsors about 60 cultural events a year. Some black students select to live in "African House," a residence in East Campus.

As for sports, the "school has done some losing," a student warns us. The Columbia Lions are not scaring many folks on the gridiron after a long losing streak a few years back. The basketball team is also described as "only so-so." One problem, some say, is that the soccer field and Baker Field are more than 100 blocks away. Four-level Dodge Gymnasium, an underground facility, does have basketball courts, swimming pools, and exercise and weight rooms.

Well, sports aside, when you leave campus, the cultural "mecca" of New York City awaits—from nearby Harlem to Broadway. You can travel to the city's museums, theaters, clubs, restaurants, and beyond. Columbia has also been the home of many movers and shakers of all races, including Paul Robeson, Langston Hughes, and Melvin Van Peebles.

Academic Realities

Columbia has several undergraduate schools. There's Columbia College, the School of Engineering and Applied Science, and the School of General Studies. Columbia is known for its "broad range of innovative multidisciplinary programs," but the academic focus here is still on the core curriculum, with a focus on Western history and literature and the sciences. Some of the required courses include Literature Humanities (Lit Hum), Art Humanities (Art Hum), logic and rhetoric, and a two-semester focus on "major cultures." Not only will you interact with a renowned faculty, but you'll also be facing more than a bit of academic rigor. Columbia has a very bright, intellectually focused student body.

You register by phone. Amazingly, there are usually more than 3,000 courses available to select from. Once seated, you may find yourself in a very large introductory class. But smaller, more congenial settings are the standard. The administration says that only 10% of the classes have more than 50 students. The most popular majors at Columbia are: English and Economics (14% each), History (13%), and Political Science and Psychology (8% each). There is also an African American Studies program. Historian Manning Marable is the director of the program and teaches the introductory course. It's one of 61 courses taught by 23 faculty members each year for the department.

Getting In

The acceptance rate at Columbia, a school usually ranked among the top 10 national universities by most accounts, is about 23%. In a recent year, 11,192 students applied, and only 1,943 were accepted. The average SAT score is 1370. Nearly 70% of the students arrive from out of state, with more than 90% residing on campus. There are about 5,700 undergraduate students, with approximately 9% of that total being African American. International students are a little over 4% of the student count.

CORNELL UNIVERSITY	410 Thurston Avenue Ithaca, NY 14850 (607) 255-5241 Web site: www.cornell.edu	**Application deadline:** January 1 **Financial aid deadline:** Submit as soon after January 1 as possible; the FAFSA, school aid form, and copies of parents' tax returns must be filed **Early decision deadline:** November 1 **1999–2000 tuition:** $23,848*; room and board, $7,035

College Ranking

Cornell is a member of the highly selective Ivy League and consistently ranks as one of the top 10 premier academic universities in the United States in independent surveys.

The Campus

Cornell is in Ithaca, New York, where there are relatively few people of color visible besides our students. Compared with the size and scenic view of most other schools, this campus is huge and breathtaking—it's the largest school in the Ivy League. The school makes all the "most beautiful campuses" lists. The 745-acre campus is hilly, with waterfalls and gorges, and it even overlooks Lake Cayuga. Including residences, there are 761 buildings. Many students say "it's too big!" When students first arrive, they think it will be too impersonal, the size overwhelming. But this feeling seems to give way to a fondness for the place (even when it rains or snows). Some say that trekking to class through puddles of water or over mounds of snow really isn't as bad as they'd anticipated.

Cornell is the sort of university that can raise $1.5 billion in a five-year fund-raising drive, so listing the college's most remarkable buildings and resources here would take pages. Suffice to say, that whatever you want or need is here. Collegetown, the "cozy" district adjoining the college, is one key hangout. It's generally described as "nice," with little shops, restaurants, and

---

*Cornell has several state-supported colleges with tuition less than half the stated above. It's a bargain! You must inquire.

bars. And yes, there's a community called Southside, where you'll find a lot of middle- to lower-class black folks. The black community (some say) has a few unfortunately common urban problems—high dropout and teen pregnancy rates, for example. Of course, Southside is never referred to in the viewbooks or catalogs, and most students rarely head that way. Still, African American students interested in mentoring and community work often visit. "Nobody seems to remember," one student of color informed us, "the last time a Southside youngster made it into Cornell!"

Campus Life

Interested (or accepted) students should visit the school during one of its "Open House Minority" weekends. Your host, an enrolled student, will familiarize you with the school and campus life. You will be your host's roommate, eat meals in several dining halls, go to classes and parties, and follow an itinerary that your host and tour guide will set up for you. You will be kept busy.

Most likely your host will be an African American. He or she probably will live on North Campus at the Ujamaa (a Swahili term meaning, "familyhood") residence, where a sizable number of students of color reside. Ujamaa is where "things black" happen. On your weekend you'll probably attend a student fashion show, hear lectures by someone such as Jawanza Kunjufu and students, and undoubtedly see a Greek-letter step show at a weekend frat or sorority get-together. Aside: there's also an all-women's dorm, Balch Hall, that has a sizable black community.

As at some other schools—Dartmouth, to name one—most Black Cornellians will remain somewhat segregated out of the classroom. Few seem to be complaining. The students at Ujamaa are involved in Big Brother/Big Sister programs, a Prison Outreach Project, a newspaper *(Umoja Sasa),* a gospel choir (Pasmoji-Ni), a spectacular dance group (Uhuru Kuamka), and numerous other cultural efforts. To gain admission to Ujamaa (many apply and a committee selects), you must write an essay about yourself. It should be noted, however, that there are many African Americans who, for whatever reason, live in other residences, "hang" with whomever they please, and are happy. The option is yours to make.

Cornellians have more than 700 extracurricular and social clubs they can join, not to mention the pleasure of a full range of sports: basketball, hockey, football, and so forth. Every night, if you dare to take your head out of the books, you can find something to do. And yes, there's an African American worship service on campus, but most black students prefer Calvary, a "jumping" Baptist Church in town. Cornell, with its visiting chefs and Hotel School, is said to have food as good as any in the nation. We have heard raves from students who have all gained weight. At meals there are all kinds of entrées.

Academic Realities

The academic climate at Cornell is usually described as "intense" or "rigorous" in discussions with educators. One guidebook says the atmosphere is more demanding than most in the Ivy League, "with the possible exception of Yale." The consensus of African American students we've talked to is that Cornell lives up to its reputation as a high-pressure school. Competition in all classes is strong, and your classmates are all honors and top students from their respective high schools (many with prep backgrounds). One smiling student told us this telling story: "In one freshman Bio class I sat down and a valedictorian was sitting to my right, a salutatorian to my left, and a Westinghouse Science winner was behind me." Indeed, it is not unusual to be sitting next to a student with stratospheric SAT scores.

Some African American students, it seems, do have an initial period of adjustment. The situation is similar to a great college basketball player graduating to the pros. Suddenly the shots you once made with ease are being blocked, and you can't score at will. Still, it is clear that the African American students at Cornell are capable, resilient, and often brilliant. Most prevail. Students who major in Engineering, to name just one major, should prepare for a demanding, academic roller-coaster ride. Swimming, on the other hand, is said to be the "only easy course," and all students are required to take it and swim two laps in a long pool.

Perhaps the most frightening thing African American students must face in some crowded classes (200-plus in some technical courses) is the "curve." For example, if you're in a class of 10 and one student gets a 100, eight get 90, and you get 80, you could get an "F." The irony is that your 80—if measured against the test knowledge of students elsewhere—would probably get you an A or honors score.

A Cornell plus: there's an Africana Studies department, with a sizable number of black courses with well-known teachers of color. Generally the professors and TA's really care about their students and often act as mentors, giving advice and help beyond their core teaching roles. At Cornell you will have well over 4,000 courses you generally can pick from. There's no course you can't find or, even, create if you are so inclined. Our tip: in your freshman year don't get sidetracked with socializing, dating, parties, and all the other distractions. Hit the books hard and get an early edge.

Getting In

Approximately 5% of the students at Cornell are African American, which may not sound too hot, but is among the best levels of black attendance in the Ivy League. In a recent year, 19,860 students overall applied and 6,837 were accepted—a 34% acceptance rate. If past years are a barometer, the school will try to maintain the black body count by taking only the best students of color who apply. To get in you should be a top student, preferably with grades at the 90 and above level, with an above-average SAT score: 1100 range or higher. You should be taking advantage of the most demanding academic programs at your high school: honors, advance placement, and whatever academic "goodies" offered that are connected to college enrollment and training in your senior year. Do not relax or take easy courses. Your transcript should include courses such as Physics, Chemistry, Biology, Calculus, and several years of a foreign language.

Whatever else happens in the admissions process, you must hurdle that first almighty question: "Can he (or she) do the work?" If the reviewer doubts or questions that, your application will be passed over. Cornell does not want any student, particularly an African American student, failing out. Your grades and class standing will say a lot about your ability and motivation. Although nobody at Cornell is going to tell you this, in many ways you are competing not only with the overall student body—the school wants diversity—but more importantly, with the African American pool of applicants. Let's say Cornell wants 250 freshman of color; they will take the 250 people they think are the most academically competent, resourceful, talented, etc. Your extracurricular activities, special skills, and other positive traits will come into play, and a subjective decision will be made. Needless to say, you should make your application stand out in any way you can. It appears that out of every 10 students of color who apply, only three are accepted.

Don't fret over the moon-high scores you generally see in the guidebooks. An "average" Cornell score is usually about 1350. Remember to sell "the total you." Your grades, class rank, and overall ability will be assessed. If you can get close to 1100, you can place yourself "in the ballpark." Higher scores, and you will undoubtedly get "consider us" letters from most of the super schools—Stanford, Brown, and so forth. Of course, you must also deal with three achievement tests (your choice), and it would be nice if you could get respectable scores.

Here's a story we think you should consider. An African American who was eventually accepted to Cornell went to take his SATs at a local high school. He sat down, laid his pencils out, and placed his wristwatch on the desk. He noticed that an Asian and many of the white students did the same. When the test began he moved quickly through the test and answered questions at a certain pace, never mulling over anything too difficult. The students with the watches did the same. When the test was over, he found that many of his fellow African Americans said that they did not finish. They didn't pace themselves, were unfamiliar with certain English and mathematical problems, and weren't prepared. If you have the money, take the same training courses you see students of other races taking.

Many of the African American students we have talked to (from New York) had their interviews at the preppy Cornell Club in Manhattan. Most had to chitchat with young, liberal, happy-go-lucky graduates. Remember: you want to give the impression that you're intelligent, well-read, and a nice character who will be a friend to everybody on campus. And if you could give the impression, also, that you might be a future resource to the nation, that would be a definite plus. Yes, it's about PR! If you leave a "sour" or threatening feeling, you might as well forget it. Needless to say, dress appropriately and don't "showcase" any hairstyle. During your interview, be ready to talk about your favorite book and how, for example, you've taken it upon yourself to help kids in the community. You're a resource, is the pitch.

The Admissions team also wants to see that "I am very special" quality in the essay. We saw a recent essay by a young woman named Karen who wanted to get into Cornell. Her essay was about her cat. The piece was well written, and cute with a creative flair. For most colleges, it would have been just fine. But for Cornell we thought Karen needed a stronger "take me" offering—one that would show, conclusively, that she was very special. Make folks love you, we said, not the cat. Imagine writing about your "campaign for Congress" as if it were happening today. Karen wrote something just as creative. And it worked.

Apply to one of the three schools that are state-supported: the College of Human Ecology, College of Agricultural and Life Sciences, or College of Industrial and Labor Relations. At these schools tuition will be approximately 25% less, and more than 50% lower if you're a New York State resident. Remember: you can (and will) take courses in all the other schools. Why empty your pocketbook if the state sections can deliver what you need and want in regard to majors and future plans? The other endowed schools are: the College of Engineering, College of Hotel Administration, College of Arts and Sciences, and College of Architecture, Art, and Planning.

NEW YORK UNIVERSITY

22 Washington Square North
New York, NY 10011
(212) 998-4500
Web site: www.nyu.edu

Financial aid deadline:
  February 15
Application deadline:
  January 15
Early decision deadline:
  November 15
1999–2000 tuition: $23,436;
  room and board, $8,676

College Ranking

New York University is one of the world's largest private universities and ranks among the top in academic diversity and rigor.

The Campus

NYU is in the middle of Greenwich Village. The Village, one of those communities that is known worldwide, never sleeps, and is as much an attraction as any in the city. A must-visit list of a tourist might read like this: Broadway, Wall Street, Central Park, the Statue of Liberty, Radio City Music Hall, and Greenwich Village. All this and more add to the uniqueness of New York University. The Village is your backyard, with Washington Square Park and its central fountain your Quad. All that's been mentioned above, are just a bus or subway ride away.

This 28-acre campus of brick has 109 buildings, including coed dormitories and on-campus apartments. Stretches of city blocks make up this space, with several structures being high-rises. This is a community of trendy shops, cafés, restaurants, clubs, street vendors, bookstores, and an endless potpourri of sightseeing outlets. Besides students, the characters you see will go from A to Z: some will look like movers and shakers, and others will look like, er, "freaks," as some students have said. You'll pass folks with briefcases and others with earrings in every imaginable place on their bodies. As one student says, "you can rub shoulders with the rich or the homeless."

To help with studies is the 12-story Elmer Holmes Bobst Library and Study Center. It sits adjacent to Washington Square Park, where you might see a juggler, a one-wheel cyclist, or hear a comic do his routine for "some change." The Math Science Library also is a stroll away. You're got more than 3.3 million books available in this "city" campus. Many of the renovated apartment buildings you see serve as dorms. Smaller brownstones with names such as Hayden, Weinstein, and Rubin also serve as living quarters.

Campus Life

NYU has more than 250 clubs, organizations, and special-interest groups on campus. Some that might be of special interest to our folks include: the African Student Congress, Black Business Students Association, Council for Unity, Caribbean Student Association, All-University Gospel Choir, Organization of Black Women, NAACP, Black Dance Collective, Black Science Students Organization, African Heritage Planning Committee, Brothers to Brothers, National Organization of Negro Women, and Dr. Martin Luther King Scholars Program. Last, several black Greek-letter groups are active on campus, including Alpha Kappa Alpha. Black groups usually coordinate a "Carnival Africa" each year, with vendors selling Afrocentric items and foods.

Rachel Lyn Johnson graduated from New York University and thinks it's "a wonderful place for African American students and *all* students of color." She arrived from California and points out that "your professors work for you!" Rachel, it turns out, is a success story. She says, "I was surprised and honored to be chosen as valedictorian. I never imagined that I would have such opportunities in a school so large, but I found multiple outlets for my interest and received incredible encouragement and support from many administrators and faculty—black and white alike." Rachel says that the assistant dean for freshmen "really took an interest in me and my success!"

The NYU Violets and its varsity teams don't make the newspapers a lot. Both the Men and Lady Violets (Division III) have played in the finals recently. One year the Ladies won a national championship. The fencing teams have had some success. On an intramural or personal level you can visit the Jerome S. Coles Sports Center. There you've got an Olympic-size swimming pool, tennis and racquetball courts, and a track.

Academic Realities

NYU has seven undergraduate schools, with more than 150 major options. There's the College of Arts and Sciences, Stern School of Business, Tisch School of the Arts, School of Education, School of Nursing/Health Professions, and the Gallatin Division. More than 16,000 bright students pursue majors in this galaxy, often sitting in large lecture classes. The most popular majors at NYU are Business (16%), Performing Arts (10%), Film Studies (7%), Psychology (6%), and Political Science (5%).

Although some still consider this a "commuter school," about 40% of the students arrive from out of state. The good news: NYU students go on to medical, law, business, and other postgraduate degrees at a very high rate.

Famous NYU alumni include Dr. Lorraine Hale, Congressman Charles Rangel, actor Lou Gossett, and filmmaker Spike Lee.

Getting In

The acceptance rate at NYU is about 54%. In a recent year 21,171 applied and 8,420 were accepted. The average SAT score was about 1280, with the lower quarter of accepted students scoring below 1190. Approximately 9% of the students are African American, with another 5% in the "international" category.

STATE UNIVERSITY OF NEW YORK AT ALBANY

1400 Washington Avenue
Albany, NY 12222
(518) 442-5435
Web site: www.albany.edu

Financial aid deadline:
March 15
Application deadline: rolling
Early decision deadline:
November 15
1999–2000 tuition: $4,453
(state residents); $9,353
(nonresidents); room and
board, $5,836

College Ranking

SUNY Albany is highly regarded. It's one of "the gems" of the state university system. Here you'll find a "best education"—laudatory academics and programs, low tuition, bright students, and a distinguished faculty. Many have called this school a "public Ivy" and have noted its growing reputation, high admissions standards, and its "cosmopolitan" student body.

The Campus

Located in Albany, the state's capital, SUNY Albany sits on a suburban 560-acre campus. The school is five miles from downtown Albany and has 90 buildings, including residences. The campus (the central uptown campus) is divided into four quads. They are called (based on periods of New York history) "Indian," "Dutch," "Colonial," and "State." Within the quads are the student dorms and "special-interest halls." The halls include those interested in math, science, and being "substance-free."

Some think the uptown campus is "attractive," while others say it looks "monolithic." Uptown you won't see any historic landmarks, but stately modern buildings of drab color and predictable lines. The uptown campus "was born," after all, in 1962. A point of discussion is "the Podium," a massive fountain of brick near the center of the campus. It's huge and apparently an eyesore or "wonder," depending on whom you talk to. In the summer, some students happily "dip in." At the downtown campus you'll find the pillars, ivy, and an "older" version of what students expect a campus to look like.

Campus Life

A lot of the recreation is centered around Greek-letter activity. All the major eight black fraternities and sororities are here, and they are active. SUNY Albany is not a "rah-rah" sports school, but intramural sports are popular.

Academic Realities

There are five undergraduate schools, which you apply to after your freshman year. There are programs of study in business, social science, education, computer and physical science, the health professions, communications and the arts, and biological science.

The preprofessional and science programs are considered excellent. Sometimes, in those areas, there is academic pressure. The most popular majors are Psychology (13%), English (12%), Business (9%), Sociology and Political Science (7% each). The career-minded students at Albany have intern possibilities galore. Government agencies offer internships in most areas, including social service, health, and public policy. There is an Afro American studies department.

Getting In

The acceptance rate at SUNY Albany is about 61%. In a recent year 14,729 students applied and 9,026 were accepted. There are approximately 9,800 full-time students, with 8% being African Americans. The average SAT score usually is about 1130. Most students are from Long Island, New York City, or Westchester or Rockland Counties.

| STATE UNIVERSITY OF NEW YORK AT BINGHAMTON | P.O. Box 6001 Binghamton, NY 13902-6001 (607) 777-2171 Web site: www.binghamton.edu | Financial aid deadline: March 1 Application deadline: rolling 1999–2000 tuition: $4,416 (state residents), $9,316 (nonresidents); room and board, $5,516 |

"Genus Variun Hederae (A Different Breed of Ivy)"
—from college viewbook

College Ranking

This is another of those "pubic Ivy" schools, with cut-rate costs and growing reputation.

The Campus

This campus covers 606 acres of land, including 62 buildings and residences. There is a pond, a 117-acre nature preserve, trails, and the view of the surrounding countryside. In the summer you will enjoy the green lawns and actually spot some ivy vines. In the winter, you'll better put on boots. You'd be wise, too, to have an umbrella handy. Expect a lot of rain.

Campus Life

Most of the students arrive from New York City, Long Island, or the upstate rural areas near Binghamton. On campus, where 53% of the students reside, there are five residential areas. The Dickinson residence is said to be "the oldest and most stately." Newing College is the "party spot." College of the Woods is, er, in the woods. Interestingly, black students complain that "there is nothing to do in Binghamton" and that it's a very small, isolated town.

Clubs and organizations that might be of social interest to black students include the Black Student Union (the oldest black organization on campus, 1968), Caribbean Student Union, African Students Club, Thurgood Marshall Prelaw Society, National Society of Black Engineers, Charles Drew Prehealth Society, Mary E. Mahoney Nursing Support Group, and Bert Mitchell Management Organization. Also all the major fraternities and sororities are on campus and are very active. Here you'll find Alpha Psi Alpha, Alpha Kappa Alpha, Phi Beta Sigma, Delta Sigma Sigma, Zeta Phi Beta, and others.

Events sponsored by students of color include Black Solidarity Day, Kwanzaa, Pan-African Festival, and Black History Month. The BSU publishes *Vanguard,* a newspaper. On campus there are more than 200 student organizations. Guest speakers have included the author Chinua Achebe.

Binghamton varsity sports include "class" tennis teams (men/women). Also, there are basketball and soccer teams that do reasonably well. For intramural fun, there's corec football (teams of men and women together), and even downhill sledding on trays when it snows. Students use both the East and the West Gymnasiums.

> Shanqua Harrison, a graduate of the State University of New York at Binghamton, is a voluntary recruiter for her alma mater. Shanqua loves her school, but notes: "For me, I know my involvement with the Greek world was just as helpful (if not more) than my college degree itself. My B.S. in Accounting is one thing. My experience in leadership, organizing, and humanity came through Alpha Kappa Alpha. Who knows which has been more helpful?"

Academic Realities

Binghamton is best known for its undergraduate arts and sciences majors. There are several undergraduate schools: the Watson School of Engineering, School of Management, Harpur College (the liberal arts division), School of Education and Human Development, and the Decker School of Nursing (which has an accelerated bachelor's program for students with other degrees). Expect to meet distribution requirements in all schools—of course, with a "liberal arts emphasis." You have to take eight credits in three distribution areas: the humanities, social sciences, and math/the natural sciences. After two years, you then pick a major. There are pre-professional programs in nursing, accounting, and psychology.

The most popular majors are Business (14%), Psychology (13%), English and Biology (10% each), and Philosophy (6%). To meet the needs of these students there are six different libraries. The Glenn G. Bartle Library is the main undergraduate hangout. For fine arts students, there's the Floyd E. Anderson Center for the Arts which includes a 450-seat recital hall and a 1,200-seat theater. Internships and travel opportunities are available. There are African American Studies and Caribbean Area Studies programs.

Getting In

SUNY Binghamton accepts about 43% of its applicants. The average SAT is 1200, but a quarter of the applying students score below 1110. The majority of students (93%) are from New York State. There are approximately 9,500 full-time students. A little over 5% are African American. Sadly, the admissions process here is by "the numbers," with academic considerations such as grades and test scores very important. Extracurricular activities and special talents also are pivotal.

STATE UNIVERSITY OF NEW YORK AT BUFFALO

Buffalo, NY 14260
(716) 645-2000
Web site: www.buffalo.edu

Financial aid deadline: March 1
Application deadline: rolling
Early decision deadline: November 1
1999–2000 tuition: $4,510 (state residents); $9,410 (nonresidents); room and board, $5,903

College Ranking

An academically intense state school with strong programs in pharmacy studies and engineering.

The Campus

SUNY Buffalo is big. There are more than 13,000 full-time students, including 8% who are African American. This is the largest school in the state university system, covering 1,350 acres with 157 buildings, including residences. There are 11 undergraduate schools, sitting on either the North Campus (home of most students) or the South campus. The School of Dentistry and the School of Medicine divide the two sides. On North Campus, where most classes are held, large numbers of students live either in the Governor's dorm or in Ellicott Complex. Some say there's "the look and feel of granite blocks." In Ellicott there are six separate units with names such as Spaulding, Wileson, Red Jacket, and Fargo. South Campus housing is said to be more amenable, with "a more modern look and private bathrooms." But your classes are three miles away, and you must take a shuttle bus. Still, on the South side, the buildings have an older "college aura," with some ivy. The Buffalo campus is about 20 minutes away from Niagara Falls.

At Buffalo they are always building, and students are used to it. The $45 million natural sciences building is one addition, and an athletic stadium that was used for the 1993 World

University Games is another. There is a tunnel—"The Spine"—that connects the Commons to the Student Union and the university's mall.

Campus Life

The winter months are a plus or a minus, depending on whom you talk to. Snowmen quickly appear when they can, and the 3,000-plus members of the school's ski club smile. When the weather's good there are plazas and the Baird Amphitheater for relaxation or concerts.

There are hundreds of clubs, organizations, and special-interest groups on campus. Some that might be of interest to us include the Black Student Union, Caribbean Student Association, UB Gospel Choir, National Society of Black Engineers, and the Office of Multicultural Student Affairs for cultural entertainment or support. Also, most of the major fraternities and sororities are here, including Phi Beta Sigma, Alpha Kappa Alpha, Delta Sigma Theta, and Zeta Phi Beta. Folks such as Cornel West and the poet Rita Dove have lectured.

SUNY Buffalo plays Division I football, basketball, and has 16 intercollegiate teams, eight each for both men and women. There are more than 19 intramural sports for each gender.

Academic Realities

Large numbers of students at Buffalo, are "preprofessional" in attitude, with some of the majors described as "very intense and competitive." Some say that the pharmacy and engineering majors are the strongest in the SUNY system.

Academically, students have many resources and state-of-the-art facilities. There are seven libraries, including the main one, Blockwood. More than 3 million volumes can be found on campus. There's an honors program for about 100 "gifted students," with award and scholarship benefits. There are, really, a multitude of special programs, including joint degrees: B.S./M.B.A., for example. The most popular majors are Business (14%), Psychology (12%), Engineering (11%), Health Sciences (6%), and English (4%). The Educational Opportunity Program offers counseling and tutoring. Helpful, too, is the Committee on Campus Tolerance.

Getting In

At Buffalo, the acceptance rate is about 72%. In a recent year 18,132 students applied and 13,124 were accepted. About 4% of the incoming students were from out of state. They arrived from about 35 states and 61 foreign countries. About a fifth of the students live on campus.

STATE UNIVERSITY OF NEW YORK AT STONY BROOK

Office of Admissions
Stony Brook, NY 11794-1901
(516) 632-9898
Web site: www.sunysb.edu

Financial aid deadline: March 1
Application deadline: July 10
Early decision deadline: April 15
1999–2000 tuition: $4,145 (state residents); $9,045 (nonresidents); room and board, $6,421

College Ranking

A solid state school with state-of-the-state facilities, renowned faculty, and highly respected social science and humanities programs.

The Campus

SUNY Stony Brook is a state-supported school on more than 1100 acres of land. It's in the "picturesque village" of a small town. The campus, some say, looks like a lot of the other state schools: relatively new, blocklike, slabs of concrete. That's the 1960s architectural style. A quick mix of cement without the flourishes of pillars or ivy. The many high-rise structures are "too cold," as one student says. Of course, the Javits Lecture Center is one of a few exceptions: eye-catching curves and design. Add, also, the five-theater Staller Center for the Arts.

Campus Life

With 113 buildings, including residences, there's always a place to go. You can stop at the Fine Arts Center, the Museum of Long Island Natural Sciences, or head to the "plush" North Shore or South Shore beaches (a half hour away).

Academic Realities

The school's social science and humanities programs get the most attention. Key schools are the School of Arts and Sciences and the College of Engineering and Applied Sciences. The most popular majors at Stony Brook are Psychology (14%), Social Sciences and Multidisciplinary Studies (6% each), and Biology and Biochemistry (6% each).

Getting In

Well, there are nearly 10,000 full-time students, and we make up 8% of the body count. The acceptance rate at Stony Brook is about 57%. In a recent year 13,589 students applied and 7,767 were accepted. The average SAT score is in the 1100 to 1110 range. About 2% of the students are from out of state, with 3% from other countries. Nearly 55% of the students reside on campus, but the school is generally considered a commuter school.

SYRACUSE UNIVERSITY	201 Tolley Administration Building Syracuse, NY 13244-1140 (315) 443-3611 Web site: www.syr.edu	**Financial aid deadline:** FAFSA and other forms as soon as possible after January 1 **Application deadline:** February 2 **1999–2000 tuition:** $19,784; room and board, $8,400

College Ranking

Syracuse is ascending, and its rank seems to get higher after each year. Here we are talking about 16 different schools and colleges, many with stellar programs. One example, is the one offered by Newhouse School of Communications, with its top Broadcast Journalism major. Notable, too, are other programs in this "galaxy" of offerings. If you are thinking about engineering, public affairs, business, and natural science offerings (to name just a few areas), you will be rewarded with top-notch study.

In one recent poll Syracuse was in the company of schools such as Georgia Tech, Boston College, and the University of California at Davis. *Nightline* host Ted Koppel is a graduate of Syracuse, as is singing star Vanessa Williams.

The Campus

Syracuse University is a private school that's often mistaken for a SUNY state school. It is on a high hill (200 acres) and overlooks the city of Syracuse. Your walk on campus will be scenic: there are buildings designated as historic, as well as many modern dwellings, including newly renovated dorms and science labs and facilities. There's the Ernest Stevenson Bird Library (more than 2.8 million books) and the Schine Student Center (with its auditorium, food court, and student service offices). From "the Quad," the center point on campus, you can face the pillared Hendricks Chapel and see the Carrier Dome (the school's 50,000-seat stadium). Indeed, there are more than 170 buildings on campus. Walkways, grass, and trees surround these structures (many modern, and some Gothic in style). If you live on "the Mount," the highest point on the hilly campus, you'll get to climb many stairs. And in the winter, all this is usually covered with snow (an average of more than 110 inches over the winter period).

The dorms are described as "nice" and well maintained, and they form an outer ring around the campus. The better dorms are the Day, Flint, and Brewster-Boland Halls. Some have dining halls and fitness centers, and most are equipped with computer stations, TV lounges, and game rooms.

Campus Life

There are more than 300 clubs and organizations you can look to for entertainment, intellectual fulfillment, or hands-on involvement here. Extracurricular activities abound. There are the student-run *Daily Orange* newspaper and on-campus radio and cable-access TV stations. There's a debate team, theater and drama groups, an investment club, literary magazines, intercollegiate sports, and ice rink and tennis interest groups. You can head to the Archbold or Flanagan Gyms. Or, if you're headed to one of the campus food courts, to Burger King or Sbarro.

Syracuse is a Division I powerhouse, where athletics (both basketball and football) are very big. The Carrier Dome can hold 50,000 people, and it's often full. The lacrosse team is an attraction.

We've got, too, the African Student Union, Jazz Ensemble, and Diversity in the Arts groups. Also, look for the NAACP and Urban League units, the National Society of Black Engineers, the Black Celestial Choral Ensemble, or the Office of Minority Affairs for moral and tutoring support. Finally, you can go to Sims Hall, the home of the African American Studies Department and Martin Luther King Memorial Library.

And—oh yes—all the African American fraternities and sororities are here—from Alpha Kappa Alpha to Zeta Phi Beta. And, of course, the city of Syracuse is just a walk or a bus ride away. There, you've got restaurants, parks, museums, art galleries, theaters, and shopping malls.

Academic Realities

Academic intensity—or lack of it—varies among the many different schools. The professional schools—Engineering, Architecture, and Communications—are the toughest. The general consensus seems to be that the academic environment is not cutthroat, too rigorous, or too demanding. Students usually talk more about sports or dorm life than about books, if our informants are to be believed.

All freshmen must complete a writing seminar. Also, be aware that the application procedure and core requirements differ among schools. In the Arts and Science Division, the largest, students must complete work in math, the sciences, the social sciences, and the humanities. Inquire. That said, the most popular majors are in the social sciences, communications, business, engineering, and the performing arts areas.

Sample majors at specific schools:

- School of Education: Secondary, Music, and Art Education
- College of Arts and Sciences: Biology, Psychology, English
- College of Engineering and Computer Science: Computer, Civil, and Chemical Engineering
- College for Human Development: Child and Family Studies, Nutrition
- College of Nursing: baccalaureate program in nursing
- School of Social Work: Social Work
- College of Visual and Performing Arts: Drama, Music, Art

Getting In

The Syracuse acceptance rate for applicants is usually about 60%. And always, the application pool is large: approximately 10,600 applied recently, with about 6,400 accepts. This is a big school, after all, with more than 10,400 undergraduates (with about 4,200 graduate students). A third of these students graduated in the top 10% of their high school class. The average SAT score was 1170. Note, however, that the lower quarter of the accepts had scores below 1070. Very important here is your preparedness. A college preparatory track and advanced placement courses are important, as well as your "unique" personal qualities. Your essay and recommendations should definitely sell you, if your standardized test scores fall short.

This student body is pulled from 50 states and 100 foreign countries, with about 44% from New York State. Massachusetts is next, with also large numbers from other northeastern states.

UNIVERSITY OF ROCHESTER	Wilson Boulevard Rochester, NY 14627 (716) 275-3221 Web site: www.rochester.edu	**Financial aid deadline:** February 1 **Application deadline:** January 15 **Early decision deadline:** November 1 **1999–2000 tuition:** $22,845; room and board, $7,512

College Ranking

Well, we hope you like snow, because students at the University of Rochester see a lot of it. Still, it's a highly regarded national university with a growing reputation. Not only is there a distinguished faculty, and academically capable students, but also the university has superb facilities.

The Campus

Located about two miles from downtown Rochester, the university is on a 600-acre campus with more than 143 buildings, including residences. Students say their campus is "attractive" and can point to the Eastern Quadrangle, where you'll find the main library (there are seven libraries). Another eye-catching spot is Wilson's Commons, the student "do it all" center designed by architect I. M. Pei. It's glass-framed and built around a four-story atrium, with eateries and game rooms inside. Older Georgian buildings and modern structures are everywhere. The Chemistry and Biology departments have state-of-the-arts facilities, including 25 electron microscopes. For sports buffs, there's the $8 million Zornow sports complex. Another plus is the renowned Eastman School of Music, which is a part of the University of Rochester.

Campus Life

Clubs and organizations that might be of special interest to us include the Black Student Union, which sponsors a Pan-African Exposition each year during Black History Month. The group also hosts a Kwanzaa dinner, workshops, and discussions. Other groups are the African Caribbean Cultural Club, the Association of Black Drama and the Arts, and the Black Greek Council. All the major black fraternities and sororities are also on campus and are active.

U of R varsity teams (11 for men, 10 for women) have, in the past, done well. There's a 5,000-seat stadium, and a gym that seats half that total. Still, intercollegiate sports do not "rock the house" here. For a workout you can head to the fitness center, weight room, or strut to the jogging path.

Academic Realities

Once accepted, students will enter one of four undergraduate schools: the College of Arts and Sciences, the School of Engineering and Applied Sciences, the School of Nursing, or the Eastman School of Music.

The most popular majors are Biology (14%), Engineering (12%), Psychology (11%), Music (9%), and Economics (8%). If you wish, you can take courses offered by the Frederick Douglass Institute for African/African American Studies. The Office of Minority Student Affairs offers academic support.

Getting In

The acceptance rate at the U of R is about 54%. In a recent year 9,981 applied and 5,402 were accepted. The average SAT score range is 1250 to 1260. About 46% of the students arrive from out of state. With a full-time body count of approximately 4,750 students, at least 8% are African American. Three quarters of the students reside on campus.

U.S. MILITARY ACADEMY	600 Thayer Road
	West Point, NY 10996
	(914) 938-4041
	Web site: www.usma.edu
		Application deadline:
		    March 21
		Early decision deadline:
		    October 25
		Tuition and room and board:
		    It's free; graduating cadets are commissioned as second lieutenants in the U.S. Army and must serve five years of active duty

College Ranking

"West Point," as its called, is perhaps our most famous military academy.

The Campus

The dorms are "barracks." You'll have computers and study materials, and your space will be "subject to inspections." For long periods, you cannot leave the grounds. The campus is 56 miles north of New York City. It's a 16,000-plus-acre campus, with more than 902 buildings. Talk about a military complex!

Campus Life

Unlike most colleges or campus settings, you will be placed under constant scrutiny, be subject to rules and regulations, and will "belong to them," to put it mildly. At 5:00 A.M. it will be "rise and shine." At midnight, the lights go out. You will eat breakfast and lunch in "the mess hall." As a "plebe" (freshman) you will serve upperclassmen and be at their beck and call.

At 40,000-seat Michie Stadium or elsewhere you'll get to let loose, especially when Army's football team takes the field. More than 7% of the cadets are African American. There's a Cadet Gospel Choir, a Minority Advisory Group, the African American Literature Forum, and the National Society of Black Engineers.

Oh, yes, sometimes you'll get a weekend leave. But that might have something to do with a holiday, seniority, or military performance.

Academic Realities

At West Point you're a student on one hand, but you're also part of a "company" (a military unit). You'll be stationed on campus with 120 would-be soldiers. Like the others, you arrived because you're pursuing a military career.

The academic work at USMA is always demanding, if not rigorous. You must complete 40 courses, covering a very wide range of areas. It's no cakewalk. You've got to take Computer Science, English, History, Psychology, Mathematics, Chemistry, and more. In your last two years there's a five-course engineering sequence that's supposed to give you "military expertise." Luckily, most classes are small (15 to 20 students). Of course, before you take one class you're facing the "Beast Barracks"—a test of endurance—in basic training during the summer. That'll be your Camp Buckner initiation. You've got to endure two summers of that as well as maintain a very high level of personal fitness at all times. The "conditioning equipment" will be there for you. Continuous intramural sports, including swimming and gymnastics, is a day-to-day activity.

To say the least, high ambitions are the standard at West Point. The most popular majors are Engineering (36%), Behavioral Sciences (15%), Foreign Languages and History (8% each), and Mathematics (4%). The students aim to excel, achieve, and succeed. There are more than 23 degree fields of study to select from. All that, while you get to ride in helicopters, parachute, or direct a tank.

Getting In

To gain admission to USMA is probably as hard as getting into Harvard. The acceptance rate is 13%. In a recent year 11,808 students applied and 1,609 were accepted. The average SAT score is about 1250, with a quarter of the students scoring less than 1160. The male-to-female ratio is 88:12.

To apply to USMA you must "get nominated," and it's a process that should begin during the second semester of your junior year. You must initiate the process. You must get nominated by an "approved source." That list includes members of Congress, as well as the president or vice president or the Department of the Army. At the same time, you must request a Service Academies Precandidate Questionnaire from the school. Contact the Admissions Office as soon after January 1 as possible for materials and instructions. Essential here are factors such as academic ability, character, your contributions to society, and how physically fit you are. Recall some of the basic training scenes you've seen in the movies. Can you hang tough?

VASSAR COLLEGE

124 Raymond Avenue
Poughkeepsie, NY 12601
(914) 437-7300
Web site: www.vassar.edu

Financial aid deadline:
February 1
Application deadline:
January 1
Early decision deadline:
November 15
1999–2000 tuition: $24,240;
room and board, $6,770

College Ranking

This very selective college is world renowned and regarded as one of the top liberal arts colleges in the nation.

The Campus

Located on a beautiful 1,000-acre campus in upstate New York, you can take pictures of pond-size lakes, marvel at the flowers, visit an arboretum, or take a stroke on a golf course. It's rumored that they still serve afternoon tea in the Main Hall, the oldest building on campus and a historic landmark.

Campus Life

A little elitist? Vassar, some say, attracts students with "eclectic backgrounds" who are academically capable. There are about 2,300 students, with a little over 5% of African American descent. The good news is that the name "Vassar" opens doors. The bad news, for many, is that most folks still think this college is a women's school. It's been coed since 1969, but the sisters complain that "the brothers don't know that."

Although there are no Greek-letter groups on campus, we do have a Black Student Union, the Vassar College Intercultural Center, Paul Robeson Men's Band, Ebony Theater Ensemble, Caribbean Student Alliance, and the Black Student Leadership Network. Other spots that we find amenable—besides the "family" atmosphere of the campus—are the main library (more than 660,000 volumes) and the "ACDC," the All-Campus Dining Center. The Retreat, inside the ACDC, is the popular snack bar. Also on campus is the Vassar College Art Gallery, Frances Lehman Loeb Art Center, and Hallie Flanagan Davis Powerhouse Theater. Jewell, one dorm, has a tower with a great view. Of course, every residence on campus has a Steinway piano in its parlor.

For sports activity you're got tennis and about 24 other intercollegiate possibilities. But forget about that spectacular marching band, or football or basketball teams. There is, thankfully, a new rowing team that you can see practicing on the Hudson.

Actress Meryl Streep is a distinguished alumna, as well as the late Jacqueline Bouvier Kennedy Onassis.

Academic Realities

Although the work is often called "moderate to intense," there are no "core" requirements to straitjacket your course selections. And the professors are accessible, most residing on campus. If you wish, you can design your own major. The most popular majors are English (14%), Psychology (12%), Film Studies and Art History (about 7% each), and Political Science (6%).

Once done, Vassar grads go on to law, medicine, or graduate programs at an astounding rate. A plus, too, is that Vassar has an undergraduate Twelve-College Exchange Program. Students can spend a semester or more at colleges such as Amherst, Williams, or, yes, Spelman.

Getting In

The acceptance rate here is about 42%. The male-to-female ratio is about 38:62, which is irregular compared to other schools of its size and reputation. An application from a brother or sister with a strong college preparatory record and good test scores would probably get a receptive review. The SAT average here is in the 1280 to 1300 range, but we can garner an accept with scores that are considerably less. Your high school record, essay, and recommendations can carry the day.

NORTH CAROLINA

BENNETT COLLEGE

900 East Washington Street
Greensboro, NC 27401
(336) 273-4431
Web site: www.bennett.edu

Financial aid deadline: March 1
Application deadline: rolling
1999–2000 tuition: $8,460; room and board, $3701

"Because I am a woman, strength, wisdom, and compassion are my gifts. Because of my faith, I have the courage to move mountains. Because I am a Phenomenal Bennett Belle, whatever I can envision, I can achieve!"

—The Belle's Creed, Bennett College.

College Ranking

Bennett College is the "other" historically black college that takes only women of color. The school is private, affiliated with the United Methodist Church, and is in southeastern Greensboro. At Bennett, with only about 600 full-time students, you've got a "sisterhood" around the clock.

The Campus

Only a mile from downtown Greensboro, the school is on about 55 acres of land. At the edges of the campus you'll see magnolia trees that have been "planted by each graduating class" to symbolize "the southern ideal of feminism." There are 31 buildings, including the residences.

You'll also find on campus the Thomas F. Holgate Library, which has 95,000 volumes, as well as an art collection that includes work by Jacob Lawrence and Aaron Douglas. The "fresh-women" all get to see the line of four oak trees on campus that remind all who arrive to "be strong."

Campus Life

Some of the clubs, organizations, and special-interest groups include: the Belles of Harmony Gospel Choir, debate team, Business and Accounting Club, National Council of Negro Women,

Bennett Scholars, Student Government Association, Students in Free Enterprise, and the Delta Sigma Theta sorority (Omicron Delta chapter). Three other sororities are active on campus. With all that's been noted, students still get a chance to do volunteer work. For example, students have worked at the Children's House and Hampton Elementary School, both in Greensboro.

The Bennett College Choir performed for President Bill Clinton during the 1994 Anniversary Gala of the United Negro College Fund. Kelly Teresa Cole, a Belle, was named National Miss UNCF in 1997.

In intercollegiate sports there are basketball, swimming, track and field, tennis, and softball teams. This is a school with lots of spirit, proud of its cream and gold colors, its songs, and its traditions (it was founded in 1873). And yes, Dr. Maya Angelou has donated money to Bennett and the "Bennett Belles."

Academic Realities

Bennett has Humanities, Sciences, and Professional Studies Divisions. Within those boundaries you can major in Business, English, Biology, Education, Computer Science, Secretarial Studies/Office Management, Music, and more. A support vehicle is the Center for Academic Achievement and Retention (CAAR), which was set up to "recruit and enroll qualified students" and nurture them. Note that Bennett has 3-2 B.A./M.A. programs in nursing and engineering with nearby North Carolina A&T, which is also located in Greensboro (population 190,000).

Getting In

The acceptance rate to Bennett is about 70%. In a recent year 754 students applied and 538 were accepted. The average SAT score is in the 970 to 980 range. The ACT is approximately 20. The stats say that about 22% of the Belles are from North Carolina, with 76% of the out-of-staters arriving from 30 to 32 states. About 2% of the students are from countries such as Kenya, Ghana, South Africa, Zimbabwe, and Angola.

DUKE UNIVERSITY

Director of Undergraduate
   Admissions
2138 Campus Drive
Durham, NC 22206
(919) 684-3214
Web site: www.duke.edu

Financial aid application: February 1; recommendation: submit as soon after January 1 as possible; FAFSA and CSS profile required
Application deadline: January 1
Early decision deadline: November 1
1999/2000 Tuition: $23,921; room and board, $7,088

College Ranking

Duke has been called the "Harvard of the South," a phrase that is said to perturb many who live below the Mason-Dixon Line, who'd prefer it if Harvard's ambition was to be the "Duke of New England." Whether it's considered a term of endearment or not, the implied message is indisputable. Duke is a top-notch school, a powerhouse in the rankings game. You can say "Duke" in the same breath with names likes Yale or Stanford. In the *U.S. News & World Report* rankings, Duke has been ranked in the top 10 for at least a decade if not longer. As late as the 1970s, African Americans were an afterthought if that, at Duke. Now, a combination of factors makes this southern institution an appealing pick. Indeed, more than 800 freshmen of color arrive each September. It's clear that Duke, with its solid academic programs and reputation, deserves a close look for students looking for a top-tier university.

The Campus

The campus of Duke has been described as "beautiful," "majestic," and a "visual delight." Situated beside a 8,300-acre forest, it has two sides. The West Campus has a Gothic air and was formerly a men's college. Today this is the hub of where most of the 230 buildings, including some residences, are located. There's the bell-chiming chapel (with a tower more than 210 feet tall), the "gargantuan" medical center, and the 4.5-million-volume Perkins Library. You can use your Duke Card (debit) at the Bryan Center, the all-purpose student union. There you've got three theaters, eateries, a bookstore, game room, check cashing outlet, lounges for socializing and watching TV, student stores, art galleries, conference rooms, and more.

On the West Campus you'll also find the Math-Physics Building, Cameron Indoor Stadium, and tennis courts. On the East Campus, where only women used to dwell, you'll find a lot of Georgian architecture. There's the Lilly Library and the Academic Advising Center. Arts facilities include the Mary Duke Biddle Music Building and Museum of Art. Since 1995, the East Campus has been the home of most freshmen. Shuttle buses connect the two campuses. On Campus Drive you can walk or drive the one mile. All this is in Durham (population 100,800), about 25 miles from the state's capital, Raleigh. Yes, Durham is home to many of our folks, and perhaps why some Duke write-ups give little lip service to "the neighborhood."

Students reside in a number of "quads" (e.g., Clocktower, Craven, Edens). The quads stretch from East Campus to North Campus, and each is composed of several dorms. Look for names such as Camelot, Westminster, Lancaster, Stratford, Windsor, Canterbury, and Stonehenge. Generally, these buildings (there are 26 residences) are all stately in appearance. Most are three floors high, of gray or brown stone, and are ivy-covered. Tall trees usually are nearby.

Among the regular (coed, or single-sex) residences are "selective" or theme houses. In Mitchell Tower you'll find arts students. In Decker Tower, they'll be students interested in the study of languages. And fraternity and sorority houses are available. In the Craven Quad you'll find the black Alpha Phi Alpha residence. Many black students choose to reside in housing along Campus Drive, which is often called "Central Campus." There are locations that are with or without air conditioning. The *Resident Hall Survival Guide* can tell you more. In one "cool" setting a single costs $6,023 and a triple is a much lower at $4,055. All the dorms have common rooms or studies, and condoms are "available in vending machines throughout the resident halls."

Campus Life

Some might recall that there was a past segment on "self-segregation" on *60 Minutes* about Duke. Of course, this is not that unusual at many of the highest-ranked schools. At Duke, students of the same race do seem to "hang together."

There are a wide number of clubs and organizations for students of color. Key stops at Duke include the Mary Lou Williams Center for Black Culture (a meeting place in the West Union Building), the John Hope Franklin Research Center for African American Documentation, and the Office of International Affairs. The Black Students Alliance (BSA) is a growing presence, as well as Ashanti, Sister to Sister, Brother to Brother, Bench and Bar Society, The Future Is Now, Students of the Caribbean (SOCA), *Prometheus Black* (a literary magazine), Black Campus Ministries (BCM), African Student Association, Hoof & Horn (theater), and the National Society of Black Engineers. All the major eight black fraternities and sororities are on campus, including Delta Sigma Theta, Omega Psi Phi, Alpha Kappa Alpha, Kappa Alpha Psi, and the others.

Also on campus are more than 350 other social, cultural, and entertainment outlets. There's the Duke Players (theater), the visiting Carolina Ballet, concerts and readings (e.g., Ntozoke Shange), a radio and a TV station, jazz band, chess club, chorale groups, debate teams, and dozens of other special-interest, entertainment, and cultural possibilities.

Of course, we all know of Duke's basketball legacy and its perennial success. This school has managed to combine its high academic programs with excellent sports components. Very strong soccer and tennis teams as well as very competitive groups in football, hockey, baseball, golf, and fencing are the rule. Duke's scholar-athletes (basketball star Grant Hill, among others) are credits to the school. Besides the varsity football stadium, students have two gymnasiums, more than three dozen tennis courts, indoor and outdoor pools, a golf course, and tracks and recreational fields.

Academic Realities

Duke is said to be academically laid-back compared to some of the other highly ranked schools that make the top 25 lists. Do note, however, the comments of student Richard Jones, writing in the new online black journal *The Talking Drum*. He writes:

> You work hard! It has been a long, stressful week. You have a 10-page English paper due. You are up all night studying for the chemistry test. You run on four hours of sleep, and find it hard to stay awake during class. You live during the week by looking forward to the weekend. You play hard! Friday night finally rolls around. You hang out with your friends, go to a few parties, let loose. . . .The stress of the week has finally disappeared, only to return with a vengeance.

Duke's "Curriculum 2000" organizes your course of study into modes of inquiry. You must achieve competencies in a foreign language, writing, and research. You do this by taking courses (beyond major requirements) in four areas: the natural sciences and math, the social sciences, arts and literatures, and civilizations. For your degree, you must complete 34 courses.

The most popular majors are Biology (15%, with many in premed tracks), Psychology (10%), Economics (9%), and Public Policy and History (about 7% each).

For those so inclined, there's an African American Studies Department, where you can take either a major or a minor. In a given year, approximately 45 different courses are given. Here's a sampling: Film and the African Diaspora, Islam in West Africa, Black Women and the Civil Rights Movement, Religions of the African Diaspora. Note, too, that the department often sponsors conferences under it's W. E. B. Du Bois Lectures banner. A recent affair was called "Race and Representation." The keynote speaker was Nobel Prize–winning author Toni Morrison. A prior event was called, "African-American Women: The Body Politic."

Duke also has an exchange program with Howard.

Getting In

Getting into Duke's undergraduate schools (either the Trinity College of Arts and Sciences or the School of Engineering) won't be easy.

The acceptance rate at Duke is a little over 30%. In a recent year approximately 13,700 students applied and about 4,030 were accepted. The full-time undergraduate body count is usually about 6,300. African American students make up 8.1% of that number. The median SAT score is about 1,380. In one survey by the *Journal of Blacks in Higher Education,* it was noted that (on average) we score about 180 points lower than the Duke median. The *JBHE* analysis then goes on to demonstrate how we still do the work and graduate. The message here: apply, even if your score falls below the average.

It's said that the Duke admissions team is very thorough, always using more than one reviewer to make its decisions. It's not only about grades and/or test scores, although those are very important. Your personal qualities, essays, extracurricular activities, and teacher recommendations also help and define your profile. Taking a very strong college preparatory sequence of advance placement and honors courses (especially if you are considering an engineering degree) is essential.

Only about 15% of the students are from North Carolina. Others arrive from the 49 other states, the District of Columbia, and more than 30 foreign countries.

JOHNSON C. SMITH UNIVERSITY	100 Beatties Ford Road Charlotte, NC 28216 (704) 378-1000, ext. 10 Web site: www.jcsu.edu	**Application deadline:** rolling **1999–2000 tuition:** $9,974; room and board, $3,875

College Ranking

Johnson C. Smith University is a nice choice for a student looking for a golden opportunity and perhaps a second chance.

The Campus

This private school is in an urban neighborhood in Charlotte, on a 105-acre campus that has 32 buildings, including residence halls. On campus is the very lovely Biddle Hall, with its tower and clock. The Jane M. Smith Memorial Hall is pillared and sits beside flowers. There's also the Banking and Finance Center, the Language Lab, and a career placement location (handling internships and cooperative education assignments). On a visit you'll see that the outer line of the campus is actually decided by the shape of the city blocks, divided by several streets with "neighborhood" stores. It's an urban setting. A satellite branch of the Medical School of the Carolinas is nearby. Driving away, you'll find yourself passing beautiful homes lined with huge trees and see fewer of our faces.

Campus Life

More than 90% of the students reside in either single-sex, coed, or Honors College dormitories. Carter Hall, a men's dorm, was one of the first at this college.

At Johnson C. Smith you have more than 40 clubs and organizations to keep you occupied. There's the Student Government Association, NAACP, Spiritual Choir, Student Christian Association, Shaki/Shaki Dance Club, drama and dance groups, debate team, jazz and marching band, Radio WJCS and a TV station, chess club, school newspaper, political science club, and more. Also, the major eight black fraternities and sororities are on campus and are very active. About 20% of the men and women pledge. Important campus events include West Fest and Founders Day.

For physical recreation there are two gyms, the larger one with a seating capacity of about 3,200. A city-owned stadium with 25,000 seats is available for Golden Bulls football games and other sporting events. JCSU plays schools such as North Carolina Central and Virginia State. On campus there's also a pool, basketball and tennis courts, a weight room, and more than 250 computer terminals for your use.

Academic Realities

While JCSU is not difficult to get in, it will take you as far as you're willing to go. About 25% of the students go on to graduate school within six months, with a larger percentage employed within that time frame. For students enrolled in the Engineering major, there are 3-2 cooperative programs with historically black colleges North Carolina Central and Florida A&M University. After three years at JCSU you can get that B.S., and a Bachelor in Engineering degree from one of the other two schools after two years of further study.

The most popular majors here are Business (23%), Communications (16%), Biology (8%), Computer Science (7%), English (6%), and Sociology in the "social services" category. There is an African American Studies track.

Getting In

JCSU is a relatively easy school to get into, with an acceptance rate of nearly 71%. The median SAT score is about 900. If you are an "average" student taking college preparatory courses (e.g., Biology and Chemistry), you would be a very desirable candidate. For admission, the school's minimum requirements are: a "2.0 GPA, 650 SAT, and 14 ACT."

More than a quarter of the approximately 1,280 students are from out of state, with the college attracting most students from the Northeast. The demographics look like this: 19% of the students are from North Carolina, 18% from South Carolina, and the balance (63%) from other states.

NORTH CAROLINA A&T UNIVERSITY

1601 East Market Street
Greensboro, NC 27411
(336) 334-7946; (800) 443-8964
Web site: www.ncat.edu

Financial aid deadline: March 15; NCAT wants both the CSS profile and the FAFSA submitted; try to get these forms in as soon after January 1 as possible

Application deadline: June 1; again, apply much sooner than that

1999–2000 tuition: $1,889 (state residents); $9,159 (nonresidents); room and board, $4,010

"NCAT is recognized as having 'one of the best'—some say the best—engineering schools among historically black universities."

—Beth McMutrie, *Greensboro News Record,* 1998

College Ranking

This is the alma mater of the Reverend Jesse Jackson and the late astronaut Ronald McNair. In recent *U.S. News & World Report* rankings this public college has been placed in the favorable "second tier," ahead of nearly 60 other colleges in the southern university group. *Black Enterprise* ranks NCAT ninth its "top 50 Colleges for African Americans" list (1999).

In the Black Excel newsletter we picked NCAT as one of our "10 best" historically black colleges. At the time, we wrote: "In 1993, NCAT was awarded an $8 million grant to establish an aerospace research center. This grant is typical of the kind of attention this comprehensive university (with its engineering and science emphasis) attracts." Other indications of their strengths include its number one ranking in 1996 in USDA fiscal allocations to HBCUs and its number one ranking in 1998 in schools producing the most minorities with degrees in Science, Mathematics, Engineering, and Technology.

The Campus

North Carolina A&T is located in the city of Greensboro, about 9 blocks from the downtown area. About 30 miles from Winston-Salem and 90 miles from Charlotte, N.C., the main campus is on 187 acres of land, including 107 buildings and student residences. This state-supported school is located near major shopping centers, restaurants, theaters, and medical facilities. The shared sentiment seems to be that "the area's mix of industry, with schools and universities, contributes to its economic and cultural diversity." NCAT's farm, east of the city limits, covers another 600 acres of land, with several modern farm buildings.

On campus there is the F. D. Bluford Library, named after the third president of the university. This is a four-level structure with more than 670,000 volumes, including a special collection in the Archives and Black Studies sections. Other essential locations on campus include the Learning Assistance, Computer, and Audiovisual Centers. Also, there's a radio station, a television station, a language laboratory, a planetarium, and the Reed African Heritage Center. There is an outstanding art museum, featuring special exhibits throughout the year.

Other notable sites are "The Oaks," which is the chancellor's residence; the Dudley Memorial Building (with its pillared columns); and the Richard B. Harrison Auditorium. Several of the class and laboratory halls also deserve mention. There's Ron McNair Hall (College of Engineering); Crosby Hall (College of Arts and Sciences); and Frazier Hall, where art and music majors hang out.

The residence halls are set up to "provide opportunities for personal, social, and intellectual companionship." The women's dorms include Curtis, Morrow, Zoe Barbee, Holand, Morrison, and Vanstory. The men's include Scott, Cooper, Alex Haley, and the Gamble Complex. Only about 44% of NCAT students live on campus.

Campus Life

There are more than 150 clubs and organizations on campus, including all the major fraternities and sororities, as well as countless "social fellowships." You'll find Alpha Phi Alpha, Phi Beta Sigma, Delta Sigma Theta, Zeta Phi Beta, to start.

Important days on campus include Founder's Day, Homecoming, and Ronald E. McNair Memorial Day. The Memorial Union Building includes lounges, a ballroom, a dining area and snack bar, a beauty shop, music and games rooms, and facilties for large cultural and recreational events. The Union is the student activity headquarters and the spot where forums and workshops take place.

You can join or get involved with the Biology Club, the Richard B. Harrison players, the symphonic band, Tender Loving Care of the Nursing School, the A&T Karate Club, the A&T Fellowship Gospel Choir, Caribbean Student Association, Jazz Ensemble, Pan-Hellenic Council, NAACP, or actually join one of the "hometown clubs"—the Durham, Maryland, Raleigh, Virginia, or Rocky Mount groups, to name a few.

Of course, at football games there's the Blue and Gold Marching Machine, a 163-member band that is sometimes said to be "the small band with the BIG sound. This band is the reigning Atlanta Battle of the Bands Champion.

Academic Realities

There are six undergraduate schools: the Schools of Education, Technology, Engineering, Nursing, Agriculture, and the College of Arts and Sciences. Within these schools there are at least 44 departments, all obviously asking you to develop your "powers of critical and analytical thinking." While one student might be discussing heath care, another might be studying the "theory of equations," while still another student might be working on an independent study project. At NCAT, students face a very wide range of study and adjustment levels. Some students, in fact, will even be working with the Learning Assistance Center, strengthening their reading, communication, and computational skills.

Whatever your major, however, there are core requirements: you must take at least six credits in each of the following areas: English, Social Science, Natural Science, Humanities, and Mathematics. A two-credit Health or Physical Education class also must be taken. At NCAT the most popular majors are Engineering, Nursing, and Business.

Getting In

Nearly 61% of the students who apply to NCAT get accepted. In a recent year about 4,600 students applied and approximately 3,040 were accepted (an additional 300 transfer students enroll annually). Of these students, the median SAT score was about 900, with accepts obviously presenting a very wide range of scores. For example, about 25% of the entering Aggies have scores in the 1020 or higher range. A large group of "second chance" applicants (the bottom quarter) have scores below 820.

Note that about 85% of the students are from North Carolina, and are obviously happy about the relatively low tuition this public university charges its state residents; out-of-staters must pay considerably more. Still, students arrive from 38 states and 25 foreign countries. Most students are from the Carolinas, Virginia, and Washington, D.C. Countries such as Nigeria, the Bahamas, South Africa, China, and India are represented. About 89% of the Aggies are African Americans.

NORTH CAROLINA CENTRAL UNIVERSITY

Office of Undergraduate
 Admissions
Durham, NC 27707
(919) 569-6080
Web site: www.nccu.edu

Application deadline:
 July 1
1999–2000 tuition: $1,774
 (state residents); $8,902
 (nonresidents); room and
 board, $3,475

College Ranking

NCCU is a public institution and one of the country's top historically black universities; they offer a top-ranked teacher program and a caring faculty.

The Campus

NCCU is in Durham, North Carolina (population 140,000-plus). Durham also is the home of Duke University. NCCU is on 110 acres, with surrounding sloping hills, "verdant green," and lovely blossoms (azaleas) much of the year. On campus you'll find 57 buildings (both modern and Georgian in style), including residences that accommodate more than 1,900 students. Dorms include McLean, Rush, Chidley Hall, Eagleson, and Latham. The school is about 25 miles from Raleigh.

On campus you'll pass McDongald House, which is the home of undergraduate admissions and the oldest building on campus. Clyde R. Hoesy is the administration building. The James E. Shepard Memorial Library has more than 600,000 volumes. The Alfonso Elder Student Union is a popular gathering place. Students have access to bowling lanes, the Eagles Nest Food Court, a bookstore, and a game room, as well as the use of a post office. The W. G. Pearson Cafeteria is the main eating spot. The cafeteria is connected to a walkway that leads to the C. Ruth Edwards Music Building. In the latter, students enjoy classroom and rehearsal space. The marching and concert bands, jazz ensemble, and choir practice at this location. The Department of Art, with its studios and computer graphics lab, is in the Fine Arts building. At the B. N. Duke Auditorium you can hear lectures or sit in on concerts. There's the 300-seat University Theater. Adjacent to each other are the Robinson Science, Hubbard Chemistry, and Lee Biology Buildings. The new Biomedical and Biotechnology Research Institute is under construction.

Campus Life

On campus, there are about 60 social, cultural, and special-interest clubs and organizations. There are 11 major Greek-letter groups, including Delta Sigma Theta, Kappa Alpha Psi, Alpha Kappa Alpha, Sigma Gamma Rho, and Omega Psi Phi. You've got a Greek Affairs Program, countless Greek-letter related activities and parties, and step shows galore. There's a student symphony, theater group, touring choir (it's been to Carnegie Hall in New York), WNCU radio (90.7), *Ex Umbra* (a literary magazine), the International Students Association, the National Society of Black Engineers, a jazz ensemble, a string ensemble, and the Sound Machine (a marching band with 100-plus members). This group does the expected drill and dance routines. Also, there's the *Eagle* (the yearbook) and the *Echo* (the school newspaper). Important events are Family Weekend and Homecoming.

The Division II basketball and football teams (the football team plays its home games at the 12,000-seat O'Kelly-Riddick Stadium) are popular. The school plays teams such as Bowie State, Winston-Salem State, and Johnson C. Smith. There's the McDougald-McClendon 4,500-seat gym, a swimming pool, and a weight room. For intramural sports there's flag football, volleyball, aerobics, bowling, swimming, racquetball, and more. There's also Army ROTC.

Academic Realities

NCCU has three undergraduate schools: the College of Arts and Sciences, the School of Business, and the School of Education. The most popular majors are Business (14%), Criminal Justice (13%), Political Science (12%), Nursing (9%), and Education (8%). For strong students, there is the Rising Star Leaders Program.

Annually, about 740 students receive bachelor's degrees, and many leave résumés with any of hundreds of recruiters that visit the campus before graduation.

Getting In

The acceptance rate at NCCU is about 70%, with most students arriving from the Southeast. Approximately a quarter of the students are from out of state. A recent state sampling included New York (88 students), Maryland (64), New Jersey (50), the District of Columbia (37), Georgia (23), and Florida (17). Ideally, the school says that a combined SAT score of about 950 is a desirable goal. The actual SAT average of entering students, however, is about 897. ACT: 17. In a recent year, about 2,016 students applied and 1,418 were accepted; 736 actually enrolled. The undergraduate full-time body count is about 3,350. There's an optional Early Orientation Program for admitted students that's always run in the summer. There's academic advisement, placement testing, a cookout, discussions about money matters, and an "introduction to campus life."

| **SHAW UNIVERSITY** | 118 East South Street
Raleigh, NC 27601
(800) 214-6683
Web site: www.shaw.edu | **Application deadline:** July 31
1999–2000 tuition: $5,746;
room and board, $3,824 |

College Ranking

Shaw University has been called "the mother of African American colleges" in North Carolina. After all, it's the oldest historically black college in the South.

The Campus

Located in downtown Raleigh, this private liberal arts college, is on 18 acres of land. There are 18 buildings, including residences. On a stroll, you'll pass the James E. Cheek Learning Resource Center, which is two stories high. Inside you'll find the library (with 126,000 volumes) and the John Wilson Fleming collection of "African and African American black papers." The building also has a radio station and a radio and television studio. Pass "the Yard" and you'll be at the Willie E. Gary Student Center. Also, there's the Drama Building, the Boyd Chapel, the International Studies Building, and the Talbert O. Shaw Learning Center.

Campus Life

At Shaw there are approximately 2,100 full-time students, with 96% being African American. About 44% of the students are from out of state, and 70% of all students reside on campus. Some of the student organizations include the Future Black Scientists of America, AYA Dance Ensemble, Accounting Club, Criminal Justice Society, Mass Communications Club, Shaw Players, Choir, Band, and WSHA-FM 88.9. All the major black fraternities and sororities are on campus and active.

Academic Realities

There are 23 departments and 31 degree possibilities at Shaw. The most popular majors include Business (26%), Criminal Justice (21%), Social Sciences (21%), Liberal Studies (7%), and Communications (5%). This is an actual breakdown of some "major clusters" in a recent typical year: Business Management (488 students), Psychology/Sociology (327), Criminal Justice (294), Education (198), Mass Communications (85), Liberal Studies (88), Music (29), Theater Arts (4), and Biology (7).

Getting In

The acceptance rate at Shaw is about 76%. In a recent year 1,131 applied and 862 were accepted. The average SAT score was in the 870 to 880 range.

UNIVERSITY OF NORTH CAROLINA AT CHAPEL HILL	Chapel Hill, NC 27599-2200 (919) 966-3621 Web site: www.unc.edu	**Financial aid deadline:** March 1; please file earlier **Application deadline:** January 1 **Early decision deadline:** October 1 **1999–2000 tuition:** $2,262 (state residents); $11,428 (nonresidents); room and board, $5,160

College Ranking

The University of North Carolina at Chapel Hill is one of the most prestigious, highly ranked universities in the United States. In recent polls this school was as highly regarded as prestigious private universities such as Emory and Georgetown. What makes it particularly attractive is that it is a state school (low cost, relatively speaking) with an Ivy League aura: stellar programs, topnotch students and faculty, and a track record of achieving students that rivals most schools. For example, since 1980 there have been 10 Rhodes Scholars and an impressive list of Luce, Truman, and Marshall awardees.

The Campus

This 730-acre campus is the site of the oldest public university in the United States. The campus is often described as "beautiful" or "lush." You'll find tree-lined walkways, azaleas, and sometimes an ancient oak overlooking the green quadrangles that fit into the design of the campus. Often the buildings have a southern flavor: those white pillars, red brick exteriors, and large glass windows. If there's a Carolina sky, it's soothing.

You'll see buildings and dorms of varying styles, from Gothic to modern. Quite a few will be soothing to the eye. There are more than 190 permanent buildings, with many designated National Historic Landmarks. For example, there's PlayMakers Theater (1852), and Person Hall (1797), still used as a student residence.

Davis Library also sets a record as the largest educational building in North Carolina. It has nine levels and all kinds of amenities inside: computers, labs, study cubicles, the books (more than 4.2 million, when you count those also available at the Wilson Library). The Student Union has several floors. There is a cafeteria, lounges, 12 bowling lanes, billiard tables, the offices of the *Daily Heel* (the school newspaper), and even a barbershop. For astronomy lovers there's Morehead Planetarium. If you're interested in journalism, you'll settle down in Howell Hall. For living there are the Kenan, Alderman, McIver, Old East (another of those historic sites), and Spencer dormitories, among others. Off campus you can head to Research Triangle Park, a research and corporate community, to assist thinkers for extra income.

Campus Life

No discussion of campus life can begin without mention of Tar Heels basketball. It's basketball country here, with rivals Duke and North Carolina State and the yearly run toward a possible NCAA championship. Football is also a big favorite, with also track, swimming, fencing, lacrosse, and wrestling teams to mention just a few At UNC there are also hundreds of clubs and organizations to keep you occupied. There are fraternities and sororities, many with their own houses. There are theater drama groups; a literary magazine; a radio and television station; intercollegiate sports clubs, including tennis, badminton, bowling, handball, and soccer; religious associations; musical ensemble groups; the Black Student Union; the age-old Black Student Movement; and the Association of International Students. And if these are not enough there's the town of Chapel Hill, with its delights: restaurants, clubs, bars, and nearby Durham, where Duke awaits you. Also nearby is HBCU North Carolina Central, where we sometimes head for interaction with students of color.

Academic Realities

Generally, you will you find some academic pressure and stress, as you'll find at most any of the highest-ranked colleges. You will be challenged, to be sure. You're going to be in classes with bright and ambitious students. UNC offers first-rate academic programs and facilities, including a 4.2-million volume library system. There is certainly a commitment to vital teaching and cutting-edge research. As the admissions office says, the university is large enough to grant you individuality, yet small enough for you to find your niche.

You'll be required to take two semesters of English composition, and perspectives (two courses each) in categories that cover literature/fine arts, science, and the social sciences. Count, also, necessary courses in math and a foreign language. Finally, all students must fulfill a cultural diversity requirement, which might include a course such as Black Women in America. For a student with the ambition and grades, there's an honors program (more than 120 courses to choose from) that some consider one of the best in the country. A typical course might be Ethnicity, Race, and Religion in America. As a senior, if you wish, you can choose to do an independent research paper—usually 60 to 80 pages long—that you must defend before a faculty committee. The most popular majors are Biology, Psychology, Business, Journalism, and Political Science.

Note that there's a Black Studies Department and that a $1 million black student and cultural center is scheduled to be built.

Getting In

Keep in mind that North Carolina's guidelines have a major impact on admissions. The freshman class, by law, must be filled with 82% of state residents. This means that out-of-staters must face the most stringent review decisions—a more rigorous review of their high school records, tests, and achievements. Interestingly, outsiders generally send in more applications than do those from North Carolina. For example, in a recent year North Carolina residents forwarded 7,095 applications for admission, while the outside total hit the 8,330 mark. With such an imbalance, 60% of the residents were accepted, while a paltry 16% of the outsiders gained acceptance.

For anyone to gain an accept a student should have completed a rigorous college-preparatory courseload that includes courses in physics, chemistry, and a foreign language. Supplemental materials (essays, recommendations, and test scores) should signal that you are very capable.

The college presents its evaluation breakdown as follows:

- 60%: course difficulty, performance, quality of school program
- 20%: leadership, special talents, personal statement, diversity, involvement, recommendations
- 20%: SAT and ACT scores

North Carolina CH accepts about 37% of its applicants, with more than 67% of these students having graduated in the top 10% of their high school class. The median SAT score is in the 1330-plus range. African American students comprise 11% of the student body. If you are a student who can forward a total package, you'll get a good look.

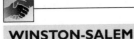

WINSTON-SALEM STATE UNIVERSITY	601 Martin Luther King Jr. Drive Winston-Salem, NC 27110 (336) 750-2000; (800) 257-4052 Web site: www.wssu.edu	**Application deadline:** rolling **1999–2000 tuition:** $1,631 (state residents); $8,049 (nonresidents); room and board, $3,403

College Ranking

Winston-Salem State University is a state-supported liberal arts college and an HBCU with solid academics.

The Campus

WSSU sits on 94 acres of land. Located in Forsyth County (population 168,470), there are 30 buildings, including residences. There are 2,270 full-time students, with 80% being African American. On campus, important gathering places are the WSSU Student Center, Academic Computer Center, O'Kelly Library (with 163,000 volumes), Blair Building, Administration Building, and the Diggs Gallery, with its art exhibitions. The residences are named Brown, Dillard, Moore, and Wilson Halls. The latter is coed and new. The school can accommodate 1,104 students in on-campus housing; 42% reside on campus.

Campus Life

Traditions at WSSU include Greek Week, the Coronation Ball, Black History Month, Mr. Ram Pageant (the ram is the school mascot), and Casino Night. Some notable clubs/organizations include all the major eight black fraternities and sororities, Pan-Hellenic Council, JOVE, the band, the Chemistry Society, *Ram* yearbook and *Argus* newspaper. In 1997 WSSU hosted a National Black Theater Festival.

Flying its "red and white" colors, WSSU is a member of the CIAA Conference. The school completes against teams such as North Carolina Central, St. Augustine's, and Virginia State.

Academic Realities

There are four undergraduate schools: Arts and Sciences, Education, Health Sciences, and Business and Economics. The most popular majors are Nursing, Business Administration, Elementary Education, and Biology. This is one recent breakdown of the majors clusters: Business Administration (283 students), Accounting (133), Nursing (491), Physical Therapy (193), Computer Science (107), Mass Communications (96), Biology (118), Elementary Education (177), Art (38), and Music (33).

Getting In

The acceptance rate at Winston-Salem is about 75%. In a recent year 1,353 applied and 1,080 were accepted. The average SAT was about 870. Approximately 94% of the students are from North Carolina.

OHIO

CASE WESTERN RESERVE UNIVERSITY	10900 Euclid Avenue Cleveland, OH 44106 (216) 368-4450 Web site: www.cwru.edu	**Financial aid deadline:** February 1 **Application deadline:** February 1 **Early decision deadline:** January 1 **1999–2000 tuition:** $19,354; room and board, $5,470

"Of the 100 most wired colleges, Case Western says, 'We're no. 1.'"

—from Yahoo's 1999 annual survey

College Ranking

Case Western Reserve University is an academically powerful private school; it has been ranked among the top 50 colleges in the nation by various experts.

The Campus

Case Western is about four miles from downtown Cleveland. It is a school with "two identities." Due to the 1967 merger of the Case Institute of Technology and Western Reserve University, we're left with technological-scientific students on one side and liberal arts folks on the other. Indeed, Euclid Avenue separates the South Campus and the engineers from the North Campus humanities aficionados. Altogether there are 132 acres here, with 87 buildings, including residences.

On campus you'll see architecture that ranges from old Gothic to modern. Although some students say the surroundings are "attractive," enough say it's just the opposite, even "ugly." One state-of-the-art facility is the Kelvin-Smith Library. It has 1.9 million volumes, mobile book-shelves, and computers at study tables, with the Internet only a finger-push away. A gathering place is the Thwing Student Center, where you'll find the Student Union, a bookstore, a game room, and a post office. To eat, you've got the Fribley Cafeteria in the South and Leutner in the North. On South Campus, most tech students live in coed dorms that have "six-person suites." The North Campus has standard "doubles" with shared hallway bathrooms and showers.

Campus Life

This is a school with a solid reputation. There's a heavy emphasis on careers, and academics are a first priority. But there is more. At the eastern edge of CWRU is "University Circle," the cultural center for the city. There you've got parks and gardens and more than 30 cultural outlets. Within a short stroll are the Cleveland Orchestra, the Cleveland Museum of Art, the Cleveland

Institute of Music, the Cleveland Museum of Natural History, and nearby is the Rock and Roll Hall of Fame (1995).

Groups that might be of special interest to us include the African American Society, Daniel Hale Pre-Med Society, National Society of Engineers, CWRU Gospel Choir, Caribbean Student Association, Minority Student Nurses Association, and Black Women's Society. *The Observer* is the campus newspaper. WRUW is the radio station. Students interested in pledging with any of the black fraternities or sororities usually do so at nearby Cleveland State University or other local colleges. Off-campus students head to "The Flats," where there are nightclubs and a water-side strip. In the Coventry area there are small shops.

Varsity sports are not big at CWRU. Some say there is "little team spirit" in regard to their Spartans. Still, there are competitions between the "divided" campuses.

Academic Realities

The academics at CWRU are rigorous, particularly in the tech areas. The Minority Scholars Program (MSP), however, offers a summer orientation program, as well as tutor and peer support. The Minority Engineers Industrial Opportunity Program, also is important. You can head to Educational Support Services (ESS), for tutorial assistance. The most popular majors are Engineering (38%), Nursing (11%), Biology (9%), Psychology (8%), and Chemistry (6%).

There is a core curriculum. If a student is interested in engineering, computer science, or any of the other technical areas, intensive work in mathematics and science is necessary. Still, "supplemental" work is required. The arts and sciences students need 33 hours in a wide range of disciples: humanities courses, literature, and the natural and social sciences. "A breadth of choices" is the goal. The "Weatherhead" core, named after the business school and designed for those majoring in Management or Accounting, has added requirements.

Getting In

The acceptance rate at CWRU is about 79%. This high percentage, doesn't tell the real story. In a recent year 4,427 students applied and 3,509 were accepted. Approximately 22% of that total enrolled. This indicates that many of those "strong" and "very capable" students select to go to other top schools. Note that the average SAT score of enrolled students is about 1200.

African Americans and international students each make up 6% of the student body. With Asians making up about 12% of the body count (nearly 4,000 full-time undergraduates), this school has a lot of diversity. Most students are from Ohio and elsewhere in the Midwest. Good numbers also arrive from New England, New York, and Pennsylvania.

OBERLIN COLLEGE	Carnegie Building Oberlin, OH 44074 (216) 775-8411 Web site: www.oberlin.edu	**Financial aid deadline:** February 15 **Application deadline:** February 15 **1999–2000 tuition:** $24,264; room and board, $6,178

"The education of the people of color is a matter of great interest and should be encouraged and sustained in this institution."

—the trustees, 1835

College Ranking

If you're academically sharp, self-motivated, and don't need the "rah-rah" of the typical social life that many of us look for at our selected colleges, this highly ranked liberal arts school might be for you.

Oberlin is known as one of the best colleges in regard to having a good environment for black students. In a recent *Black Enterprise* poll Oberlin was second to only Stanford and Georgetown University among predominantly white schools in that regard.

Oberlin is the college that graduated the first African American woman, and it actually was a stop on the Underground Railroad. Today it's highly ranked in most categories, and is also the home of the world-renowned Conservatory of Music, which includes approximately 20% of the enrolled students, all accomplished musicians.

This is a highly selective school.

The Campus

The look of this rural campus—with its Gothic buildings—has not made any of the "most beautiful" lists. It's located in the small, midwestern town of Oberlin, surrounded by farmland and corn. The last time we looked there was one movie theater, and a surrounding community that students describe as "ethnically diverse." Others say that the college is "in the middle of nowhere." Oberlin's population is about 10,000, if that. Your quick getaway destination is Cleveland (about a half hour away by car). You can also visit Cleveland State, Case Western Reserve, or nearby museums, restaurants, or clubs. Oberlin's campus covers more than 440 acres and has a wide range of impressive facilities. On North Campus there's the Wright Physics Laboratory, Kettering Hall (biology and chemistry), and Sperry (neuroscience) buildings. There's Phillips Gym, with three full-size basketball courts, and NCAA-regulation swimming and diving pools. You can also visit the Nautilus Center, where there are six racquetball and nine squash courts. Dill Field is a football and track stadium. For those who play tennis, you've got 12 all-weather tennis courts. The old Hales Gymnasium has a billiards ballroom and bowling alley. A portion of the gym now serves—while students complain of its inadequacy—as the Jazz Studies Department.

At Oberlin there are many residential options: single-sex, coed, and cooperative (you share the cooking and housekeeping) housing. The residence halls generally follow two models: the "traditional" for 230 students, and the "familylike" Victorian houses for 18. The Barrows is the all-first-year dorm. East Hall is the "quiet" spot, and Zechiel House is the all-male location. The African Heritage House is a favorite residence and social meeting place.

If you wish, you can study at the "very in" Mudd Library. There you can socialize, go to the computer center (more than 160 computers are available around the campus). Another nice visit would be to the Allen Art Museum on campus.

Campus Life

There are more than 100 clubs and organizations at Oberlin, many with offices in the Wilder Student Union, including the Multicultural Resource Center and the Experimental College (Exco). During January of each year, students can take a short, "fun," or "nontraditional" course at Exco. It's always a "breather," students say. At the Wilder, you'll also find a snack bar and The Disco, known as "Sco." There's a student-run newspaper, a radio station, and a theater/dance group. More fun? There's "reading," tossing a Frisbee, playing volleyball. Sometimes, if the weather is okay, you'll see a juggler or two.

The Cleveland Orchestra has performed at Oberlin, and students present concerts and recitals almost daily. Each year, more than 200 films are shown at the school theater, and usually there are more than 25 theater and/or dance performances yearly. Students interested in film can study at the internationally renowned film school at New York University for a semester.

There's not much emphasis on sports.

Academic Realities

With a pool of more than 1,000 courses to motivate you, the most popular majors are English, History, and Biology/Biological Sciences. *U.S. News & World Report* has ranked the school's science programs as among the best in the nation. In fact, most of the programs are "good" to "outstanding."

There's an African American Studies Department that offers a related major. You can take courses such as The Heritage of Black American Literature or Colloquium: Malcolm X and Martin Luther King Jr. Visiting lecturers have included Cornel West, bell hooks, Angela Davis, and Shirley Chisholm, the first African American woman elected to Congress. Desmond Tutu spoke at the commencement in 1987.

Also of interest have been events called the Kuumba Festival, the African Market, and the People of Color Festival at the Third World House.

Getting In

Oberlin's acceptance rate is 54%, but this application pool is undoubtedly stronger than many schools with lower rates. Many of these students are also applying to schools such as Yale (their first choice, perhaps) or institutions such as Brown or Wesleyan. This strong liberal arts college must consider its "yield"—that is, how many students will decide to actually enroll.

According to Oberlin's own (class of 2002) stats, the median GPA of enrolling students (to the Arts and Sciences School) was 3.48 on a 4.0 scale. The average SAT score was about 1308. Of the enrolling group, 27 were valedictorians and 47 were National Merit scholars. 52 African American students enrolled in the Arts and Sciences School, while 10 enrolled at the Conservatory. African Americans make up about 9% of the student body.

Looking at all entering freshman, note that about 50% graduate in the top 10% of their high school class. Nearly 90% graduate in the top 25%. These college students, of course, all did well on a college preparatory track. They were and are capable academically.

African American students should forward a package that demonstrates intellectual assertiveness, with essays and recommendations that say you will fit the Obie model: a thinker, perhaps verbal, because this is a school of speak-outs, debate, and "ideas."

In regard to your SAT or ACT score, just "get in the ballpark." Scores of 1100 and above are desirable. Of course, if you are one of those people with great musical talent who is applying to the Conservatory, your campus or regional addition will be the pivotal factor. You must be masterful!

The class of 2002 is from 45 states, most (in descending order) from New York, Ohio, California, Massachusetts, and Pennsylvania. Foreign students arrived from 15 different countries.

| **OHIO STATE UNIVERSITY** | Lincoln Tower, Third Floor
1800 Cannon Drive
Columbus, OH 43210-1200
(614) 292-3980
Web site:
   www.acs.ohio-state.edu | **Financial aid deadline:**
   February 15
Application deadline:
   February 15
1999–2000 tuition: $4,137
   (residents); $12,087 (nonresi-
   dents); room and board,
   $5,446 |

College Ranking

An enormous, top-tier public university known for its wide academic selections, with particular strengths in its engineering and social science programs.

The Campus

Ohio State is on 3,200 wooded acres. Yes, there's a North Campus and a South Campus, and a third area near the river, where the students live. On one side, you can look over the Olentangy River; on the other, you can just about walk into downtown Columbus. There are 352 buildings, including residences, and you've got a centrally located lake. You won't get to know everybody. There are more than 35,000 undergraduates. With the green grass, it's rather pleasant. There are ivy-covered structures, and those that are ultramodern. There's the Central Classroom Building, which has "presentation rooms." University Hall, with ivy, has its clocks, arch, and lanterns. There's the Wexner Center for the Arts and the Chadwick Arboretum. At last count there were 24-plus libraries holding more than 4 million volumes.

Campus Life

At OSU there are hundreds of clubs, organizations, and special-interest groups. Some cultural outlets that might be of particular interest include the African Student Union, which has sponsored *Wake-UP* (a newsletter), "Black Soul—A Night of Black Art," an "All-Star Comedy Jam," and an actual "Justice March." Other groups are African Women Global Network, Black Undergraduate Council, NAACP, Black Undergraduate Engineering Council, and African American Media Association. Groups have also had a Spring Quarter Spades Tournament. There's also the Hale Black Cultural Center, which is a gathering place, and the Office of Minority Affairs. All the major eight black fraternities and sororities are on campus and are active. Other hangouts include the Drake and Ohio Student Unions, where there are convenience shops, food courts, banks, and recreational outlets (game rooms, billiards).

For sports mania there are Bill Davis and Ohio Stadiums. In 1997 OSU won the Rose Bowl, with more than 90,000 folks going crazy. This is football country. Basketball is also gigantic, and a new 19,500-seat arena helps. Men and women have 19 varsity teams each, all with strong followings. The intramural program offers more than 62 club sports.

Academic Realities

There are 19 undergraduate colleges that offer more than 11,000 courses. More than 200 majors are offered. The most popular majors are Psychology (6%), and English, Communications, Criminology, and Marketing (about 4% each).

To handle the huge numbers, the university has set up a touch-tone registration system called BRUTUS. There's no other way. There are many reputable areas of study offered. If you wish, you can pursue a career-oriented track in such areas as engineering, accounting, nursing, or business. To ensure that students get a broad-based liberal arts education, students are required to take courses in the humanities, writing, the arts, math, and other areas. OSU's African American Studies Department, one of the first created in the country, is said to be outstanding. Teachers at OSU are often "distinguished." The university can point to Nobel Prize winners, members of the National Academy, Rhodes Scholars, and other well-known "stars." Add state-of-the-art facilities and the Frank W. Hale Black Cultural Center on the South Campus and you've got a "familylike setting." At the Hale Center, you'll find the African/African American Hall of Fame (a gallery of outstanding OSU graduates). They include Faye Wattleton of Planned Parenthood fame and, the two-time Heisman Award winner Archie Griffin.

All of the above for bargain prices, particularly if you're a state resident.

Getting In

The acceptance rate at OSU is 79%. In a recent year 18,912 students applied and 15,033 were accepted. About 8% of the students on campus are African American. The average ACT score is between 23 and 24. About 6% of the students are from out of state. Approximately 22% reside on campus.

OHIO UNIVERSITY	Office of Admissions Clubb Hall 120 Athens, OH 45701-2979 (614) 595-4100 Web Site: www.ohiou.edu	**Application deadline:** February 1 **1999–2000 tuition:** $4,800 (state residents); $10,101 (nonresidents); room and board, $5,484

College Ranking:

A large public university with an array of course and major selections that provide an academic challenge. This school has been rated a "best value" in a recent *Kaplan Review* survey of grade advisers.

The Campus

Located in a small town in southeastern Ohio, the school covers 1,700 acres. There are 201 buildings, including 40 residences. At OU you'll find pillared architecture (Georgian), rolling hills, tree-lined walkways, landscaped lawns, and the nearby Hocking River. The school is about 75 miles from Columbus. Within 40 miles are 12 state parks and an endless national forest.

OU is a "midsize university," some say, probably thinking about gigantic Ohio State. We say that OU is big. The Alden Library has more than 2 million volumes, and there's a state-of-the-art aquatic center. The Ping Center (1996) is a gathering spot with bowling lanes, billiard tables, and game rooms. The new recreation center covers 165,000 square feet and has weight facilities, basketball and tennis courts, a track, and lounges.

Campus Life

There are more than 360 clubs, organizations, and special-interest groups on campus. Some that might be of particular interest include the African American Student Union, Lindley Arts and Cultural Center (a gathering location), Black Student Business Caucus, Shades of Color radio,

Romeo Club, Black Student Cultural Programming Board, Society of Black Engineers, and Black Film series. All of the major eight black fraternities and sororities are active. Alpha Phi Alpha (Phi chapter), for example, has sponsored a Paul Robeson Oratorical Contest, a "Tribute to African American Women," a voter registration drive, and an orientation for incoming freshmen.

The OU Bobcats have a strong hockey team. There's also a reputable basketball team. Football "is big." A major pleasure is seeing and hearing the 101 Marching Band. Flag football and "broomball" are popular intramural sports. Also, there is an Olympic-size pool, fitness center, ice rink, and lighted intramural tennis courts and fields.

Academic Realities

There are nine undergraduate schools, accommodating about 15,300 full-time students. African Americans make up nearly 4% of that total. Among the schools, are those of Engineering and Technology, Arts and Sciences, Business, and Communications. Majors abound.

The most popular majors are Communications (16%), Business and Education (13% each), Engineering (8%), and Biology (6%). There is an African American Studies program. Besides pursuing a major, students must take courses in "three tiers" (e.g., one in the humanities), to meet degree requirements. Including taking a writing course, the goal is to create a broad-based liberal arts education. Helpful support is available from the Office of Minority Student affairs, Affirmative Action Office, the Multicultural Access Program (MAP), and the Ohio University Recruiting Society (OURS). There is also the Honors Tutorial College (and smaller class settings) for about 40 students with super academic credentials.

Getting In

On the Athens campus of Ohio University, we're about 600 strong. The acceptance rate at Ohio University is about 75%. In a recent year 11,789 applied and 8,880 were accepted. The average SAT is 1190, and the ACT 24. OU doesn't ask for essays, or factor in extracurricular activities in their admission reviews. They do say, however, that they are looking for "historically underrepresented groups." Only 11% of the students are from out of state, with approximately 42% of all students living on campus.

WILBERFORCE UNIVERSITY	1055 North Bickett Road
	Wilberforce, OH 45384
	(513) 376-2911;
	  (800) 367-8568
	Web site:
	  www.wilberforce.edu
		Application deadline: June 1
		1999–2000 tuition: $7,820;
		  room and board, $4,100

College Ranking

Wilberforce is a small liberal arts college religiously affiliated with the African Methodist Episcopal Church. It is not an overly selective college, but it offers good academics.

The Campus

The college is on 125 acres of land about 20 miles from Dayton, and has 21 buildings, including residences. Some say the campus is "beautiful." It is said that the "old Towne Creek winds its way through the entire site between the crest of two rolling hills." Bring your camera. Nearby is John Bryan State Park, Clarence Brown Reservoir, and less than an hour's drive away, the "famed" King's Island Amusement Park.

On campus you'll find the Rembert Stokes Learning Resources Center. Inside you can study media technologies and visit the university library (60,000 volumes). There's the Walker Center, and the King Classroom–Science Building with its modern labs, lecture halls, and computer rooms. You'll pass the "famous" Wilberforce University fountain. Registering, you'll enter the Wolfe Administration Building. Timken Court, the newest addition to the campus, is composed of 67 redwood condominium-style dwellings. The Athletic and Student Recreational Complex cost more than $2.2 million. On the "old" campus of Wilberforce, about a mile away, is the National Afro American Museum.

Campus Life

The are about 40 clubs, organizations, and special-interest groups on campus. All the eight major black fraternities and sororities are active. Also, include the Poet Society, Debate Club, Engineering and Computer Science Club, *Brainstorm* (a literary magazine), Black Women United, Campus Ministries, *I-Sight* (an online magazine), Ladies of Heart, National Student Business League, two national honor societies, and WU Gallery II (for student art exhibitions). A big campus event is the Fall Festival, which includes Homecoming and the crowning of Miss Wilberforce.

For intercollegiate sports there is basketball, track and field, and several other sports for both men and women. For intramural play there is the Alumni Multiplex, which contains a 1,500-seat gymnasium.

Academic Realities

Wilberforce programs lead to degrees in liberal arts, business, engineering, communications, fine arts, computer sciences, music, and other areas. You can get educational certification in some areas by taking some courses (by arrangement) at neighboring Central State University. Two popular majors are Business and Communications.

Getting In

Wilberforce accepts more than 95% of the students who apply. In a recent year 1,223 applied and 1,021 were accepted. Of the accepts, about a third eventually enrolled. Approximately 64% of the students are from out of state, the majority from Illinois, Michigan, Indiana, Pennsylvania, and New York.

PENNSYLVANIA

BRYN MAWR COLLEGE	101 North Merion Avenue Bryn Mawr, PA 19010-2899 (610) 526-5152 Web site: www.brynmawr.edu	**Application deadline:** January 15 **Early decision deadline:** November 15 **1999–2000 tuition:** $23,360; room and board, $8,100

College Ranking

Bryn Mawr is a private, liberal arts college for women. Located in a suburb of Philadelphia on a 137-acre campus, this college is one of most selective in the country.

The Campus

The campus, a short drive from downtown Philly, is also within walking distance of the train station. "It's peaceful and self-contained," some say, pleased with the modern buildings. The Louis Kahn structure, for example, looks like it's covered with slate and "is cool." Many of the older Gothic structures "have personalities" but are a turreted gray in color. Besides climbing an occasional hill, you will see trees, green lawns, and (depending on the season) daffodils and azaleas on campus. There are 57 buildings here, including residences such as Rockefeller, with a couple of fireplaces, and Pembroke East, with "very nice" views from the windows.

Campus Life

Bryn Mawr is known for attracting "intellectuals." Here, folks are well-read, ambitious, and will debate at the drop of a hat. Some say you'll get a "melting pot of ideas and personalities," with feminists forever present. The school is known for its diversity, and large numbers of students will head to graduate and professional schools. Asian Americans make up about 18% of the student body, and African Americans make up a little over 4%.

A positive here is Bryn Mawr's "sense of community." Once in, you'll be very much a part of Haverford College, which you can walk to. Students at the two schools often cross-register for classes, and can choose to live in the other's dorms. Some say "it's the best of two worlds," with the latter school being coed. Both schools share an honor code—sometimes you can take exams home—which students take very seriously. Even with some men around, the two schools "share a sisterhood." There are also close ties (a scholastic exchange) with nearby Swarthmore and Ivy Penn. Buses run to Haverford and Swarthmore daily.

At Bryn Mawr groups of special interest to us include COLOR, The Sisterhood (with about 35 members), Tri-College Summer Institute, NUBIA (Network Utilizing Black Individuals' Achievements), On Target Tutoring Program, Minority Women in Science, and Minority Coalition. Perry House (the African American Cultural Center) is our meeting place. "The House" has a library and living quarters. Of course, besides "study" and campus activities and recreation, Philly offers many options. Visits to the Philadelphia Museum of Art, theaters, clubs, and restaurants are possibilities. Temple University, too, is reachable. At Bryn Mawr there are no official fraternities or sororities.

Bryn Mawr has bragging rights! It is the 1995 badminton national champion. Other sports include basketball, swimming, tennis, rugby, field hockey, and soccer. If you are interested in fencing, diving, sailing, squash, or track and field, there are club sports.

Academic Realities

At Bryn Mawr students must take a writing composition course, math, and be proficient in a foreign language. A year's study in the humanities, laboratory sciences, and social science also is required. The work is challenging, and hard study is a given. The most popular majors are Biology and English (10% each), History (8%), and Mathematics and Psychology (each 7%). Also, there is a relatively new Africana Studies program.

Getting In

The acceptance rate at Bryn Mawr is about 58%, with the average SAT score in the 1290 to 1310 range. A strong high school record and recommendations—indicating how smart you are, and how you'd be a "perfect match"— are pivotal. The bottom quarter of students do get accepts with scores below 1190. Of course, make that essay do its sales pitch.

CARNEGIE MELLON UNIVERSITY

5000 Forbes Avenue
Pittsburgh, PA 15213
(412) 268-2013
Web site: www.cmu.edu

Financial aid deadline:
February 15
Application deadline:
January 1
Early decision deadline:
November 15
1999–2000 tuition: $22,230;
room and board, $6,500

College Ranking

Carnegie Mellon University is a highly regarded, top-ranked private institution with specialties in engineering, computer science, and the performing arts. When you think of CMU you think of driven engineering students, rows of computers, and the Internet. You think, too, of art students in smocks, and of actors and actresses reciting Shakespeare.

The Campus

CMU is on a 103-acre campus about five miles from downtown Pittsburgh, near affluent Oakland. You can walk to 500-acre Schenley Park, the city's largest. You are also close to Phipps Conservatory, the Frick Fine Arts Museum, and "The Carnegie" (which is a cultural complex with several renowned museums). There are 60 buildings on campus, including residences. Many of the structures are Beaux Arts style, and those that are more modern are described as "just there." There's the University Center, the Roberts Hall of Engineering, Hunt Library (907,000 volumes), the new Purnell Center for the Performing Arts, and Highlander Café (the main cafeteria). Stroll over the well-tended lawns and you'll pass six undergraduate schools: the Mellon College of Science, the School of Industrial Management, the School of the Fine Arts, Carnegie Institute of Technology, the School of Computer Science, and the College of Humanities and Science. Freshmen dorms include Morewood Gardens, Donner, and Resnik, said to be among "the best." The Worst? Perhaps Hammerschlag, which is for "guys only." Last, there is SPIRIT House, where a small number of African Americans reside.

Campus Life

Clubs, organizations, and special-interest groups that might be of special interest to us are SPIRIT, the African American student organization, National Society of Black Engineers, the Gospel Choir, Summer Bridge Program, and Carnegie Mellon Action Project (helping us to focus and adjust academically). Broadway plays such as *Godspell* and *Pippin,* are said to have been first presented in enthusiastic but less polished form at CMU. All thanks are due to Scotch 'n' Soda, the drama club. For those interested in acting, your famous alumni include Blair Underwood, Shari Belafonte, Ted Danson, George Peppard, and Albert Brooks. For scientific types you've got astronauts Edgar Mitchell and Judith Resnick (killed in the *Challenger* accident). Popular events are Homecoming Week and Spring Carnival (with its buggy races).

CMU has varsity sports, but there's really no fuss and "rallying calls," even though the men and women's soccer teams have won divisional championships. This school's greatest tradition: study.

Academic Realities

Clearly, CMU offers a superb combination of arts and technology options. Finish here, and you've got a fine liberal-professional education, great technical skills, and wonderful career prospects. The key words are "professional focus." Whether you're into engineering or visual art, the universitywide curriculum requires courses that leave you well rounded. A basic computing course is a must, plus humanities options that let you learn about "human thought and values." And since this is CMU, many of your courses (e.g., philosophy and logic) will integrate computer use. CMU, after all, was ranked fourth among "tech schools" in the 1999 survey of the "100 Most Wired Colleges" by *Yahoo Life* magazine.

The most popular majors here are Engineering (27%), Business and Computer Science (each 10%), Social and "Decision" Studies (9%), and Biology (5%). Whatever you are studying, you will have a demanding workload.

Getting In

The acceptance rate at CMU is about 43%, but the varying schools have their own requirements and needs. For example, art and drama students must present portfolios or an audition. With this in mind, note that the average SAT score (the tech folks are inflating these numbers) is about 1350. If you're a strong student, don't be daunted. The admissions people here consider your high school record first, and factor in factors such as "personality," "special talents," extracurricular activities, and geographical location. Note, too, that in a 1997 *Journal of Blacks in Higher Education* survey it was pointed out that black students actually gained admission at a higher rate than others: 46%. The numbers: 626 applied and 293 were accepted. Of the enrolled student body (approximately 4,800 full-time), we represent 5% of the count. About 75% of the students are from out of state.

CHEYNEY UNIVERSITY OF PENNSYLVANIA	Cheyney and Creek Roads Cheyney, PA 19319 (610) 399-2275 Web site: www.Cheyney.edu	**Application deadline:** May 30 **1999–2000 tuition:** $4,023 (state residents); $9,379 (nonresidents); room and board, $4,646

College Ranking

Cheyney is an HBCU with solid academics.

The Campus

You can find Cheyney on the "rolling side hills" of southeastern Pennsylvania. The college is on 275 acres of land, has more than 30 academic and auxiliary buildings, and is about 25 miles from Philadelphia. And Wilmington, Delaware, is only about 15 miles away. On campus you'll find the Dudley Center, where about 20 students recently performed a Greek comedy titled *Lysistrada,* about the "battle of the sexes." On a stroll you'll also pass Melrose Cottage,

Carnegie and Raze E. R. Halls, and the Leslie Pinckney Hall Library, with its Ethnic Studies Collection. Of course, too, there's the Ada Georges Dinner Hall. Emlen and Burleigh Halls, both being renovated, will become "living/learning" and "student service" centers.

Campus Life

There are about 60 clubs, organizations, and special-interest groups on campus. The eight major black fraternities and sororities are here. Also: a choir, radio and TV stations, student government groups, and dozens of clubs. Important events include Founder's Day Ball, picking Miss Cheyney, the Wade Wilson Football Classic, and the Black College Convention.

Football and basketball are the most popular intercollegiate sports at Cheyney. The school plays teams such as Virginia Union, Central State, and North Carolina Central. For personal and intramural activity there's an Olympic-size pool and outdoor tennis, volleyball, and handball courts.

Academic Realities

Cheyney, a public liberal arts institution, has two undergraduate schools. They offer programs in business, teacher education, communications and the arts, computer science, the health professions, and more. The most popular majors are Education (27%), Social Sciences (18%), Business (14%), Communications (7%), and Hotel and Restaurant Management (6%).

Getting In

The acceptance rate at Cheyney is about 73%. In a recent year about 1,058 applied and 777 were accepted. The SAT or ACT is required. Of about 1,000 full-time students, 97% are African American. Nearly 85% of the students are from in-state. The others arrive from 20 states and three foreign countries. About 62% of the students reside on campus. During registration, students must take placement tests to determine their academic and developmental needs. For students who enter with very strong records (1000-plus on SATs, more than 21 on the ACT), there's the possibility of getting one of 50 new Keystone Honors Academy tuition-paid-in-full scholarships.

HAVERFORD COLLEGE	370 Lancaster Avenue Haverford, PA 19041-1392 (610) 896-1000 Web site: www.haverford.edu	**Financial aid deadline:** February 1 **Application deadline:** January 15 **Early decision deadline:** November 15 **1999–2000 tuition:** $23,780; room and board, $7,620

College Ranking

Haverford is among the elite liberal arts institutions, usually ranked among the top 10, and is located among the cluster of top colleges in suburban Philadelphia.

The Campus

Sitting on 216 acres of land, there are 70 buildings, including residences. The Center of Philadelphia is only 10 miles away. On campus, you can stroll from one side to the other in fewer than 20 minutes. You'll pass a lovely "wall of trees," a duck pond, rolling fields, an arboretum, even a golf course. If you wish, you can walk or jog on a two-mile trail. A gathering place is the Campus Center, where there's a café, a pizza shop, and a game room. The residences, too, are "good places to hang out, debate, and have friendly talk." Most freshman reside in Haverford College Apartments, (HCAs), Barclay (it's got doubles), or the "singles" dorm, Gummere.

Campus Life

On campus are the Multicultural Center, the Women's Center, and groups such as Women of Color and the Black Student League. Sports at the varsity and intramural levels are popular. This school is in the Centennial Conference (NCAA Division III), with schools such as Johns Hopkins, Swarthmore, and Bryn Mawr. The men's and women's track teams are "perennial powerhouses."

There are no official fraternities or sororities.

Academic Realities

Haverford has an "honor code" that seems to be one topic all students talk about. No cheating. If it's a "take home" test and you're in your room with the class textbook inches away, you don't look. Founded in 1833, the terrain was intended for Quakers.

A key plus at Haverford is its close relationship with nearby Bryn Mawr, less than a mile away. If you wish you can cross-register for a class or classes, live in the other school's dorms, and "connect" in totality. More than 90% of the students take at least one course at the other school, taking the shuttle bus to travel back and forth. Students also can take courses at Swarthmore or Penn, two schools that are a little farther away.

Haverford students are often called "very bright" and are said to be "intellectual." Although there is no "core" curriculum, students must take three courses from three different areas: the social and natural sciences and the humanities. They must also take a "social justice" course and demonstrate capability with a foreign language. The most popular majors are Biology (14%), English and History (12% each), and Political Science and Economics (8% each).

Getting In

The acceptance rate is 44%. In a recent year 2,769 students applied and 946 were accepted. The average SAT score was well over 1270, with a quarter of the students scoring lower. There are generally about 1,150 full-time students on campus, with 5% being African American. Note that this was an all-male institution until 1980. Today it's about 50–50.

LINCOLN UNIVERSITY (PA)

P.O. Box 179
Lincoln University, PA 19352
(800) 790-0191
Web site: www.lincoln.edu

Financial aid deadline:
March 1
Application deadline: rolling
1999–2000 tuition: $5,756 (state residents); $8,264 (nonresidents); room and board, $4,956

College Ranking

When you enter the arched gateway that leads to Lincoln University, you'll be walking a path that was traveled by great alumni such as Thurgood Marshall, Langston Hughes, Nigerian

Nnamdi Azikiwe, and Ghana's Kwame Nkrumah. And poet/musician Gil Scot Heron is a graduate. The school likes to say it's produced leaders, and it has. State-supported Lincoln is a college that is known worldwide for its "international" favor and commitment.

The Campus

Lincoln is in southern Chester County and is on 422 acres of land. The school (surrounded by farmlands and hilltops), is in a rural community. Both Philadelphia and Baltimore are about 50 to 55 miles away. About 20% of the students have cars and swear that "it's a necessity." Several students have told us they "feel isolated." Most students live in one of the 18 resident halls (11 for women, 7 for men), and most remain on campus during weekends.

On campus you'll find 37 buildings including the noted residences. The new Thurgood Marshall Learning Center was completed in 1996 and cost about $17 million. The International Cultural Center, also new, covers more than 51,000 square feet and has a 2,000-seat auditorium, art gallery, and conference rooms. The Langston Hughes Library has more than 180,000 volumes. John Miller Dickey Hall is a humanities and computer complex. A gathering place is the Student Union, which has a dining hall. Also, LU has a Life Sciences Building, Mary Brown Chapel, African Museum, and the Ware Center (dedicated to the fine arts). Manuel Rivero Hall has an Olympic-size pool, a 2,400-seat gymnasium, a bowling alley, a dance studio, and a game room.

Campus Life

All the major black sororities and fraternities are on campus (about 20% of students join), as well as more than 85 cultural, social, and special-interest clubs and organizations. There's the NAACP, Jazz Ensemble (hear their "We Three Kings"), a gospel ensemble, the Tolson Society (a discussion group), the *Lincolnian* (school newspaper, now online), Fashion Club, yearbook, radio station, band, drama and dance groups, Mu Phi Alpha (a musical-social organization), and more. Popular events include Homecoming, Founder's Day, and the annual Christmas Concert.

LU has intercollegiate sports (nine for men, six for women), including basketball and football teams. For students there are handball and tennis courts, a soccer and football field, the Wayne Coston Track, and the gym already noted. For bird watchers, joggers, and those who like to walk, there's the Robert Garner Fitness Trail.

Academic Realities

The courses that you must take at Lincoln are usually grouped into three primary areas—the humanities, social sciences and behavioral studies, and the natural sciences and mathematics. All students must take a computer course. LU has built a reputation on its LASER (Lincoln Advanced Science and Engineering Reinforcement) program. The school recruits and mentors students for science careers. The U.S. Department of Education has ranked LU third in the nation in awarding bachelor's degrees in science to African American students. There's also a students (SOS) one-on-one advisement program that gives students a "global perspective." After all, this is the first predominantly black college to offer languages such as Arabic, Chinese, Japanese, and Russian.

The most popular majors are Business (23%), Education (16%), Biology (9%), Criminal Justice (8%), and the Health Sciences (5%). You can pursue preprofessional programs in law, medicine, nursing, dentistry, engineering, or veterinary science. For art students a portfolio is necessary, and music students must audition. For those who want to travel, you can visit China,

Taiwan, or African or European countries. A cooperative education program is available (work/study) as well as Army ROTC.

Getting In

The Lincoln University acceptance rate is about 89%. In a recent year about 1,800 applied and 1,306 were accepted. Exactly 469 students enrolled (the majority from the Northeast). The size of the freshman class was 813 (nearly half out-of-staters), including students who arrived from Ghana, Kenya, Zimbabwe, Nigeria, Jamaica, and the Bahamas. The average SAT score was about 879; ACT was between 14 and 21. LU usually has about 1,477 full-time undergraduates on campus. A typical essay topic is "Write an essay about yourself and the events in your life that have made a difference in the way you view yourself and others."

PENNSYLVANIA STATE UNIVERSITY AT UNIVERSITY PARK	University Park Campus University Park, PA 16802 (814) 865-5471 Web site: www.psu.edu	**Financial aid deadline:** February 15 **Application deadline:** rolling **1999–2000 tuition:** $6,092 (state residents); $12,908 (nonresidents); room and board, $4,536

College Ranking

Not only is PSU the home of the Nittany Lions and Beaver Stadium, which seats more than 93,000, but also there are majors and programs galore that have stellar reputations. You'll find here 10 undergraduate colleges with more than 180 baccalaureate majors. Factor in, too, state-of-the-art facilities, libraries that hold more than 2.4 million volumes, 400 clubs and organizations, 16 computer centers, and you get the picture.

The Campus

Almost 33,000 undergraduates attend college here, and it's a campus that has been described as "a behemoth." The school covers more than 5,617 acres, and there are 403 buildings, including residences.

Campus Life

Although only 3% of the students at Penn State are African American, there are still more of us at the main University Park branch than at most historically black colleges. You've got The Black Caucus, and "It's Friday" forums (talks, discussions, and debates) in a supportive atmosphere. Besides the eight major black fraternities and sororities that are very active, there are more than 30 other clubs and organizations that are specifically related to us and our needs. For "other" recreation students can head to the Stone Valley recreational area to hike, sail, or ski. You're about 20 minutes away. On campus you can use one of three gyms, several swimming pools, consider countless intramural sports options, or simply "cool out" at the Hertzel Union Building (HUB), the student center.

Academic Realities

If you don't like crowds—maybe 600-plus students in an introductory class—don't apply.

The most popular majors include Business (18%), Engineering (14%), Education (7%), Communications (5%), and Psychology (4%). There's also an African American Studies major.

Also, the Multicultural Resource Center assigns every minority student an adviser. The curriculum includes "diversity training" for all arriving students.

Getting In

PSU is competitive, always ranked among the best national universities, and accepts only about 53% of the students who apply. The average SAT score here is about 1200, with many of the lower quarter of accepted students scoring below 1100. Big numbers? In a recent year there were 22,154 applicants and 11,826 accepts.

Do note that more than two-thirds of the students arrive from more than 22 other branch locations after two years of study. A majority of the students are from in-state, Philadelphia, and Pittsburgh. About 20% of the students are out-of-state, with approximately 1% from foreign countries.

SWARTHMORE COLLEGE	500 College Avenue
	Swarthmore, PA 19081
	(610) 328-8300
	Web site:
	    www.swarthmore.edu
		Financial aid deadline:
		    February 1
		Application deadline:
		    January 1
		Early decision deadline:
		    November 15
		1999–2000 tuition: $24,190;
		    room and board, $7,500

"Anywhere Else It Would Have Been an A, Really!"

—A T-shirt sold in the Swarthmore bookstore

College Ranking

If not the best, then Swarthmore College is only a breath behind as one of the nation's top-ranked liberal arts colleges, along with an elite group of schools including Amherst, Williams, and Wellesley. And with its top-notch academic programs and very bright student body, there's more to rave about.

The Campus

The Swarthmore campus has been described as "gorgeous," and makes all the "great-looking" lists.

Located in the western suburbs of Philadelphia, Swarthmore is on 330 acres of land. If you're taking photos, you might want to head to stately Parrish Hall which is at the center of campus. To get there you'll pass tree-lined roads, flowers, and shrubbery. Parrish houses the school's administrative offices and is one of 46 buildings including the residences. On campus there's the McCabe Library, which has 1 million volumes (when you count the other four libraries). At the Tarble Social Center students gather to socialize, chat, and be "Swatties": bright and opinionated.

Campus Life

At Swarthmore there are more than 150 clubs, organizations, and special-interest groups. The Black Cultural Center is the central meeting and gathering spot for our folks. We are involved

with the Swarthmore African American Student Society (SASS), Students of Caribbean Ances-
try, Women of Color, African American Student Association (AASA), and the Gospel Choir. A
cappella groups include the Sophisticated Gents, Sistahs, and Black Coffee. Visiting lecturers
have included Spike Lee and Harvard professor Cornel West. Prominent graduates: Eugene
Land, the founder of the "I Have a Dream" Foundation. The late novelist James Michener, who
recently left his "tens of millions estate" to the school, also was a graduate.

Swarthmore has varsity sports but, sorry, none of its teams is televised. Still, this school has
had some winning moments in swimming, women's lacrosse, and field hockey.

Academic Realities

At Swarthmore, with its $610 million endowment, you can earn a B.A. in the arts and sciences
(there are two dozen majors available), or a B.S. in engineering. Some create their own interdisciplinary majors. Although there is no "core requirement," you must take two PDCs (primary
distribution courses) in each of three areas: the humanities, social sciences, and national sci-
ences/engineering. After two years of getting "rounded," you then pursue your major in earnest.
The most popular majors are Biology and Economics (13% each), Political Science (11%),
English (10%), and Engineering (8%). Students can cross-register at Bryn Mawr, Haverford, or
the University of Pennsylvania.

Getting In

At Swarthmore, the acceptance rate is about 23%. In a recent year 4,270 applied and 994 were
accepted. More than 88% of the students were from out of state. Of the 1,370 full-time students,
6% were African Americans and 5% were from other countries. The average SAT score was in
the 1320 to 1330 range.

UNIVERSITY OF PENNSYLVANIA	34th and Spruce Streets Philadelphia, PA 19104 (215) 898-7507 Web site: www.upenn.edu	**Financial aid deadline:** February 15 **Application deadline:** January 1 **Early decision deadline:** November 1 **1999–2000 tuition:** $24,230; room and board, $7,362

College Ranking

"UPenn," as it's usually called, is a preeminent, Ivy League university, often considered among
the top 10 universities in the nation. Penn is also the home of the world-renowned Wharton
School of Finance and Commerce. And its School of Nursing, with its Center for Nursing
Research, is the only one of its kind in the Ivy League cluster.

The Campus

UPenn, one of the oldest universities in the United States, is in Philadelphia. This 260-acre campus is "pedestrian"—free of cars—and circled by the fifth-largest city in the nation. The school
has a very collegiate but "urban" feel. More than 119 buildings are on campus, and the first one
you'll probably see is the old, ivy-covered College Hall. It's the central structure on campus, the

house of the Admissions Department and the administration. The Main Library, or "The Button"—that it's nickname, because of the shape of its insignia—is another very important spot. The last time we counted, there were 3,576,227 volumes.

On campus you'll pass many buildings that shape or comprise the four undergraduate schools. You'll pass the Wharton School, with students who are into financial analysis. Across the street there's the Lauder Institute, an adjunct center for seminars and other business-related matters. The School of Nursing is near the Johnson Pavilion. The School of Arts and Sciences (with more than 50 majors available) is comprised of a cluster of buildings. Last, there's the School of Engineering and Applied Sciences, where some say the students must work "harder than anyone else." Near South Street you'll find the Museum of Archaeology and Anthropology. There are the Van Pelt and Fine Arts libraries, only two of many. Remember that there are extra graduate and professional schools on this campus (e.g., Law, Medical, and Veterinary Schools) with resources available to you at every turn. Yes, you'll be told that it was all the idea of Benjamin Franklin, who chartered the school in 1755.

There are 12 residence locations on campus, but the W. E. B. Du Bois House is of central importance to African American students. Not only does this theme house serve as a residence for 175 black students, but also it's the center of activity for events, lectures, and performances sponsored by faculty, staff, and students of color. The house also serves as a meeting place for West Philadelphia community leaders.

The Du Bois House is a "do everything" resource. Inside this earth-toned, textured concrete and brick structure, you'll also find the Uchoraji Gallery—where students congregate—as well as a library, computer center, and seminar rooms where tutoring takes place. In regard to the living conditions, a student describes Du Bois as "a pleasant relief from academic and social pressure," as well as a "learning experience." There are carpeted suites (with single, double, and triple bedrooms), and lounges for living and relaxation.

Of course, the Du Bois House hasn't been without its controversy. According to an article about black theme houses in the *Journal of Blacks in Higher Education* (Winter 1997–1998 edition), many white students at UPenn feel that the residence "is divisive" and an example of "segregated housing." The complaints arose after a student newspaper did a story on the residence. Interestingly, more than 500 black students reside in fully integrated campus housing. A pivotal question might be, however, "Where would they select to live if Du Bois had more space?" After all, more than 28% of the black students call it "home."

Other residences include the Goldberg, Hill, Kings Court, and Spruce residences. These are like typical dormitories, sometimes with nearby oak or elm trees. The most popular dorms are in what is affectionately called "the Quad." These dwellings frame a huge, grassy courtyard that often serves as the grounds for college-sponsored festivals such as "Spring Fling." That's your yearly carnival, with vendors, food, live music, Frisbee, volleyball, and other games. The Hamilton (very much like the Harnwell and Harrison Houses), is a "skyscraper with many floors and sunset views," says one student. The suites have carpeted or wood floors and have air conditioning and private baths. More than 750 students live in the Hamilton with a house dean, twelve RA's (resident advisers), and a "faculty master."

Campus Life

At Penn there are 350 clubs, organizations, and special-interest groups, not to mention the social and cultural outlets available in downtown Philadelphia. Back at the Du Bois House there's the creation of the black yearbook and *The WEB,* a monthly newsletter. Also, there's the Academic Lecture Series, and the annual Souls of Du Bois Conference.

At other locations there's the Black Wharton Undergraduate Association, Sister-Sister, Bicultural Inter-Greek Council, African Rhythms Dance Troupe, Black Prelaw Society, Black Drama Ensemble, Caribbean Cultural Association, and related outlets. For brothers and sisters interested in pledging, there's no problem. From Alpha Kappa Alpha to Zeta Phi Beta, they're all at Penn, stepping and very visible.

Besides Spring Fling, popular events on campus include the annual Hey Day (Moving Up to Senior) event. There are also art, chess, jazz band, choir, debate, cheerleading, student government, newspaper and literary magazines, and dozens of other activity and involvement options.

Sports lovers can visit the Palestra—the "Philadelphia basketball landmark"—and watch Penn's championship basketball team play. For football there's Franklin Field, and for baseball, Bower Field. For those interested in track, there are the famous Penn Relays. This school has lots of team spirit, and sports are a big part of the campus excitement. Just bring in Princeton, and there's a frenzy.

For students interested in intramural sports, you can play tennis at the Hunter Loft tennis courts, or head to the Gimbel Gymnasium. At Penn there are swimming pools, squash courts, an ice rink, weight rooms, and more.

Academic Realities

You will find some rigor in class, as well as (if you're lucky) take notes in front of a distinguished Nobel Laureate or two. Study here is serious business and is not for the insecure or fainthearted. The Wharton (undergraduate unit), nursing, and engineering shadows perhaps fall on everyone. You'll be getting high-quality instruction, and will feel the presence of that preprofessional drumbeat, even if your major is strictly in the liberal arts.

The most popular majors are Finance, History, English, Psychology, and Biology. The Anthropology Department is said to be as strong as the one at the University of Chicago. In Engineering, you'll get "exposure to emerging technologies." Exciting, too, is the Penn idea of the "interdisciplinary major." Combine, for example, that engineering track of courses with a related psychology component. And if that's not enough, all students must demonstrate proficiency in at least one language.

Getting In

The statistics for the class of 2002 say a lot. The acceptance rate was 29%. There were 16,658 applicants, and 4,873 students were accepted. Look for these totals, if anything, to indicate harder admission odds in the future. In the noted grouping there were 2,125 early decision applicants, and only 897 were accepted. Of 905 valedictorians who applied to the overall class, 64% were accepted. Of the salutatorians (448) who applied, 51% were accepted. Obviously Penn is looking for other variables besides GPAs in its admissions reviews. Black freshman who enrolled (144) were 6% of the admissions total. We notice that this total generally stays steady year after year.

Most students arrive from the Northeast (New York, New Jersey), and California. Pennsylvania enrolls about 21% of its own. Students also journey from Asia, Canada, Europe/British Isles, Africa/Middle East, Central and South America, the Caribbean, and elsewhere.

The median SAT scores at Penn are about 1420. Black students should not blink at such a score, but submit an application and package that dares them to say, "deny." Your supplemental material—essays and recommendations, for example—can really be a major factor here. Note that about 16% of the enrolling students have scores in the 1140 range, with some lower.

UNIVERSITY OF PITTSBURGH	4200 Fifth Avenue Pittsburgh, PA 15260 (412) 624-PITT Web site: www.pitt.edu	**Financial aid deadline:** March 1 **Application deadline:** rolling **1999–2000 tuition:** $6,698 (state residents); $14,014 (nonresidents); room and board $5,766

College Ranking

Very large and public, the University of Pittsburgh (a.k.a. Pitt) is a solid, second-tier public university with a strong academic history stretching back to 1787.

The Campus

The 132-acre school is on a hill in the Oakland district. Think large here. The Hillman Library seats more than 1,500 readers, and resources abound. If you decide to live on campus, there are 11 residences. You are only three miles from downtown Pittsburgh, an urban community.

Campus Life

On campus, the William Pitt Union is a favorite campus hangout. We've also got the Black Action Society, Kunta Repertory Theater, Yotep, Caribbean American Association, National Society of Black Engineers, African Drum and Dance Ensemble, Students for a Free Africa, and other cultural outlets to ease any transition. Pitt, too, is home to all the major black fraternities and sororities, and they are very active on campus. Students tell us "you'll feel at home." Read the *New Pittsburgh Courier* and listen to WAMO radio.

If you're into sports, you'll climb "Cardiac Hill" to attend Panther football games. And basketball will undoubtedly also bring on the cheers. Of course, to relax you can visit 456-acre Schenley Park which sits beside the campus. Last, you can take the shuttle bus to Pittsburgh's cultural, sports, and social outlets.

Academic Realities

Pitt has traditionally been supportive of our needs. About 10% of the approximately 13,500 students at this branch are students of color. We're "in the mix," a junior says. In regard to academics and majors, you have about 96 ways to go. This is a school with a legacy. Its laboratories produced the Salk polio vaccine, synthetic insulin, and have been involved with other breakthrough research and findings. The most popular majors are Engineering, Nursing, and Psychology (about 9% each), Business (7%), and Communications (6%). There's also an African American Studies major. For "super" students there's the prestigious Honors College, with its small classes and individual attention.

Getting In

The acceptance rate at Pitt is about 79%, with the average SAT score in the 1090 to 1100 range.

The university has many programs and support services. Some admissions goodies include Upward Bound, Quest, Investing Now, Future Minority Engineers Weekend, and the Nurse Recruiting Coalition Program. These programs supplement others that try to reach, recruit, and prepare students who are capable (and often disadvantaged) and want to benefit from a college education. Scholarships such as those offered in the names of Helen Faison and Donald

Henderson are a help. It's a wide net. Although about 87% of the student body is from the state, Pitt has its eye on African Americans from the Middle Atlantic states and beyond. Indeed, students arrive from 50 states and more than 100 foreign countries. Nearly 40% of the students live on campus.

RHODE ISLAND

| **BROWN UNIVERSITY** | 45 Prospect Street
P.O. Box 1876
Providence, RI 02912
(401) 863-2378
Web site: www.brown.edu | **Financial aid deadline:**
February 1
Application deadline:
January 1
Early decision deadline:
November 1
1999–2000 tuition: $25,186;
room and board, $7,094 |

College Ranking

One of the top 20 national universities, Brown is a highly selective Ivy League school with a top-notch academic reputation.

The Campus

Brown (with the smallest endowment among the Ivies, with more than $410 million), is on the "middle-class" East Side of Providence, the capital of Rhode Island. The school is atop College Hill on 140 acres. It's a storybook picture of lush greens and of stately modern and historic buildings. There are 243 buildings, including residences. The surrounding neighborhoods are full of tree-lined streets and Victorian houses. If you head downtown, it's about a 10-minute walk.

On campus you will walk down Thayer Street, which some say is a "miniature Harvard Square." You'll pass coffee shops, restaurants, and "chic" shops. Along the way you'll find the student center, Bear's Lair. Stop and enjoy the video game room, the play tables (Ping-Pong and field hockey), billiards, the coffee corner, dance floors, and the exercise space and equipment. Other gathering places on campus include The Ivy Room (vegetarian food) and Josiah's (a snack bar). "The Rock," the name students call the John D. Rockefeller Library, is one of several. Another study location, with exceptional lighting and some "quiet," is "sci-fi," the Sciences Library. There are more than 3 million volumes on campus. An important spot is the Multimedia Lab, where you can put to use the emerging computer technologies for graphics, video, animation, and more. The Sheridan Center for Teaching and Learning and the David Winton Bell Gallery (art) are also resources for students.

"Ratty" or Sharpe Refectory is one dining hall, and Verney-Wooley ("V-Dub") is another. At the Keeney Quad dorm there are lots of freshmen. The "singles" are at Andrews Hall. Perkins Hall and Littlefield Hall—"the mansion"—are popular. At the Wriston Quad dorms you'll live "around lots of noise."

Campus Life

The are many clubs, organizations, and special-interest groups on campus. Some that might be of special interest to us include the African Students Association, *African Sun* (a magazine), Black and Latino Premedical Society, Shades of Brown (an R&B jazz singing sextet), 360 Degree Black Experience in Sound (radio), National Society of Black Engineers, Brown Sisters United, The Brotherhood, Sister 2 Sister, Harambee House, Pan-Hellenic Council, United African People, and Minority Peer Counselors. All the major fraternities and sororities are represented, including Delta Sigma Theta (Lambda Iota chapter), Alpha Phi Alpha, Alpha Kappa Alpha, and Zeta Phi Beta. A key cultural spot on campus is the Third World Center, which sponsors events such as Black History Month and a lecture series. A popular event is Funk Night, the weekly Thursday "gig" of bands and partying. As in the past, students from the Rhode Island School of Design (within walking distance) usually are around.

At Brown, varsity sports are popular. There's football. Also, there are men's soccer, women's ice hockey, and lacrosse. You will get involved. Pizzatota, one gym generally used by Brown's athletes, is called "The Pizz." Students, however, prefer the Olney Margolis Athletic Center for exercising and workouts. On campus you'll find an Olympic-size swimming pool, a weight room, and many tennis courts.

Academic Realities

This is the Ivy school that has "no core requirements," that allows you the freedom to pick and choose your courses. It's the school that many high school students think is "less stressful" than the others academically. Of course, they've got it all wrong. At highly regarded Brown University, you will be challenged and intellectually stimulated.

What some call the school's "innovative" approach is what makes it so special. In recent years the school has been called "hot," with very large numbers of applicants. As a student, you can decide what your primary focus will be and pursue special interests. You can even, if you wish, take courses in pass/fail mode. You can, as one student excitedly says, "go for it!"

At Brown there's an Afro American Studies Program that the *Journal of Blacks in Higher Education* has listed as one of the strongest in the country. Eight faculty members have been involved, teaching about 6% or approximately 300 students in a given year. A key component has been the Rites & Reason Theater, which presents original dramas about African Americans. Past presentations include *Ophelia's Cotillion* (about upper-class blacks) and *Mystic Falls,* a musical set in the Caribbean.

As an alumnus, maybe the very rich industrialist John D. Rockefeller, is the best known. But the late John F. Kennedy Jr., a more recent graduate, is more of the kind of student we expect to see at Brown: bright, adventurous, active. Hey, where's the Frisbee?

Getting In

The acceptance rate at Brown is about 18%. In a recent year 19,000 applied and 2,670 were accepted. There are more than 2,220 full-time students. Of this total, about 6% are African Americans, and 7% are arrivals from other countries. The average SAT score is about 1380, but the admissions team makes it clear that other factors are pivotal: the high school record, extracurricular activities, special talents, and your essay (very important). Apply if you feel bright, energetic, and have a strong record. Most arriving students are from the East Coast, mainly from New York State and California. At Brown the most popular majors are: Biology (11%), English, History, and Engineering (6% each), and Psychology (4%).

SOUTH CAROLINA

**CLAFLIN
COLLEGE**

700 College Avenue
Orangeburg, SC 29115
(803) 535-5339
Web site: www.claflin.edu

Application deadline: rolling
Early decision deadline:
November 1
1999–2000 tuition: $6,978;
room and board, $3,812

College Ranking

Claflin is a private, liberal arts HBCU, considered among the upper echelon among southern liberal arts colleges.

The Campus

About 40 miles from Columbia, on 32 acres of campus, is Claflin College. It's in Orangeburg, South Carolina (population 15,000). Near the business district, this small, private liberal arts college has 18 buildings, including residences. On campus there's the H. V. Manning Library, which has 458,000 volumes. There's also the Living and Learning Center and the Center for Excellence in Science and Mathematics. The last site is set up to "recruit, retain, and graduate students who plan to pursue careers in the fields of science, engineering, mathematics, and technology."

Campus Life

Clubs, organizations, and special-interest groups on campus include: the honor society Alpha Kappa Mu, Banneker II Mathematics Club, Student Christian Association, Science Club, NAACP, Pan-Hellenic Council, International Students Association, Vogue, Esquire, Oxford Club, Jazz Ensemble, and all the eight major black Greek-letter groups.

Claflin has a sports program that includes basketball. There's a 2,000-seat arena on campus as well as running tracks and tennis courts.

Academic Realities

At Claflin there are Humanities, Business, Education, and Natural Sciences and Mathematics Divisions. Within the framework of 24 possible majors, you can get preprofessional training in dentistry, law, engineering, and medicine. The most popular majors are Education (28%), Psychology (8%), and Biology and English (6% each). There are also specific programs in business administration, physical education, art, music, chemistry, computer science, and religion and philosophy. Claflin is affiliated with the United Methodist Church.

Getting In

The acceptance rate at Claflin is about 64%. In a recent year 1,055 students applied and 679 were accepted. The average SAT score is about 875. There are approximately 680 full-time students now on campus, with 97% being African American, and 3% from other countries. About 70% reside on campus.

SOUTH CAROLINA STATE UNIVERSITY

300 College Street, N.E.
Orangeburg, SC 29117
(803) 536-7185
Web site: www.scsu.edu

Financial aid deadline:
February 15
Application deadline: July 1
1999–2000 tuition: $2,550
(state residents); $5,030
(nonresidents); room and
board, $2,836

"We are large enough to offer almost 60 degree programs but small enough to value the importance of a caring and nurturing learning environment."

—Leroy Davis, president, South Carolina State University

College Ranking

This competitive HBCU offers a quality education and a nurturing atmosphere at a most reasonable cost. Notable alumni include Dr. Benjamin Payton of Tuskegee University and the renowned Dr. Benjamin Mays, president emeritus of Morehouse College.

The Campus

South Carolina State University is on a 160-acre campus in Orangeburg (population 14,400), about 40 miles from Columbia. The SCSU campus is said to be "attractive," and is shaped like a boot if you're looking at a map. On campus there are 60 buildings, including nine student residences (approximately 2,250 students can be accommodated). There's the 280,000-plus volume Miller F. Whittaker Library, with its Students' Computer Lab of 25 stations. Also, there's the Crawford Industrial Engineering/Technology Building. At Nance Hall you can hear a debate on slavery or see "how a computer module works."

The Student Union is a "most popular" gathering place, as well as the Washington Dining Hall. At Belcher Hall new students sit in on admissions orientations. The Henderson-Davis Theater sometimes presents Broadway-style student musicals. On campus, too, you'll find the Stanback Museum, Martin Luther King Auditorium, a planetarium, and (among others) the Williams, Earl, and Miller dorms.

Campus Life

Most of the major sororities and fraternities (Delta Sigma Theta, Omega Psi Phi, Zeta Phi Beta) are on campus and are very active. For example, the Alpha Kappa Alpha sorors are involved in the following events annually: AKAfest, Mr. Ivy Ghent Pageant, Miss Fashionetta Pageant and 25 Buds and Roses, with support to the nearby Rivelon Elementary School.

Other organizations, clubs, and special-interest groups include Cooperative Education Club, Life Savers/Peer Education, Student Union Board, National Society of Black Engineers, Psychology and Sociology Club, Mays I Hall Club, United Voices of Christ, Pan-Hellenic Council, Marching 101 Band (said to be one of the best in the Southeast), Collegiate Chorale, Jazz Band, International Students Club, NAACP, and more. Each year there's a Miss SCSU Pageant (Homecoming), Bulldog Fest (football), a Halloween Haunt, and an Annual Student Art Exhibition.

The school has an Honors House, a "meeting place for honors students." The house is "equipped with a multimedia center, a presentation room for exhibits and displays, and project rooms where small groups of students study and carry on discussions together." Army ROTC is available.

In 1994 the SCSU's footballers (the Bulldogs) were the Heritage Bowl champions, while the basketball team played in the 1995–1996 NCAA tournament. SCSU teams play schools such as Bowie State, Fayetteville, Savannah State, and Johnson C. Smith. In a recent Annual Labor Day Classic (at Oliver Dawson Stadium) the school played Norfolk State in football. Students also can participate in about 15 intramural sports.

Academic Realities

You'll find a familylike atmosphere, that emphasizes "developing the total student." The SCSU undergraduate schools include Arts and Sciences, Human Sciences, Engineering Technology, Business, and Education.

The most popular majors are Business, Education, Engineering, and Criminal Justice. A recent sampling of student enrollment in majors placed 356 students in Education. Also: Business Administration (261), Accounting (195), Marketing (116), Engineering and Related Technologies (300), Nursing (213), Criminal Justice (234), Social Work (107), Computer Sciences (218), Home Economics (92), Psychology (139), Biology (103), English (69), and Sociology (50).

The schools offer preprofessional programs in law, medicine, dentistry, and veterinary science.

Getting In

This competitive school accepts about 59% of those who apply. There are about 4,100 undergraduates. In a recent class 3,452 applied and 1,940 (most from the Southeast) were admitted. The average SAT score is about 880, with a GPA of approximately 3.0 (a B). About 85% of the students are from South Carolina. Beside the out-of-staters, about two dozen international students also are on campus, arriving from places such as the Bahamas and Nigeria.

TENNESSEE

**FISK
UNIVERSITY**

1000 17th Avenue
North Nashville, TN 37208-
    3051
(615) 329-8717
Web site: www.fisk.edu

Financial aid deadline: the
    FAFSA must be submitted,
    and well as Fisk's own finan-
    cial aid form; the deadline is
    April 20
Application deadline: April 20
1999–2000 tuition: $8,770;
    room and board, $4,930

College Ranking

Fisk University usually is listed as a "best buy" school by *Money* magazine. In the 1999 *Black Enterprise* pick of the "top 50 schools for African Americans," Fisk gets a nod at no. 23.

Fisk leads the nation in preparing black undergraduates earning Ph.D.'s in the natural sciences. Nearly 60% of Fisk graduates go on to get higher degrees. A significant number are physicians, dentists, and attorneys. Experiments developed in Fisk's physics laboratories have orbited the earth in the space shuttle. Last, some experts think that no single institution has played a greater role than Fisk "in the shaping of black learning and culture in America."

The Campus

The urban, 40-acre campus of Fisk University is on a hill overlooking downtown Nashville. It's about a two-mile drive to the capital, which is best known as being a tourist mecca and "Music City," for its reputation as the home of many in the recording industry. It is the third-largest metropolitan area in the United States.

This liberal arts college has 21 buildings—eight considered Historic Landmarks—including the residence halls. It's a mix of the "historic and modern." At the Academic Building you'll find administrative officers, a computer laboratory, and radio station WFSK-FM. The Physics and Chemistry Departments are at Talley-Brady Hall, as well as lecture halls and classrooms. Park-Johnson is another academic building.

The Fisk University Library has more than 200,000 volumes, including manuscripts by Langston Hughes and Marcus Garvey. The Aaron Douglas Gallery of African American Art, inside the library, is considered "renowned." Also, there are more than 50,000 titles on African Americans and their descendants in America and the Caribbean. The modern library also has student and faculty carrels, computer and study rooms, and lounges for reading. In the Instructional Technology Center, on the first floor, you'll find audio, graphic, and video equipment for student/faculty projects and presentations.

At another location there's the Fisk Special Collection, which has paintings by Picasso, Cézanne, Renoir, Toulouse-Lautrec, and other notable artists. Also you'll find a wealth of memorabilia from the life of W. E. B. Du Bois, W. C. Handy, and some of the music and personal papers of composer George Gershwin.

Nearly 90% of the students are from out of state, with most residing in Fisk housing (three residences for women, two for men). Housing is guaranteed for four years, but the dorms are generally described as "only passable," the same comment you often hear about the campus food.

Campus Life

Magna cum laude graduate Jamika D. Burge, now working on a master's degree in computer science at North Carolina A&T, says, "Fisk forever! My activities on the great campus of Fisk University have been senator for the freshman and sophomore classes and chairperson of Activities Committee in Jubilee Hall my freshman year. I was also a member of the Fisk University Gospel Choir—modern black Mass—serving in the capacity of president for two consecutive years. I was also an active member and officer of the Computer Science–Fisk Club (Miss Georgia-Fisk '96–'97). And I'm an active member of Alpha Kappa Alpha Sorority, Inc.!" You go, girl!

Fisk has many clubs and organizations, but the Greek-letter groups play a pivotal role in regard to campus events. There's the Orchesis Dance Club, Stagecrafters (and the Little Theater), University and Modern Mass Choir, student government, a literary magazine, and special-interest groups.

There's also the Fisk Memorial Chapel, where there are concerts, arts festivals, academic convocations, lectures, and conferences. Important events also include Homecoming (with Miss Fisk), W. E. B. Du Bois Day, and Jubilee Day.

Another major event is the Fisk Spring Arts Festival. During the 70th annual affair there was a Fisk Faculty and Student Art Exhibition at the Carl Vechten Art Gallery, the Fisk Jazz Ensemble performed at the Fisk Memorial Chapel, and there was a musical review of *Sophisticated Ladies,* at the Henderson A. Johnson Gymnasium. The gym was transformed into the Cotton Club, with cozy tables, dim lights, and the music of Duke Ellington. Last, there was a Fisk Jubilee Singers concert by the world-famous traveling group.

Fisk is an NCAA Division III, WIAC school. It is not a "big" sports school like Grambling or Florida A&M, but there are basketball (men and women), football, tennis, and track teams. Intramural sports usually are confined to basketball, tag football, and track.

Distinguished alumni include W. E. B. Du Bois, a graduate of the Fisk class of 1888, the eminent historian John Hope Franklin, and poet Nikki Giovanni. Major literary figures who have taught at Fisk include Arna Bontemps, James Weldon Johnson, Sterling Brown, and Robert Hayden. At one time, Booker T. Washington served on the Board of Trustees.

Academic Realities

The introductory classes will have no more than 40 students at most. At upper class levels you might have 10 to 25 classmates. At this small school there's an intimate air to your studies, with nobody feeling anonymous. It's not unusual to be invited to a professor's home for dinner or a private talk. You're in an "assessable" situation, often nurturing in nature. Most students are into the preprofessional majors—in premed (Biology, Psychology) and business, for example. But there are core requirements for all students. There's a freshman orientation class—you're going to get an overview of the Fisk legacy—and courses that must be taken in literature, math, history, and the natural and social sciences. You'll get, within the framework of all your study/learning, however, some Afrocentric focusing.

There's a dual-degree pharmacy program with Howard University, and five-year joint degree programs in business management (B.A./M.B.A.) or science/engineering (B.A./B. Eng.) with Vanderbilt University. Also, there are similar programs with Florida A&M and the University of Alabama at Huntsville.

A large number of students (more than 60%) go on to study at schools such as Emory, Vanderbilt, and Marshall. Of this total, most enter medical, dental, or law school. The remainder of students go on to work in business and industry at companies such as IBM.

Getting In

Fisk enrolled 230 freshman for the 1988–1999 academic year, its largest freshman class in four years. This influx of students (a 45% increase over the previous year) increased enrollment to 825 students. Among these students were valedictorians, salutatorians, members of national honor societies, student government leaders, newspaper editors, and varsity athletes. The school's dean of academic affairs says that a Fisk priority is to "attract more of the nation's top high school students," who will carry the school's "legacy of academic excellence" into the future.

In a recent year, Fisk accepted 76% of its applicants, students who averaged about 1000 on their SAT tests. About 760 applied, and 580 were accepted. An often-heard question: "Where are the men?" The men to women ratio of students is 30:70.

Generally, about 25 transfer students arrive each year. About 150 degrees are awarded annually.

TENNESSEE STATE UNIVERSITY

3500 John A. Merritt Blvd
Nashville, TN 37209
(615) 963-5000
Web site: www.tnstate.edu

Application deadline:
August 1
1999–2000 tuition: $2,610
(state residents); $7,436
(nonresidents); room and
board, $3,650

College Ranking

Well, Oprah Winfrey is a graduate. And Tennessee State University has an Olympic tradition with more than 29 gold, silver, and bronze medals won. Some might remember the Tigerbelles, TSU's triumphant women's track team. Or do you recall Wilma Rudolph (three gold medals in Rome in 1960) or Ralph Boston, our long-jump specialist? This state-supported historically black college (with its white enrollment at nearly 20%) has been a resource. Today the school is trying to maintain its "racial identity" as legal decisions develop and evolve. Stay tuned. In the meantime, there are more than 31 alumni chapters nationwide, and many of our folks are animate. They say, "we must maintain the cultural heritage" of the school.

The Campus

TSU is in Nashville, the capital of the state. It's called "Music City U.S.A.," by many. The main campus is on 465 acres of land with landscaped courtyards and surrounding farmlands. There are 65 buildings, including six residences, three each for men and women. Only about 28% of the students reside on campus, accommodating about 26% of the arrivals from more than 40 different states.

TSU has state-of-the-art facilities. The Otis L. Floyd–Joseph A. Payne Center (costing more than $16 million) has a gymnasium, offices for registration and career development, a post office, a hair salon, a 15,000-square-foot bookstore, dining facilities, weight and exercise rooms, and space for student organizations. The game room section has a bowling alley, video games, card and table games, billiards, Ping-Pong, and more. The Brown-Daniel Library, with more than 405,000 volumes, has a "galaxy of worldwide information." The University Career Center prepares students for "the world of work." On campus you'll also find an art gallery, learning resource center, radio station, and 450-plus computer workstations.

Campus Life

On campus there are many clubs, organizations, and special-interest groups that are available to students. The fraternities and sororities—Omega Psi Phi, Alpha Phi Alpha, Sigma Gamma Rho, and Alpha Kappa Alpha, for example—are active here. There's the marching "Aristocrat of Bands," which has performed at the Heritage and Blue Bowls, as well as the 52nd Inaugural Presidential Parade. There are the Sophisticated Ladies (majorettes), Baptist Club, African Student Association, Players Guild, Bebop Society, choral groups, jazz band, student newspaper, string ensemble, and more. You can join the Army, Navy, or Air Force ROTC.

TSU has competitive intercollegiate sports for both men and women: football (men), and track (both sexes). For basketball and convocations there's a 10,000-seat complex with facilities for a 35-meter swimming pool, 220-yard indoor track, and racquetball courts. The basketball team has won Ohio Valley conference and tournament championships.

In Nashville, students have access to entertainment of all types: the Nashville Symphony, clubs, restaurants, plays, films, and dance troupes. There are also public parks and other recreational outlets nearby.

Academic Realities

TSU has seven undergraduate schools. There are the Colleges of Arts and Sciences, Education, Business, Engineering and Technology, Nursing, Allied Health Professions, and Agriculture and Home Economics. Their schools offer 42 different degrees. Keeping "in tune," speakers such as Kweisi Mfume (president of the NAACP) and Julian Bond (civil rights activist) have recently addressed students at the Thomas E. Poag Auditorium in the Humanities Building.

Getting In

The acceptance rate at TSU is about 50%. In a recent class 5,555 applied and 2,775 were accepted. Exactly 1,165 enrolled. In data supplied by TSU, 5,430 undergraduates are African American, and 1,039 are classified as "white." The SAT average was not reported, but the average ACT score is said to be 19. Reportedly a 2.25 minimum GPA is necessary for admission consideration for those residing in the state. For others, at least a 2.5 is required. The most popular majors are Business (26%), Education (20%), Engineering and Psychology (10% each), and Computer Sciences (8%). About 32% of the students are enrolled in preprofessional studies.

Most students are from the Southeast. Students also arrive from other countries, including Nigeria, India, Jordan, Saudi Arabia, and the Bahamas.

TEXAS

PRAIRIE VIEW A&M UNIVERSITY	P.O. Box 3089 Office of Admissions and Records Prairie View, TX 77446 (409) 857-2618 Web site: www.pvamu.edu	**Application deadline:** August 1 **1999–2000 tuition:** $2,028 (state residents); $7,140 (nonresidents); room and board, $3,828

College Ranking

A nonselective HBCU with solid academics.

The Campus

The school, in Waller County, is on a 1,440-acre campus and is about 40 miles from Houston. Texas Highway 290 is about a mile away. There are 36 buildings, including nine residences. On campus you'll find the Memorial Student Center and the J. B. Coleman Library, which holds 240,200 volumes. You'll also find University Village which went through "three building phases" and can accommodate 1,877 students. The "Village" is two stories high and has carpeting, air conditioning, and central heating. There's also Drew Hall, Banks Hall, and Evans Hall (where honors students can room two to a room). "The Place," another dorm, encourages "academic success" and has in-house mentors and tutorial services.

Campus Life

About 94% of the students live on campus. PVAM can place about 3,400 students in campus housing. There are many clubs, organizations, and special-interest groups on campus. PVAM has a Miss Prairie View A&M University Pageant, a Queens Ball, and KPVU-FM 91.3 is the radio station. Since 1989, the Classic Dance Ensemble has been a joy to watch in performance. Also, you have the Charles Gilpin Players. *Southern Living* magazine called the PVAM Marching Storm Band one of the "top 12 in the country." This school plays in the Southeastern Conference against schools such as Grambling, Texas Southern, and Southern University.

Well, let's not talk about the recent 77-consecutive-game losing streak in football. There are winning teams at Prairie View A&M University. There are seven intercollegiate sports for men and five for women. Go Panthers!

Academic Realities

Count about 4,270 full-time students, with 91% being African American. There are six colleges and two schools here. The colleges are Arts and Sciences, Business, Education, Engineering, Nursing, and Agriculture and Human Sciences. The Schools of Juvenile Justice and of Architecture complete the picture. At PVAM the most popular majors are Engineering, Business, and Nursing.

Getting In

The PVAM acceptance rate is about 93%. In a recent year 2,545 applied, and 2,369 were accepted. About 10% were from out of state (approximately 660 students from 40 states). About 2% of the students were from 44 foreign countries. The average SAT score was between 820 and 840.

Jenerica Wilson was the "only black and only female" in her first engineering course at a predominantly white college. She says the professor never directed his attention to her, and "taught the other side of the class." Her next semester she transferred to Prairie View A &M University, a historically black college.

Of one of her new teachers, she said this: "Dr. Freddie Frazier broke Calculus I & II down not only for me, but the entire class. He made it interesting and exciting. He incorporated life experiences into every class. He rhymed certain integral equations so that they stuck in your head. I never had Geometry nor Trigonometry and I caught on to the fundamentals of Calculus, an "A" for my final grade. I'm not good, he's GOOD. He was also pleasant to see dressed down to the 't.'" Jenerica received her degree in Mechanical Engineering and works for General Electric.

RICE UNIVERSITY

6100 Main Street MS-17
Houston, TX 77005-1892
(713) 527-4036
Web site: www.rice.edu

Financial aid deadline:
March 1
Application deadline:
January 2
Early decision deadline:
November 15
1999–2000 tuition: $14,746;
room and board, $6,600

College Ranking

This southwestern school, yet another college often called the "Harvard" of its region, makes all the "best buy" lists. Rice University gives you more bang for the buck because of its top-notch programs in the liberals arts and sciences and its (relatively speaking) low tuition.

The Campus

Located in suburban Houston (where we are 28% of the population), the school is on a 300-acre campus. One sales pitch is that the school's residential setup is patterned after the one at Oxford. There are eight coed colleges, each with about 225 students and a faculty "master" to keep order. These schools have their own "personalities," dining halls, and common rooms. Outside, there are stone paths, oak trees, rows of hedges, and buildings that some say are "Mediterranean" with a Spanish flavor.

Campus Life

Clubs and organizations at Rice that we might have special interest in include: the Office of Multicultural Affairs (OMA), which coordinates tutoring and support programs. This group also sponsors Minority Leadership Weekend. There's also the Black Student Union, which sponsors talks about issues relevant to us. The Black Student Association (BSA) assists with programs during Black History Month. Overall, it seems that very few of the many groups on campus cater to our particular interests. Yes, there is a chapter of the National Society of Black Engineers on campus. But there are no "official Greeks." We must head to either Texas Southern, a historically black college, or the University of Houston to pledge.

At football games, at halftime, you've got the exciting MOB (Marching Owl Band).

Academic Realities

At Rice there are six schools: Humanities, Architecture, Engineering, Natural Sciences, Music, and Social Sciences. On "Majors Day" you pick your school and your choice in regard to the direction you want to take. You're encouraged to create a broad liberal arts program. There is no core curriculum, although you must take at least 12 credits each in the humanities, social sciences, and natural sciences/engineering. Double and even triple majors are fine. At Rice the most popular majors are Engineering (19%), Economics (8%), Biology and English (6% each), and History (5%). Expect a very competitive, stressful academic environment.

Getting In

The acceptance rate at Rice is 27%. In a recent year 6,375 applied and 1,748 were accepted. The average SAT score falls in the astounding 1420 to 1430 range. With 4,263 full-time students, about 6% are African American. Interestingly, President Malcolm Gillis says, "No university is working harder than we are to compensate for the adverse effects of the Hopwood [anti-affirmative-action] decision." In 1997, according to a *Journal of Blacks in Higher Education* survey, 28% of the African American students who applied were accepted. Yet, in the Hopwood climate, 12% fewer African Americans decided to enroll. Stay tuned.

But perhaps a Texas bumper sticker says it all: "I Must Be Smart, I Got into Rice."

UNIVERSITY OF TEXAS AT AUSTIN	Main Building, Room 7 Austin, TX 78712 (512) 475-7475 Web site: www.utexas.edu	**Financial aid deadline:** April 1 **Application deadline:** February 1 **1999–2000 tuition:** $3,128 (state residents); $9,608 (nonresidents); room and board, $4,854

College Ranking

The University of Texas is a gigantic, state-supported school with a wide array of course selections and a strong reputation.

The Campus

Think "bigger" and you're in the right mind-set. Behind Harvard and Yale, it has the third-largest library collection in the nation, the Lyndon Baines Johnson Library. More than 34,000 undergraduates use the 350-acre campus, which is near downtown Austin, just off the interstate. There are 109 buildings, including residences.

Campus Life

Besides the pivotal Black Student Alliance (BSA) and the major black fraternities and sororities—two with Greek-letter houses—there are more than 750 student clubs and organizations on campus. You can play chess, or join the Innervisions Gospel Choir. You can socialize in the Texas Union, the student center, or do community work in Austin. At 4% of the student count, we are visible. Take a head count and we're over 1,300. Approximately 15% of the students live on campus.

Of course, Texans love their sports. After a football victory, for example, the UT Tower is lit in Longhorn orange. The big opponents here are Texas A&M and Oklahoma.

Academic Realities

Generally, academics are said to be challenging on the one hand and "pleasurable and laid-back" on the other. You have 11 undergraduate schools and more than 109 bachelor degree programs to select from. Thousands of courses are available. The most popular majors are Business (14%), Engineering (11%), Psychology (7%), Education and Biology (5% each).

Getting In

UTexas has an acceptance rate of about 78%. In a recent year 14,974 students applied and 11,708 were accepted. The average SAT score was about 1180. Students with higher scores, however, sometimes enter honors programs. There are, after all, always many National Merit finalists on campus. Although all states are represented, more than 88% of the students are Texans. International students arrive from more than 100 countries.

Be aware that there has been a dramatic dip in African American applications here as an aftermath of the legal anti-affirmative action rulings.

VIRGINIA

HAMPTON UNIVERSITY

Hampton, VA 23668
(804) 727-5328;
    (800) 624-3328
Web site:
    www.cs.hampton.edu

Financial aid deadline:
    March 1, but apply early as
    possible; FAFSA required
Application deadline:
    March 15
Early decision deadline:
    September 1; note that a B
    average and a combined 1050
    SAT are desirable here; you
    should also be in the top
    quarter of your graduating
    class
1999–2000 tuition: $10,076;
    room and board, $4,442

College Ranking

Historically black Hampton University is undoubtedly one of our most prestigious colleges, ranking in reputation and rank beside schools such as Howard, Spelman, and Morehouse. When we think of Hampton we think of a "class" institution (Booker T. Washington was a graduate), where proven or "promising" achievers are striving to better themselves. Our impression at Black Excel is that Hampton has created "an image," deservingly so, that makes the school a desirable place to grow and shape your future. Indeed, Hampton includes both undergraduate and graduate schools that cover a wide range of majors: Business and Management, Communications and Education, Health and Social Service, as well as other areas of study. More than 400 corporations have recruited at Hampton in recent years, and usually there is a waiting list on Career Day because demand to see and talk to students is so high.

This school's endowment is valued at $102 million. It ranks behind only Howard and Spelman among HBCUs.

The Campus

Hampton's urban campus is scenic, with an air of hospitality. Some students laud it as "Hampton by the Sea," because waters (Chesapeake Bay) border the 204-acre campus on three sides and you often see boats and mariners. Hampton sits off a major highway and is not far from Norfolk, Virginia Beach, and Colonial Williamsburg. You must drive through a gate when you reach the grounds. On campus there are more than 120 buildings, including the Pure and Applied Sciences, Arts and Letters, Nursing, Education, and Business buildings (some designated National Historic Landmarks). One, "The Mansion," was build before the founding of the college. Odgen Hall, on campus, is the home of the Virginia Opera and other symphony companies.

There are also single, coed, and honors dorms. The newest dorm for females is eight stories high, and there's a relatively new male dorm. There is also a natural history museum, art gallery, learning resources center, main library (with its Peabody Collection of African American resource material), gymnasium, Olympic-size pool, and an 11,000-seat stadium. In the Student Union Center, there is a recreation area with arcade games, pool tables, and a snack bar. On campus you will pass tennis and basketball courts as well as magnolia and orchard trees. Wherever you go, you'll generally find a pleasant view.

Hampton University has installed six touch screen booths—"kiosks"—around campus, which will offer college and community data at a touch. Students will be able to get information about restaurants, theaters, the school calendar, and course offerings.

Campus Life

The students Black Excel has talked to are very happy with HU. They have a beautiful campus. But if you're not in the "classy" honors dorms, the rooms are often described with terms such as "dull" or "livable." In Davidson Hall, one dorm we visited, the hallways were painted green, and the rooms had those to-be-expected beds, desks, and lamps. Our opinion: the standard, no-frills college setting. Most students are said to be "nice," easy to get along with, and do exhibit cultural pride and self-esteem. The majority of students are from the South, Northeast, and Middle Atlantic states. At Hampton these students involve themselves in many recreational and social activities. There are enough parties to "keep everybody happy."

There is a marching band of 276 members, an orchestra, a gospel choir, fraternities and sororities (with their step shows), a Student Union hangout, the Hampton University Players (drama), and more than 100 other student organizations available. Students show strong support for the school's basketball and football teams. There are also Homecoming and Career Days, which are well attended. *The Hampton Script* is the school newspaper. A major rivalry is with nearby Norfolk State.

Girls outnumber the boys, seemingly, "5 to1," says one female. Another informant explains, "most of the males move off campus after freshman year, so it feels like it's 7 to 1 on campus, at times. The real deal: 62.8% women, 37.2% men.

At present there are campus curfews: 11:00 P.M. from Sunday through Thursday, and 1:00 A.M. on the weekends. Some students complain, saying that they "don't have such restrictions" at home. Campus security will question you if you break curfew, especially if you're a female.

There are two cafeterias. Years ago, the food was described as "southern and excellent": chicken, biscuits, grits, black-eyed peas, collard greens, and the like. Now students complain that the food is unsatisfactory, with the best meal being breakfast. After a recent student survey that knocked the food, the administration is reportedly looking for a new caterer. Students utilize meal plans but can, if they wish, buy snacks and goodies such as hamburgers at the snack bar in the Student Union.

Hampton's fine football team usually plays in several classics, including the Coca-Cola Classic at RFK Stadium in Washington, D.C., and the Whitney Young Classic at Giant Stadium in New Jersey. HU is the first historically black college to sponsor an intercollegiate sailing team. The coach is Gary Bodie, former coach at the Naval Academy, where he guided the midshipmen to four national Championships. Scheduled competition includes the University of Florida, Old Dominion, and SUNY Maritime.

Academic Realities

Many students who were A students in high school do mention some adjustment problems. One Computer Science major whom Black Excel talked to says students with strong college-preparatory backgrounds have an advantage. He also says that a "little seriousness" and "hard work" won't hurt. The rule: any malingering or goofing off usually results in poor grades. For students who are having difficulty, there is a tutorial program that is said to be helpful. Both students and teachers instruct.

Generally, the size of any introductory class will be 50 students or less. Usually you'll find 10 to 15 students sitting in on upper division classes. Majors offered include Education, Engineering, Business, Music, Architecture, Art, Communications, Health, Nursing, Drama, Sociology, Home Economics, History, and Mathematics. Baccalaureate degrees are available in 47 areas. Do review the college catalog for extensive degree and specialization options. The most popular majors are Biology (11.4%), Psychology (8.8%), Mass Media (7.6%), Business Management (7.6%), and English (5.6%).

Computers are available around the campus, and the main library (nearly 400,000 bound volumes) is more than adequate. The ratio of students to teachers is about 16:1, so there is a lot of close interaction and attention. The ratio of white to black teachers is approximately 50:50. There is a wide range of majors (from business to the social sciences), and there are preprofessional programs in dentistry, law, medicine, pharmacy, and social work. For students interested in Engineering, there are 3-2 programs associated with Old Dominion and George Washington Universities. At Hampton, more than 63% of the students graduate in five years. That retention rate is far greater than at most HBCU schools, and is indicative of the commitment of the administration to "getting the job done."

All 1,500-plus freshmen must take University 101, which is a class run by computers. "I wanted all Hampton students to have an appreciation of the role of technology in the global economy," says Dr. William Harvey, the college president. The school is calling its innovation an "ATM" (Academic Technology Mall). The 80-seat electronic classroom, where each student can hold a computer in his hands, is a mall. You can shop at a learning center, a language lab, and do distance learning from your seat. Sophomores must continue their orientation to technology by taking Humanities 201, another addition to a revised core requirement.

Getting In

Getting into Hampton University has been described by some as being "moderately difficult." We agree. In one recent year 7,211 applied and only 3,200 were accepted (1,181 chose to enroll). In the near future, HU's acceptance rate will probably remain between 50% and 52%, if not drop lower.

A combined SAT score of at least 900 is said to be "desirable," but the SAT median score for applicants is in the 1000-plus range. Average ACT: 20. Of the students who are accepted, at least a quarter of the freshman admits are in the top 10% of their graduating class. The average GPA of admitted student is almost 2.9. The eventual good news: 25% of HU graduates head for higher degrees within a year.

A Black Excel insider's tip: HU is looking for students who demonstrate academic seriousness, leadership, and a strong commitment to community service. Many of the applicants also will be applying to schools such as Spelman and Florida A&M University.

If you are a good student but are a bit discouraged by Hampton's stats and search for strong students, do consider this note from Hampton Admissions: "Students whose potential and promise may have been inhibited by a lack of economic, social, and educational opportunity are also considered for admission." Make your essays and recommendations resonate.

Hampton now requires an essay and recommendations. If you feel that you have leadership qualities or special talents that could carry you over the "acceptance" line, you must let the school know. If you were a leader in student government, for example, that would be a major plus. Playing an instrument or having singing talent also could be a factor. If you feel that an interview could help, call the school and make arrangements for one. Keep in mind that Hampton does have a Summer Bridge program for some preadmission students. It might be an option in "questionable" cases. Do inquire.

HU declares says that a "minimum 2.3" in prior college work is required for transfer. Like other top-ranked schools, since relatively few upper-class students leave, transfer spaces are limited. Be aware that the acceptance rate for a transfer student is lower than that for regular applicants. That 2.3 transfer? Perhaps it's a student from UPenn. Got the picture? Apply with gusto, as if you're a freshman candidate.

NORFOLK STATE UNIVERSITY	2401 Corprew Avenue Norfolk, VA 23504 (757) 683-8396 Web site: www.nsu.edu	**Application deadline:** August 1 **1999–2000 tuition:** $3,335 (state residents); $7,540 (nonresidents); room and board, $4,992

"This is where I learned about the real world. I love Norfolk State.
I'm a Spartan for life . . . Can't hide that Spartan pride!"

—A student

College Ranking

Norfolk State University is a state-supported school and a good "second chance" choice. TV actor Tim Reid is a graduate.

The Campus

The school covers more than 120 acres of land, has 34 buildings, including residences, and is near a port city and water. It is in the Tidewater area of Virginia, which is a hub for navy, army, and air force personnel. NU has a sizable ROTC program. From the college, you can drive to Chesapeake, Virginia Beach, or visit nearby Old Dominion University, the more famous neighbor.

On campus you won't miss the Lyman Beecher Brooks Library. Maybe you'll visit its museum with its display of West African artifacts. The William P. Robinson Technology Center has rows of computer workstations. In one materials lab building, the school brags that it has "the best-equipped laser laboratory" in the nation. For entertainment there's the L. Douglas Wilder Performing Arts Center. For eating there's the Mary Scott-Dozier Dining Hall.

Campus Life

About 1,360 students reside in residence halls in either the East Campus or the West Campus. Students are separated by sex, and the "no-coed visitation rule" is a major complaint of just about everybody. A men's residence hall (Samuel F. Scott) is near the West Campus Dining Hall. There are the Twin Towers North and South, which serve the women.

All the major sororities and fraternities are on campus. For example, you'll find the Alpha Kappa Alpha sorority (Delta Epsilon chapter), Delta Sigma Theta sorority (Epsilon Theta chapter), and Alpha Phi Alpha fraternity (Epsilon Pi chapter). Students are also involved with the Baptist Student Union, Gospel Choir, *Spartan Echo* newspaper, Legion Marching Band, *Reflections* yearbook, NGOMA African Dance group, University Players, Chess Club, Biology Society, WNSB radio station, and Thurgood Marshall Prelaw Club. The club scene? Some students say Big Momma's, Shadows, and City Lights are popular hangouts.

Varsity sports also are popular. Norfolk plays teams such as Florida A&M, Virginia State, and Hampton in football. NSU has won CIAA and NCAA Division II championships in other sports.

Each year NSU has an Open House, where its dance, jazz, and other groups entertain students and their parents. The grand tour includes a visit to academic departments, a cookout, and an admissions and financial aid seminar.

Academic Realities

Norfolk has seven undergraduate schools, including the Schools of Arts and Sciences, Education, Social Sciences, Health, Communications, Engineering, and Business. Many majors are available. NSU is the home of the Doretz National Institute for Minorities in the Applied Sciences (DNIMAS). This program was created to address the shortage of minorities in the applied sciences. Also, there's the Retention Enhanced Education Program (REEP). This program is designed to help "provisionally admitted freshmen" develop the skills to do college-level work. Students who need a little nurturing and guidance take required university orientation courses during their freshman year. These students generally make a fine adjustment, and go on to perform as well as or better than regularly admitted students. There's an honors program for very capable incoming freshman (3.5 GPA).

Getting In

The acceptance rate at NSU is more than 97%. In a recent year 2,864 applied and 2,753 were accepted. Nearly all transfer students are accepted. SAT or ACT scores are used for placement purposes.

Norfolk has about 5,800 students, with approximately 88% being African American. Most students (about 72%) are Virginians, with other students arriving from nearly 50 states and nine foreign countries.

UNIVERSITY OF VIRGINIA

P.O. Box 9017
Charlottesville, VA 22906
(804) 982-3200
Web site: www.virginia.edu

Financial aid deadline:
March 1; the FAFSA and the the institutional form are required
Application deadline:
January 1
Early decision deadline:
November 1
1999–2000 tuition: $4,130 (residents); $16,564 (nonresidents); room and board, $4,589

College Ranking

The University of Virginia is often called the "finest public university in the nation," sharing space with schools such as the University of California at Berkeley and the University of North Carolina at Chapel Hill. At the University of Virginia you'll find a cadre of top-notch professors, from Pulitzer Prize–winning poet Rita Dove to Fulbright, Humbolt, and National Book Awards honorees.

The Campus

Thomas Jefferson, the founding father of the University of Virginia, created the master plan. The nation's third president actually laid out the idea for his academic village in architectural drawings. Well, it's quite a sight. More than 1,131 acres, with 557 buildings, including residences, this school has made many "most beautiful campus" lists.

In a 1997 survey of the 25 highest ranked universities as picked by *U.S. News & World Report*, the *Journal of Blacks in Higher Education* made some startling findings. Charting the top schools, it was clear that the University of Virginia had enrolled next to the highest number of black freshmen, 309 for the fall 1997. A total of 1,381 students of color had applied, and 747 had been accepted. The acceptance rate was 54.1%. The yield (students who decided to enroll) was 41.4%. UVA had beaten UMichigan (400).

The Rotunda, undoubtedly the most famous building on campus, is the school's centerpiece. The structure sits on the northern end of a great lawn and seems supplanted from Rome. Imagine, perhaps, the White House: a dome, pillared columns, rising marble steps, elegance. It's hard to believe, but esteemed faculty and honored students still reside inside.

On the campus of UVA, situated east of the Blue Ridge Mountains, you'll find colonnades and Georgian brick everywhere. There are six undergraduate schools: the College of Arts and Sciences, as well as the Schools of Engineering, Architecture, and Nursing. The final two schools are the McIntire School of Commerce (a rival to Penn's Wharton School of Finance and Commerce) and the Curry School of Education. These schools admit achieving students after their sophomore year. Within the framework of these schools there are many nationally recognized departments.

Around the Rotunda and the lawn, are 10 pavilions. This area is called the Central Grounds, and it's circled by dozens of halls. There's Monroe Hall (the Commerce School), Bryan Hall (the English Department), and other buildings with names such as Peabody, Madison, Minor, Fayerweather, and Brooks. From this section, you can see the chapel, visit the president's office, the Alderman Library (there are more than 4.4 million volumes in UVA libraries), or the Health Services Center. Note that UVA has an endowment of more than $1 billion.

At other locations you'll find the Fiske Kimball Fine Arts Library, the McCormick Observatory, as well as Ruffner Hall (Education School) and Thorton Hall (Engineering School). A key gathering spot is Newcomb Hall/University Student Center. Inside you'll find a dining hall, movie theater, game room, bank, post office, art gallery, lounges, a ballroom, and offices for the Student Council and the school newspaper, the *Cavalier*.

About 1,400 students live in the Alderman Road residence halls. These are 12 buildings with suite-style settings. One location is Cauthen House, which is a first-year residence. In the Gooch/Dillard residence area, you'll find four-story houses with air-conditioned suites. About 650 students reside in this section. On Emmett Street near Memorial Gym you'll find the Munford/Gwathmey residences with their beautiful lounges.

Hereford College (1994) is a 500-bed residential college. Brown Residential College (1986) is on Monroe Hill. This complex accommodates 300 undergraduates, with 12 portals that house 22 to 30 students. These miniresidences (with suites of two rooms) are named after distinguished professors of the 19th century. Some are named Davis, Tucker, McGuffey, and Mallet. The residences open into quads and have green spaces where you can study, cook, or play games.

Campus Life

Some say that UVA is "very segregated," while others say "there has been improvement." In the Black Student Alliances' publication *Black Pride,* there was a recent article titled "Self-Segregation vs. Forced Integration." Undoubtedly, diversity is an issue. Interestingly, the editors of the college viewbook are eager to say that the "rich collection of traditions unites members of the student community with each other and with generations before them." Ironically, UVA was only integrated in 1971. Indeed, this author found it curious that the viewbook then goes on to mention the Curry School Bridge. There freshmen might note strange insignias or "ages-old graffiti that mark the presence of the university's secret societies."

The Luther P. Jackson Cultural Center is an important location for students of color. There you can find the African American Affairs Office and helpful academic, social, and extracurricular information. The center presents Nommo Cultural Workshops, the Heritage Poetry Series, and sponsors celebrations for African American History Month and Kwanzaa. At a recent event, "Jazz Fest 1999: At the Millennium," world-renowned pianist Herbie Hancock appeared. Some groups that operate out of the center and/or appear on campus include the Black Student Alliance, Black Fraternal Council, Association of African and Caribbean Cultures, Black Business Student Forum, NAACP, Black Commerce Student Network, National Society of Black Engineers, Black Empowerment Association, Black Voices (a 70-plus member gospel group that has performed at Hampton University, Virginia Commonwealth University, and at UVA's women's basketball games), African Dance and Drum Ensemble, UV Jazz Ensemble and Vocalists, the Mahogany Dance Troupe, Black Nurses' Association, Multicultural Issues Committee, and the Daniel Hale Williams Black Premed/Predental Society.

Black fraternities and sororities are also active on campus. The Zeta Phi Beta sisters (Tau Theta chapter), recently sponsored a forum, "Women in Leadership: At the University and Beyond." Delta Sigma Theta, Alpha Kappa Alpha, Sigma Gamma Rho have been involved with mentoring. One contribution is the Madison House Big Sibling program. And, of course, there's the annual "Greek Explosion Stepshow Competition."

UVA has more than 300 other clubs, organizations, and special-interest groups on campus. There are radio and TV stations, the daily *Cavalier* (newspaper), the student-run University Union (social events), and groups such as the Madison House Organization (volunteer work in the community).

Varsity sports are big. Often the basketball team is nationally ranked. Also, the soccer team has been a national champion. There's Scott Stadium, for football, with more than 44,000 seats available. This school competes in the tough Atlantic Coast Conference. There are 24 intercollegiate teams (12 men, 12 women), including soccer, swimming, lacrosse, tennis, and other teams.

Some reports say that more than 85% of the students participate in club or intramural sports at some time. Four recreational centers are used, including a new aquatic fitness center.

Academic Realities

Students at UVA are said to be "laid-back" in regard to academics. There is not the sense of overwhelming rigor that some students feel at some other highly ranked schools. It's been said that usually students in your classes won't be overly competitive or cutthroat. Still, the work is generally described as challenging. These students, after all, are obviously very bright. If you are at UVA, you are capable.

Black students say the distribution requirements keep you sharp, though there are a lot of "directions you can go." Students have more than 1,000 course selections a semester. Still, you must take math and science courses (at least 12 credits), courses in the humanities and social sciences (six credits each), and a two-semester composition sequence, plus history and Western perspectives classes. There is, too, a foreign language requirement. Beyond the above, 18 to 42 credits must be taken in your major. You have one of 61 areas of study to consider.

However, if you've been selected to enter the Echols Scholars program—about 180 super students are so honored each year—you can go on an approved journey of 120 credits without any distribution restraints. During freshman year you'll reside together, and you can create what some call your "master program" or cluster. In fact, you might decide not to select any major, but "a plan."

The Distinguished Majors program allows "qualified" upper-class students to do independent study during their last two years. The Interdisciplinary Majors program allows students to mix or integrate disciplines while creating a comprehensive thesis for their senior year.

Some popular majors are Commerce (11%), English (9%), Biology (8%), Psychology (8%), History (6%), and Economics (5%).

Students also can major in African American Studies, while taking courses such as The African Cultural Past, The Harlem Renaissance, Third World Nations, and Race and Ethnic Relations. The problem here is that there is no actual department. About 30 faculty numbers are pulled from the whole of the university to form a working nucleus. Established in 1981, the African American Studies Initiative (under the guiding eye of the Carter G. Wooden Institute) was created to support a "more aggressive program of minority recruitment." In a recent year only nine undergraduates completed the major, perhaps a sign that some kind of upgrade is necessary.

Getting In

The acceptance rate at UV is about 34%. In a recent year 16,055 students applied. Of that total, 6,107 students were Virginians. The out-of-staters forwarded an astounding 9,948 applications for admission. As in the past, the Virginians were rewarded. They were accepted at a rate of about 48%, while the possible "visitors" got in at a paltry 25%. Like most public universities, the "homies" get a tremendous advantage. And of the 2,095 students who were placed on UV's wait list, only 25 were eventually admitted. Clearly, gaining an accept is *not easy.*

In that recent year the median SAT of accepted students was about 1310. Still, we should heed these comments from the Admissions Office: "We don't have a minimum GPA [and] we don't have a minimum SAT score . . . students are more than the sum of two numbers, no matter how important those numbers may be." So although your stats are pivotal, remember that UVA will try to "take into account all of the information we see in each application."

Of a full-time student body count of about 12,384 undergraduates, 10.3% are African Americans. That's a higher total than most similar-size institutions.

Students arrive from all the states and the District of Columbia. In a recent applicant pool, the top 10 non-Virginia state student totals were as follows: New York (109), Maryland (86),

New Jersey (85), Georgia (53), Massachusetts (46), Florida (45), Connecticut (39), Texas (38), North Carolina (35), Tennessee (34), and California (32). International students (usually more than 300) also arrived, from more than 90 foreign countries.

Launched in 1995, the Office of African American Affairs (OAAA) established the Faculty/Student Mentoring program. This caring effort was created to provide students of color at UVirginia with "a supportive and caring environment." Based on common interests (academic orientation or professional goals), freshmen are paired with either upper-class students or a faculty member in a mentoring relationship. The goal is to "enhance the growth and development of the students at the university and beyond."

The new students meet their mentors at a Meet-and-Greet Reception in the fall and beyond, communicating in person and via e-mail. The program has its own web site and helpful newsletter. Also, a valuable component is a calendar of events. A recent event was a visit and performances by a highly acclaimed New York dance troupe, the Nicholas Leichter Dancers.

VIRGINIA STATE UNIVERSITY	1 Hayden Place P.O. Box 9018 Petersburg, VA 23806 (804) 524-5000 Web site: www.vsu.edu	**Application deadline:** May 1 **1999–2000 tuition:** $1,951 (residents); $6,430 (nonresidents); room and board, $4,910

College Ranking

This public historically black college is another good choice for students looking for a solid academic experience at a school with fairly noncompetitive admissions.

The Campus

The university, about 25 miles from Richmond, covers more than 236 acres. On campus there are 52 buildings, including residences. The VSU campus is shaped in a rectangle, and students say it's attractive. You'll see lawns, trees, and shrubbery. Visiting, you'll note the president's residence and the "The Student Village," which is a complex of half a dozen buildings where upper-class students generally live. One residence is Powell Pavilion (with its computer labs and lounges). In the southwestern section of campus, you can stop at the Johnson Memorial Library, with its nearly 300,000 volumes. On the eastern side, you'll see woodlands. On the western side, you can walk to the nearby "neighborhood of homes." On the northwestern side of the campus you've got a view of the Appomattox River. At only two locations on campus (a sore point) you'll find arrangements of flowers. The flowers spell out the words "VSU" and "Trojans" (the school's mascot). Other notable structures are Alumni Fountain, the Career Placement Building, and Jones Dining Hall, a gathering place. Also note that VSU also has 460 extra acres of farmland that is used by agricultural students for research, and is located about a mile from the main campus.

Freshman residences include "The Branch," which has 194 beds for "the sisters." Other female living quarters include Howard and Byrd Halls. Williams Hall is one male, freshman unit. Langston Hall is the living quarters for honor students. Puryear Hall (for men) also serves as a home for Army ROTC students. More than 1,500 commissioned officers have graduated from VSU over a 50-year period. At Commencement exercises you're always treated to the grand entry of marching students in uniform.

Campus Life

VSU has over 60 organizations, clubs, and special-interest groups on campus. There are 10 major fraternities and sororities available, from Delta Sigma Theta to Omega Psi Phi, for example. Other outlets include a marching band, drama club, Betterment of Brothers and Sisters, NAACP, Big Brothers/Big Sisters, Baptist Student Union, ROTC band, Muslim Student Association, Trojan Cheerleaders, *The Virginia Statesman* (school newspaper), Orchesis Dance Group, New Generation Campus Ministries, and a debate team.

Varsity sports (CIAA Conference) also are popular on campus. VSU plays teams such as Bowie State, North Carolina Central, and Johnson C. Smith in football and basketball. The school has Rogers Stadium, an Olympic-size swimming pool, tennis courts, a dance studio, a gym, and other recreational facilities.

Major events on campus include Homecoming, Commencement, Honors Week (Nikki Giovanni was a keynote speaker), and VSU Day.

Academic Realities

Since 1995, VSU has restructured its offerings, reducing its schools from seven to four. Now there are the Schools of Business, Science and Technology, Education, and Arts and Sciences. The most popular majors (out of 27 degree areas you can pick) are: Business (22%), Education and Sociology (about 10% each), Psychology (7%), and Political Science (5%). Here's one sampling of recent student enrollment in specific areas: Management and Marketing (366), Sociology and Social Work (342), Accounting (224), Psychology (196), English and Literature (192), Political Science (191), Engineering Technology (132), Hotel Management (69), and Chemistry (26).

Getting In

The acceptance rate of students who apply to VSU is about 86%. In a recent year 2,561 students applied and 2,194 students were accepted. Eventually 872 enrolled. Since 1995 the enrollment at Virginia State University has increased by about 8%, and interest in the school is likely to continue. The average SAT scores usually are in the 810 to 840 range. Most students are Virginians. In the year noted, here's a sample breakdown: in-state (520 students), New York (133), New Jersey (58), Maryland (42), Pennsylvania (39), Connecticut (17), and the District of Columbia (16).

**VIRGINIA UNION
UNIVERSITY**

c/o Director of Admissions
1500 North Lombardy Street
Richmond, VA 23220
(804) 257-5856
Web site: www.vuu.edu

Application deadline: rolling
1999–2000 tuition: $9,110;
   room and board, $4,120

"As we review applicants, we consider more than grade point averages; we look at [a] prospective student's character and at his or her demonstrated interest in person growth."

—VUU Admissions

College Ranking

Virginia Union is an academically sound school and a good "need a second chance" option for black students.

The Campus

Private Virginia Union is in Richmond, the capital of the state. The climate is described as "mild and healthful." This urban campus is on 100 acres in the city's Northside section. There are 18 buildings (some are Historic Landmarks), including residences. Women can live at Hartshorn, MacVicar, or Newan Halls. The coed and honor dorm is named "Huntley." Males only live at Storer Hall. You can live off campus after your freshman year. You are minutes from downtown, and Colonial Williamsburg is an hour's drive away.

Campus Life

The major fraternities and sororities (from Alpha Kappa Alpha to Zeta Phi Beta) are very active. Also, there are more than 50 clubs and organizations on campus. Students are encouraged to attend events such as the President's Reception, Coronation Ball, Winter Concert, Visiting Lectures Series, and Parents' Weekend. Off campus, there are many cultural advantages, including museums, theaters, concerts, restaurants, and clubs. Twice a year there are career fairs with more than 100 employers available for interviews. Intercollegiate sports also are an important part of life at VUU.

Academic Realities

At VVU there are about 1,100 full-time students. They enroll in either the School of Arts and Sciences or the Sydney Lewis Business School. Students can earn degrees in 27 different areas, including business, engineering, biology, education, music, philosophy, and religion. The most popular majors are Business (30%), Education (12%), Biology and English (10% each), and Psychology (9%). Each year, approximately 150 students are awarded degrees. Graduates have gone on to medical (Albert Einstein, Meharry), law (University of Virginia, Howard), business, and other graduate schools. Famous graduates include NBA star Charles Oakley and former Governor of Virginia L. Douglas Wilder.

Students are encouraged to participate in the school's cooperative education program (work/study). Also, there's ROTC. Popular gathering spots on campus are the L. Douglas Wilder Library, with more than 148,000 volumes and "The Square" (patio) in front of the Henderson Center. There you will get to see step shows, musical performances and concerts, and Homecoming ceremonies.

Getting In

The acceptance rate at VUU is about 97%. The average SAT average is about 700, ACT 15. You can get a "second chance" fit here and apply online. About 52% of the students are from Virginia, while the rest arrive from about 27 states and four foreign countries.

CHAPTER 17

BLACK ARTS

Colleges of Art, Film, and the Performing Arts

Many African American students have interest and talent in the arts and are intent on pursuing their career goals and aspirations. Often they consider colleges and professional schools that have majors in their fields of interest. These students and their parents generally have concerns about making a living, also known as "the starving artist syndrome," and how to maximize their chances for stardom or acclaim. There are, too, other considerations (both good and bad) that have to do with such a career choice. Many such students won't be deferred, can't live without expressing themselves creatively, and it's a no-brainer. They are "going for it" no matter what the odds might be.

As they pursue their dreams, some students hedge their bets by seeking related degrees or certificates in teaching or other areas. It's general knowledge that some of these students (with a bachelor's degree in Fine Arts, most likely), do eventually go on to law, business, and medical schools. Possibilities abound. Great numbers of colleges have sterling reputations for "birthing stars." If you go to Juilliard School, you'll see that Wynton Marsalis is a graduate. Holly Robinson and Robin Givens (actresses) are graduates of Sarah Lawrence. Angela Bassett (actress) hails from Yale. So does filmmaker Warrington Hudling. Spike Lee is from Morehouse and New York University. Singer/actress Vanessa Williams is from Syracuse. Debbie Allen (actress, dancer, and choreographer) is a Howard University graduate. Wesley Snipes (actor) and Ma$e (rapper) are from SUNY Purchase, a state school with both art and performing arts majors.

A number of the schools profiled in this chapter are major universities with very strong art and performing arts divisions. Sometimes the number of students enrolled at these schools is relatively small and can be overlooked by counselors. For example, Carnegie Mellon (for fine arts) and Yale (for drama), would be cited by experts as excellent places to learn your craft. Those colleges offer an oasis for talented and determined students. At Carnegie Mellon, which has approximately 4,800 full-time students, there there are only a select 200 or so studying art. If you investigate, you find that there are other art, film, and performing arts gems. At Howard there are about 180 students studying art. At the University of Michigan at Ann Arbor (with more than 23,000 full-time students), only about 500 study art annually. At Florida State there are only 20 to 25 students in its Professional Actor Training Program (PATP). Yes, some of the big-name and prestige colleges can be vital and respected arts resources. You've got to read on if you have a dream and are not fazed by the sometimes daunting odds of making it.

The profiles presented in this chapter are of a small group of schools with programs that have opened doorways in regard to the arts. Some are schools within larger universities; some are small, specialized schools. All are highly regarded. Review the profiles that follow, and write for the catalogs (while requesting information about your desired area of interest).

Good luck, maybe you'll be the next Judith Jamison, Wesley Snipes, or Jacob Lawrence.

ART SCHOOLS

THE COOPER UNION FOR THE ADVANCEMENT OF SCIENCE AND ART

30 Cooper Square
New York, NY 10003
(212) 353-4120
Web site: www.cooper.edu

Cooper Union is in the Greenwich Village section of Manhattan, New York City. This is the highly regarded engineering and art school that makes all the "best buy" lists. Gain admission and you're awarded a full-tuition scholarship. At Cooper there are about 990 undergraduates each year, with approximately 250 visual arts majors. About 5% are African American. January 10th is the application deadline.

Art students can pursue majors in Painting, Printmaking, Sculpture, Graphic Design, Film/Video, Photography, and Calligraphy. To get in, however, is the hardest part. Unlike most art schools, a stellar and rigorous academic record really matters. Your SAT scores and your high school record must be very strong. An "outstanding" portfolio is necessary, as well a strong showing on a take-home exam that includes five or six "projects." You've got about a month to create something good enough to impress the admissions folks.

Here you'll find state-of-the-art facilities, including studios and computer labs. You'll learn to silkscreen, do litho work, and more. After freshman year you'll be assigned your own studio space. Also, you'll eventually get a chance to intern at New York City museums and art galleries.

You have Greenwich Village, SoHo, and the wonders of cultural Manhattan to explore. You won't exhaust or get to visit every chic café, restaurant, or theater. New York's creative and cultural outlets are limitless. There are Lincoln Center, Radio City Music Hall, boutiques, and fashionable shops galore. You've got, too, more than 50 campus clubs to consider when you're not in skylighted rooms learning your craft or listening to artists in residence.

The Bachelor of Fine Arts degree is awarded.

FASHION INSTITUTE OF TECHNOLOGY

Seventh Avenue and 27th Street
New York, NY 10001-5992
(212) 217-7675
(800) GO-to-FIT
Web site: www.fit.edu

FIT, as it's commonly called, is an art school that places a strong emphasis on the world of fashion and its needs. At one time it was simply a fashion college, but today this internationally known school of art and design has stretched its wings. Beyond programs in fashion you can study advertising design, illustration, packaging and interior design, restoration, and toy design. If fashion is your thing, there are fashion design, fabric styling, fashion buying and merchandising, fashion management and marketing, and more. A plus, too, is FIT's location. It's in the heart of an area where the fashion community and industries flourish. Students are trained to enter the fashion world at a creative and/or business level.

The majors are Business/Merchandising Management (52%), Visual Arts/Fashion Design (40%), and Engineering Technologies (8%).

To gain admission to FIT, which is on eight acres of concrete in Manhattan, you should possess artistic talent and a "level head." With your school record, a portfolio must be presented, as well as an essay. Once in, there are eight modern buildings, including residence halls, that await your use. In a recent year 1,973 students applied and 1,417 were admitted. Eventually 996 enrolled. A total of 12% of the students are African American. At last count there were 5,537 full-time students—4,434 women, and 1,103 men. About 16% of the students are from out of state, and 10% from other countries. About 21% of the students live in FIT apartments or dormitories, but most students commute.

At FIT there is a museum, textile and costume collection, studios, a lighting lab, and computer-aided design and communications facilities. There are also about 60 clubs, organizations, and special-interest groups on campus.

INDIANA UNIVERSITY (HERRON SCHOOL OF ART)	1701 North Pennsylvania Street Indianapolis, IN 46202 (317) 923-3651 Web site: www.iupui.edu

The Herron School of Art, though part of public Indiana University, has retained its own identity. It's been around for more than 90 years. The school is about three miles from downtown Indianapolis, the Indianapolis Museum of Art, and Union Station. It's close, also, to the main Indiana–Purdue University campuses, where you'll find that 11% of the students are African American. There are 500 undergraduates studying art at Herron, with about 170 new freshmen arriving yearly. These students can pursue study in painting, ceramics, printmaking, sculpture, wood, graphic design, photography, commercial art, and more. If they wish, they can also major in Art Education or Art History. The faculty includes 45 full- or part-time practicing artists. The student-to-teacher ratio is 9:1.

To gain admission, students must present a portfolio of 10 to 15 pieces of art. This work can be brought to the Admissions Office or mailed in a study binder. There is a required interview. Applications can be mailed between January and July of the entry year. Residence halls are available.

A Bachelor of Fine Arts degree is awarded, or a B.A. in either Education or Art History.

PARSONS SCHOOL OF DESIGN

66 Fifth Avenue
New York, NY 10011
(212) 229-8910; (800) 252-0852
Web site: www.parsons.newschool.edu

Parsons is an internationally known art school that aims to train "tomorrow's art and design professionals." Through many of the students take those traditional majors of painting and sculpture, there is a very heavy emphasis on art in the real world. On one hand, you might work with wood, glass, clay, and paper, and on the other hand, there's talk of marketing and the great advertising agencies. Here you can take courses in product and graphic design, creative and commercial photography, layout and production, illustration, fashion, and interior design as well as art education. And this is just a sampling of possibilities. A plus is that besides the artwork, you'll get a chance to take your academic courses at the New School for Social Research, a well-known college only blocks away.

Parsons has state-of-the-art facilities, studios, and equipment. The fashion design and marketing departments are in the David Schwartz Fashion Education Center, in the center of New York's garment district. At the main location is Manhattan's largest public gallery. As you enter the school, you can veer left and look at some stunning work.

Parsons has more than 1,700 full-time students. Approximately 3% are African American. If you live within 200 miles of the school you must present an original portfolio and have a personal interview. If you live farther away, a slide portfolio in a plastic sleeve is okay. Generally your work should be in "various media and styles." A take-home exam is required.

Students are delighted that the campus is near New York's Greenwich Village. In any direction, you'll find fashionable shops, restaurants, boutiques, and more. New York University, famed Broadway, Madison Square Garden, and the world of New York's concerts and industries are at your disposal.

A Bachelor of Fine Arts degree. is offered.

PRATT INSTITUTE

200 Willoughby Avenue
Brooklyn, NY 11205
(718) 636-3669
Web site: www.pratt.edu

Pratt Institute is a world-renowned art school. Located on 25 acres in Brooklyn's historic Clinton Hill section, there are 22 buildings, including an "advanced" computer arts center. Each year the surrounding community becomes more and more chic, with new cafés, small shops, and street-by-street renovations. Students are just a subway ride away from New York's Manhattan and its museums, Broadway, galleries, and design and business firms.

Students at Pratt can study painting, sculpture, printmaking, ceramics, jewelry/metals, fibers/textiles, illustration, graphic design, film/video, animation, photography, package design, fashion design and merchandising, art history, art education, architecture, and more. There are more than 130 faculty members, with a teacher-to-student ratio of 1:13.

To gain acceptance, students must present a portfolio in person or send slides. In the past, you had to draw a self-portrait as well as complete at least two other specific assignments. If you live within 150 miles of the school, an interview is suggested. An essay and recommendations also are required. Note that besides being an art school, there's a school of architecture here. When applying, follow the instructions on your application.

In a recent year 902 art students applied to Pratt and 570 were accepted; 409 freshman art students enrolled. The full-time student body usually is about 2,104 students, including students of architecture. A total of 8% of the students are African American, and 20% are international students. For admission, the application deadline is February 1.

Students at Pratt intern at companies such as ABC, Time-Life, and the Museum of Modern Art. There are endless work/study possibilities. The facilities at Pratt are state-of-the-art. There's a 4,000-square-foot gallery, and a building for sculpture, ceramics, and printmaking. Students also have semiprivate and private studio space. On campus there are five residences. You'll have a social life. There are clubs (art, radio, yearbook), organizations (eight), and special-interest groups (24) available.

A Bachelor of Fine Arts degree is awarded as well as B.A. and B.S. degrees in Art History and Art Education.

RHODE ISLAND SCHOOL OF DESIGN	2 College Street Providence, RI 02903 (401) 454-6300 Web site: www.risd.edu

Just a stroll away from Brown University, in the College Hill area of Providence, the Rhode Island School of Design is considered one of the most prestigious art schools in the country. Students at RISD can study painting, printmaking, film/video, photography, graphic design, architecture, sculpture, industrial design, art education, and more. There are 40 buildings, all with state-of-the-art facilities. The nearly 770 full-time undergraduates have studios, dark-rooms, ceramic kilns, glass furnaces, printing equipment, and more to work with. Besides a 50,000-square-foot Design Center, the RISD Museum of Art, and art galleries, there is a 600-seat theater. You can also cross-register at the Ivy school Brown. Each year, more than 200 artists, critics and/or lecturers visit the campus.

To get into RISD (approximately 1,850 usually apply, with about 860 accepts), you must present an original portfolio or send slides. Beyond that requirement you must forward several recommendations, an essay, and also present three actual renderings, using a medium pencil. About 370 freshman will eventually enroll. You'll be given instructions on the RISD application. The application deadline is January 21, unless you are applying for early admission, then it's December 15.

Students at RISD have more than 60 student-run organizations to choose from. There's an Artist's Ball on Halloween, and many activities that are shared with students at Brown. The faculty members are practicing artists. The professor-to-student ratio is about 7:1. Off campus, you have theaters, clubs, restaurants, and other cultural outlets. If you wish, you can head to the Tillinghast Estate, a 33-acre recreational area for students on Narragansett Bay. There you can visit the beach.

RINGLING SCHOOL OF ART AND DESIGN

2700 North Tamiami Trail
Sarasota, FL 34234
(813) 351-4614
Web site: www.rsad.edu

This highly regarded art school is in Sarasota, Florida. Students have the use of 18 buildings, with studios for painting, sculpture, printmaking, graphic design, and photography (with the necessary darkrooms and labs). Computer animation also is taught here, with the necessary equipment for state-of-the-art work. Students showcase their work in the 3,000-square-foot Selby Gallery.

To get in, you must forward a portfolio of 10 slides, an essay, and recommendations. In a given year about 660 students apply and 450 are accepted. Of this total, about 230 enroll. Approximately 3% of the students are African American. There is a rolling deadline, and SAT and other test scores are optional. At Ringling, students study art under practicing artists. Other faculty members teach the humanities and related courses. The final degree will be a Bachelor of Fine Arts. This is a "professional" school.

Ringling is near theaters, ballet and opera companies, as well as the John and Mabel Ringling Museum of Art. Students also enjoy the beaches, swimming, horseback riding, and art festivals. There are resident halls.

RUTGERS, THE STATE UNIVERSITY OF NEW JERSEY (MASON GROSS SCHOOL OF THE ARTS)

358 George Street
New Brunswick, NJ 08901
(908) 445-3370
Web site: www.rutgers.edu

The Mason Gross School of Arts (MGSA) is a small art school in New Brunswick, New Jersey. The school is part of the larger Rutgers campuses, which include four towns and cities and well over 30,000 students. At Mason there are only about 200 undergraduates, with about 45 freshmen being admitted each year. It's a very competitive admit. In a recent year 349 aspiring artists applied and 96 were accepted.

Students can pursue study in painting, ceramics, sculpture, film/video, illustration, graphic design, photography, and other areas. Your studio and artistic skills are honed, but there is also a lot of emphasis on theory and critical analysis. Study-abroad programs are offered in England, France, Italy, Spain, and Portugal.

To gain admission, students must submit at least 20 pieces of original artwork. You must also include a one-page essay/statement about your goals and background. If you reside in the state, you will be asked to bring your portfolio when you appear for an interview. If you are an out-of-town applicant, you can send slides by mail. The application deadline is February 15.

The new building (1995) is in downtown New Brunswick. It has state-of-the-art facilities, including four painting areas, a darkroom, photo classrooms, film/video studios, computer workstations, a theater, and sculpture tables. Also, there is equipment and supplies for welding and ceramics. The Rutgers Center for Innovative Printmaking also is a resource. Students have six galleries for presentations. Art students can avail themselves of the hundreds of clubs, organizations, special-interest groups, and related activities at Rutgers, a public university. At the Rutgers campuses African Americans usually make up 8% to 22% of the student body count.

A Bachelor of Fine Arts is awarded, or a B.A. degree (in Art History or Education) from either the Rutgers, Livingston, Douglas, or University College branches.

SCHOOL OF THE ART INSTITUTE OF CHICAGO	37 South Wabash Avenue Chicago, IL 60603-3103 (800) 232-7242; (312) 899-5100 Web site: www.artic.edu

SAIC is a highly regarded school of art. It's in the downtown Chicago Loop area. Here you'll find all of the most important theaters, galleries, and cultural outlets. The school is part of that scene, and the public is aware of the school's legacy and presence. After all, the Art Institute of Chicago also serves as an internationally acclaimed museum. At this art school there are nearly 1,500 talented and aspiring artists "in house."

To get in you must present an original portfolio of 15 samples or slides for review. An essay and recommendations also are necessary. Portfolio reviews and interviews in a number of cities is also an option. Of the full-time students, approximately 5% are African American. Call for information. Application deadlines are March 15 (fall) and November 15 (spring).

This school has comprehensive facilities for all areas, including painting, ceramics, fibers/textures, sculpture, film/video, and photography. Fashion design, interior architecture, and majors such as Art Education, Art Therapy, and Art History also are available. Students can (and do) work in the school's studios, darkrooms, and labs around the clock. There are single-room residence halls with kitchens. For recreation, students have the city's professional art world at their fingertips. Just jump on Chicago's EL train.

SCHOOL OF VISUAL ARTS	Director of Admissions 209 East 23rd Street New York, NY 10010 (212) 592-2116 Web site: www.schoolofvisualarts.edu

The School of Visual Arts, the largest art school in the United States, is in midtown Manhattan. A cluster of five buildings comprise the school, and there are about 2,700 full-time undergraduate students. Of this total, approximately 700 new freshman arrive each year. SVA has students from 40 states and 23 countries. African Americans are 5% of the body count.

Students study painting, sculpture, printmaking, advertising and graphic design, film/video, animation, computer graphics, cartooning, art therapy, and more. At SVA there is a state-of-the-art computer art center, a Stop-Motion Control Studio, Oxberry stands, 69 Bolex cameras, "flatbed suites" for post production, an Avid lab, rows of IBM-compatible PCs, a Digital

Imaging Center, movie cameras (8 and 16mm), silicon graphics stations, book and slide libraries, and studio space and workstations. The library has 95,000 art slides and a picture collection of more than 250,000.

To apply, students must present a portfolio of 10 to 15 pieces of artwork. If the student lives within 250 miles of New York City, it is desired that he or she report for an interview and work presentation. Beyond that distance (or by arrangement), slides can be sent by mail. A high school transcript, essay, and recommendations also must be presented with the application. The application deadline is March 17. SVA housing for about 600 students is available.

SVA aims to "educate the artists and designers of today" to meet the challenges of the "competitive market." Students are put in tune with the "many studios, galleries, and museums nearby" as they train. The world and needs of design firms and advertising agencies are part of this orientation. The school says that "85% of the young men and women who graduate from SVA are working in their field within one year." Not surprisingly, the faculty is composed of working professionals. SVA has a Visual Arts Museum and eight student galleries, including one in SoHo for student exhibitions. The Bachelor of Fine Arts degree is awarded. Besides taking courses in their majors, these future "working professionals" (generally) must take 12 credits in art history and 32 credits in the liberal arts. There is also an art education track for students interested in teaching.

The most popular group on campus is the Visual Arts Association, but there's a Black Student Union and African American Artists organizations. "The total mix," one student says, "adds to a very good experience in this, the art and design capital of the universe."

TEMPLE UNIVERSITY (TYLER SCHOOL OF ART)	7725 Penrose Avenue Elkins Park, PA 19027 (215) 782-ARTS Web site: www.temple.edu

The Tyler School of Art is part of Temple University but is in suburban Elkins Park, which is about two miles from the facilities of the main campus. Outside Philadelphia, the school occupies 16 acres. Although Temple has a full body count of more than 14,000 undergraduates (28% African Americans), the Tyler School has only about 625 art students. They experience the "intimacy of an art community."

Students can study painting, ceramics, sculpture, fibers/fabric design, illustration, graphic and visual design, photography, printmaking, art education, and more. Students will work with wood, metals, glass, plastics, or any combination of materials. The faculty-to-student radio is about 1:11. The teachers are all practicing artists, some "world-renowned."

To gain an accept, students must present a portfolio for review. Generally, 15 to 20 pieces of original artwork should be forwarded. Slides may be sent by mail, but a personal interview is encouraged. There are "rolling" admissions, but a March 29 deadline is desirable.

At Tyler there are computer labs and modern work studios. Also, there are three galleries and an auditorium.

The Bachelor of Fine Arts degree is awarded, and a Bachelor of Science degree in Education from the College of Arts and Sciences.

UNIVERSITY OF THE ARTS	320 South Broad Street Philadelphia, PA 19102 (215) 875-1100; (800) 616-ARTS Web site: www.libertynet.org/~uarts

The University of the Arts has one of the most beautiful college catalogs we've ever seen. The cover is colorful, well designed, and has a cutout. Inside that window you can see the upper bodies of students, many of color. When you lift the cover the surprise is that you discover hundreds of students looking like a crowd out of the movie, *Fame*.

The University of the Arts is located in the heart of Philadelphia. Students can study art, including painting, ceramics, sculpture, photography, graphic design, film/video, animation, printmaking, and more. On campus are state-of-the-art facilities that include darkrooms, typography and computer labs, glass/ceramic kilns, and a bookbinding and Oxberry animation studio. Of approximately 1,200 students, about 700 are art majors. Approximately 10% are African American. The Bachelor of Fine Arts degree is awarded.

Generally there are about 100 Drama majors, 115 Music majors (Andre Watts is a graduate), and 170 Dance majors (Judith Jamison is a graduate). These students have the use of several theaters, including the 100-seat "black box," and the 1,660-seat Shubert Theater. Six wood dance floors are available. A Bachelor of Theater, of Music, and of Dance degrees are awarded.

Art students must present 10 to 20 pieces of original work for consideration. To gain admission to the noted Dance, Music, and Theater departments, auditions are held on campus from October to July. Auditions are also held at regional locations. Call the school for information. VHS formatted videotapes of students performing also can be submitted if need be, after consulting with the school. For all divisions, there is on-campus housing.

Exhibitions and performances of all kinds are held throughout the year. Students take advantage of historic Philly, where there are museums, theaters, concert halls, and all kinds of cultural outlets.

UNIVERSITY OF HARTFORD (HARTFORD SCHOOL OF ART)	200 Bloomfield Avenue West Hartford, CT 06117 (203) 768-4393 Web site: www.hartford.edu

The Hartford School of Art is on the 200-acre campus of the University of Hartford. The school is about two miles from many Hartford museums and the downtown area. The School of Art is a 50,000-square-foot facility, with state-of-the-art studios, labs, and equipment. Here you'll find a wood shop, kilns, welding and stone carving stations, and printmaking tools (for silkscreen, etching, lithography, offset block printing, and more). Also, there are video studios, two galleries (one, the Joseloff Gallery, also serves as an auditorium), and student workstations. The Anne Bunce Cheney Library has more than 10,000 art books. More than 40,000 slides are available for student use.

The University of Hartford has more than 4,100 full-time students, but generally the School of Art accommodates only about 360 students, with approximately 103 freshmen arriving yearly. Students can pursue study in painting, ceramics, sculpture, metalsmithing, printmaking, photography, film/video, illustration, fibers, graphic design, and art history. To gain admission, students must present a portfolio of 15 to 20 pieces of original work. The presentation can include pictures, photos of 3-D work, and/or videotape cassettes. An SAT score, essay, and recommendations also are required. Although a personal presentation/interview is preferred, you can forward slides by mail. Contact the Admissions Office for an appointment. The deadline is rolling, with December 1 for early decision. Dorms are available, including "art apartments."

Internships and cooperative programs are available at nearby corporations, museums, and galleries. A Bachelor of Fine Arts degree is awarded.

THE MUSIC SCHOOLS

BERKLEE COLLEGE OF MUSIC	1140 Boylston Street Boston, MA 02215 (617) 266-1400; (800) 421-0084 Web site: www.berklee.edu

Are you interested in jazz or popular music? Or you would like to step into the shoes of Quincy Jones or Branford Marsalis, both of whom are graduates? Well, the Berklee College of Music, in the historic Back Bay section of Boston, may be the school for you. There is training in just about all instruments except the harp and the harpsichord. Here, you can perfect your skills while learning about composition and how to score movies. You can learn, too, about the business of electronic music, and even study jazz technique and theory. The emphasis is on "contemporary musical idioms."

To get in you must submit an audiotape or videotape that can run for more than 20 minutes. Recommendations, an essay, academic record, and musical background and activities are important. Usually there are about 2,700 undergraduates (70% from out of state), with more than 300 full- and part-time faculty members, many practicing musicians. There is rolling admissions until March for the fall term, but it would be wise to get in your application and FAFSA about January 1 for scholarship consideration. To get a scholarship, you must audition in person in Boston or at another "regional" location. A majority of the arriving students reside on campus. Over 25% of the aspiring artists arrive from 70 countries, including Italy, Japan, Germany, Canada, and Brazil. A little over 5% of the students are African American. At Berklee there's the Concert Performance Center with 1,200 seats. From this location students and faculty will give more than 200 concerts a year. At the CPC there are state-of-the-art equipment and facilities. There are recording studios, synthesizer and film scoring laboratories, as well as 75 private-instruction studios, 40 ensemble rooms, and 250 practice rooms. You will receive a Bachelor's degree in Music after completing a Core Music Curriculum (e.g., a study of harmony, notation, and "ear training"). You must also complete a "general education" track that includes courses in the humanities, writing, and more.

Berklee is a member of the Professional Arts Consortium (ProArts), which includes schools such as the Boston Conservatory, Emerson College, and the Massachusetts College of Art. If you wish, you can take courses at these schools, and those of the other members. Berklee is located close to world-class performing centers such as Symphony Hall and the Wang Center in Boston. After a short ride on public transportation, you're part of the cultural hot spot of Boston.

On campus, the Student Organization and Activities Program (SOAP) will keep you busy with unending clubs and special-interest outlets. Our guess is that you'll probably find the Black Student Union and head to the reggae, jazz, and other clubs in the vicinity.

CLEVELAND INSTITUTE OF MUSIC

11021 East Boulevard
Cleveland, OH 44106
(216) 791-5000
Web site: www.cim.edu

The Cleveland Institute of Music, in Cleveland, is a small school that has nevertheless been listed as one of the superior music conservatories in the country. There are about 270 undergraduate students, with approximately 19% from abroad (e.g., Germany, Taiwan, China, and Japan). African Americans make up about 7% of the body count. At CIM there's a very strong emphasis on "orchestral training."

Students here get fine-tuned on orchestral instruments, including the piano, clarinet, bassoon, oboe, French horn, trumpet, viola, tuba, and guitar. Voice is also taught (song, oratorio, opera), along with composition, choral and orchestral conducting, music theory, audio recording, eurhythmics (dance), and music performance. Working closely with Case Western Reserve University, students can also play with wind and/or jazz ensembles. Many faculty members are members of the Cleveland Orchestra. Interestingly, CIM is the sponsor of the acclaimed biennial Cleveland International Piano Competition.

Students take repertoire classes, give recitals, and have the use of electronic music studios, audio recording facilities, and 16,000 records, tapes, and CDs. Kulas Hall is the school's concert auditorium. It has two Steinway grand pianos. Cutter House is the coed residence.

Students must audition between February and early March. Applicants must also take a Music Theory and Music History assessment exam. In some cases an audiotape or videotape can be submitted. The application deadline is December 15.

Most students are awarded a Bachelor of Music degree. A smaller number earn a Bachelor of Science in Music Education diploma.

THE JUILLIARD SCHOOL

60 Lincoln Center Plaza
New York, NY 10023
(212) 799-5000
Web site: www.juilliard.edu

Well, if it was good enough for Wynton Marsalis, shouldn't you take a look? When you talk about the performing arts, The Juilliard School might be one of the most famous and prestigious schools in the world. Most college guides don't even mention Juilliard because it's a specialty school. It may be a secret to some, but to the informed, bachelor's degrees in the arts—and careers—are to be had at this prestigious school.

The school's campus is part of the enormous Lincoln Center for the Performing Arts, on the Upper West Side of Manhattan. From your room in the Meredith Wilson Residence Hall next door, you can walk to New York Philharmonic and the Metropolitan Opera House. From your window, you can see the Vivian Beaumont and New York State Theaters. Talk about artists in residence! You are there, living it.

On campus are 200-plus pianos, 84 practice rooms (22 in the resident halls), 34 private studios (15 in two-story setups), classrooms, and the Lila Acheson Wallace Library (with its two-story reading rooms). Year long, you'll practice and perform. And oh, you'll eat at the SAB cafeteria in the Samuel B. and David Rose Building adjacent to Juilliard.

There'll be student recitals at Alice Tully and the 278-seat Paul Recital Halls. Student soloists, ensembles, and orchestras will perform. There will be, too, both small and full-scale theater and dance productions. The calendar for family, friends, and the public will be full. Recreation? It's called *practice!*

At Juilliard there are Divisions of Music, Dance, and Drama. Sure, you should be a good student but, first and foremost, you are a student of the arts. It's a professional school. Study is intense, sometimes lasting all day and deep into the night. When you're finished you'll have 24 credits in the liberal arts, and the bulk of your other credits in your majors and minors.

In dance, students learn ballet, modern dance, ballroom dance, dance composition, and history, as well as stagecraft and production. One teacher is Carolyn Adams, who was the cofounder of the Harlem Dance Studio. The drama students will learn "voice and speech," "movement," "audition techniques," and different acting styles and theories—for example, the "Alexander" and "Suzuki" approaches, to name just two. Students will be taught to refine a phrase or a gesture. Also, singing and comedy are taught as part of the dramatic approach.

In music, there's an array of instruments, techniques, and theory taught. And yes, there's a lot of emphasis on "orchestral instruments" such as the harp, violin, and trumpet. Does all this work? Besides Marsalis, who is listed as a faculty member, graduates include Robin Williams and Patti Lupone. Just check out the Juilliard Hall of Fame wall of photos. Yes, it's where Christopher Reeve got his start. And sure, that's Luciano Pavarotti, who's taught "master classes."

Getting the nod is not easy. Admission or denial are based on your performance at a "competitive audition" before a committee of faculty and professors. At Juilliard they don't ask for SAT or ACT scores. Your talent level must be exceptional, with every indication that you will most likely excel in your field. The numbers tell the story. In a recent year 1,522 students auditioned, but only 123 made the cut. That's a tougher percentage than applicants to Harvard must face. At Juilliard there are only about 460 full-time students—12% African American—enrolled at any given time. The training and focus on technical mastery are, after all, personal and individualized.

MANHATTAN SCHOOL OF MUSIC	120 Claremont Avenue New York, NY 10027-4698 (212) 749-2802 Web site: www.msmnyc.edu

When the auditions are over, only about 52% will be given good news. In a recent class, 568 students applied, but only 204 were accepted. It's no walkover, and talent will matter here.

Besides your sterling musical performance, you'll need to present a strong academic record and write an essay. For a March audition your application should arrive before December 15. For a May audition, forward it by March 15. If you live outside North America or play the tuba, bass, or are a cellist, you can submit audiotapes or videotapes. Accepted students can cross-register at Barnard College, or eventually spend a semester at the Royal Conservatory in Toronto, Canada.

At the Manhattan School of Music you'll get to study with faculty members who have international reputations. There are majors in Jazz (bassist Ron Carter is a graduate), Piano/Organ, Voice, and Instruments (String, Wind, and Percussion). Some of these instruments include the violin, classical guitar, harpsichord, vibraphone, organ, clarinet, French horn, oboe, flute, and bassoon. Note that some of Juilliard's faculty also teach at MSM.

MSM has state-of-the-art equipment and facilities. There's Borden Auditorium, a 1,000-seat theater. Hubbard Hall is a 250-seat recital hall with an organ. There's a 60-seat recital room in Pforzheimer Hall. A recording studio is in Myers Hall.

At the MSM there are 431 full-time undergraduates from 36 states, including 5% who are African American. About a third of the students are from other countries: England, Israel, Japan, Germany, Canada, and elsewhere. About 100 students reside in campus "assigned" housing. The others commute. There are about 250 full- and part-time faculty members. To get your Bachelor of Music degree you must perform at a "senior's recital." If you are a composer you must complete an original symphonic work. Students also must complete some core requirements in the humanities, which generally include eight courses. Note that the most popular majors are Voice (23%), Commercial Jazz (21%), and Piano (21%).

Some of the student organizations on campus include the Pan-American Student Union; Composers Now, a choral group; and a dozen or more musical clubs. Off campus, the world of Manhattan and the rest of New York City are available to you. There are Broadway, Lincoln Center, Radio City Music Hall, clubs, cafés, restaurants, museums, parks, and hundreds of other possibilities available to you. Enjoy!

FILM SCHOOLS

BARD COLLEGE

P.O. Box 5000
Annandale-on-Hudson, NY 12504
(914) 758-7472
Web site: www.bard.edu

Besides film, Bard also has programs in art, drama/dance, and photography. This is a "university without walls" to many. The students (about 1,150 full-time) are creative types who "love to think" and who particularly enjoy their 600-acre campus, where you're encouraged to use your imagination. It is one of the first small private schools in America, and you can see the Catskills and the Hudson from your dorm room. And the dorms are all said to have personality, one way or another. Shapes and sizes vary, from cottages to converted mansions. There are 70 buildings, including residences. You've got your trees here, flowers, and your ivy-covered walls. Now, try to imagine taking a year-long freshman seminar that takes you from Rome to modern Europe. You've got the idea. In your second year you'll write an "educational autobiography," outline your objectives, and pick a major. With Bard being picked annually as a top "best national liberal arts college," you know something is working.

At Bard, the school of actor Chevy Chase, about 75 students major in Film, seeking that B.A. The Film and Electronic Arts Program, emphasizes production and editing, often "experimental." The courses will be taught by working media artists. The students will use 16mm production equipment, including screening rooms, sound transfer equipment, JVC and S-VHS cameras, animation stands, and more. Screenwriting, documentary work, and animation tracks are available. Internships can be had.

The acceptance rate for all students at Bard is about 51%. In a recent year 2,283 applied and 1,155 were accepted. A total of 76% of the students arrive from out of state and 49 countries. The school doesn't require SAT or ACT scores but looks for students who are academically strong and creative. All freshmen must reside on campus. The female-to-male ratio is 41:59. About 3% of the enrollees are African American. Here there is the Bard Black Student Organization. There's also a varsity sports program, including basketball, cross-country, swimming, rugby, and other sports. To gain admission at Bard, an interview is required. Scholarships are a possibility.

CALIFORNIA COLLEGE OF ARTS AND CRAFTS	5212 Broadway Oakland, CA 94618-1487 (510) 653-8118 Web site: www.ccac-art.edu

This school is said to be the "only regionally accredited school of art, architecture, and design on the West Coast." Fine arts and graphic design attract most of the students. Here we're focusing on the film and video department.

On the four-acre campus of the California College of Arts and Crafts, you'll marvel at the garden setting and the modern and Victorian structures. You're about three miles from the University of California at Berkeley. From the campus of CCAC you can see the city of San Francisco, the Golden Gate, and the hills of Marin County. A Bachelor of Fine Arts degree is awarded. The study emphasis for about 40 students out of about 870 is on creating "independent film and video projects." On campus, African American students make up only about 2% of the body count.

The school has the Oakland Gallery and sponsors a film series and festival. Students sometimes produce for cable television. Professional instructors guide you in the use of 16mm equipment and teach you production and postproduction theory. The film studios have Super-8 and 16mm cameras. There are editing systems, portapaks, and Sandin image processors.

To gain admission, students must present a portfolio, personal essay, and their school records. In a recent year, 274 students applied and 171 were accepted. The male-to-female ratio is 41:59. More than 83% of the students are from in-state, and only 6% (about 60 students) reside on campus. Most classes have fewer than 20 students. There are weekly student exhibitions and receptions.

CCAC has rolling admissions.

CALIFORNIA INSTITUTE OF THE ARTS	24700 McBean Parkway Valencia, CA 91355 (805) 255-1050 Web site: www.calarts.edu

Cal Arts is essentially an art school. There are also majors in Dance, Music (jazz), and Theater/Drama. Walt Disney founded the school in 1961. A key major is Graphic Design. Here, however, we're focusing on the Film and Video Department. The degree awarded is a Bachelor of Fine Arts. Each year there are about 700 students, including about 5% who are African American. Approximately 210 students are majoring in film and video areas. Very large numbers are studying animation, with about 30 into live action. The emphasis is to produce innovative films, with a hands-on approach. Generally, folks are learning experimental and character animation. Instructors with professional experience, including special effects, guide you.

Cal Arts, about 30 miles from Los Angeles, is on the crest of a rolling hill. The school overlooks the community of Valencia, and is on 60 acres of land. There are three buildings, including a modular theater, galleries, a library with 70,000 volumes, and residences. The faculty is composed of "working artists and eminent educators." The goal, for students, is artistic professionalism.

Cal Arts has a visiting professionals and artists program. It also sponsors a student film festival. Work by students is produced for cable and on-campus television. Students have the use of state-of-the-art equipment: screening and editing rooms, a video studio with CMX, animation labs, optical and video synthesizers, and a library. Super-8 and 16mm cameras are used. Internships are also a pivotal part of the program.

To gain admission, students must present a portfolio (or audition) and forward a "statement of purpose." In a recent year 1,124 students applied and 445 were accepted. The male-to-female ratio is about 60:40. Aspiring artists arrive from more than 54 states and 38 foreign counties. A majority live in campus housing. For interested students, there's a three-day orientation program.

At Cal Arts, talent and potential are the keys.

GEORGIA STATE UNIVERSITY	University Plaza 1 Park Place South Atlanta, GA 30303 (404) 651-2365 Web site: www.gsu.edu

Georgia State is located in the middle of Atlanta. It is on 57 acres, and has 45 buildings, including residences. With 18,000 full- and part-time students walking around, it sometimes gets crowded. GSU is big enough to be called a comprehensive university. At 30% of the student body count, African Americans are everywhere.

Not only are there six undergraduate colleges, but also there are 250 majors available. The most popular areas of study are business, education, and the health sciences. Students love the low cost—it's a public school with no tuition for state residents—and 94% of the students are residents of the state. Generally, we're getting a good vibe. There are organizations galore, including those that cater to our special needs and interests. There's the Black Student Alliance, Black Life and Culture Committee, Caribbean Students Association, the major black Greek-letter groups, and support services from the Office of Minority Affairs and Incept Orientation Program. Note, too, that there's an African American Studies Department.

At GSU there's a Department of Communications, which offers a B.A. in Film and Video (not to mention degrees in Theater and Journalism also). In the Film major there are about 160 students. These students will get involved with "Cinetest, a program of daily screenings." They will also listen to guest lecturers, be involved in an annual film festival, and create material for both on-campus, public, and commercial television stations. They will get to use professional cameras and related equipment, screening and editing rooms, animation stands, and will have access to a film/video library. Studying film history, theory, and criticism will also be part of their orientation.

Some of the courses that will be pivotal include A History of Motion Pictures, Contemporary Hollywood Cinema, American Film and TV Industries, Filmmaking 1, Documentary Film, Acting for the Camera, Postproduction, and African Americans in Film. Last, students will have an opportunity to intern.

To get into the film and video track, your admissions requirements will be higher than those of regularly admitted students. For example, the acceptance rate at GSU is about 60%. To gain admission to the small Communications Department, it's about 48%. A 3.0 GPA is desirable, as well as a score of a least 500 on the verbal section of the SAT. The undergraduate application deadline is rolling. For information about film and video try (404) 651-2000.

ROCHESTER INSTITUTE OF TECHNOLOGY	P.O. Box 9887 Rochester, NY 14623-0887 (716) 475-2411 Web site: www.rit.edu

RIT is generally known for its engineering emphasis and majors. Few realize that art/fine arts are also among their most popular concentrations. The Film and Video Department deserves attention.

The Rochester Institute is on 1,300 suburban acres and has more than 231 buildings including residences. It's a highly regarded school for technology-driven students, and there are more than 200 majors. Generally, we're talking about fields such as electrical and mechanical engineering. Options abound. You've got eight undergraduate schools that can take you, A to Z, in many directions: marketing, physician's assistant program. There's also a small College of Liberal Arts.

One quietly kept secret? You can get a Bachelor of Fine Arts in Film and Video. Although there are more than 8,000 full-time undergraduates, about 12% are pursuing Fine Arts degrees. Of that total, about 140 students are specifically honing their skills in the art of filmmaking. Students here get hands-on experience while working with professional cinematographers, film producers, and postproduction executives. Students learn about animation, documentary work, and "fiction narrative." Writing and directing are also factored into the course of study. The are internship possibilities, and work is produced for commercial television and cable. RIT sponsors visiting filmmakers' programs, film festivals, and encourages students to enter national competitions. RIT students have access to state-of-the-art equipment and facilities. There are Super-8 and 16mm cameras and screening, sound mix, and postproduction rooms. Also, there are "animation systems" and stands, computer graphics generators, a film library, and more.

To gain admission, students must present a portfolio, have good grades and SAT scores, and present a writing sample. In a recent year, 6,525 students applied to all programs and 5,109 were accepted. Although most students were interested in engineering (28%), and a good number in business (10%), artsy types are always on campus. About 21% of the students are fine arts or photography majors. More than 60% of the students are from out of state, and 55% reside on campus. The male-to-female ratio is 66:34. African Americans make up 4% of the body count. The admission/application deadline is rolling.

TISCH SCHOOL OF THE ARTS (NEW YORK UNIVERSITY)	721 Broadway New York, NY 10003 (212) 998-1900 Web site: www.nyu.edu

"Student profile: NYU student filmmakers have consistently earned the respect of industry professionals. Since 1992, seven Student Academy Award gold medals have been presented to NYU student freshmen."

—from the Tisch School catalog

"The department's Future Filmmakers Program identifies gifted high school students from groups traditionally underrepresented in the industry, and provides them with an intensive 12-week training program where they learn the craft of filmmaking."

—from the Tisch School guidebook

New York University, in Greenwich Village in New York City, is a top-rated national university; its Tisch School of the Arts has garnered its own reputation worldwide. Its film program is recognized internationally as the premier site for professionals in film, television, and radio. Students are required to perform "all crew positions (director, cinematographer, editor, etc.) as they produce works that are reviewed and evaluated by faculty and fellow students." This school delivers. Oliver Stone, Billy Crystal, Martin Brest, Chris Columbus, Joel Coen, Nancy Savoca, and Jonathan Kaplan are some of the distinguished undergraduate alums. Although this profile is focusing on that B.F.A. level, do note that students at the graduate level include Spike Lee, Martin Scorsese, Martha Coolidge, Ernest Dickerson, Ang Lee, Ron Maxwell, Susan Seidelman, and others. If you're seriously interested in making movies, this is a can-do-it-for-you school.

To get in is not easy. Generally, there are about 1,000 applicants to the undergraduate school. Fewer than 300 are accepted. You'll get a "creative review" after you forward your "audition portfolio," application, high school record, SAT scores, and recommendations. "Meaningful" extracurricular activities also are important. You should definitely write or call the Tisch School advising it of your interest in film and asking for application instructions. For fall entrance, all supporting materials should be on file by January 15. Early decision: November 15. Notification of your status usually occurs around April 1.

Once accepted, undergraduates will be offered training in all film production phases, including directing, producing, writing, even acting. You will learn about view editing, video post-production, and sound mixing. Another positive is that you will most likely intern at one of a host of companies or programs that utilize Tisch students: Paramount Pictures, Universal Pictures, the TriBeCa Film Center, *Saturday Night Live, Dateline NBC,* and any number of other independent and smaller companies. While you progress, you will have the use of state-of-the-art facilities. There are 25 film and video screening rooms, animation studios, 60 editing rooms, a cinema studies archive, television studios and film sound stages, and the University radio station, WNYU-FM. The faculty at Tisch includes Academy, Peabody, and Emmy Award winners and other stars of the industry.

The film students must complete, for example, a "seven-point, 16mm film production workshop" during one semester. Five short black-and-white films must be submitted by "the crew" of students, with each one rotating to get hands-on experience in all aspects of the project. Of course, students must also take courses in cinema studies and screenwriting. Last, there are humanities and related requirements, that must be fulfilled by attending NYU classes.

Graduates have signed with companies such as Warner Brothers, ICM, and CAA while still completing their degrees. Indeed, expect more news flashes like this: "Five NYU Filmmakers Capture Awards at 1999 Sundance Festival" and "Three NYU Filmmakers Awarded at the 26th Annual Student Academy Awards."

<table>
<tr><td>

UNIVERSITY OF SOUTHERN CALIFORNIA, UNIVERSITY PARK

</td><td>

Cinema-Television Student Affairs Office
Los Angeles, CA 90089-2111
(213) 740-2311
Web site: www.suc.edu

</td></tr>
</table>

What African American graduate can we point to here? Well, John Singleton. He wrote and directed *Boyz N the Hood, Poetic Justice, Rosewood,* even Michael Jackson's video for *Remember the Time.* While a student at the University of Southern California's film school, Singleton was signed by Creative Artists Agency. Other great alumni of USC include George Lucas of *Star Wars* fame, and other giants in the industry. The list of credits and work by graduates (that the school makes available) is outstanding.

USC's School of Cinema-Television was the first ever film school. Today the goal is to give students professional training in all aspects of film. It's not just an exercise. Although USC as a whole has an undergraduate enrollment of approximately 13,900 students, only about 400 of that count will study at the film school. Each year the admissions process is selective. To gain an accept, you need a strong academic record, a minimum 1000 score on the SAT (ACT 22), three recommendations, and a one-page "character profile" of yourself. You must also "briefly describe the most emotionally intense moment you have experienced." That can be no more than two pages. Last, your supplemental application must also include a list of your related art projects and accomplishments with short descriptions. No portfolio and/or tape is required. Truly, students will get an intense liberal arts education here, but cinema theory, hands-on production, and technique will be first and foremost.

The degrees that are offered include a Bachelor of Fine Arts in Filmic Writing (that was

Singleton's concentration), or a B.A. in Film/Video production, Still Photography, or Critical Studies. Students have the use of 35mm and 7mm screening rooms, computer and animation labs, editing suites, studios for sound mixing, a cassette/laser disc library, and more. Note that the Computer Animation Laboratory has produced material for IMAX films.

With the study framework, there are guest speakers, visits from film directors, screenwriters, cinematographers, and critics. The school has gotten support from such industry powers as Sony Entertainment, Hanna-Barbera, and Warner Brothers.

There's an African American Film Association run by students.

THEATER AND DANCE SCHOOLS

THE CATHOLIC UNIVERSITY OF AMERICA	620 Michigan Avenue, N.E. Washington, DC 20064 (202) 319-5305 Web site: www.cua.edu

Catholic University has been picked by experts as one of the "fifteen best colleges for the aspiring actor." It's a private school on 144 acres near the Capitol in D.C., with 50 buildings, including residences. There are seven undergraduate schools, including the School of Arts and Sciences, Engineering, Nursing, and Architecture. The key majors here are Business, International Relations, Communications, Criminal Justice, and Political Science. A majority of the students (85%) are from out of state and the Middle Atlantic region. Of the approximately 4,750 students, 8% are African American. About 15% of the students are from other countries.

CUA has programs that lead to majors in Drama, Dance, and Music. Some famous CUA drama graduates include Jon Voight, Ed McMahon, and Susan Sarandon. Generally, only about 20 drama students enter yearly. They study under a professional faculty, learning speech, the "Alexander technique," and other methods. From four to eight plays are presented a year, as well as several workshop presentations. CUA is affiliated with a theater company, for there are learning and intern opportunities.

The dance students learn ballet, tap, jazz, movement techniques, and performance and auditing rules. Music students study in a "conservatory setting" and can study on the bassoon to the violin.

Students pursuing these majors must audition in person or present a video. Strong test scores, recommendations, and an essay also are necessary.

GOUCHER COLLEGE	1021 Dulaney Valley Road Baltimore, MD 21204 (410) 337-6000 Web site: www.goucher.edu

Goucher College has dance, drama, and music paths that lead to a B.A. degree. This small liberal arts college has about 1,030 full-time students, with 8% being African American. It is on 287 acres of land, with 18 buildings; about 72% of the students reside on campus. Goucher is about eight miles from downtown Baltimore. At GC there are many pathways. The most popular majors are Psychology, Biology, Management, Communications, and English. It's the School of Communications and the Arts, that we're focusing on here.

Studying dance, you'll study choreography and composition, modern dance, ballet, jazz, dance theory, "Labanotation," stagecraft, and some specifics: anatomy, Pilates, pas de deux, pointe. Of dance students applying, about 33% are accepted into the program. About five students graduate annually. The dance students produce two full concerts and several informal presentations a year. You'll also tour at times. There are four Gerstung floors of varying sizes.

The drama students (about 10 each year) take courses in acting, dramaturgy, drama criticism, speech, movement, and voice. There's an Action Theater Residency involved. Each year two to six plays are performed. A "black box theater" and conference rooms are available for use. With other theaters on campus, the maximum seating capacity is nearly 1,000.

The music group also has a small constituency of students, with nine full- or part-time faculty members. Study is available with one of more than 25 different instruments, including the clarinet, piccolo or flute, organ, violin, guitar, French horn, trumpet, saxophone, oboe, and piano. You can also study electronic music, jazz, and orchestral conducting.

Call the college for applications and audition instructions. The acceptance rate at Goucher is about 78% for students in other major areas.

HOWARD UNIVERSITY (COLLEGE OF FINE ARTS/DEPARTMENT OF THEATER ARTS)	Sixth and Fairmont Streets, N.W. Washington, DC 20059 (202) 806-7050, ext. 51 Web site: www.howard.edu

The focus here is on Howard's Department of Theater Arts, which offers degrees in Drama and Dance. The College of Fine Arts also offers majors in Art and Music.

The College of Fine Arts at Howard University occupies Childers Hall, a four-story building on campus. Inside you'll find the Aldridge Theater, the home of the Howard Players. The Bachelor of Fine Arts degree from the Theater Department can be in one of seven areas: Acting, Directing, Musical Theater, Theater Education, Administration, Technology, or Dance. Students who pursue a dance major sometimes audition for (and make) the Howard University Dance Ensemble. Besides an acceptable academic record, Howard asks that students interested in theater or dance audition as "evidence of ability to successfully pursue college-level work" in their chosen major. Prior to an actual audition, students can submit a videotape (VHS format) to assist the faculty with their evaluation of talent and potential. Students must also submit two letters of recommendation and a résumé.

The theater program combines "classroom instruction with rehearsal and performance techniques." There's training for students who want to combine voice and acting. In the directing area students are taught how to integrate the "script, the actor, the stage, the production company, and the style."

In dance, the emphasis is on performance skills, with a strong theoretical classroom backup. Students get to work with guest artists, and intern with major performance companies. There's a senior "practicum experience" that is mandatory.

The theater audition requires the performance of two "contrasting monologues" of a least two minutes. They should be selected from published plays.

Interested students should call Howard's College of Fine Arts for specific instructions and applications.

ILLINOIS STATE UNIVERSITY	Director of Admissions Campus Box 2200 Normal, IL 61790 (309) 438-8284 Web site: www.ilstu.edu

Illinois State University is in the small town of Normal. It's an 850-acre campus, with 153 buildings, including residences. Look for 15,865 full-time students, 99% from the state, with 8% African American. There are five undergraduate schools: Arts and Sciences, Applied Science and Technology, Education, Business, and Fine Arts. The largest majors groups are Education (21%) and Business (17%). Also popular are Communications (8%), and Heath Services and Criminal Justice (5% each). The acceptance rate is about 79%, with about 40% living on campus. The best spot on campus is said to be the "central quad," where the academic buildings stand and the "dorms circle." The Milner Library is six stories high, and you can study in the Prairie Room at the Bone Student Center. Recently our folks went crazy because the ISU basketball team made the NCAA tournament. To stay in touch there's the Black Student Union, all the major black Greek-letter groups, and support services. There's a Multicultural Center, Minority Student Phone-a-thon, and the Minority Retention Committee.

There are many options available to students of color at this school. Our focus here is the Communications and Arts Department. Dance students must take courses in choreography and composition, dance theory, ballet, jazz, research and criticism, modern dance, stagecraft, tap, music, rehearsal and performance, and more. At times students will be taught "Cunningham, Graham, and Limon" based approaches. Movement, body conditioning, and proper eating and nutrition, also are part of the training. There are at least two concerts a year, as well as informal and workshop presentations. The dance team, on occasion, will tour. Practice locations include Marley wood floors. To apply, you must forward an application and do a solo audition, using a CD or cassette player.

Drama students (about 240) only have to audition if they are interested in getting a scholarship. Required courses will include those in acting, scene study, makeup, directing, Stanislavski exercises, voice, and more. Electives might include courses in improvisation, audition preparation, and study in regard to musicals. Internships with Steppenwolf and other affiliated theater groups are possible. There are about 10 productions a year, not including workshop and informal presentations. The drama uses, at times, all four of the theaters on campus. The largest has a seating capacity of 1,200. Usually the entering freshman drama class is about 85 students.

At ISU there is also a music major. About 260 students are in the program. You can get training on one of many instruments. They include oboe/English horn, clarinet, flute, piano, trombone, saxophone, trumpet, violin, organ, French horn, and more. Orchestral conducting or work with electronic music also are possibilities. There's a long list of renowned alums. There are 32 full-time faculty members.

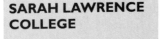

SARAH LAWRENCE COLLEGE

One Mead Way
Bronxville, NY 10708
(914) 395-2510
Web site: www.slc.edu

Of course, highly ranked Sarah Lawrence College is a "best national liberal arts" school. It's known for its innovative academic programs, very bright students, independent study projects, and villagelike atmosphere. We're focusing here, however, on its performing arts components. The Dance and Theater departments, for example, have gotten the experts' nod. Also note that there's a music program here.

We know that Robin Givens and Holly Robinson are graduates. They didn't do too badly. Neither did Joanne Woodward, or dancers Carolyn Adams and Lucinda Childs. Private Sarah Lawrence College, if you can afford the price tag, has delivered in the performing arts area.

The school, in the affluent suburb of Bronxville, New York, is on 1,000 acres. The scene is described as "self-contained" and "beautiful," with 20 buildings, including residences. On any stroll you'll see lovely trees, flowers, hills, rocks, and be able to breathe the fresh air. This liberal arts institution caters to students who have "their own visions," don't want to feel academic restraints, and are driven. In the SLC environment, for example, students officially take three courses a semester. This is said and done loosely. Those credits amount to exciting, independent projects that are designed after faculty interviews, discussions, and student input. During freshman year you will have class responsibilities. But along the way the process involves a lot of research and writing while studying alone. Your road map? To get your degree, you must manage to take one course in at least four deciplines: the humanities, social sciences/history, natural sciences/math, and the creative arts.

Students majoring in dance (about 90 of a full-time count of approximately 1,400) study dance choreography, composition, and technique. Varying styles are taught: dance and jazz, for example. The faculty includes professionals who have worked (or still work) in the field. Their résumés include performing for groups such as the Dance Theater of Harlem, and the Dan Wagoner and Kathryn Posin Dance Companies. The department has at least six produced concerts a year. There are also workshops and other related performances. The department has two Harlequin dance floors, studios, and room for audiences. Besides actually dancing, students must do research about dancing and study criticism. There are no formal auditions. A recommendation and essay are required.

Students in the Drama Department (about 200 students) study the "Alexander" technique, improvisation, comedy, speech/voice, "Stanislavski exercises," movement, directing, dance, dramaturgy, audition preparation, "how to make a musical," and more. At SLC there's a main proscenium stage and two studio theaters. A recital hall seats 350 people. Under the guidance of a renowned faculty, several plays are performed each year. Students also have many internship opportunities, including possible work with the All-Seasons Theater and Ensemble Studio.

About 5% of the students at SLC are African American. Harambe, a cultural group, is composed of our folks. The students celebrate Black History Month and have had singer Rachid and the Barnard/Columbia Gospel Choir on campus. In 1998 the school had its first Jazz Festival. Poet Amiri Baraka has also read on campus.

At SLC you can also study music (orchestration, theory, and composition) and writing (poetry and fiction).

STATE UNIVERSITY OF NEW YORK AT PURCHASE

735 Anderson Hill Road
Purchase, NY 10577-1400
(914) 251-6300
Web site: www.purchase.edu

At Purchase, drama (theater) and dance get raves, and the Music and Art Departments are highly recommended. It's a total package for creative folks. SUNY Purchase, the school where the New York Knicks of basketball fame practice, is a "sleeper" school. Purchase is on 400 acres of land in Westchester County. Founded in 1969 by the governor, the buildings are rather bland in appearance, modern, and without personality. Indeed, in the past dozen or so years, this state school has been making all top lists for its performing arts school, particularly in the areas of dance and drama. Although the school is officially divided with arts and sciences students, the visual and performing arts half has the "look of artists, dancers, creative types." You can feel the energy. Interestingly, it's almost as if the academic part of the Purchase community is an aside. People talk about Wesley Snipes, Mase, Terese Capucilli (Graham Company), Hernando Cortez (Taylor Company), and other graduates who are blazing a trail of success in the world of the arts.

At Purchase there are Conservatories of Dance, of Music, and of Theater Arts and Film. Also, there's the School of Art and Design. The College of Arts and Sciences completes the equation.

To gain admission to the Purchase Arts Departments, you must audition. The students we knew who were accepted in dance, for example, were exceptional in form, style, and execution. To gain an accept in dance it's important to have prior training, obvious talent, and the "potential as a performer." Students who are interested in drama (acting and the theater) must also demonstrate stellar talent in an audition. The film folks must present a portfolio. A recent graduate won an Academy Award for his movie in cartoon form. The visual artists must present a package of 10 to 15 slides for review.

Generally, the auditions are held at the Westchester campus between December and June. Regional auditions also are held in various locations throughout the city. Purchase has rolling admissions to July 15 for the fall semester. January 1 is the recommended deadline.

The conservatory and art programs are small enough so that the faculty/studio ratio can have impact. Of about 2,470 full-time students, perhaps 40% fall into the arts categories. Approximately 7% of the students are African American. At least 10% of the other students arrive from counties such as Japan, Taiwan, and Korea, as well as from South America, and Europe.

Dance students learn performance and choreography, dance history, improvisation, and the skills of modern dance and ballet. Those in theater get to perform in a series of plays such as Shakespeare's *A Midsummer Night's Dream* and Gertrude Stein's *A Manoir*. All the techniques of acting and its related theories are taught. The music majors learn about performance (instrumental/vocal). Graduates now perform with the New York Philharmonic, and the Baltimore Symphony, as well as in the areas of rock, rhythm and blues, and jazz. The visual artists are trained in gallery and museum work and study painting, printmaking, computer graphics, photography, illustration, and more.

On campus is the Performing Arts Center, with four theaters (one with an experimental stage). There are also eight dance studios with wood and Marley floors. You'll find, too, practice rooms for musicians, a photography lab, multitrack synthesizers, typesetting and computer graphics labs, and printmaking equipment.

Another plus is its multicultural environment.

APPENDIX A

I Am Somebody:
Actual Essays and a Student Résumé

named this appendix "I Am Somebody" because that's what your essay is supposed to demonstrate. That's the first step you must climb. The second step is to demonstrate your mastery of grammar, technique, and style. The third step should be to show resonance, creativity, and to put your special signature on your work. You are more than "somebody." You are unique, priceless, a princess, a prince, a student who's destined to make a name for yourself and your alma mater. "Ordinary" is not where you want to go.

You've got to think good, better, extraordinary. After you've read chapter 6, on writing the essay, look at these actual essays and excerpts. Although it's rarely said in college guides, your slamming personal statement can sometimes lift a "maybe" application to the "admit" grouping or touch someone so that he or she might fight for you in an admissions review. At Spelman. At Yale. At that "second chance" school. Give your essay everything you've got. Shape it. Toil over it. Take your time.

Essay 1

What Person Had the Greatest Influence on You?

by Kristin S. Black, Cornell University

When I am asked to give an inspirational speech to teenagers, I am never at a loss for words. I have repeated this true story dozens of times, not only to friends and teachers but also to groups at churches, college fairs, and cultural events throughout New York City. My grandfather, who passed away due to heart failure when I was 12, was one of the most influential people in my life. Granddad was a storyteller who often held me spellbound as I sat on his lap or listened beside his rocking chair. Many of his tales would leave me aghast, happily startled, or laughing. He told me about FOR COLORED ONLY signs, how it was to ride a horse and buggy, and how it felt to pick cotton or peas. When he spoke I could see scarecrows, chestnut trees, and could almost smell the odors of South Carolina. Teachers were respected and wonderful, sometimes teaching in shanties to hungry brown faces. Everybody seemed to walk "five miles to school." And the town doctor (whom you might pay with a pie or fruit) was caring, and always traveling with an old black sachet. I was fascinated.

Of all the stories that Granddad told, however, the one that gave me the greatest inspiration and determination follows. When he was in his late teens, Granddad told his father he wanted to go college. His father was opposed, telling him that he had to farm the land and "gather the crops." Without encouragement or help, Granddad saved. He went to school and worked around the clock, saving money in jars. Eventually he sent a single application to a historically black college, Savannah State in South Carolina.

When an envelope returned, he opened it and lifted his arms to the sky. He was accepted. But his father was outraged, shouting that a degree wouldn't put food on the table. But it would, Granddad tried to say. Townsfolk loaned Granddad money, and he filled a lone suitcase. At Savannah State he worked but barely survived. He was called the boy in "the white suit." His bill grew, and his white suit (washed and pressed every few days) began to fall apart. A good student, some wept when he had to leave, broke and without clothing. My children will get my total support, he vowed to himself when he left, and will get their degrees. Then, God willing, I'll go back and get mine.

Granddad kept his word. His three children, including my father, received a total of eight degrees. He guided and supported them every step of the way. But the beautiful thing was that in 1985 he rose to the cheers of his children and grandchildren to accept his Bachelor's degree in Business at Medgar Evers College. That day, though he was suffering from angina, he took the time to give me that look. He didn't have to say a word. Nobody, and no odds can stop you, was the message in his eyes. When I enter medical school he will be smiling, but not because he is surprised.

> *Kristin comments: "I don't recall which college I eventually forwarded this essay to, but I remember that writing it made me feel teary-eyed. As with every essay I wrote, I gave it everything I had. The essay went through at least six or seven drafts, with me reading and rereading it until I felt like I couldn't do any better. That was my way with every essay. In the end, I had been accepted to seven or eight colleges, including Spelman and Cornell. I went Ivy. I think an interesting point here is my ending. Here, I am in high school and yet I conclude by saying, "When I enter medical school . . ." I bet the readers noticed.*

Essay 2

Swimming with Dolphins (an excerpt)

by Daemond Arrindell, University of Michigan

My first love has always been the sciences. As I got older, my growing interests focused on a narrower scientific range. I have always felt a certain connection between myself and the animal world. Having pets in the family and the constant viewing of *National Geographic* specials managed to keep my mind occupied. Several years ago I experienced the most amazing occurrence of my life, something very few people can boast about. While visiting relatives in Aruba, I had the privilege to swim with wild spotted dolphins. It was at that moment that I knew what I was meant to do. I wanted to become a veterinarian and eventually specialize in the care of marine animals.

Black Excel comments: Daemond's entire essay was strong, but this section has always stood out in my mind over the years. I've frequently read or mentioned it in lectures. Daemond separates himself from the pack: he mentions the animal world, shows the intensity of where he's at, then BLOWS everybody away with his swim with "wild spotted dolphins." How many students, black or white, could relate such a story? After I read the essay I said to myself, "Admit, admit, admit!" And, of course, the admissions people said the same thing.

Essay 3

Why Is PENN Good for Me?

by Sherice Perry, University of Pennsylvania

"I love it here" were the words I heard as a voice echoed away. My head quickly turned to see who it was, and I caught sight of a small figure jogging into the distance. A brown, busy ponytail bobbed up and down, and the red and blue "P" on the back gradually grew smaller and smaller.

"Yeah, sure," I thought. "You haven't spent two hours in the car smooshed between your two sisters." When I got out of the car to take a deep breath and to stretch, my mother looked around and noticed tennis courts. *"Look, Sherice! You can play tennis in the afternoon. Do you see all the people jogging? You'd always have someone to work out with."* As I looked around, I realized she was right. Although it was early on a Saturday morning, you would never know it. Scattered like ants, people were jogging with Walkmans and proudly wearing PENN T-shirts. Those walking were laughing and talking, like carefree birds flying in the sky. This is what I first remember of PENN.

I love people. During my college search, the students on each campus helped me to determine whether that university was a place I could attend. My first impression of a campus helped me discern fact from fiction. Every school provided shiny brochures that contained beautiful landscaping and smiling faces. They all agreed, "I love it here!" But a PENN student said, "There's ALWAYS something to do." And still another advised, "I've made so many new friends here." One junior even let my family see her dorm room while one of my little sisters used the bathroom! This school spirit and excitement were what sold me. . . .

Writing has always been a passion of mine. It has allowed me to express the thoughts that dance around in my head. Perhaps writing for *PENN Review* or *Red and Blue* will give me that opportunity. I hope to continue writing throughout college as a way of exploring a career path that I have considered while in high school: journalism.

Throughout my high school career I've had the opportunity to interact with others through sports and volunteer work. Although my varsity status will be left behind in high school, the passion to play will not be. I look forward to playing intramural sports and fueling that competitive engine once again with energy, enthusiasm, and excitement.

Children have fascinated me for as long as I can remember. I love being around them. Being able to teach children and become a role model is an experience that has changed the way I see small children as well as myself. Having the opportunity to mold young minds was a great responsibility as well as a great pleasure. A program such as PENNPals would allow me to continue to share these experiences with younger children and hopefully to make a difference in their lives.

Although I plan to be involved in activities, I also intend on making my presence felt inside the classroom. I will be more than just a number. I'm often seen as a small student in the back of the classroom who asks the big questions. I want my professors, as well as other members of the faculty, to know who I am. I am not afraid to approach a teacher for casual conversation or for extra help. I love to learn, and my studies always have been a priority for me.

Many students often attend a particular school because their mother or father once did. Although I have no legacy to follow, I will create my own. Years from now my grandchildren may say, "Hey, Grandma worked hard and went there. Maybe I can, too!" Hopefully a couple of months from now I will be that jogger. I'll shout to prospective students, "I love it here!" And while jogging down Locust Walk, I'll glance over at Ben Franklin and think, "The legacy begins now!"

Black Excel comments: I'd seen several of Sherice's essays, and they are all creative and touching. You can hear her voice. I've marveled, too, about how I always go back for a second and a third reading. Sherice takes chances, and her work takes you on a ride. It's like returning to a good book and discovering a deeper nuance. Here Sherice is saying "PENN is perfect, and I am a perfect fit." She's as much of the story as is PENN. And she closes with finesse, as it's all just the beginning for her. I can almost hear the admissions people saying, "We've got to take her, she'll be an asset here." And she will be.

Essay 4

I Am on a "Rescue" Mission!

by Kristin S. Black, M.D., Cornell University, Mount Sinai School of Medicine,
Harvard Arthur Ashe Fellow

The following essay has evolved from its shorter version—a successful college essay to several undergraduate schools—into one that Kris keeps updating, reshaping, and sending out as she continues. I believe the essay says who she is, and lays out what her "mission" is. You could say it's a "living" essay. The key is that Kris tells her story with heartfelt commitment, and you get a sense that she won't be denied. Would you want her on your team? Do birds fly?

I care, first and foremost:

As I pursue my goal of becoming a family physician, my intent is to make contributions in communities where there is a need. In my applications to medical school, I quoted a sobering article in the *New York Times*. There are only 38 qualified doctors serving 1.7 million people in some poor urban sectors of the city. My essay theme was that I could make a tremendous difference, although there was a shortage of black physicians. My intent was to hold, heal, and have impact (spiritual and physical) in underserved communities.

Accepted to Cornell, I was selected as a "National Scholar," based on what I had already achieved. I believe my success lifted above raw scores and grades. I was president of a youth chapter of the NAACP and coeditor of its well-read newsletter. I wrote about issues like teen pregnancy and depression. A school leader, I was often called on to give speeches by community leaders. I won awards while participating in the Queens Bridge to Medicine and Mount Sinai's Secondary Education Through Health Programs.

At Cornell I continued to be involved with service-oriented projects. While a Resident Advisor, I designed weekly programs consistent with the theme of "giving back" to the community. I developed and ran many seminars that addressed health problems, and I was even a participant (and curriculum contributor) in Cornell's Homeless Education Program. I taught students in Ithaca about poverty and homelessness. I was, too, an administrator/mentor for Urafifi, a Big Brother/Big Sister Program at my school.

In Cornell's Urban Semester Program, I worked at the Women and Children's Health Center in Queens. I visited the community with outreach workers and physicians to provide care to the people of the Ravenswood and Queens Bridge Housing Projects. I gathered information and conducted health-related workshops. I summarized my findings in a paper called "Health Care Issues in an Undeserved Community." Graduating from Cornell, I was named a Recognition Tradition Fellow (the school's highest honor for college and community contributions), and a scholarship was named after me.

At Mount Sinai I immediately conducted workshops on health issues like breast cancer and the dangers of smoking for the East Harlem community. I became involved in the Mount Sinai Moms Program (for teenage mothers). Not only was I a lecturer, but I was also confidante and friend to many of the young women. As a mentor for the Mount Sinai Scholars Program, I spent at least one hour a week with a New York City high school student who is now away in college.

In the Urban Health Care Program I did an elective at Women in Crisis, a program in Harlem for women with HIV/AIDS. I did workshops in churches, beauty parlors, and nail salons. I stood on corners distributing condoms and literature. I talked to women for hours, not just about HIV/AIDS but also about other issues affecting their health and/or well-being: self-esteem, safe sex, drug/alcohol abuse, the importance of an education. The following summer, I also participated in the AMSA/NHSC Health Promotion/Disease Prevention Project at the Institute for Urban Family Health in New York City. I developed lower literacy material on a variety of health topics.

During my clerkships, I believe that I was able to bring all my skills—and caring—to fusion. Patients at all age levels and genders seemed to take to me. My most rewarding clerkship (among many successful ones) was an elective I did at the Phillips Family Practice at Jefferson Medical College. I felt like a doctor, perhaps the way they were portrayed in old movies: like a family confidante, like a friend. I worked in an office and even made (my pleasure) home visits. I spoke to middle-aged patients about Diabetes and Hypertension and to adolescents about sex, social, or cultural issues—the death of a rap star, for example, why an eight-year-old shouldn't be drinking Kool-Aid. At Phillips, I felt that my life's résumé was sending a resounding message: Family Practice would be my choice. But with a heart!

I will earn my M.D., and "come to the rescue" as a primary care doctor. My residency (and eventually my practice) will preferably be served in an urban setting like New York City, Philadelphia, or Washington, DC. Across this country, "economically disadvantaged people" need help and support. At the next step, I will expand my knowledge on urban health and community needs (e.g., family dynamics, or trends in drug use). In a few weeks, I will be off to Harvard as an Arthur Ashe Fellow. And with my eventual residency and four-year responsibility to the National Health Service Corps, I intend to take advantage of every learning experience. After all, I am on a "rescue" mission!

SAMPLE RÉSUMÉ

Here's Sherice again, with a résumé that has impact. Of course, we've seen and recommended a number of different formats. The key is that it's another knockout punch. In this example, narrative is inserted to powerful advantage. Essentially the writer says "I am special" and will "be a wonderful addition" to your student body. It's a reecho of the message in her essay: *Admit!*

Sherice begins with her name, address, and phone number, with the words "Honors Track" in a corner.

A. Awards at Kellenberg Memorial High School

Certificate of Educational Development—National, 9

Commended National Achievement Scholar, 12

Excellence of Character Award, 9, 10, 11

Honor Roll, 9, 10, 11

Long Island Math Fair participant, 9

Macy's Scholar, 10, 11

Math Fair, 2nd place

Perfect Attendance trophy, 9, 10, 11

U.S. National Mathematics Award, 9

Who's Who Among American High School Students, 10, 11

B. Activities

Cheerleading

- Captain, 9
- Freshman letter, 9
- MIP Trophy, 9
- UCA All-Star, 10

Communications Clubs

- Letter, 9, 10, 11

GS0

- Letter, 9, 10, 11

Gymnastics

- Letter 9, 10, 11
- 2nd place JV All-Around, 9
- JV All-Around Champion, 10
- Coaches' Award, 9
- Commitment Award, 11
- Captain, 11, 12
- All-League Selection, 11
- Women in Sports Award Dinner, 12

Leaders' Club

- Letter, 9, 10, 11
- Vice president, 11
- President, 12

Phoenix Newspaper

- Staff Writer, 9
- Sports Editor, 11

Spring Track

- Junior Varsity letter, 9, 10
- Varsity letter, 11

Winter Track

- Varsity letter, 11

C. Participation in Kellenberg Activities

Advent Prayer Service, 11

Big Sister, 12

Cheerleading Club, 9

Communications Club, 9, 10, 11

GSO, 9, 10, 11

Gymnastics, 9, 10, 11, 12

Innkeepers, 12

Junior Retreat Staff, 11

Leaders' Club, 9, 10, 11, 12

Lenten Prayer Service, 11

National Honor Society, 11, 12

Newspaper, 9, 11, 12

Spring Track, 9, 10, 11

Triple "A" Orientation, 10, 11, 12

Winter Track, 11

Writers' Guild, 12

D. Activities Outside of Kellenberg Memorial High School

Athletic: Gymnastics, 9, 10, 11

Nonathletic: Day-care worker, 9; McDonald's 10, 11

E. How I Prefer to Use My Time

When I have free time I enjoy reading, listening to jazz, and being with my friends. Sports are very important to me because they offer relaxation, exercise, and focus. Gymnastics training as well as work consume a great deal of my time during the off-season. During vacations I like to travel, whenever possible, especially to Martha's Vineyard. While in New York I also like to travel to places I don't see often. Rockefeller Center is my favorite.

F. Focus

As a person, I am honest. As a student, I am determined. And as a friend, I am loyal. These are three key things I believe all individuals must possess. I was not born with super powers, but I do believe through hard work and persistence I have reached super heights. Throughout my life I was never handed anything. I have worked for all that I have achieved. My family is not rich, yet I attend a quality Catholic school. I was never naturally talented in gymnastics, yet I have received many awards.

Athletics has opened a new world to me. Not only is it enjoyable, but it also disciplines. I would like to continue to have exposure to the athletic world; therefore I would like to become an orthopedic surgeon. My main objective will be to heal the injured physically as well as mentally. I understand the mind of the hurt athlete since it is something I've experienced.

I would like to study psychology to help athletes deal with their injuries and the feelings they may be experiencing. One of my goals is to be the doctor of a professional team, and to open a rehabilitation complex complete with facilities for fitness, rehabilitation, and counseling. I also hope to continue writing because that is something I have enjoyed for many years. Not only does my writing help others to understand me, but it also helps me to learn about myself.

G. Letters of Recommendation

- Mrs. Dugal
- Mr. Huggard
- Mrs. Trentacoste

APPENDIX B

Gateway to the Internet: Additional Scholarships, Black Excel, and More

Homes, high schools, colleges, and libraries are now wired. The odds are high that if you are reading this college guide, you at least know some rudimentary things about computers and the Internet. The information highway offers all sorts of valuable data, so you'd better get aboard if you want to be informed and beat the odds in regard to navigating the college admissions process.

If you've been to our web site, www.blackexcel.com, you've got a general idea of what the possibilities are: unlimited resources offering you access to a netherworld of college-related wonders for hours, if not days.

FINANCIAL AID RESOURCES

Here are some online financial aid resources.

FastWeb: Your 180,000-Plus Free Scholarship Database (www.fastweb.com)

Some say it's a money bonanza, others that it's the best free database of scholarships on the Internet. It's FastWeb (Financial Aid Search Through the Web). Go to the web site and fill out a personalized profile, including your grade-point average, test scores, and interests. This "largest free scholarship search" then matches you with the scholarships in its database, and provides you with a hit list of potential scholarships. The list sometimes arrives into your e-mailbox within minutes.

FINAID: The Financial Information Page (www.finaid.com)

It's a web site that's often described as the "granddaddy" *(Boston Globe)* of all financial aid and scholarship web sites. Like FastWeb, Mark Kantrowitz's super page has garnered nationwide attention and awards, counting more than 1,000 reviews and testimonials to its credit. You'll find Mark's page to be a treasure chest of financial aid and money tips. Get the lowdown on scholarships and related scams, for example. Here you can type in FAFSA and find yourself looking at the interactive web version of the Free Application for Federal Student Aid form.

Other useful sites include Peterson's College Quest (www.petersons.com), Sallie Mae/Cash Online Scholarship Service (www.salliemae.com), CollegeNet (www.collegenet.com), or the College Board's Fund Finder (www.collegeboard.com). All of these locations offer more free information about financial aid and scholarship sources.

APPLYING ELECTRONICALLY

If you go to the College Board's web site you'll discover that you can apply to hundreds of schools electronically, using a specific school's application thanks to the College Board's partnership with CollegeLink (www.collegelink.com). Other sites that offer electronic applications include:

- Embark.com (www.embark.com)—more than 160 applications
- Xap (www.xap.com)—mostly applications from the western states
- Peterson's (www.petersons.com)—more than 1,000 possibilities

You can also use APPLY, a free CD-ROM that can be requested at www.weapply.com. Using APPLY, you'll have more than 500 applications at your disposal.

OTHER INFORMATIONAL SITES

Aside from applying electronically or getting scholarship information, the web offers sites that have information on every aspect of the college admissions process. Here are some of the best.

The *U.S. News* Web Site (www.usnews.com)

This web site is your gateway to the magazine's yearly college rankings, as well as a wealth of other information. You can peruse many lists of schools, including those in the regions of the country (North, South, Midwest, West) that you are targeting. Find out what schools are ranked highest in a particular survey, which schools have the highest and lowest acceptance rates, which leave you with the most or least debt. It's all valuable.

You'll find, too, important information on affirmative action and where we're headed. A typical article is titled "Diversity Declines in California and Texas." You're given a feel for the impact *Hopwood* v. *Texas* and Proposition 209 in California had on those states and the nation. For every African American and student of color, this reading is an eye-opener.

And there's more: you can go to "writing the essay," learn about campus interviews, and SAT prep courses, and check out oncoming test dates.

The international student section, too, is useful. You learn that "Boston University has the most international students—4,603 at last count—following New York University." And the "transfer student data finder" will locate your chosen college and tell you how many students applied, how many were accepted, and how many enrolled.

The NACAC's National College Fairs (www.nacac.org)

Every African American student who is interested in mainstream colleges, or who would like to sit in on a financial aid seminar, should look at the NACAC's web site. There you'll find valuable college information, including the dates and times of more than 33 sponsored college fairs nationwide.

These fairs generally attract more than 300,000 students each year. If you show up, you can stop at any number of more than 150 college tables and talk to representatives of the particular schools. There you can add your name to inquiry lists, and pick up viewbooks, as well as financial aid, scholarship, and special-program information, and discuss such matters as SAT scores and admission requirements.

Unfortunately, if you're looking to find a large clutter of HBCU colleges at these NACAC affairs, you generally won't. In recent years at the New York fair, we were lucky to find a half dozen of our schools. Suggestion: if you visit a fair, bring a knapsack to collect and save viewbooks and related materials. Plastic NACAC bags are distributed as you enter, but won't hold what you can collect if you are seriously collecting material for later study.

Here's a sample listing of NACAC-sponsored college fairs:

- New York City National College Fair at Madison Square Garden, New York, NY—usually held about May 1
- Philadelphia National College Fair, Pennsylvania Convention Center, Philadelphia, PA—usually held about October 31
- Washington, DC, National College Fair, Washington Convention Center, Washington, DC—usually held about November 15
- San Diego National College Fair, San Diego Convention Center, San Diego, CA—usually held about April 21

The NACAC also sponsors college fairs in 27 cities that are specially targeted to students interested in music, theater, dance, art, and design. These are very important to us because we have no such college fairs, and majors in these creative areas are generally limited in scope—if available—at the historically black colleges.

College Web Sites

Most colleges are "wired" to the Internet highway, and you can visit after a few pushes on the button. For example, if you go to Brown University's web site (www.brown.edu), you can find information on:

- Admissions
- Financial aid
- Student clubs
- The school's newspaper (the *Brown Daily Herald*)
- The *Brown Alumni Monthly*

And that's only a starter. You're really going to learn about the history of Brown, not only with photos but also via special reports. One section is called "A to Z." You can stroll and browse at countless stops—Applying, Egyptology, Resident Life, Student Organizations, Tutoring—and get information on the Women Writers' Project.

One of the best items at the Brown web site, however, is its search engine. Type in the words "black student" and more than 118 African American–related posts will appear. These posts, written by students, staff, and faculty, will give you a feel for what it's like to be a black student at this Ivy League school. The posts are pullouts from student papers, letters to the editor, and elsewhere. It's a telling read.

At the Fisk web site (www.fisk.edu) you can get an overview of the college and actually visit about a dozen of the student home pages. It's an informative journey that even takes you to the school's Race Relationship's Institute (RRI) and its significant mission statement. Another glowing spot is the Fisk University Class of 1972's home page. It warms your heart to note that the group recently celebrated its 25th Year reunion. Go see the photos. The page opens with these words: " . . . Her sons are steadfast, Her daughters true . . ."

Collegiate Choice Walking Tours (www.register.com/collegiate)

This site is valuable, although there's a cost. A group of independent advisers has collected more than 330 amateur videos of colleges and universities across the United States and abroad. The tapes average about an hour in recorded time, are unedited, and sometimes are very rough.

Just imagine visiting a college and holding your camcorder. The tapes were actually created during student guided tours and cost $19.95 apiece. Watching is a very real experience, and if you simply want to get a "feel" for the look and character of a school, a tape or two might be a bargain.

Note that only a few HBCUs are available—Spelman, Howard, and Fisk, for example—but there's a wealth of other worthwhile tapes: Emory, Wesleyan, UFlorida, Johns Hopkins, Penn State, Rhode Island School of Design, UIllinois, Georgia Institute of Technology, Wellesley, UMaryland, and Duke, to name about a dozen or so.

The Black Collegian (www.black.collegian.com)

This is a great site for exploring career opportunities and gathering college information for students. It's the cyber companion to the *Black Collegian* magazine.

HBCU Alumni Center and Student Discussion List (www.hbcu-alumni.com)

Here you will find alumni and student discussion forums, information on college events, and more. There's a listserv (discussion site) you can join: HBCUTALK-L. Here you exchange college news and talk about national issues.

Black Excel: The College Help Network (www.blackexcel.org)

Black Excel is your Internet gateway to the college resources mentioned in this chapter and much more. Our web page delivers, A to Z, all the great links and original material you will ever need to navigate the college admissions process. An award-winning site, we have a "top 10" educational pick.

APPENDIX C

Historically Black College Tours

The following is a list of organizations that sponsor tours of historically black colleges. For tour updates or additions go to BlackBlack on the net: www.blackexcel.org. Generally we recommend that you write for information packets. Many sponsors and volunteers here are not working out of nine-to-five offices in regard to these tours.

ALPHA PHI ALPHA BLACK COLLEGE TOUR

Alpha Phi Alpha
P.O. Box 501
West Hempstead, NY 11552
(516) 733-0442 or (516) 234-8952

APA (Eta Theta Lambda chapter) sends a black college tour group out every October. The price is about $500, paid in installments. The tour includes bus transportation, hotels, some meals, and SAT and financial aid workshops. The tours take seven days and the students visit a dozen colleges. Call or write for information. The tour covers Morgan State, Hampton, Alabama A&M, Clark-Atlanta, Alabama State, Morehouse, Virginia State, North Carolina Central, Howard, Oakwood, Spelman, Tuskegee, and Johnson C. Smith.

ANNUAL MBC HISTORICALLY BLACK COLLEGE TOUR

Metropolitan Baptist Church
1225 R Street
Washington, DC 20009
(202) 483-1540

The annual tour heads to Tuskegee, Clark-Atlanta, Georgia Tech, Morehouse, Morris Brown, Spelman, Florida A&M, and Florida State. The cost is about $300, which you can pay in installments. For information call Brother Tracy Brower, Coordinator, at MBC (College and Career Ministry). He can be reached at (301) 853-1776 or at the church number.

AYA'S BLACK COLLEGE TOUR

AYA (African Youth in Action)
G.P.O. Box 1376
Bronx, NY 10451-1376
(212) 884-2270

African Youth in Action invites you to join them on one of their yearly tours (10 to 14 schools). The tours usually take place semiannually, in February and October. The cost of the tour is about $400. Traveling with AYA will be chaperones. All students and family members must attend an orientation prior to the trip. AYA uses deluxe motor coach transportation. All individuals attending the trip must have medical coverage. Payment plan: usually a first payment of $75 (nonrefundable), and then two installment payments. There's always a stop at the Martin Luther King Jr. Memorial Center. Sample schools visited: Howard, Morgan State, Hampton, Virginia Union, Morehouse, Spelman, Clark-Atlanta, and Morris Brown. Call or write for details.

CALIFORNIA COLLEGE CONSULTING AND TOURS

P.O. Box 2456
Pasadena, CA 91102-2456
(626) 284-0400
e-mail: edinfo@calcollegetours.com

This group hosts a black college tour as well as northern and southern California college tours, and tours including the Ivy League. The price is $895, which includes airfare, lodging, and ground transportation. The fee also includes a consultation for the student. In addition, if the student is in southern California and the parents would like a home visit, an adviser will visit the home and speak with the student and parents.

The black college tour is usually scheduled for June. Planned visits include schools such as Howard, Spelman, Morgan State, Clark-Atlanta, and Hampton. They plan for meetings with financial aid officers, an overnight stay in a college dorm if space permits, a visit to a college classroom to experience a college lecture, and a general overview of the city or town where the college is located. Tours are chaperoned by teachers and counselors to provide as much guidance as necessary to the student.

If you need information, please contact this group. The director is Henrietta L. Williams, who has several years' experience as a student adviser for an academic enrichment program at the University of Southern California.

COLLEGE BOUND HISTORICAL BLACK COLLEGE TOUR

Fellowship Covenant Church
720 Castle Hill Avenue
Bronx, NY 10473
(718) 829-2116

Tour sponsored by the Ujamaa Shute Nelson Mandela Learning Center. This tour usually takes place in mid-February and lasts about six days. Twelve colleges are visited, including Lincoln, Morgan State, Howard, Virginia Union, Hampton, South Carolina, Benedict, Allen, Spelman, Morehouse, Clark-Atlanta, and others.

You can reach the Ujamaa Shute Center at 212-283-2687. The fee is about $400, with counseling, chaperones, and hotel accommodations. Over a three-year period, more than 300 students have taken the tours. The tour includes 11 black colleges and universities.

COLLEGE VISITS, INC.

207 East Bay Street, Suite 304
Charleston, SC 29401
(843) 853-8149 or (800) 944-2798
Web site: www.college-visits.com/schedule.htm

Since 1991, College Visits has been organizing college tours for high school students from around the world. Students and counselors from all ethnic origins have participated, traveling to schools across the United States. Our students, we realize, might be interested in the scope of schools that could be targeted here, from state and private institutions to schools such as Yale and the University of Michigan. This group sponsors at least one totally black tour a year, generally given in June. Call for details.

Southeast tour:

Clark-Atlanta University, Morris Brown College, Spelman College or Morehouse College, Florida A&M University, University of Florida, Bethune-Cookman College, Johnson C. Smith University, North Carolina A&T University.
   Cost: $855. Originating city: Atlanta GA
   For any tour information, you can go to the site noted, call the number given, or contact Rober Rummerfield, director of College Visits, at cvisits@aol.com.

COMMUNITY UPLIFT THROUGH PERSEVERANCE, INC. (NEW YORK)

Xi Phi chapter of Omega Psi Phi fraternity (annual college tour). Usually a six-day tour of 10 historically black colleges: North Carolina A&T, Bennett College, North Carolina Central, Shaw, St. Augustine's College, Norfolk State, Hampton, Virginia State, Howard, and Morgan State. For information call (212) 877-1737.

DELTA SIGMA THETA SORORITY, INC.

Queens Alumnae Chapter—New York
Orientations sometimes held at:
St. John's University, Council Hall
800 Utopia Parkway
Jamaica, NY 11439
(718) 276-5233

This chapter runs historical black college tours I and II. Some schools visited (Part I): Delaware State, Morgan State, Bowie State, Virginia Union, and Virginia State. Included in these packages: college prep, SAT prep, tutorial program, career development, talent show. Contact information: Roslin Spigner, (718) 468-8990.

EAST NEW YORK KIDSPOWER YOUTH SERVICE

420 Georgia Avenue
Brooklyn, NY 11203
(718) 342-3401

This youth service organization sometimes has black college tours. Call for information.

EST (EDUCATIONAL STUDENT TOURS)

16850 Gresham Street
Sepulveda, CA 91343
(818) 891-8087

Educational Student Tours (EST) is a black tour company run by Gregory and Yasmin Dela-houssaye. The journey takes off from Southern California. The price, about $550, does not include the airfare, which EST can arrange. Prospective students visit schools such as Howard, Hampton, Spelman, and Morehouse. It's a six-day trip that covers nine schools. Students will chat with admissions people and students on campus. Usually at least three trips are scheduled, the first in about April. Call or write for details and information.

HARLEM YMCA BAI MENTOR PROGRAM
BLACK COLLEGE TOUR

The tours usually occur in April. The tour visits 10 black colleges in Atlanta, Virginia, Maryland, and Washington, D.C.: Hampton, Howard, Morehouse, Morgan State, Morris Brown, Norfolk State, North Carolina A&T, Spelman, St. Augustine's College, and Virginia Union. The fee is $350. Contact Hope Bright or Tisa Howard at 212-281-4100, ext. 201 (Monday through Friday, 9:00 A.M. to 5:00 P.M.).

HISTORICALLY BLACK COLLEGE UNIVERSITY TOUR CONSORTIUM

c/o Manchester High School
134 East Middle Turnpike
Manchester, CT 06040

This college tour group visits Hampton, Howard, Coppin State, Norfolk State, St. Paul's, North Carolina Central, North Carolina A&T, Virginia State, Morgan State, and Johnson C. Smith. The coordinator is Lou Irvin, who can be contacted at work at (860) 647-3531 or at home at (860) 282-0224.

THE LIVING CONSORTIUM OF THE NEW YORK URBAN LEAGUE

204 West 136th Street
New York, NY 10030-2696
(212) 234-2610

This Urban League group gives an annual college fair and also sponsors a black college tour. Call for extra information. E-mail to Mark W. Payne, project director, at awo@mindspring.com.

LOS ANGELES BLACK COLLEGE TOUR

This tour visits 20 historically black colleges and universities in the eastern and southern regions of the United States. The tour takes place from about mid-March to April. For an application and extra information call (213) 290-9850.

MINNEAPOLIS URBAN LEAGUE

(Black College Tour)
2000 Plymouth Avenue N.
Minneapolis, MN 55411
(612) 302-3100

This group visits schools in the DC, Maryland, and Virginia areas. The stops include Howard, Morgan State, and Hampton. Call Linda at the Minneapolis Urban League Street Academy for more information: (612) 874-9667.

NASHVILLE ANNUAL BLACK COLLEGE TOUR
(IN CONJUNCTION WITH JACK & JILL OF AMERICA, INC.)

This Tennessee-based tour heads to "the Mid-Atlantic portion of the great United States." The colleges visited include Virginia State, Virginia Union, St. Paul's College, Howard University, University of DC, Coppin State, Morgan State, and the University of Maryland at Eastern Shore. Dates change.

Contact the president of the Nashville chapter of Jack & Jill via e-mail at PTHOMjjDST@ aol.com.

PAN-HELLENIC COUNCIL OF MONTGOMERY COUNTY, MARYLAND
ANNUAL THERESA SUGGS MEMORIAL BLACK COLLEGE TOUR

This tour heads to Morris Brown, Morehouse, Clark-Atlanta, Spelman, North Carolina Central, North Carolina A&T, Hampton, and Virginia State. The cost is about $300 and includes transportation and lodging (three dinners, four breakfasts). The contact person is Albert Roberts at (301) 588-8883.

PROJECT ENRICH (GAMMA PI OF OMEGA PSI PHI FRATERNITY)
ANNUAL BLACK COLLEGE TOUR

Prince Georges County
P.O. Box 4072
Capitol Heights, MD 20791

Sponsors college tours. Write for information.

QUEENS CADET CORPS

Queens, NY

Each year there's an eight-day tour to Morehouse, Spelman, Clark-Atlanta, Morris Brown, Norfolk University, Hampton, and Howard. The trip is usually in April. Other sightseeing includes the Martin Luther King Jr. Center, Ebenezer Baptist Church, the U.S. Supreme Court, the Vietnam Memorial, the FBI Building, the White House, and more. For information call the Cadet Corps at (718) 712-6148.

ROOSEVELT HIGH SCHOOL

Mr. James Johnson
Coordinator of College Tour
Roosevelt High School
Tuckahoe Road
Yonkers, NY 10710

Mr. Johnson and the African American Club at Roosevelt High School sponsor this tour. The trip usually takes you to 11 colleges/universities. About 30 to 40 students take this trip, many from surrounding school districts and beyond. The trip usually starts in April. Schools: Clark-Atlanta, Duke, Georgia State, Georgia Tech, Hampton, Howard, Morehouse, Morgan State, Spelman, North Carolina Central, and Virginia State. Call for information and details at (914) 376-8500. Or write.

TEEN LIFT BLACK COLLEGE TOUR OF DELTA SIGMA THETA SORORITY, INC.

New Orleans Alumnae Chapter
P.O. Box 52862
New Orleans, LA 70152
(504) 433-0702

This group sponsors college tours.

THEATRE OF DANCE MOVEMENT, INC.

200-29 Linden Boulevard
St. Albans, NY 11412
(718) 525-6847

Schools visited: Spelman, Clark-Atlanta, Bennett, North Carolina A&T, Norfolk State, Hampton, Howard, and Morehouse. Also stops at Black Wax Museum, Baltimore Harbor, Martin Luther King Jr. birthplace. Contact: Mrs. Lucile Hill, president.

APPENDIX D

Organizations

Here are educational organizations that will offer you additional help. We have included the names and addresses of the major black Greek-letter organizations in this listing. They are excellent resources for helpful educational information as well as scholarships.

HELPFUL EDUCATIONAL ORGANIZATIONS

A BETTER CHANCE, INC.

419 Boylston Street
Boston, MA 02115
(617) 421-0950

Seeks and finds our talented and motivated children, then provides them with access to college preparation and academic enrichment.

ACT-SO

(Afro Academic, Cultural, Technological, and
   Scientific Olympics)
Okaloosa County Branch 5633
Fort Walton Beach, FL

ACT-SO is a major youth outreach project of the NAACP. This "Olympics" spotlights our youngsters in a competition that includes the humanities, sciences, and visual and performing arts. The NAACP information hot line is (410) 521-4939.

   Motto: "If you THINK SO, you will BELIEVE SO. If you BELIEVE SO, then you will ACT-SO!"

AFRIKIDS

108 William Howard Taft Road
Suite 2
Cincinnati, OH 45219
(513) 569-8286

Afrikids offers educational books for our children, ranging from preschool to junior high level.

AMERICAN FOUNDATION FOR NEGRO AFFAIRS

117 South 17th Street, Suite 1200
Philadelphia, PA 19103
(715) 835-1470

Recruits motivated students after the 10th year and helps with educational experiences aimed at students through college and professional school.

ASSAULT ON ILLITERACY PROGRAM (AOIP)

231 West 29th Street, Suite #1205
New York, NY 10007
(212) 967-4008

This is a coalition of more than 90 black organizations working to help eradicate illiteracy.

ASSOCIATION OF BLACK ADMISSIONS AND FINANCIAL AID OFFICERS OF THE IVY LEAGUE AND SISTER SCHOOLS, INC.

c/o Lloyd Peterson
Yale University
149 Elm Street
New Haven, CT 06520
(203) 432-1916

Information and help to students seeking admission to this collection of "elite" schools.

ASSOCIATION OF BLACK WOMEN IN HIGHER EDUCATION

c/o Lenore R. Gall
234 Hudson Avenue
Albany, NY 12210
(518) 472-1791

ASSOCIATION OF CARIBBEAN STUDIES

P.O. Box 22202
Lexington, KY 40522
(606) 257-6966

BLACK EXCEL: COLLEGE HELP NETWORK

28 Vesey Street
MPB 2239
New York, NY 10007
(212) 591-1936 (Voicemail)
e-mail: ijblack@blackexcel.org

College help resource telling you the "how to" of getting into the college of your choice. Also, medical school and scholarship help and more.

BLACK STUDENT FUND

3636 16th Street, N.W., Suite #AG15
Washington, DC 20010
(202) 387-1414

COALITION OF HISTORICALLY BLACK COLLEGES AND UNIVERSITIES

c/o Kenny Ray
P.O. Box
Manhattanville Station
New York, NY 10007
(212) 234-8408 or (212) 978-3795

Alumni and college fair group nationally known for its participation in the Annual Harlem Week and Urban League college fairs held in New York City. Write coordinator Kenny Ray for information.

CONCERNED EDUCATORS OF BLACK STUDENTS

Fayetteville State University
School of Education
Fayetteville, NC 28301
(919) 486-1181

COUNCIL OF INDEPENDENT BLACK INSTITUTIONS

P.O. Box 40519
Pasadena, CA 91103
(818) 798-5406

COUNCIL OF NATIONAL ALUMNI ASSOCIATIONS

Delaware State College
Dover, DE 19901
(904) 561-2408

NATIONAL ALLIANCE OF BLACK SCHOOL EDUCATORS

2816 Georgia Ave, N.W.
Washington, DC 20001
(202) 483-1549

NATIONAL ASSOCIATION OF BLACK PROFESSORS

P.O. Box 526
Crisfield, MD 21817
(410) 968-2393

NATIONAL ASSOCIATION FOR EQUAL OPPORTUNITY IN HIGHER EDUCATION

400 12th Street, N.E.
The Lovejoy Building, Second Floor
Washington, DC 20002
(202) 543-9111

A membership group that includes 117 historically black colleges.

NATIONAL BLACK CHRISTIAN STUDENTS' CONFERENCE

P.O. Box 4311
Chicago, IL 60680
(312) 722-1441

NATIONAL BLACK LAW STUDENTS' ASSOCIATION

1225 11th Street, N.W.
Washington, DC 20001
(202) 642-3900

NATIONAL BLACK MBA ASSOCIATION

180 North Michigan Avenue, Suite 1515
Chicago, IL 60601
(312) 236-2622 or (312) 644-6610

More than 2,000 members and 25 chapters of African Americans with M.B.A.'s or pursuing that degree.

NATIONAL COUNCIL FOR BLACK STUDIES

Memorial Hall East 129
Indiana University
Bloomington, IN 47405
(812) 335-6581

NATIONAL COUNCIL OF NEGRO WOMEN

633 Pennsylvania Avenue
Washington, DC 20004
(202) 737-0120

NATIONAL ORGANIZATION OF BLACK COLLEGE ALUMNI

4 Washington Square Village, Suite 15E
New York, NY 10012
(212) 982-7726

NATIONAL ORGANIZATION FOR THE PROFESSIONAL ADVANCEMENT OF BLACK CHEMISTS AND CHEMICAL ENGINEERS

c/o Department of Chemistry
Howard University
525 College Street, N.W.
Washington, DC 20059
(202) 667-1699

NATIONAL SOCIETY OF BLACK ENGINEERS

1454 Duke Street
Alexandria, VA 22314
(703) 549-2207 or (703) 549-2207

NATIONAL STUDENT BUSINESS LEAGUE

7226 East Forest Road
Kentland, MD 20785
(202) 895-3926

A communications center for students interested in business. There are more than 50 chapters, at 45 colleges.

OFFICE FOR THE ADVANCEMENT OF PUBLIC BLACK COLLEGES

1 DuPont Circle, Suite 710
Washington, DC 20036
(202) 778-0818

Group spreading the word about black schools and their value. Looking for national support for black colleges, "a primary source of talent."

100 BLACK MEN OF AMERICA

The Chandler Building
127 Peachtree Street, N.E., Suite 704
Atlanta, GA 30303
(404) 525-7111

RON BROWN SCHOLAR PROGRAM

1160 Pepsi Place, Suite 306B
Charlottesville, VA 22901
e-mail: mmallory@ronbrown.org
Web site: http://www.ronbrown.org

STUDENT NATIONAL MEDICAL ASSOCIATION, INC.

1012 10th Street, NW, Suite 1000
Washington, DC 20001
(202) 371-1616

Information and help to African American students interested in medical school.

UNCF NATIONAL ALUMNI COUNCIL

8260 Willow Oaks Corp Drive
P.O. Box 10444
Fairfax, VA 22031
(703) 205-3400

UNITED NEGRO COLLEGE FUND

500 East 62nd Street
New York, NY 10021
(212) 326-1100

Our major fund-raising organization, helping more than 50,000 students yearly and 41 HBCU member schools.

VISIONS FOUNDATION

1538 Ninth Street, N.W.
Washington, DC 20001
(202) 462-1779

THE GREEK-LETTER ORGANIZATIONS

ALPHA KAPPA ALPHA SORORITY, INC.

5656 South Stony Island Avenue
Chicago, IL 60637
(312) 684-1282

More than 820 chapters and 120,000 members. Strong educational help and assistance here. College-educated women on a mission. Nearest chapter could assist you.

ALPHA PHI ALPHA FRATERNITY, INC.

2313 St. Paul Street
Baltimore, MD 21218-5234
(410) 554-0054

Strong educational involvement here. Nearly 700 college and alumni chapters that help with scholarships, guidance, and community projects.

CHI ETA PHI SORORITY, INC.

3029 13th Street, N.W.
Washington, DC 20009
(202) 232-3858
This sorority has more than 70 undergraduate and graduate chapters, with more than 6,000 members. It's a national nursing association.

DELTA SIGMA THETA SORORITY, INC.

1707 New Hampshire Avenue, N.W.
Washington, DC 20009
(202) 986-2400

This sorority encourages academics and does assistance. More than 185,000 members and 850-plus chapters.

ETA PHI BETA SORORITY, INC.

16815 James Couzens
Detroit MI 43235
(313) 862-0600

This is a national business and professional women's organization.

IOTA PHI LAMBDA SORORITY, INC.

P.O. Box 11609
Montgomery, AL 36111-0609
(205) 284-0203

This group "unites business and professional women," with one key area being students in high school and college who are interested in pursuing business careers.

KAPPA ALPHA PSI FRATERNITY, INC.

2320 North Broad Street
Philadelphia, PA 19132
(215) 228-7181

Has more than 600 undergraduate and graduate chapters, with over 90,000 members. Has a "Guide Right" national service program.

NATIONAL SORORITY OF PHI DELTA KAPPA, INC.

8233 South King Drive
Chicago, IL 69615
(312) 783-7379

This is a group of more than 5,000 "professional educators" who promote educational advancement.

OMEGA PSI PHI FRATERNITY, INC.

2714 Georgia Avenue, N.W.
Washington, DC 20001
(202) 667-7158

This fraternity is generally referred to as the "Ques." This fraternity has over 660 chapters. It focuses on "achievement, youth and community uplift."

PHI BETA SIGMA FRATERNITY, INC.

145 Kennedy Street, N.W.
Washington, DC 20011
(202) 726-5434

More than 600 chapters here, with 90,000-plus members. This fraternity promotes education, with scholarship and tutorial services. A key theme is "brotherhood and community service."

SIGMA GAMMA RHO SORORITY, INC.

800 Stoney Island Avenue
Chicago, IL 60617
(312) 873-9000

This sorority has more than 70,000 members and 400 chapters. Slogan: "Greater Service, Greater Progress!" Promotes community service and academic achievement, as well as "educational development" for our youth.

ZETA PHI BETA SORORITY, INC.

1734 New Hampshire Avenue, N.W.
Washington, DC 20009
(202) 387-3103

More than 600 chapters, with 60,000-plus members. This sorority promotes "academic achievement" with college and community projects.